DORSET
COAST

DORSET COAST

FROM LYME REGIS TO MUDEFORD QUAY

Interviews by JAMES CROWDEN
& RUBY WRIGHT

Photographs by GEORGE WRIGHT

Transcriptions by RUBY WRIGHT, DAHLENE ROOD,
SIGRUN APPLEBY *&* NELL BARRINGTON

FLAGON PRESS

First Published in 2007
Flagon Press
14 Whitelackington, Ilminster, Somerset TA19 9EF

Layout by Andrew Crane
www.axisweb.org/artist/andrewcrane
Printed by Remous Limited, Milborne Port, Dorset DT9 5EP
www.remous.com

Text typeset in 11/14pt Octavian, headings 14/15pt Octavian and Octavian italic.
Cover font Baskerville Old Face

www.james-crowden.co.uk

ISBN 978-0-9557073-2-2

Stone boatman text on page 19 © Lyme Regis Museum 1991
Geological text on page 19 © GM Davies 1935

Painting opposite: *Portland – Clearing Storm* © Michael J Chappell 2005   www.chappellstudio.co.uk
By strange coincidence, in these very same waters *The Earl of Abergavenny*, an East Indiaman, was lost
in similar conditions on 6th Feb1805 with 240 hands. Her Captain John Wordsworth
was the younger brother of the poet William Wordsworth. For further details see page 175.

Cover photo: *Alan Lander at Chapman's Pool*

This book is dedicated to all those who have spent
their working lives on the Dorset Coast, whether they be fishermen or
quarrymen, coastguards or lifeboatmen, boat builders or swanherds…
the diversity is enormous.

Jim Miller on the look out for stray mines and torpedoes

CONTENTS

INTRODUCTION

Dorset Coast is a fitting sequel to *Dorset Man* and *Dorset Women* and completes the trilogy. It records the working lives of a large cross section of people who are intimately connected to the Dorset Coast. There is always something very special about being close to the sea, an interface with the ocean whose beauty and unpredictable storms create a sense of wonder and awe, as well as providing a hard-earned living for fishermen.

At the western end of Dorset lies the ancient and quirky port of Lyme Regis with its Cobb. Here I was spoilt for choice. So much history: stone boats and aquariums, day tripping and mackerel fishing, a cliff tumbling into the sea, boat building and whelks, crumpets and first editions, lobsters, fossils and ice creams. Lyme Regis has it all. Often, whenever I visited the writer John Fowles for tea, I came to realise that the sea was an important part of his writing, it was his horizon and he could not bear to be parted from it. The sound of shingle moving in a storm is, as on Chesil beach, a deep unconscious force which works upon the imagination in mysterious ways.

Dorset Coast has concentrated on the oral history of fishermen. To provide fresh fish on the quayside, day after day, week after week is a dangerous calling which is often deeply underrated. Like farmers they are constantly having to manoeuvre between ever increasing piles of paper work, inspections, quotas and satellite tracking. The Southern Sea Fisheries Committee have very wisely chosen to limit the size of their boats to under 12 metres. This gives the smaller fisherman a fighting chance and this will hopefully keep stocks abundant.

Also I have taken various key places along the coast from Lyme to Mudeford Quay via West Bay and Abbotsbury focusing on Weymouth and Portland, Lulworth and Purbeck, Swanage and Poole. The variety of scenery is enormous and a whole range

of geological strata are laid bare like an open book from one end to the other. No wonder the Jurassic Coast has recently been given World Heritage status. But what concerns me most is not the fossils but the present day workings of a marine economy.

Here are tales of smuggling and tragedy at sea, daring rescues and foreign trade, fishermen and fish merchants, lobster men, quarrymen, crabbers, boat builders, geologists, divers, chefs, oysters, swans, artists, seine boats, tank training, live firing, gig racing, submarines, prisons, lifeboats, oil exploration, mullet fishing, poaching, Punch & Judy, net makers, sculptors, scallopers, coastguards, sailing close to the wind, landslips, wrecks and dinosaurs. Such enormous variety but what impressed me most was the depth and breadth of the stories. Such vitality and enthusiasm for the sea, such commitment and passion, such a sense of history.

My own family connection to the Dorset Coast goes back to the 1840s when my great-great-grandfather, also called James Crowden, was stationed at Lulworth Cove as a coastguard. He had previously been in the navy for eight years and had been to South America in HMS *Druid*, a 46 gun 5th Rate and round the Mediterranean in HMS *Endymion*, a 50 gun 4th rate. So he was happy to stay put in Lulworth for a few years. The 1841 census shows James there with his young wife Mary Anna Trick. Their first son, my great-grandfather was born here in 1843. Twelve other coastguards and their families were based there as well as a naval Commander and a Lieutenant. So there was quite a nautical presence. No doubt everybody was watching everybody else. Smuggling was rife and the rewards were rich.

But it wasn't all plain sailing. Only ten years previously a coastguard had been pushed over a cliff at Durdle Door and killed. In one sense Lulworth was an idyllic location for a newly married couple but in another it proved a moral dilemma, for the real purpose of being a coastguard was to save life, not to take it. The number of coastguards stationed at Lulworth, Worbarrow and White Nothe was legendary. Their cottages are now much sought after. Whilst talking to Jim Miller in Lulworth Cove I soon realised what my great, great grandfather was really up against. A rich tradition of seamanship, native cunning, story telling, sheer hard work and bravery. Ironically it is Jim Miller who lives in the coastguard cottages now. I suspect that my ancestor, who had more than his fair share of Cornish blood in his veins, was slightly in sympathy with the smugglers. Smuggling was a real and lucrative tradition on the Dorset coast.

Interestingly James Crowden's father, Dennis Crowden had been a gunner's mate in the Navy during the Napoleonic war and had been up the Adriatic in 1809 on special boat operations just as Jim Miller had been in the Second World War. After a few years James Crowden was posted from Lulworth to Looe and finally to Muchals in Scotland where in 1868 he won the Albert Medal and RNLI Silver medal for saving 13 lives at sea.

Time and time again on the Dorset Coast you are brought back to fishing, whether it be stories of seine netting off Chesil beach, lobster potting or bass fishing off Portland Bill. Recently I was talking to Dick Dalley's wife, Betty, in Abbotsbury and she showed me a picture of herself and her sister pulling on a rope, the 'lawn' end of a seine net. One of the few women's crews working on the beach, if not the only one. What also fascinated me was the Portland and Purbeck tradition of quarrying in the winter and fishing in the summer. More than anything else this tradition is peculiar to Dorset. Where else can you find such high quality stone next to the sea, ready to be shipped up to London for the likes of Inigo Jones and Christopher Wren. A major industry that has kept men busy for at least 400 years.

My own acquaintance with the Dorset coast really began in the early 1970s whilst in the army at the Royal Engineers Bridging Camp at Wyke Regis. Here we did battle with Bailey Bridges, floating pontoons and heavy ferries as the eight knot tide drained from the Fleet which, we were told, simulated the Rhine in Germany. We also played around with medium girder tank bridges on Portland in the early hours testing our skills crossing the steep ravines of the old incline railways. I started sea cliff climbing on Purbeck near Dancing Ledge and my stag party was held at Durdle Door on the beach. Later on when I worked on the land in Dorset I ended up shearing many coastal flocks, from Lyme and Charmouth through to West Bexington and Abbotsbury. I once sheared in a quarry on Portland, the stone dust blunting the cutters very quickly. I also had a half share in a small fishing boat, a Norwegian Rana, with Simon Eastwood. It was kept on the beach at Burton Bradstock. Often we would row out and lay nets under the cliffs at dusk. Fresh mackerel made a fine breakfast cooked on a driftwood fire. Once we sold a 9lb sea bass to Arthur's Riverside Café. The fish was weighed, still flapping, on the old post office scales at 8.30 in the morning.

What has really impressed me about doing the research for this book is the sheer depth of knowledge of local people. Their stories and their connectedness not just with the sea, but with each other. A fisherman at one end of Dorset will have a pretty good idea what a fishermen at the other end is up to. So long as there are fish in the sea and men build boats, lay nets or weave lobster pots, there will always be a fascination for what lurks beneath the surface. Not just men building boats these days.

James Crowden *November 2007*

ACKNOWLEDGEMENTS

My main thanks are due to the many men and women along the coast who have freely given their time to be interviewed and photographed. Many are very active and when you are fishing, time is of the essence. In particular I must mention Dave Sales of West Bay who first featured in Dorset Man. As a key member of the Southern Sea Fisheries Committee he was able to furnish me with a short list of interesting fishermen and their phone numbers. Many of these now appear in the book. They are the main characters left along the coast and he quite rightly felt that it was important for their stories to be heard. Without his help the book would not be as colourful as it is. Hopefully the next generation will be able to fish these waters which have traditionally provided much needed food. The preservation of small fishing boats and ports where they can land the fish is a vital part of our local coastal economy.

I am grateful to the Philpott Museum for permission to use the extract about stone boatmen written by John Fowles which appears in the interview with Roy Gollop. The actual text originally derived from 'A Short History of Lyme Regis' by John Fowles © Lyme Regis Museum and published by The Dovecote Press 1991. The list of geological layers comes from 'Dorset Coast - A Geological Guide' by GM Davies published in 1935 by A&C Black Ltd. I am grateful to Sarah Fowles and J R Fowles Limited for permission to reproduce this adaptation.

I am very grateful to Michael J Chappell for permission to reproduce his painting 'Portland – Clearing Storm' which he painted in situ during just such a storm at Osmington Mills.

A few days before we went to press with *Dorset Coast* in November 2007 I found myself at a lecture on Rudyard Kipling's early years at the Eype Centre for Arts. I was slightly late for the lecture, took one of the few seats left at the back of the church and found myself sitting next to this delightful painting. My eye kept being drawn to it as it exactly encapsulated the light and vicious quirky squalls that can suddenly blow up in Weymouth Bay. Curiously enough where the patch of light is on the painting, is almost exactly where the *Earl of Abergavenny* went down in 1805, two hundred years earlier.

For more details of *The Earl of Abergavenny* and other tragic disasters see 'Dorset Shipwrecks' by Maureen Attwooll published by the Dovecote Press which has many other excellent books related to the Dorset Coast.

My thanks go to George Wright, the Dorset photographer who has again managed in difficult locations to come up with some excellent shots. My thanks also to George for finding the Weymouth postcard in a junk shop. Also to Ruby Wright for recording five of the interviews. She helped with the transcription, a major task, as did Dahlene Rood, Nell Barrington and Sigrun Appleby. Transcription is not an easy task, but a vital one. I must thank Carol Trewin and Nell Barrington for proof reading, and my father, Guy Crowden, for collation and work behind the scenes. My thanks to Fergus Byrne of the Marshwood Vale Magazine for supporting the project. Thanks to Andrew Crane for his patience in laying out the book and to Keith Sparks and Remous for printing.

LYME REGIS

1. Ken Gollop — Local historian, fisherman, pleasure boatman, lifeboatman & Keeper of the Marine Aquarium. Born Lyme Regis 1936.

There was a little trip boat we had built called 'Later On' that was named because whenever you asked someone on the Cobb if they wanted a trip, they'd say 'Later on,' so you'd say 'Well this is the boat for you'…

Father was a pleasure boatman and fisherman. In those days the pleasure boats were more important, they made the most money in the summer, and then he did an odd bit of fishing, trawling in the winter months when the weather was fine, and if it was a rough period they'd get a job ashore for a while. The pleasure boats were where the money was. He had a motor boat 22 foot long. Luckily he sold it just before the second war broke out and after the war he bought another one.

He was a retained fireman at the start of the war stationed in Lyme. They were 24 hours on, 24 hours off. That's when they weren't down at Plymouth Blitz or Exeter Blitz or Portsmouth docks or Southampton docks. They used to get sent off to relieve the local men. They'd ride all the way on the fire engines to Plymouth. Mother was born in Exeter so all her family was in Exeter. Mother's sister married a Plymouth man so they could ferry the news between each other. They'd get plenty of tea.

Sometimes they'd come back black as the ace of spades. But when he was on 24 hours on, 24 hours off in Lyme, he used to go out to sea with an old chap called Billy Raffle one of the old fishermen. So we had plenty of fish during the winter to eat. At the beginning of the war fishing was restricted and then only two people had licences to go to sea during the war, and that was Jim

Homyer and Billy Raffle and they used to go out and do a bit of potting. All the seafront was barbed-wired off, and you had to have a permit to go along the sea front. The cliffs down near Seaton were mined and the cliffs up near Golden Cap were mined, but our local cliffs, I don't think were. Of course we had the Air Force here during the war, they had five air sea rescue boats here, the smaller type. The military were here all during the war, they regrouped from Dunkirk here, because they had all the hotels you see, not the two best ones, but virtually all the hotels. And then the Americans came in 1943 and built a big tented camp, that was where the modern housing estate is, that was all fields during the war, and they were stationed in all the boarding houses. And all the Americans that were first ashore at Omaha, they had a really rough lot, they actually came from Lyme Regis. They lost a lot. Our lot, they were grouped up at Winterbourne Abbas, at Wellbottom Woods, the Americans from Lyme, that was the 16th Infantry. I've got lots of memories of the Yanks here, your boyhood revolved around the war. Lyme wasn't bombed, just a couple inland. They were just strays really.

Grandfather came from Charmouth when he was a young lad. His mother was a Hunter, Frances Hunter, and the Hunters were a big fishing family in Charmouth, in the area, and they go way back. Grandfer's mother was Frances, and then I think there were four generations before that who were fishing out of Charmouth, so you're going back to the 1750s at least. And they were catching everything, herrings and that, seine netting for mackerel, they were potting, they were long lining, they were hooking, and they didn't do any trawling of course, they had very small boats. The fish would have been sold locally, if it reached Bridport or Axminster they were lucky. They were probably sold before that. If they seined loads of mackerel on Charmouth beach probably some merchants would get to know

Roy and Ken Gollop on the Cobb

about it and they'd haul them off. They just got them out the boat and out on the beach, that was it. If it didn't go locally it'd go off on a horse and cart.

I don't think the women round here took much part in the fishing. My grandfather's father married into that family, he was a stone boatman, my great-grandfather, they used to quarry stone from the ledges and ship it onboard ships out in the bay or in the harbour. And that was taken away and used for building or for making cement. Down where the barracks are now there was a cement factory and that ran from the early 1850s making cement. The limestone here, the lias, is very rich in silica, so when you make that into cement the silica makes the cement harden in damp conditions. They used Lyme Regis cement when they built the Grand Union Canal. It was quite well known. The cement works went on until 1914. Great-grandfather and Grandfer Gollop used to quarry stone and knock it up into manageable bits, take in the boats at low tide, fill the boats up and row them out to the ship. It was real hard work and there was probably about 18 stone boats working in Lyme. Lyme's never been a big fishing port, that went on until 1914 when local pressure forced the owners to close down, because in a sou'westerly wind the smoke blew all over Lyme and some days you couldn't put your washing out. Stone went out and timber came in.

Of course in the 19th century everything came in by sea, they used to bring in cargoes of timber for Luff's in Axminster, the builders' merchants. Baltic timber, and they'd bring in flat packed butter boxes, wooden ones for the milk factory at Chard Road, in fact that was one of the last cargoes that came into Lyme in 1939. Of course we had no industry, all the stuff that came into Lyme was things people needed, like coal.

The Cobb? We think it was built sometime in the early 1200s. They used to unload the ships over by the river mouth until they got too big, and there was some storm damage. So they built a new harbour, totally artificial, totally against the elements, where the harbour is now. If you look at it at low tide, it's the biggest rock pool we've got. It's got rocks either side and a darn great sandy bottom, and the shape of the harbour is defined by that as well. I think it was built like it is now, but it kept getting damaged by the storms. That's where the pressure point is, over there by the shore so they said 'Bugger it, we'll leave it open,' so the water could flow through. It's a relief valve. It remained an island until the 1750s, and then they got fed up with it so they connected it, and ever since then the beach has been building out. The beach, when they built the harbour first of all was literally the bottom of Cobb Road, and that's all shingle, all that square over there, all those houses are actually built on shingle.

Getting back to the family, Great Grandfer married into the Hunter family and Grandfer married into the Gorge family, they've got a long history going right back to the 1400s. They were coast watchers or coast riders for the customs, tide waiters. Stanton St Gabriel they lived, in West Hay Farm, and they came into Charmouth and got into the civil service. They were parish clerks for several generations. Going back to early times, they have sea connections in Plymouth. There were loads of Gollops in the Marshwood Vale in the 1700s. They were all farm peasants. If you draw a line from Exeter to Taunton to Dorchester, that triangle, right until the early 19th century, the Gollops were all enclosed in that triangle. Then they spread out.

After the war I was at grammar school and Mother wouldn't let us go on the boats because it was a haphazard way of living, and going to the grammar school you had to get a proper job. So I went away for nine years and worked for a government department that did hydrographic surveying for research purposes, that was based at Wallingford. Seamen and civil servants don't mix. You've got the practical and the intellectual, they just don't mix, and in the end, I was the first one to leave and within three years the whole department had folded. They all went and worked at Wimpey and places like that, so I came back, and we had a little trawler built. Father had more or less finished by then. After the war he finished with the fire service and he did a little bit of tripping and that. Then we came home and we had father's boat and our boat, tripping in the summer with a little bit of potting, and trawling in the winter. Then we got a fish shop, that was in the old market below the Guildhall, and we had two big trawlers, and then we saw the light of day.

The trawlers' names? *Sweet Promise* was the one we had built, then there was a little trip boat we had built called *Later On*, that was named because whenever you asked someone on the Cobb if they wanted a trip, they'd say 'Later on,' so you'd say 'Well this is the boat for you,' then we had a little trawler, a 32 footer built up at James & Caddy up at Weymouth, that was called *Early On* to go with *Later On*. Then we bought the *Torbay Star* from Browse Brothers down at Paignton, that was a crabber, 42 foot long, longest boat they've ever had in Lyme, and then in 1970 we had the *Sea Soldier* built down at Mevagissey. Then we packed up the fish shop and we decided that by 1974 we'd had enough of rough living. It's long hours and not family friendly, so my brother Roy started making nets and I had a new trip boat built. We'd always been involved with the aquarium because it was opened in 1958 by Oliver Farnworth, it was designed by Les Jackman from Paignton who opened his own aquarium a few years before. Les came up with Oliver and set up this. Father provided some of the fish and fish food. It was a warehouse before, used as storage. So we came along in 1959. I

started looking after the technical side of the aquarium for a few years, besides going to sea. Then in 1980 we bought it when Oliver retired, and we ran it for 25 years, and then when I finished my nephew Max took it on and he's running it now.

The quality of the water is something you've got to keep looking at. Max has all the technical side of it all up to date, whereas we were working in 1958 mode, which suited me just fine. We had a good time at fishing but with the EEC regulations and everything, we'd had enough of hard living, so we decided to make it a little easier. We've got half a dozen good lads now, who keep the fishing up, which is good. Then in 1967 they decided to have a lifeboat here, we had the rubber dinghy, the 'rubber duck' as we called it. Father was in the last of the rowing lifeboats, Grandfer and his brother were in the old rowing lifeboats, so we've got a bit of a history there. The worst is when you're looking for someone and you can't find them. As long as you can draw a conclusion and find their body you're all right, not happy, but they know what's happened. But when they don't find the body… People have no sense of responsibility. You see them up on the Cobb in gale force winds with a buggy, you try and tell them and they just abuse you.

I did 20-odd years. We had pagers. I don't know what the range was, if you were out of Lyme it was hardly worth coming back. There was one hilarious story about a lad who was in Exeter shopping with his wife and when the bleeper went he rushed back to Lyme, by the time he got here, the rescue had been washed up and everyone had gone home. If the blokes are around the Cobb and that, you can be in the water in five minutes. The boats were for three, but you'd need another three to launch them. Especially before the tractor. Then of course the Air Force closed down in 1964, and we got the range safety contract from that. The range is all Lyme Bay. The range safety base here closed because of helicopters, they could do all the work virtually that the boats could do, except be on the spot continually all day long waiting to pick up someone. So they employed us on a daily basis, as and when, to be ready to go out. We did all the 'over-sea' trials for the Nimrods, they were testing all the gear, dropping parachutes and that, that was an interesting job. That went on until 1974. We also did a ten year research programme when they did the Bridport sewer. They did the sewer out in the 1960s or 70s, they extended it and did tests on it periodically, so we had a good contract there. A third of the year was not actually fishing, it was doing research which was a nice change from hard graft. Mines in the trawl nets? Brother had a couple of mines which they had to blow up. I never had one.

Plenty of filming has happened here. That's brought Lyme a lot of money. John Fowles, The French Lieutenant's Woman and Persuasion are very good advertising. The French Lieutenant's Woman was made in 1980 or '82, and we're still making money out of it. When they made The French Lieutenant's Woman, it was an American company that made it, they just steamrollered over Lyme. We learnt a lot about filming. They very rarely employ locals as extras, but they've got to shop in town, they've got to feed, they've got to sleep, so they spend money. Lyme is the type of place that attracts a certain type of person. We have a lot of walkers, there are wonderful walks. Of course Lyme is a wonderful touring centre. You've got Dartmoor, Exmoor and Hardy country, and all the lovely towns and cities in between.

Fossils? My grandfather used to do a lot of fossilling because when they were stone boating, knocking up the ledges they found a lot of fossils. If someone found a big fossil, sometimes they'd get Grandfer to clean it up, what they call 'develop it' nowadays. He was quite well known as a cleaner of fossils. I'm sure he found interesting things. The Cobb is mostly made of local stone, but it's been repaired so many times that there's all sorts of things in it now, but in the late 1700s they decided to used shaped blocks of Portland stone. Originally the shape was determined by the rock pool they built the harbour on, the round bit there, the actual shape of the walls was designed to reflect the shape of the waves, bearing in mind you've got nothing between us and Brazil if you look out south west, so you get some hell of a big waves come over. We have all these lovely records going back to the 1200s of the town petitioning the Crown to give them money to repair the Cobb.

Lyme became Lyme Regis in 1284 I think, there was a charter. A lot of the town was destroyed in the Civil War because it was all thatch. There was a lot of trading with the Channel Islands, a lot of cattle went over in the 1700s, 1800s. There was the wool trade abroad, it was wool out and wine in, that's what the old phrase was, but as exploration discovered more of the world, there were Lyme ships going to the Mediterranean and to West Africa, then the Indies and they were coming back to Lyme, then of course ships got bigger… Salt cod? That didn't last very long in Lyme, they were involved in it but that was left to Poole. I don't think there was a big trade back from the West Indies. George Somers was wrecked on Bermuda, that made him, they celebrate that every year with a little parade round here.

It's all changed. We're losing our hotels, they're turning them into apartments. They can't get the staff. The trouble was in the old days when I was brought up, you'd never find a hotel or a pub or a guesthouse up for sale, it was always taken over by the family. Now of course the family don't want that sort of tie, so places come up for sale. They can't sell them as a business so they sell them to a developer and he gets permission to turn it into flats and second homes. The cost of housing is terrible.

2. Roy Gollop – Royal Marine, netmaker, fisherman and boat builder. Born Lyme Regis 1932.

Grandfather was a coastguard, Frank. I was his shadow. By the time I went to school when I was five, all my peers already called me Boatman Gollop.

I was born at the Old Mill House in 1932 and the Old Mill House is the one more or less in the back of Lyme, the nickname of the road was Monkey's Rough, but it was actually called Windsor Terrace. My family had just moved from the coastguard's cottages on the Cobb here because they were condemned at the time. Subsidence. They were condemned, but they're still here now, all these years later. I don't think they've ever done much to them.

Grandfather was a coastguard, Frank. I was his shadow. He taught me how to row a boat, how to handle a boat and everything before the war. I was down on Cobb Gate Beach from the age of three years. He just missed his hundred years, but he taught me from the age of three years old, so by the time I went to school when I was five, all my peers already called me Boatman Gollop. I've got more time now to teach things to my grandson, when he's interested, which is a different kettle of fish these days. My father was working hard so grandfather and I had this bond and even during the war when we weren't allowed on the beach, we still did things together, we went for long walks and he still taught me things about the sea. Handling boats, making up gear and lines, splicing ropes and pots.

They were stone boatmen but they were fishermen as well. They did herring drifting, the stone boating was mainly done when there wasn't much fish about. I believe it was something between half a crown a ton and five shillings a ton. They would work the cliffs both side, and at Broadledge, on the eastern side of Lyme, Broadledge is like an island of ledges because my grandfather and his mate cut a channel so that the stone boats didn't have to row right the way round. The channel goes right alongside the jetty, and my grandfather and his mate cut that by hand. He did have explosives but he was the last chap in Lyme to have an explosive licence, and I always remember that when he moved from his house in Mill Green, when I was in the marines, and Father cleaned out his shed, there was still explosives in that shed from all those years ago, whereas now they would have cleared Lyme Regis of people, all my father did was put it in a wheelbarrow, bring it down to Cobb Gate jetty, load it aboard a boat and take it out to sea and dump it. That's how he got rid of all that. It was probably black powder in those days. I always remember the tale where Grandfather blew a tree down on Cadbury's land, just here, and he bored it, and he put that tree down exactly where he wanted to put it. He was my mentor, he was my main man, really. He was an old man all my life.

Sadly his father had a fatal accident under the cliffs down there. This is one of the things that I'm always wary of. Families digging fossils out of the cliffs and that. I used to get quite uptight and go and tell them about the things that can happen, but unfortunately now you get so much abuse that you tend to leave them.

KILLED BY FALLING STONES, A SAD DEATH

'An inquest was held at Mr B. Warren's Pilot Boat Inn on Tuesday morning to enquire into the circumstances surrounding the death of William Gollop, age 53, a stone boatman who met with his death on Monday whilst at work below the sea cliffs. The enquiry was conducted by Mr CGA Nantes of Bridport, the district coroner, and the following were sworn on the jury: Messers E Wallis, Foreman, WG Berry, R Warren, J Speed, H Love, W Manfield, CG Renvill, CO Stell, E Sprackling, N Launton, W Lang and WD Cornish,' and I might come in here and say they are all local names.

'William Gollop, son of the deceased said his father was at work breaking stone at about nine am on Monday under the cliff between Devonshire Hedge and John Caddy's orchard' That's just this side- of Devonshire Hedge

'He was working about five yards from the base of the cliff which was at this point something like 60 feet high. The cliff was composed of lias stone and marle, similar to the specimen of hard clay now produced which fell from the top. The witness was working about ten yards from his father, and hearing a rumbling noise turned and saw a portion of the cliff falling. He shouted to the deceased and said 'Look up.' His father looked up and the falling stone struck him, apparently about the head and back. The witness at once picked him up and carried him a distance of ten yards from the cliff. He was unconscious, and the witness dipped a cloth in the sea and put it over his head to try to revive him, but without success and the deceased apparently expired in about two minutes. Witness hailed a passing boat, and James Gratton came to his assistance. The fatal accident happened about three-quarters of a mile from the Cobb. They did not keep a boy watch for falling earth, but such precautions had been observed at more dangerous spots. They had no warning of any dangers of the dry state of the cliff beyond the usual crumbling. James Gratton, stonebreaker, said he was rowing from Lyme in the direction of the spot where the deceased was working on Monday morning when he heard the last witness call out to his father. He looked round and saw Gollop waving his jacket. He did not see any portion of the cliff fall. He ran his boat ashore and saw the older Gollop lying as described, without any sign of life. He saw blood on one eye and understood the man's leg was broken. He went and procured assistance from Mr Porter and he conveyed the deceased to Lyme in a hand barrow. Gollop was dead. Richard Hickshop was in the witness' company that morning, but he remained in the boat. Mr William Porter, deceased's employer, corroborated with the evidence of the witness. Sergeant Ham who superintended the removal of Mr Gollop to his home said the deceased's back and one of his legs was broken. A verdict of accidental death was returned. Gollop leaves a widow and several young children and on the proposition of Mr Wallis the jurymen and the witnesses gave their fees to Mrs Gollop. Dr Dorin saw the deceased when he was brought from blue lias ledges to the Cobb.'

One of the things was that they didn't have the boy watching the top of the cliff. Now we all take chances, I take chances, and that was one of those things. This other bit was included in the Bridport News on the 2nd of June 1893:

'The mayor, Mr Z. Edwards convened a meeting at the Guildhall on Monday to consider ways and means for raising a wedding present in favour of Princess May and the Duke of York. Mr F. Radford thinks it more wiser and more homely to consider ways and means for raising a contribution for Mrs Gollop and her family. Her husband was killed under the cliff a fortnight ago.'

'Fishing: During the last week, only a few hundred mackerel have been landed. A few weeks ago numerous shoals of fish were visible in the bay. It is hoped the fishermen will be more fortunate'.

I can remember the stone boat. That was double hand rig. You had to double load. Not only that, you had to really time it, if you started when the boat was light you had to lift it a phenomenal way. If you could get there when someone else had two or three loaded, then it was better. My father used to go and take my grandfather's breakfast down of a morning, on Church Cliff jetty, where they cut through, and he'd be waiting for them, and one day he was so hungry he ate his father's breakfast, and then ran away for two days.

As to the stone boatmen and the beds, here's an interesting piece of writing by John Fowles and G M Davies:

Throughout the 1800s and up to 1914, blue lias limestone was quarried from tidal ledges and cliffs and exported for cement making, building and paving stone. The stone was ferried back to the harbour or waiting ships by stone boats. These heavily built double-ended boats were about 24 foot or 7 metres long with a crew of two and carried up to 5 tonnes of stone. If no ship was waiting the stone was stored in heaps in the pool on a little beach behind the aquarium. Some stone can still be seen here at the base of the beacon post rocks. The toughness of the stone boatmen has become legendary. They were notoriously independent and worked in all conditions, often up to their waist in water. With their great strength and stamina they formed the nucleus of the lifeboat crew. One did not lightly start a quarrel with a stone boatman and their language was famously broad.

The bands or layers of lias were of different thicknesses and quality. The men gave them different names for identification. Below the 26 named layers listed opposite were another 45 unnamed. Some of the names were table ledge, grey ledge, glass bottle, top quick, vents, best bed, second bed, rattle, second quick, gumption, third quick, top tape, second tape, top copper, mongrel, second mongrel, speckity, upper white, upper skulls, iron ledge, under copper, under white, lower skulls, lower ventry, pig's dirt or soft bed, brick ledge.

So that was that. Father was more involved with the pleasure boating. He did a little bit of fishing. My father was called Tom. My son is Tom again.

The war? I was eight. I remember the East Surreys coming, but I have one memory of being down on the beach before the war, well, at the start of the war in 1939, and one of my most vivid memories at the start of the war was that we had a young student who used to come to Lyme and work on the deckchairs. I never knew his nationality, but we had a little bit of chit chat. Anyway, war was declared and one night, signalling from up on Ware Cliffs, these Surreys caught the young man signalling to a U-boat. He was a German spy, and I can always remember the last I saw of him. He was interned in the basement of the Monmouth Hotel, and I can remember vividly seeing him talking to the lady who used to be in charge of the deckchairs, a local lady, talking to him up through the bars. There's glass there and there's bars, talking to this lady before they took him away. I can only presume that he was executed, as all spies were executed in those days. No more was ever said. I should imagine he was late teens or early twenties. I believe he came for two seasons.

What I can remember at that young age? I remember different regiments coming to Lyme, my mother used to do bundles of washing for them, she used to get a shilling a bundle or something. They built Nissen huts up under the copse up there. Defence, it was, and later on, when the Americans arrived, I was a young army cadet then, 12 years old and I used to do running for the Home Guard and things like that. I can remember the Americans filling up the hotels and different places. They treated us children, we used to go in all their army camps, all their bases. These days you'd never allow it, all the army chaps treated you well and they were always giving you sweets and rations that we didn't have. And so it came to the day before D Day, and we didn't know it was going to be D Day or anything like that, but my most vivid memory is the place being full of American troops, and the next day there was nothing. The streets of Lyme were so quiet, the tents were still there, and we went through all the tents and picked up bits and bobs. I believe they went to Omaha. There's a plaque on one of the buildings. I don't think many of them survived from Lyme Regis. A few of the local girls married Americans, and a few of the survivors went to America. They have been back and they've gone back again because they've made their home there.

The Air Force came in 1933. One of the things I can remember is there used to be three ports to allow the stone to go through at the entrance to the harbour. One of the things the RAF did, was to have them blocked up because they couldn't afford to have stones rushing across their slipway when they had their launches up there being repaired. So that was the start of the denuding of the Lyme sea defences. But I can remember RAF boats coming, I can remember some of their numbers. 1515 and 1564. There were air sea rescue launches and range safety boats to start with, or sea plane tenders as they were known. Then were the smaller ones, and then a bigger version came which were the real Air Sea Rescue. I remember seeing the German pilots being brought back in, and I remember my father going out, this must have been the day before D Day or D Day, he was in the fire service then, and they were taken out by the RAF boys. These gliders had crashed and they used their axes to beat the side of the glider and get the lads out. I can remember that. There's a bit of controversy about a plane crash in Uplyme, but it never was a plane crash because there were bombs being let go by this German aircraft, he was trying to lighten his load before he came back, and I went out with my grandfather to see the craters. There was no aircraft crashed at Uplyme.

Grandfather was too old for the first war, so he became coastguard. The oldest sons of his family, like my uncles, they went to sea during the First World War and my father was slightly too old for the Second World War, so he went in the fire service. He went to the Plymouth Blitz. Plymouth took a hammering. It so affected father that he got a Plymouth family up to live in our house. They were evacuated to Lyme. They were so good, they just went to work as they normally did in the morning, but of course they were at the Plymouth Blitz for nearly a fortnight before they sent the relief crew. And in those days they didn't know if they were dead or alive, and my father had a near miss with a wall collapsing, so the crew told me. My father never told me, and they thought my father had died. They said the wall collapsed and the mist and everything rose up, and out of the mist after a few minutes came my father, running. And they dumped him in a 40 gallon drum of water. I always thought, because grandfather lived until he was that age, that my father would live to that age, but unfortunately cancer took him from us when he was 72. I'm older than my father was now, which is strange.

They also went to London, and of course in those days they had taken all the signposts down, and if you can think, chaps from Lyme Regis like my father had probably never been out of the town. I can always remember before I joined the Royal Marines, the furthest north I'd been was Chard. I bought a pushbike out of the earnings of the boat and rode to Chard, but there was no signs you see. And so they did their job in London and got their leave, they left London in the early afternoon and it was in the summer, this is in a fire engine of sorts. In actual fact it was a car that my uncle had brought up to Lyme, it broke down so he sold it to the garage in Lyme. The garage did it up and the fire service got it then to pull a pump. So it was this car and this pump, and coming out of London there was no signs as such, and father and his knowledge of fishing pointed at the sun, and being the afternoon he said 'Follow the sun,' so forever after that in Lyme if father saw the crew, it was always 'Hello Tom, follow the sun!' They got back here on that.

I can remember finding... I mean us boys had so much ammunition, one or two had guns, there was two guns found in the American camp, we had everything. I always remember going to another boy down by the river, and his wooden gate faced across the river to the field, and he had this Yankee ·300 ammunition and he bored a hole in the gate, and he got a centre punch or a hammer and he was firing across the river. I thought 'That's good,' so I went home and bored a hole in the gate and did the same. There was a house opposite with the door open and this ·300 ricocheted up the stairs of this house opposite, I was in big trouble. That's the sort of life it was then. We had the army rations, 24-hour ration packs.

Another incident I can remember, I had an older friend, Jack Beavis, he was a notorious character in Lyme. He had heart problems so he couldn't go in the service, but he was in the Home Guard and he was a farm labourer at the back of Lyme, and there was an incident where there was a dog fight above Lyme and the British pilot got shot down. He came down and Jack was haymaking in a field above, and the pilot was on the deck and Jack comes over and stands over him with his pitchfork, and just says 'English or German?' this pilot met him

afterwards, and said 'I've never been so bloody glad to say English in my life,' so that was that little story.

Straight after the war we were allowed to bring the boat back on the beach and start fishing. One of the earliest things I had was Yankee ration tins, like five gallon drums, I got a centre punch and punched holes in them, put a neck in them and I caught lobsters in them. There was a stone blockhouse at the end of the cart road there, which we had to get the boats up and over down onto the beach. And like I say, they all had to be registered in Portland, even the small ones because it wasn't quite the end of the war, then I was the age that I had to go to work, I was 14 and I went to Lavis's down at Exmouth, boatbuilding and other little jobs. I knew more or less what I would be doing in life and I thought I wanted to see a bit of the world and that, and I chose to join the Royal Marines in 1950 for 12 years. I only went to Stonehouse for training and prior to going to 40 Commando.

At the end of my training there was a few chaps went to Korea to 41 Commando, but 41 Commando took such a hammering that they disbanded it and those lads came back to Malaya with us. I did a full spell there, we had our share and we did our share. The Ghurkhas relieved us in Taiping and they got hit the next day, and they thought they would teach them a lesson, but you don't teach Ghurkhas lessons. I always remember we had these Iban trackers and we hit these communists in the Taiping cemetery and this Iban, he threw his knife and hit this communist in the back as he was running away and it was his grandfather's knife, and so the job was done. He was making a lot of fuss, we took him to the sergeant, but I just liked this bloke. We got on well. We couldn't speak much language and that, he wanted to go and get his knife, and I said 'No way,' and we carried on the patrol, killed two of them, and we carried on, and at night everybody beds down in the jungle, nobody moves. So at

4 o'clock, regular as clockwork, we'd try and get down before the rain came. Rain came down at 5 o'clock regular, and it bucketed it down. Anyway this night comes along and Lancock, that was the name of this Iban, and he got down and in the morning he wasn't there. Two days later he came back with his grandfather's knife. What a boy. What a man. We were lucky to have him. There was no front line, that was the problem. Like Iraq. It was easy to go in, it was bloody hard to get out.

We came back then to Malta for a rest and I did a signals course and stayed with 40 Commando, then we went to Egypt. There was a panic on then, we had to run the canal and things like that. This was prior to the invasion. People don't realise that prior to 1954 when we cleared out, I came home in 1954, there was over 300 servicemen killed by terrorists. The amphib side of the Royal Marines was tying up the ships and piloting the ships and things like that. And I was on one of the landing craft and I can always remember this propeller of this ship that was light, slicing down through the engine room of our ship, just turning over, and we were sucked in under and it sliced down through the engine. I've never seen a stoker come out of an engine room as quick!

I came back to this country, my mother had died in between. She died when she was 47, and then I went to the amphib school and then they opened Poole up in 1954 and I was one of those that went down. I was a young sergeant then, and we cut all the Nissen huts and that out of the bushes, and Poole was good to us. I think the marines have been good to Poole and Poole has been good to the marines. They gave us a welcoming do, the SBS were alongside us, and I did an SBS course but my main thing was landing craft. I was an instructor up there for a couple of years. I always remember, I was here in the morning, we weren't supposed to live the distance I was living. You were allowed to live out 15 miles from the camp, but everyone knew I was 47 and a half miles from the camp, and I went back this morning when the panic was on of the Suez Canal, and there was a chief petty officer in my cabin, he said 'You'd better look at the notice board, Roy, it went up midnight time,' he'd know because he'd been in the bar until after midnight, and there it was. We formed this assault squadron, I was a senior NCO and where they seem to want three months to get ready these days, we flew out that night from Southampton Water in the old flying boats, they were the Sunderland flying boats, and they did about 250 knots, a massive great plane, no seats of course. They weren't meant for carrying troops, and we got out to Malta the next morning, the *Anzio* was in dry dock being repaired and all the LCAs were on a floating dock and they had last been used for D Day and they were in a hell of a state and we had to get them ready as best we could.

So eventually we did that job in November quite successfully, we landed half of 42 Commando on the beach and my job then, another funny little story, if it was funny. I was to go as soon as I'd landed, I had to take an LCA down to Navy House, which is about three miles down the canal, and I had to prepare to tie up *HMS Diamond*, which was our fire ship going in. The idea, she was going to be the command ship, but as I went down through the canal I thought 'This is going to be dodgy, I don't think they'd like to bring a warship round through here,' because they'd sunk all the vessels, but anyway, being a Royal Marine I had to go to Navy House. When us gets there all hell breaks loose. So discretion being the better part of valour, I had four marines and I had a sten gun and three rifles, and Navy House was full of these 'Gypos,' full of them. And they didn't take Navy House until the next morning, and they lost more marines taking Navy House with a full company of marines.

And they'd sent me there with two or three marines to stand up on the quay and wait for this ship to come in. I withdrew to the middle of the canal and after a while I went back and joined the unit.

Oh there was one other little thing I'm quite proud of. I was the last uniformed man to leave Egypt when we withdrew. It was done at night and the reason I was the last man is that my job was to take off the beach master, and he was a four ring skipper that had been in all the war, and I remember saying to him 'Are you going to be the last man off, sir, or shall I?' and he turned round to me and said 'No, sergeant, you can be the last man off, I've got enough to tell my grandchildren.' I can remember his very words, and at that particular time, there was a young lieutenant who had been captured, and the name slips me at this moment, he was an army lieutenant, they found him afterwards and the Egyptians had locked him in a cupboard, he'd died in this cupboard, and the United Nations troops who were covering our withdrawal were either Swedish or Norwegian and they held us back a minute saying they thought this lieutenant had been found, so this four ring skipper said 'We can hang on a few minutes' but bearing in mind that all the ships had withdrawn three miles…

We had a landing craft, 44 foot LCA. And also the Gypos were baying for our blood. There were only three or four of us on the quay and then there was this ring of blue helmets from the United Nations, anyway, we hung on, but then we did withdraw, and I dropped the skipper on to the mother ship and then I had to go out and pick up our ship, it was quite a rough sea. It was just before Christmas 1956 because we had Christmas Day at sea, because I'd had an abscess under the tooth, and I always remember going to the doctor and he wouldn't take it out, and I said 'Three months ago you were instructing me on how to give

morphine to a bloke who'd had his head blown off. Surely you can take this tooth out?' 'No,' he said 'you've got the sick bay to yourself, keep out the way,' because as a senior NCO I was almost crying but you couldn't do that, so they gave me a bottle of rum. We got a tot in Malaya, I always remember that was tinned Australian rum, we got the tot of rum or thruppence a day in lieu. I took the tot of rum. Always. As a senior NCO you had it neat, and you were allowed to keep it until rounds at night, eight o'clock in the evening. It was issued at about 11 o'clock, 12 o'clock.

Then I did a commission on the *Sheffield*. I came out in 1959 and did my last three years on reserve, but then my brother got our own boat, and we carried on fishing. I still regard the marines as my second family and when I go down there I get treated as one. I wouldn't have come out of the Royal Marines to go into a factory. I came out to carry on fishing. And then I came ashore after several years to make up fishing gear, and I'm still making up fishing gear. I've got a workshop at home now, I come down and do Saturdays for Max now.

I also teach traditional boat building and wire work and rope work. I've never built a boat of plywood or glue or anything. Lyme has changed in my short lifetime. There's not a nucleus. I suppose the war brought a few strange people here, the RAF did their share of infusing new blood into the town. I think it was getting so inbred. I'm related to a huge number of families in Lyme. I always remember somebody saying 'Here, I hear you've upset the Gollops,' I said 'No,' he said 'Well you've upset the Hodders so you've upset the Gollops!' that's the way it goes. But I can remember we were at Cobb Gate before the war. Father had the first tripping boat there, *The Wanderer*, and the bloke built it with so much beam that they had to knock the wall down to get it out. And it was nicknamed *The Frying Pan*. It was the dryest boat in Lyme Harbour because when it went down on the sea it threw the sea either way, so if you were a boat close by you'd had it. They used to do shilling trips, prior to that they used to book boats by the day, the gentry used to come down and book a sailing boat, but we never used to come down the Cobb very much, and if I said to my father 'I'm going down the Cobb, Dad,' he'd say 'Don't you go upsetting any of them Cobb men.'

The Cobb men? There was the Hodders, the Homyers, the Boalshs. I can remember the last few commercial vessels coming in, and of course they used to draw on casual labour. They were mainly bringing in timber and coal and they would take off all sorts of ballast. Prior to when the cement works closed down they would pick up cement, but as soon as chemical cement came that finished the hydraulic cement. It closed very early on. I can remember the mayor, he was one of them, and of course father used to have to move his mooring if there was a vessel coming in. Fishing was still here, off the beach and Church Cliff Beach, the Curtis's were there, they were an old Lyme family. You didn't go up Church Cliff Beach, you just didn't go there. They had a nickname, they were called the Bears, and their house is being done up now, it's a nice house on Church Cliff Beach, but in the early days they had galvanised partitions in the house, that's all it was. It was a nice place to grow up. Brilliant. Us kids used to go right down the cliffs during the war. There was barbed wire on the beach and that, there was a lookout post on the headland there, but we'd go off down there for the day and nobody would worry about you or anything else. You'd come home when you were hungry and that was that. We'd go down and get a loaf of bread in John the baker's, go down and pick up a bucket full of winkles on the beach, boil them up and have your winkles and

bread on the beach, lovely. We carried on fishing and then our turn came to come ashore and now my son's got the aquarium, and my brother and I are still involved in it.

There's only really the tourist trade now in Lyme, a few lads work at Westlands, there's a small building trade, other than that there's not much. We've got a good nucleus of fishing, the Wason boys are the boys now, they're doing very well in keeping it going, it's not easy.

To make a trawl? You need a fair bit of space to rig it, joining all the pieces of net together from a pattern you've got in your head. It's a well known fact that to make a successful trawl you've got to fish, if you get a factory-made trawl it's just two pieces of netting put together and that's that, if you get it from the Bridport Gundry, places like that mostly sub it out to me. I used to make a 12 fathom trawl in 50 hours, fully rigged. But this one now took me 70 hours, but of course I only charge Chris for 50.

My grandfather would be very proud of me, netting and boat building. This is what I say to people when they see me making a piece of net, that my granddad taught me how to do it, but what he kept to himself was that I'd still be doing it when I was 75. He kept that to himself, but he has given me good stamina. I still look up to him as my mentor. He had a lot of patience with me, that's the thing. I always remember when I came out the marines and started making willow pots, he was blind then and he was living up our house, I was quite proud to take him up a pot. He went around that pot and said 'That's all right, boy.' I was 27, 28 then, and I was quite proud to do that. It kept him a bit interested.

3. Max Gollop – Marine Aquarium, The Cobb. Lyme Regis. Born 1957.

It's an interesting way of life - different from financial services…

I grew up in Lyme, I went to Woodroffe, left there in 1975 and went up to Bridport Gundry and did a two-year course in netmaking and ended up on their sales team. Around about that time my father came ashore and we both set up a netmaking business making trawling gear. Since my father retired I went into financial services, ended up as an area manager for Pearl Assurance. I was in financial services for 15 years and still do a little bit of introducing. In 2001 I bought the aquarium off my uncle. Running the aquarium is a full time job.

In the aquarium? Lots of different things, conger eels, lobsters, crab, mullet, crayfish, everything is caught locally and everything's native to Lyme Bay. We buy it off the fisherman. We have families coming back year after year. There's not many small aquariums in the country now, so that's what makes it special. A lot of the big sea life centres are going over to tropical fish, but people like to be able to see what's caught locally.

The volume of water? The actual amount is 3,000 gallons which fills up the whole aquarium. We change about 20 per cent, per day, we pump it from the harbour. If the water comes in and it's a bit sandy, we've got a sand filter which cleans it and also an ultraviolet system that cleans any algae.

The water varies. In winter the water is crystal clear, the water quality is fantastic, the specimens look fantastic, the only problem is there's no people about. So when the people are about in July and August the maintenance of the tank is a lot greater. Algae? The worst sort, it's a planktonic bloom in May and June,

which the UV will sort out, but it's just the general maintenance is a lot higher. We pump it straight in. Sometimes we have to come down in the evening, like last night I was down here until ten o'clock cleaning tanks, whereas in the winter you don't have to touch them. It's been a big learning curve. Every three months we change the fish over, put them back in the sea.

Feeding? Again, depending on the water temperature and the time of the year. In the winter they hardly eat anything, in the summer it's every other day, but the fish will tell you when they're hungry. We feed them on sprats cut up, and whiting fillets. We feed whelks to the lobsters. Small crabs we catch in the pots which we feed to the octopus. Basically they're living on what they'd eat in the sea. It's an interesting way of life. It's different from financial services. What I like about this business is that people come to me, whereas in financial services I was always knocking on doors. The pressure in the aquarium is making sure the fish are OK and the tanks are clean.

We open about the 7th March and we close at the end of October. I'm down here five days a week. My wife does a day a week and my father does a day a week, but really, although I'm not here I've still got to come down and check everything before I open. It's a long season. I find the season is starting later and sliding into September and October it's still busy, but you always look forward to the last week in October which is the October half term, and after that it goes dead quiet. Any work we've got to do in the aquarium, ie new tanks or new displays, we get those done in the winter. In 2004 we had the whole aquarium re-plumbed. We've got backup pumps and that.

We try and make the displays as interesting as possible. You get some families that are in there for ten minutes and others that are in there for two hours. We get school parties. I get visitors who say 'Where are the sharks?' and I say 'Most of them are working in the gift shops over there!' The old lobster pots are quite interesting and photographs of the filming 'The French Lieutenant's Woman.' Those pictures have been up there for quite a number of years now but there's different people coming through this aquarium every year, and people never tire of seeing those photographs.

This is called the 'Dark House,' they used to lay the bodies out. That was upstairs I think. But these have been little warehouses, net lofts, part of the building used to be an isolation hospital so there's a lot of history there. It's a nice place to work, nice views. And you meet a lot of interesting people, strange people, 95 per cent of them are ok. It's quite rewarding in both senses. When it's all up together and the tanks are A1 it's a nice feeling.

Yes, there's certain species, like a red gurnard, we can't keep them, they don't survive, yet the tub gurnard, the one with blue on its fins, that's fine. Flat fish, brill and Dover sole, they won't last. I think it's to do with their breathing, they need to be out to sea, but most of the small fish, you'd find in rock pools, that's OK. As far as the weather's concerned, I don't want it too hot. In July and August I don't want it red hot because people just collapse on the beach. I need weather like this, a little bit of rain, it keeps people moving around and it keeps us busy. The other nice thing about this is that you can have a laugh with people because they're all in holiday mood.

A lot of the members of the public who come in, especially the younger ones, they love to see big fish. Large conger eels, large lobsters, big crabs, so really it's keeping in touch with the fishermen to give me the top species. Large lobsters don't make a lot of money on the market because they're tough, so it's ideal for me. We've had a couple of lobsters in, I'd say they were about 80 years old. We've tried putting seaweed in for decoration purposes, but we find that it breaks up and clogs the filters. You can decorate the tanks so much but not go over the top. The actual water in all our tanks is circulating all the time. It's being dropped in the top and it goes out the back, so the actual fish are never ever in their own water. It keeps everything fresh.

The scallops here in the sack, I'm just waiting for the scientist to come and pick them up. You'll have to ask him what research he's doing. He's come from Lowestoft.

4. Dr Ewen Bell – Marine scientist, Cefas Centre for Environment, Fisheries & Aquaculture Science, Lowestoft.

The main aim of our project is to better understand the timing and location of spawning.

I was collecting a sample of scallops from Lyme Bay as part of a study into the spawning of scallops in the English Channel. This is a five-year project being run by Cefas and funded by Defra. Scallops are a highly valuable fishery for the UK and each year since 2002 have been in the top four most valuable species. In fact, the total value of scallops landed into England between 2002 and 2006 is the largest of any species.

Scallops release their spawn directly into the water, allowing oceanographic currents to disperse the resulting larvae that settle onto the seabed after a period of 3 to 6 weeks. There are many factors that might affect the probability of a scallop successfully breeding in any one year: the condition of the adult, the oceanographic currents and the type of seabed that the larvae eventually settle onto.

The main aim of our project is to better understand the timing and location of spawning so that we can then predict where the scallop larvae will be transported to and the likelihood of subsequent viable fisheries. Once these relationships have been investigated we will use likely scenarios for climate change to investigate how scallop populations may change with the changing oceans.

Initially the project focuses on sampling commercially caught scallops throughout the year to look at their condition in relation to spawning activity and to predict the optimal time for collecting larvae from the water. Once the timing and location of spawning has been pinned down we will then use a research vessel to collect samples of larvae from the water, and newly settled larvae from the seabed, to study the factors that lead to successful scallop populations.

The sampling scheme is being greatly helped through the active co-operation of the local scallop fishermen and the South West Inshore Scallopers Association (SWISA).

5. John Wason — Fisherman, Lyme Regis. Born Glastonbury 1935.

Oh I'm just after crab, lobster, a few whelks and bass fishing. Yes bass is fun, with rod and line. I shall keep on fishing till the Government will stop me I suppose.

John Wason, born 1935, in Somerset Glastonbury. I didn't know nothing about my father. Mother, she was working in Clarks factory when they was doing the war effort, making torpedoes wasn't it? Gyroscopes. Yes that's right, they was doing that in Street. I was only a little kid wasn't I? Whitehead torpedoes from Ferrybridge and that was in Clarks factory, the shoe factory.

Her mother, she worked when she was a young girl, she was looking after children, like a nanny, she was in service in Bath Mother was, and of course when she got married she lived on the moors, Butleigh Moors, she lived out there. Very bleak, very very bleak, yes. Well she lived in Moor House for a while, which is right up on the moor by Wason's Bridge, there is a bridge named Wason's Bridge. That's our family bridge, where our family lived, all the family come from out there, see, that way.

Well my earliest memories as a kid: I lived at Wells Road, I lived in the old pub, the Wagon and Horses. That was out on the Wells Road, just outside of Glastonbury, down over Cemetery Hill, and then we moved from there just up the road a bit to a house, a red brick house, number 37, Wells Road, yes, and that is where all the tramps used to call and get their tea and Mother was soft enough to make it for 'em. We reckon they used to mark the pavement outside so that every tramp that went up through, because there was tramps everywhere they days, they used to go up through and I always used to remember when the gypsies used to come to the front door to sell her some pegs, she used to say to me as a little kid, 'you nip out the back because they will pinch the onions while I'm buying the pegs, they will have somebody out the back pinching the onions and shallots,' yes she always used to say that to me.

School? Glastonbury, I didn't spent too much time there, I didn't like school. I started work when I was 14. Yes I used to work just down the road with the Francis's, and then I went to work for a farmer out towards West Pennard. Just working on the farm, I stayed at home, and when we moved farms we moved from Brindon it was called, at Wick, and they went to Godney, out on the moors and I went to work and lived in then for a while till the floods come up one night.

We was right beside the river and it overflowed one night I been out all night with the bloody boys or sommat and I come back, had my supper, went to bed and in the morning I got up and stepped into a foot of water, under me bed, where the river had overflowed, 'cause I used to live downstairs, and it was all flooded. Mother had me back home then, she was afraid I was going to catch pneumonia or sommat.

It always flooded until they put the big pumps in down towards Burrowbridge. There's an old one, which is a museum. Yes that's right Westonzoyland.. It ain't that far from the Burrow Mound. Yes I was working with sheep, pigs, cows. Yes we used to make our own cider. Very good, hundreds and hundreds of gallons. We used to use pipes, hogsheads all sorts, you know, we had big sheds full of 'em, full up with cider and it's surprising I don't know where it all used to go but they used to bloody drink it, I never used to drink much because I was a kid like, you know. Oh yes, cider. Cider bread and cheese and a good onion or an apple, that's what we used to have. Oh yes, I used to help make it, I used to make the cider, it used to turn your hands black. The

John Wason, alias Hurricane Joe

tannin, like dye and that, yes we used to do all that. Get up in the middle of the night to run the screw to press down a few more turns. Old wooden presses, Yes, oh yes, and we used to put it in with straw, a cheese was made with straw you know, we used to have the hay knife and cut around, cut it all tidy, put that lot back on top, press it again and get some more out. Oh crikey you would press it over several days, we used to press it over quite a few days actually. Lovely to drink that. Oh yes, it used to be nice cider.

Well I worked on farms for 15 years anyway, 15 years before I took up fishing, on different farms, all over the place I worked, Bridgwater, down near Cannington, Bristol, Frome. Rampisham out here. Well they closed the pub, the Tiger's Head. There used to be a lovely stream there going by it, well it will still be there anyway, out through the water meadows and I always remember, my son, my oldest boy, he went down there trout fishing. I bought him a little fishing rod and he went down there and they seen him in the pub, they said they couldn't believe it, he had this massive trout he caught and he had it in his hands like that and he chucked the rod down and he ran up the hill to show us he'd caught this big trout, that was my oldest son, Paul. He was about four to five year old. That was his first venture in fishing. His boat now, it's called Spanish Eyes, yes all his boats is called the *Spanish Eyes* you know.

Fishing? Forty-seven years ago now, I came here. Well it started when I bought a small boat, ten or twelve foot, I can't remember actually but it's one of these with a little motor on the back and I used go out of West Bay catching mackerel, and then I came to Lyme and went out 'ere, and I bought a bigger boat, I had one built, a bigger one. And then I sold that one and got one a bit bigger. Clifford Samways he bought his first mackerel off of me when we was at West Bay, I used to go out feathering

mackerel and he had finished with Gundrys. Yes it's a hell of a business now.

My boat? I was in the pub here one day and I had a boat then called the *Three Sisters* which I had bought for £20. It leaked like a prawn bowl, it was a 20-foot boat but he leaked and I didn't know nothing about patching boats or caulking boats in them days, so it'd leak like anything. So he was in the pub one day and of course I was out in all winds and weathers and he said to me one day, he said, Mr Varnes his name was, Jack Varnes, and he said to me one day: 'Would you like a bigger boat John?' And I said 'I'd love a bigger boat but I'll never be able to afford one.' Well he said 'You find one,' he said, 'and we will see what we can do.' And I never took no notice of it 'cause he was a drinking man and I thought well…

He was retired here. And I was in the Cobb Arms a few weeks later and Jack Cawston, the landlord, he said to me 'Yer,' he said, 'have you done anything about looking for a boat?' I said 'Well no.' I said, 'I haven't done nothing about it.' 'Well,' he said, 'Jack been on to me that he told you to have a look and see if you could find a boat.' 'Well,' I said 'he wasn't serious was he?' And he said 'Yes he was serious.' So I heard of a boat for sale at Beer, *Beer Pearl*, that's what t'was, and so I told him about it and he said 'Let's go down and have a look at it.' So we went down and had a look.

That's right on the beach, so we went down and had a look at it and Newtons owned it, and he said to me 'What do you think of it?' And I said 'Cor great,' because it was magic against what I had wasn't it?

Twenty-four foot, heavily built, she had a Ruston and Hornsby engine in her. Took two of ee to start un. You get it turning with two hands, then the other bloke used to hit the lever over. That's right a decompression one, you hit it over and then he'd start. And he said 'What did ee think of it?' And I said 'I like it.' And he said 'What did he want for it?' I can't remember what it was now, it wasn't that much, well not as today's standards is, but we had it, yep. He bought it for me and he used to go out to sea with me and I used to pay him, give him his beer money, you know he used to have his beer money off of me.

I used to take him out and I used to do his lunch most days when we was trawling. He loved queens, raw you know and I used to clean up, when we were catching a lot of queen scallops. I used to clean them up and do 'em for him and he used to have them for his lunch. And then we was out there one day and he said to me 'Ere John,' he said 'I think you ought to have a bigger boat.' He said, 'I think you should have a bigger boat.' And I said 'Well it's up to you.' And we looked on the paper and that and we seen one for sale, a friend of mine owned it down at Teignmouth, a forty footer, *Early Dawn*, the name of the boat, and I do know how much we paid for that one. He said 'Let's go down and have a look at her.' So we went down and we met the owner and that, he took us out for a run out into the water. And he said 'What do ee think of un?' 'Cor,' I said, 'he's a cracking boat.' He had a five cylinder Gardiner engine in him, beautiful boat it was anyway. He said 'Well what do you think of it?' I said 'He's bloody lovely.' He said to the bloke 'What do you want for it?' He wanted just over £4,000 for it, and he said 'Well I'll tell ee what, I'll give £4,000 for it.' And the bloke said: 'Done.' Yes that was it. We shook hands on it and we took delivery. They brought the boat up here for us, all the nets. That was when I got into spratting.

Oh I must have had her in the 1960s. Yes it was the early 60s because I had him for quite a while and Jack said to me one day out to sea there 'I don't want no more money off you 'cause I don't want no beer money,' he said. 'I can't get out here so much now,' and he said 'You'm doing all right,' he said. 'Well,' he said,

'I'll give ee the boat.'

He give me the boat and it wasn't long after that he came down with cancer. He was in hospital down at Bovey Tracey which was, before that, the TB hospital. And he was in there with cancer and we thought he was getting on all right. I used to go down and see him most evenings like, and thought he was getting on all right, and he come out. He was out and about in the pub and that, and he had a cottage up Cobb Road then. And I had a phone call from the hospital in Lyme and they said 'We want you to come to the Lyme Regis hospital.' So I said 'What's this about?' 'Mr Varnes has been admitted.' And I went in there and he was in the hospital and he was pretty rough, and it wasn't long after that he died. 'Course he never had no family or nothing so everything was left to me, everything. Yes he left his cottage which wasn't a lot of money in they days, t'wasn't so much as we give for the boat.

But anyway with the money he had left, I thought 'well I am going to put that to good use.' So I had a boat built, the big one, the forty-eight footer, the *Barbarella*, yes she was built at Bideford, Bideford Bankside Shipyard, she was built. Steel ? Yes. She had a Volvo in her, a big Volvo, 250 horsepower Volvo. And you know we went on from there, I kept her for a while, she drew seven foot of water, too much water for this harbour. Yes seven foot is a lot of water for this harbour, because it's a tidal harbour but we kept her for a few years.

My son took her on. Yes Paul, he started running it when he was 14 years old and we kept it for quite a few years and then we downsized. Then we went to a boat called the *Frank Robert* we downsized. We worked that one with Leckie, yes we done a lot of pair trawling with Leckie, for sprats. Spratting was big, big money then. Clifford used to take them and he used to take 'em in they days to a processing plant at Lowestoft, a bloke at

Lowestoft used to have 'em, and it was good, we could earn good money at that you know.

Yes well we never used to sprat in they days when we had the Barbarella, we never used to sprat until October, the end of October, we'd start spratting. 'Course nowadays they go spratting too early and the sprats are like bloody jam, they been on spratting since August, yes 'course it's too hot, you want sprats to stay nice and cold. Yes that's right keeping your mackerel cold and that yes, it was the main of it you know.

Other fish? Plaice, cod, skate, a lot of skate and stuff like that. We did do potting for a while with the *Barbarella*, we were running about 400 pots then in them days but we didn't get on too well with the potting you know. We was fishing then, we was fishing from Portland right down off of Beer. Oh yes, a long stretch we was fishing yes. We had the speed with that boat see, and we had the room to carry the gear, he was such a big boat. We used to do 36 hours sometimes with that one. When me son took over he had two crew besides hisself on there, and he sacked 'em all one day. He rung me up and he was 15 years old then he was down at Brixham Market and he rung up at night and I said 'What's the matter?' He says 'You better find me another crew I've given 'em all the sack.' I said 'What do ee mean give 'em the sack?' He said 'Well they won't go to sea.' He said 'They said the weather was too bad and they wouldn't want to go to sea.' And he said 'I wanted to go lemon sole fishing down off Mevagissey.' He was fishing right down there and so he give 'em all the sack.

The nickname 'Hurricane Joe'? That was a boat I had called the *Hurricane*, that was the boat, I had after I had the small boat, I had the *Hurricane* made, that was made up near Yeovil, a clinker-built boat, and that's were I had that one made at Milborne Port. There was a boat builder there and he built it.

I had the *Frank Robert* and then when I sold the *Frank Robert*, I sold he to some Irishmen they come over and bought the Frank Robert, I delivered it for them. They came 'ere and bought the boat, and paid for him and they said would I take him to Penzance, so that they could take him on from there and go across the Irish sea? So we left here in a south east wind, in a strong wind, nearly a gale and we got down past Start Point and they said to me 'Right skipper we will take over the wheel, you go down and have a sleep 'cause you've drove all the way down here in the night like this.' And 'course the boat was going on lovely with the south east breeze wasn't it. I went down and I was in bed there and I was sort of dozy and I thought 'this boat's banging, why is he bloody banging?' Anyway I went back up because I couldn't sleep because the boat was making this banging noise, going up and down and banging. So I went back up and I said, 'What's on then?' 'Oh go back down and sleep. We'm all right skip.' 'You'm all right? You'm heading back to bloody Lyme Regis.' They was heading back for Lyme. Well they couldn't read the compass or nothing could they. Well I said 'You'm heading back to where we've come from.' So I took over and took it right down. Then I bought Leckie's boat then, called the *Why Not?*

I had the *Why Not?* for years and that was a good little French boat. I had her re-engined, I had a reconditioned engine put in her and we kept her for years, till we had the *Seeker* built. She was built at Bristol at the Albion Docks. Oh what was his name, David Abel, Abel's Shipyard it was. Just down the road from the SS *Great Britain*. There's a pub down there called The White Horse. We had the launching in there. 'Course it's all big money down there now with all the houses they built on the docks there.

Timber yard one side and the other side was the sand, Brown was the people who owned it and he had, there was 11 of 'em altogether, brothers, he had his own football team, in Bristol. Oh yes, and then you gradually seen it disappear, knocking down buildings and putting these houses up.

Well we called her *Seeker* and then we registered her, that was her name, then we got the registration people got in touch with us and said we couldn't have that name, because one of their vessels had it, the same name. So what if we put something in front? Yes that will be all right, that's why she's a *Sea Seeker*.

Well me son got her now, Christopher the youngest. Paul, he's the oldest. Paul's got the *Spanish Eyes* and Barry he's got the *Palatine*, and Christopher's got the *Sea Seeker*. Yes, at the moment they's all after different species. One's after whelks, one's after scallops and one's after trawl fish. Well the *Palatine* is the whelker, the *Spanish Eyes* is scalloping and the *Sea Seaker* is trawling, so they'm all after three different things. They vary it a bit sometimes. Oh I'm just after crab, lobster, a few whelks and bass fishing. Yes bass is fun, with rod and line.

The ground? Everybody goes on it but there it 'tis, you got to take that chance haven't you? Oh yes when I started there was some characters, there was. We had Paddy Hodder, he had one hand, Ron Crab, Crabby he was another character, Mr F, another character, we had Ron Govier, Victor Homyer, ex-mayor he was, bad tempered bastard he was, cor wasn't he just. Oh yes, he was, he been thrown in a few times, in the harbour, the other boatmen used to throw him in. When I came here there was very few boats, there was 14 licensed boats for tripping and there was only two of us fishing. That's the main thing now, 'tis our family doing it, doing that type of fishing. Yes Clive he has fish off of 'em, yes we still deal with Clive Samways. We buy all sorts off of him when we want it, you know, nearly all my bait comes from he, on the Cobb.

The sign? We was in Florida on holiday and I was out there on a fishing trip like with the wife and that, and we saw this sign so we thought right, we are going to get one of these, so we took photographs of it and that, and we had one made up then. I think the main building here so far as I can make out, was a quarantine place. But the stores there was none of this here when I came 'ere, this has all been built. The shelters out the end of the Cobb used to be the pay office where they used to pay their blokes from working on the big boats unloading coal and that, and they used to load, take a lot of stone from there, a lot of blue lias I think.

Well, when I came here, Roy and Ken Gollop were trawling then and they were very helpful to me actually, Roy Gollop gave me some ideas of what to do and whatever. To come from Somerset into fishing here? Oh yes it was one hell of a jump. I used when I started see, I used to do just mackerel fishing all the time, I used to go out here and catch boxes and boxes of mackerel. I used to have the hanging nets all along the beach like you know. We used to make all our own stuff up. All the lobster pots and that we used to make. I still bring willow up for Roy now, because he still makes 'em. Yes he makes them for visitors, so I bring the willows up from Somerset for him. I got a bloke down there sells me bundles of willows and I bring 'em up, he had some last year actually.

Keen on shooting? Oh yes, I love shooting. Wildfowl? Yes I was out last night. I had some cracking ducks last night, really high ducks, a lot of pigeons, we shoot a lot of pigeons, we clear a lot of vermin for farmers and that. Pigeons are a menace, they will drive you crazy they will, they get in a field of corn, or a field of rape, they will take the rape right down to the ground, yes, and 'course wild geese now is a vermin, Canadas. I was up in the Midlands two weeks ago, I was shooting Canadas, right up near Manchester Airport, I went up there for a few days, and we shot 52, and about 60 ducks and in one afternoon we shot 220 pigeons, they was coming in there. Pigeons was everywhere.

Keep on fishing? Oh yes as long as I can, I shall keep on fishing till the Government will stop me I suppose. I got one grandson, Luke, he's fishing with his father Paul on the *Spanish Eyes*. The other boys, we got one boy, Wayne, on the *Seeker*, been on ever since he left school, he's a terrific chap for work. Yes oh yes 'tis good to have you know, for three sons to follow into the same thing as I have done so, yes. But they don't know nothing about farming, not a bloody thing. Yes, they don't know nothing about that.

I've picked up three mines in my time and one of they's just by the Cobb Arms where you put your money in for shipwrecked mariners.

6. Clare Wason – Whelk and shellfish seller, Lyme Regis. Born Northern Ireland 1952.

I came to Lyme to work in a hotel, met a fishermen and the rest is history…

My father was an air traffic controller after the war. He was in Lancaster bombers, a pathfinder. He never talked about the war and we weren't allowed to watch war films. He was very private about it. He was decorated with a DFC. He may have talked to my elder brother but not to me. After the war my parents got married and he was transferred to Northern Ireland to the airport for a period they were there about nine years and then we were back to Manchester airport then. My grandfather came from Bolton. He was also a pilot in the First World War. That's why I like flying…. on holidays.

My mother was from Peterborough. She was a nurse and then she brought up the family. Her father was a sergeant in the Royal Engineers in the First World War. That was where she met my father because a lot of the wartime airfields were in that area. My father was Thomas Hodkinson. I started school in Manchester just outside but most of my schooling was in Blackpool. That was terrific, mainly the 1960s. Very good. There was everything to do. It was still a major holiday destination. It was safe. Not like today, a child could do anything they wanted. And it was just there, ice skating, swimming….

My first job was on the fun fair. I was collecting glasses in the fun house. There was always work in Blackpool at weekends and after school. It was lovely, just nice. In winter the pleasure beach more or less closed down. But there were a few things open. We had the lights, the illuminations, so it never closed down for long. The lights brought a different type of person and after they finished, that was the quietest time, after the Christmas, then everybody was painting ready for the following season. I have lived on the seaside almost all of my life, couldn't live anywhere else. Unless there was sea. I came to Lyme to work in a hotel, met a fishermen and the rest is history.

I have had the whelk stall for over 30 years and we did have a wet fish shop in the town. We sold that when my husband got rid of his big boat to his son, that was the *Seeker*, the last boat, he wanted to do a different type of fishing. So we gave up the fish shop and I came here permanently on to this one. We had the fish shop about 15 years. All sorts of fish. Just basic fish, we had quite a good local trade. A lot of older people would come in every day and buy a couple of fillets. They were getting whatever the boat brought in. So that was it. Occasionally they would get soles, mackerel. whiting, we used to sell a lot of dogfish, skate, you can't sell dogfish now, gurnards, all sorts of things.

This stall is totally different: prawns, crabmeat, whelks, which my husband catches, cockles and mussels, lobster today, fresh lobster meat, smoked mackerel, roll mops, I vary it if I can. Some don't sell and we have to go back to the originals. It is all ready to eat, and that is the idea, and you sit and eat it on the beach. Sometimes we open in February for the half term if the weather is any good. And we go on till the end of October, the last half term before Christmas. I get a lot of regulars. When we started, the children I served, have now got children of their own… shows we have been here a long time. And it is nice that the little ones buy for themselves, their mum gives them the money and they come and they ask for it, and that is a novelty for the little ones.

Selling fish direct is good, you make that little bit extra. People want different fish, not just from this country but from anywhere. Fish is more popular. More expensive, people

Clare Wason

experiment more. Advertising, televisions and all these celebrity chefs, that helps. Mind you some of them can't cook whelks. John won't tell a certain celebrity chef how he cooks his … It is a secret. Twenty years ago you couldn't give a whelk away. Most of them go to Korea, and there is good money to be made with whelks. If you are in the right area you don't have to do anything else.

It is hard work, back breaking, anything where you have to lift pots up is back breaking. John has his own little whelk beds and the boys leave him alone, they don't touch it. So it's fine. His sons, all three of them have got boats. *Sea Seeker* which Christopher owns, we have got *Spanish Eyes*, I have a feeling it is *Spanish Eyes* 3 that Paul owns and Barry owns the *Palatine*. They vary: Barry is doing a lot on whelks, Paul is scalloping at the moment, and Christopher is fishing, all three doing different things, all kitted out so that they can change when they need to. I don't have anything from them, just from John. They have got their own markets, but if I needed anything…

John's grandson is working with his dad Paul. His name is Luke and so he's working on the *Spanish Eyes*. Luke must be up for 30. Other fishermen? The hillbillies from Charmouth are fishing, they are full time. Father and son. And there is Brian Marks and Nicky, they are full time. And that is about it full-time fishing, but there are lots of part-timers.

September is a pleasant month, a lot quieter than August, but when you have had a packed August and the town is bursting at the seams, with big families, Lyme is very much a family place. But once September comes and the children go back to school, then you get the older people, and they have their holidays, a more leisurely pace of life and the traffic is not very busy. It is just the whole town changes, August can be very stressful if the weather isn't very good.

If mum and dad eat a pot of whelks, the children will start to eat whelks. Especially when they say 'We used to come here and eat whelks at your age with your grandad' and then they think this is good. I open anything between 10 and 11am. It takes me anything up to 3 hours before I get here. In the height of the summer I can stay till 9pm but now 7pm and 8 at the weekend sometimes.

I will continue here till I win the lottery. You never know. If people ask me 'Are you open tomorrow?' I always say 'If I haven't won the lottery tonight I will be here.' Seven days a week in the season. Now it is tapering off, I go off for a week next week, then I come back. Nobody else can do it like me so there is no point in employing a stand-in. I am modest… aren't I ?

7. Harry May – Licensed boatman, Lyme Regis. Born Ulverstone 1946.

That year there were terrible gales, so I plucked up courage, and I did buy 'Anna.' This was mackerel, taking people out, they would take them home for supper. I've been doing trips ever since and I love the job more and more as the years go on. I couldn't imagine doing anything else now.

My name's Harry May. I was born in the Lake District. My father was an agricultural adviser, he'd go round farms and tell them 'what to sprinkle on the land.' He retired early in 1950. He just happened to be working for Lancashire County Council at the time he retired. My mother and father then drove all round the south west peninsula looking for somewhere to retire and they came down Cobb Road on a fine day, flat, calm sea and the house was there. They finished up buying it for £3500. It was called The Chalet, a big place with fantastic views, 180 degrees of sea view completely and we moved in, September 1950.

The very first morning that we got here I went to St Gildas, the convent school up the road. There were all kinds of funny rules and regulations. Boys weren't allowed to play with girls. I was frowned on by the nuns because I couldn't skip. I just couldn't master it. Lots of people in Lyme will remember Sister Anthony, a lovely lady.

Sadly the house went downhill in 1962. It only slid, it was all a bit dodgy that area of Lyme. But it wasn't a natural slip, the house had been there since 1903. Lyme Regis town council gave permission for a developer to bulldoze the land next to us which was very steep, all the way along the front behind the amusement arcade. It was liquid mud, lots of slippages, there were lots of trees, a bit of a mess. They would bulldoze for hours and hours every day. They just pushed the soil straight down the cliff, across the sea front and down on to the beach. Then they'd go back and do it again. So after they'd been doing it for weeks and weeks, there was a huge wedge of mud from the top of the cliff. The seafront was completely buried, as were the lamp posts. If they hadn't messed with it, it would have probably been OK.

So on 18th February 1962, I came back from the grammar school and the house was definitely moving. It was creaking and groaning and it was making horrible noises from right inside. My parents were definitely aware of it, but not really panicking. Amazingly I went to the pictures in Seaton, saw Circus of Horrors. I came back at about half past ten. Cobb Road was closed, fire brigade there and the RAF stopped us driving down the hill. So I had to find my parents who were in Glenholme, a hotel three doors away on Cobb Road. We stayed there. In the morning our house had moved about five inches, which is enough to bring the floors up and the walls down. It had slewed to the left. It was a big rescue operation, the local RAF came up and were emptying out the house. The rescue operation went on for weeks.

My parents were devastated. My father was a lot older than my mother, he was born in 1889 and this happened in 1962 so he was 72, 73. He was getting on a bit and she seemed to shelter him from most of it. Insurance? It was an Act of God in those days, the developer went bankrupt overnight, didn't have to pay us anything. Mother went to various court cases but it was hopeless. Nothing happened. Her hair went white over this event.

So I finished up joining the Army. I was 16. I went to Carlisle to be an apprentice in the Royal Electrical and Mechanical Engineers. When I got there he said 'Oh May, there's no

Harry May

vacancies in the REME, so you're going to be a gun fitter.' They were huge guns, monsters. It was no fun. I didn't enjoy it at all. I showed my hatred of the whole thing by failing all the tests we had every fortnight on the latest bit of gun, and eventually I got sent to Driver Training in Yeovil. Then sent to Germany 1964 to '66 and went to Aden in '67. Things were hotting up then, we had to carry guns. There was FLOSY, the Front for the Liberation of South East Yemen, and the NLF, the National Liberation Front. They didn't like each other much, but they certainly didn't like the British. So there were always problems.

We had Tiger beer from Singapore, which was OK, but it was so cheap. There were crates and crates of the stuff. It was so, so hot. The locals ate this betel juice, they chewed these leaves in the afternoon. On the last day of the occupation we left by ship from Aden harbour, travelled for several days and played bingo on the ship. I wasn't really impressed. We landed in Bahrain but there wasn't any fighting, it was great. Then we flew back to England. I went to Marchwood, it was the home of the army's tugs. It was a very easy life there. I was signed on to a tug, the tug never did a thing. From stem to stern it was shining clean with everything working. The camp used to have its own railway line, rather a nice little train. We didn't really do anything. So much of my army career was just twiddling thumbs. Then suddenly somebody thought it would be a good idea to have a parade on Saturday mornings. Southampton was 80-odd miles away, it was just around the corner, and I could come home on a Friday evening. It was just wonderful. Then we had to do this parade on Saturday mornings. I just couldn't believe it. That was my decision to buy myself out. It was 1968, Northern Ireland was just starting up but that was the end of my army career, which was just the job. It cost me a mere 200 quid to buy myself out. I can remember paying 5/- more to express the cheque.

My parents had said that I could come out if I had a decent job to go to. So I lined up Securicor in Exeter. It was driving, so I left the Army and arrived at the Securicor depot as a free man a week or a fortnight later. I was told I was too young for Securicor, 'Very sorry, you can come back in a couple of years when you're old enough.' Since then I've been exceedingly lucky in this life with not having to do things that I don't want to do. I rarely wake up in the mornings and think 'Oh, I don't want to do that.'

My parents were still living at The Chalet. There is still the mobile home which their friends paid for anonymously. It is still called Sun Cottage and there was a washhouse built in the garden out of the floorboards of the house. The local rotary club took the house down and a couple of demolition experts directed them. The house was taken down beautifully.

I then started odd job gardening. I've done it for years. So odd jobs in the winter and then I got a job at an awful place, Chard Meat, it was just awful. I didn't stay there very long, but I ate a lot of fillet steak. I left and went to Glacier Metals in Chard, bearings, they were just about to move, so I was welding on the night shift and I was getting £22.10s a week, and that was the national average wage in 1970.

While I was there a friend of mine and I were going off to buy some cider on the Crewkerne road just out of Hunter's Lodge, they had some fantastic cider in there. We used to sit with a half pint glass and have a little bit of this and a little bit of that, and we were up there buying some cider for a barbecue or an orgy on the beach. He told me he was going to hitchhike to Australia. He was called Peter Waterfall. His mother was the matron of the hospital then, and on the spur of the moment, I said 'That sounds like a blooming good idea.' So I said 'I'll join you.' This was Easter so we were going to leave in September 1970.

In the meantime I carried on welding, saving a little bit. I used to have all day Friday through to Monday evening off work, so I used to wander down the Cobb to the Old Watch House. Victor Homyer who I had known for a long time employed a friend of mine, Sandy Stewart, and I would go down there. Victor had two tripping boats so Sandy and Victor would take the tripping boats out and I would sell the crabs and the lobsters. And then I took a test in June of that year with Bill Habgood who was the harbour master there, ex-police sergeant, a boat driving test, then I ran Victor's boat for him, and Sandy and I had a boat each and a very happy summer, it was 1970.

I also knew that whatever happened I was going to come back to do more tripping. I knew that was what I was going to be doing, because I so enjoyed doing it. I've never been better paid than I was then. Victor would always give me a wadge of fishy pound notes. So I learned hard from Victor, because he'd only tell you once, then he'd shout the next time. He'd shout a lot.

We took people out fishing and tripping. A bit of both. There wasn't any scalloping in those days, or if there was, there was hardly any, so the ground was in pristine condition. Since then it has since been systematically smashed up and destroyed. It's heartbreaking, the damage that is legally going on out there. I hate it. It's so flattened. There's so much money involved that the Fisheries Minister, Ben Bradshaw recently just allowed it to carry on again. I think we might be on the edge of it being banned. The bay is absolutely invaded with dogfish. They smell the blood and death from the smashed up scallops and other shellfish hit by the dredges.

And then on September 22nd 1970, I left with Peter Waterfall. We got a lift to Southampton and got on the ferry. How far did I get hitchhiking? Four and a half months later we arrived in Fremantle… It was from Le Havre to Paris. We got stopped in a town called St Dizier. We stood there the whole day long and nobody stopped. You lose your smile, and in the end at about five o'clock, we walked into the town, we had a youth hostel booked and we went there pretty fed up, far too much gear in our pack, left loads of stuff in this youth hostel.

And then we met two French men and a French girl and we got a lift with them and they took us somewhat slowly in the right direction. Then we got to the Swiss border and said 'Cheerio' to them. Then we got to Basle. We went to Basle zoo and saw a fantastic gorilla. At one point we got to the bottom of the Swiss Alps, it was pouring with rain and it was dark, there was nowhere to sleep and we got picked up by the village potter who lived at Altdorf, William Tell country. We got a lift up through these fantastic mountains and we arrived at Altdorf, pitch dark, and the potter let us sleep on the floor of his pottery while he went off home. He was going to his holiday home on the other side of the Swiss Alps, so we stayed in this cottage with him and his wife, they were so nice to us. We wrote to them for ages afterwards. Then we got into Italy, all the way down the coast of Yugoslavia. Tito was firmly in charge, his picture was up everywhere. You could knock on any door and they almost had to put you up. We went to Dubrovnik, it was beautiful. Then we went inland and saw a completely different side of Yugoslavia. It was very, very poor indeed. We went on a very rough road through the mountains into Greece.

It was very exciting arriving in Istanbul as this was our gateway to Asia. The Blue Mosque, the Bosphorus, the Galata Bridge and The Pudding Shop – the latter being a thriving café where travellers met and exchanged information. Notice boards advertised lifts east and west. The Grand Bazaar had miles and miles of shops crammed full of bargains and all in all Istanbul was wonderful.

We left to go east towards Iran on a train that seemed to stop to chat with every shepherd and there were loads on the way. We got off the train within view of Mount Ararat. Bus to the Iran border, bus across Iran stopping at various places to marvel, eat, sleep and just stand and stare. Crossing the border into Afghanistan it was like going back in time – could have stayed for weeks. Kabul Pass, the Khyber Pass and into Pakistan and then through a chaotic border post into India. Crowds, dust, water buffalos pulling huge carts, dodgy rooms, incredible trains, heat, the Taj Mahal and the Pink City. On to Nepal and Kathmandu that was everything and more, saw the sun rise over Everest, eat my beloved water buffalo, enjoyed all the sights, tastes and local produce – had a real job leaving.

Over the following weeks travelled through East Pakistan (that was), Thailand, Malaya, spent time in paradise in Penang and on to Singapore and a Russian ship to Freemantle in Western Australia – four and a half months of travel and £200 spent! Judith, my wife to be, flew out on the £10 scheme and together we settled down to life and work in Australia. The time was spent mainly in Sydney when she became a secretary and I got a job as a postman in one of the wealthier suburbs.

After two happy and eventful years we had enough saved to come back home overland – it was wonderful to be travelling again seeing Indonesia and Burma this time. It took six months to get back and cost about £250 each – it was June 1973 when we arrived back and the start of the tourist season. So I went straight back to Victor and had a very happy summer doing mackerel fishing trips and working alongside Victor, Reg and Jim Homyer, Ron and Chris Govier, Colin Cross, two Albert Hodders plus Lionel and Lewes, Jack Nuttall, Jack Brenchley, Nobby Clark, Ron Crabb, Les Haines, John Morgan, Ken and Roy Gollop and John Hodder. Some of these had retired whilst I

was in Australia but I feel it is important to record their names.

I worked for Victor again in 1974 and bought my first boat *Anna* from Les Haines at the end of that season. It took quite a bit of courage to tell Victor I was going on my own because he had a pretty bad temper and he shouted a lot but I was very fond of him and I learnt from the master how to get people in a boat even when they didn't want to go! The season for boating lasted from Easter to late September and during the winter I went odd-jobbing, usually gardening and all in all it was an ideal existence.

In 1983 during the annual inspection of my boat, the boat builder Paul Mears and his father Harold pointed out some planks in the boat that were getting a bit soft, so after much deliberations with Judith we ordered another boat exactly at the same time she was pregnant with our second son Robin, Joseph had been born in 1980, six months before my father died at the grand age of 93.

The new boat *Anna Two* was beautifully made and delivered on time – 24 foot open traditional tripping boat – oak on iroco, the hull cost £8,500.00 and the Thorneycroft engine was £4,500.00. Unknown to Paul and his father at the time, was that this would be the last tripping boat they would build, wood was to rocket upwards and fibreglass was appearing everywhere.

So the years crept by, we lived in Axminster in our own house and let it in the summer and moved back to Lyme to the garden at The Chalet and moved into the caravans that we bought since the house came down. Joseph and Robin grew up in idyllic surroundings. We all got used to the move to Lyme and six months later when autumn appeared, the move back to Axminster. For me it meant my other life as a jobbing gardener.

This carried on and in the winter of 1988 I got a job catching whelks on an Offshore 105 owned by Brian Pogson. This was a fast sleek boat of 35-foot, with a large engine, around 300hp, forward wheelhouse, loads of deck space aft for carrying a ton and a half of whelks from the fishing grounds off Lyme back to port and delivered by a Nissan Cabstar to Poole by midday where they were cooked up and picked out. Everything to do with whelks was heavy and very smelly and their reproductive habits were appalling!

I fell in love – with the Offshore 105 – and felt I could take people out fishing all year round in comfort and style so after much discussion again Brian sold his Offshore and in the early spring of '89 two brand new hulls arrived at Rousden and in two months we built two very smart, fully kitted out offshores. VHF radios, echo sounder, radar, GPS, cooker, stereo, soft seats in the large wheelhouse, 380HP turbo-charged engine and miles of space for fishermen and divers.

My life with *Predator*, as the boat was called, carried on and I soon discovered I could travel much further afield to new fishing grounds where very large congers hung out along with pollock, bass and cod. Divers would come out and dive on wrecks and reefs and I soon found the boat was booked early spring most days through to late September, early October when the weather broke. On good days in the winter I would take parties of fishermen out for channel whiting fishing which I really enjoyed. But getting out in the winter months became more and more difficult as the weather was beginning to change to wet and windy instead of long cold spells when the sea could be flat calm.

In '94 we tried a bit of shark fishing, steaming out 20 miles due south to a point where Lyme Bay meets the English Channel, a party from Rolls Royce in Bristol had booked the boat and Joseph took the day off school. The Silence of the Lambs was doing the rounds at the cinema and having seen it I was totally engrossed in the book as the fishing began. Loads of minced up mackerel mixed with pilchard oil was slowly released and to my amazement within an hour we caught and released a 70lb blue shark. Lunch appeared soon afterwards, the rods and bait were reset and spirits were very high as the afternoon slid by. Deep in my book I was brought back to reality by a reel clicking out rapidly and when I rushed out on deck the fisherman had handed the rod to Joseph saying: 'Go on, you land it!' Twenty minutes later we landed a blue of 132lb which we were to discover later was the biggest blue shark caught round the coast of Britain that year. Joseph was very proud and I never did find out what his headmaster thought when Joseph's beaming face with shark appeared in several newspapers in the days that followed.

The engine went wrong in '99 and to my horror was told I needed a new one – at £14,000.00. I had lovingly looked after that engine and was very disappointed to learn this and on the spur of the moment sold the boat, after having put in a new engine. Judith and I split up around this time and I moved in with the lovely Sylvia who was employed by Geoff Peacock at his conservation nursery growing native trees and wild flowers in Winsham. Geoff bought *Predator* and I worked the boat for him at times and worked at the nursery at other times.

To my great joy, *Anna Two* who had been owned by a fisherman Chris Wason and later by John Salter a chief engineer who had retired but still wanted contact with the sea. He had charged the name of the boat from *Anna Two* to *Marie F.* the name of his French wife and I was happy enough to leave that name with the boat. It was wonderful to be back on a small boat mackerel fishing, having *Predator* had been a major experience that I had really enjoyed, but big boat meant big bills and now I had done full circle and gone back to my roots earning the same sort of money but only using two gallons of diesel to do so.

In 2003 Sylvia and I parted which was a sad time but within a few months I met Christine who I had always known as we had children of very similar age. We did up a chalet in the garden of The Chalet and let it to holiday makers. It had views of the ocean for a full 180 degrees from the two rooms and visitors loved it and soon it was occupied summer and winter. Christine and I lived opposite the Regent cinema in Lyme at an apartment Christine owned and this would have carried on if it hadn't been around that time that West Dorset District Council brought their cliff stabilisation scheme into being. The civil engineer Mowlems got the job. Christine and I got married in November 2004 and for our honeymoon I joined the workforce two days after the wedding in the Town Hall in Lyme. The reception was held at The Harbour Inn down at The Cobb, my stomping ground. At 9.30pm that evening everyone poured out of the pub on to the beach for a spectacular firework display to the sound of Pink Floyd's classic Comfortably Numb.

From out of the ruin of our old garden that was flattened during the scheme our stunning new house emerged. As many many people discovered when I was asked to contribute to the Coast programme I had been waiting 46 years for planning permission since the first chalet had been brought down by the landslide of '62. With Mowlems putting in 100 piles and us adding another 72 the ground became as stable as it ever will be and we got permission to build.

On July 26th 2007 we moved in to a fantastic new home, beautifully designed and built, a major eco-house with a flat roof covered in Mediterranean sedums. A totally stunning house that's been a long time coming.

8. Commander Tim Gedge AFC, RN – Director, Boat Building Academy, Lyme Regis. Sea Harrier pilot. Born London 1943.

We have had people from all over the world, from Australia, New Zealand, South Africa, Argentina interestingly, Brazil, North America, Canada and quite a large number from Europe, several from Germany, Norway and Switzerland. The youngest was 16 and the oldest 71.

My childhood home was in Warwickshire. When I left school I started an apprenticeship with British Thomson-Houston in Rugby. That was a sandwich course. Then I went to university where I read engineering at Glasgow and decided, before I had completed the whole course, that I would join the Royal Navy and fly aeroplanes. My uncle was in the Royal Navy flying, he was on No 2 course just after the First War and so there was a bit of a connection there. He retired after his fifth crash, in about 1935. He was flying aircraft that were launched off ships and landed in the sea alongside where they were then picked up. They flew off the guns with launching rails on the huge barrels. So there was a bit of a seed sown. He was always very secretive. He belonged to the old school navy where you hardly admitted that you were in the Navy. It was the Royal Naval Air Service to begin with.

I went on a university expedition to Iceland which was funded by the Royal Geographical Society and The Carnegie Trust. We spent two and a half months in northern Iceland. That was 1962. After being on a glacier for about six weeks I remember going down to the nearest town called Akureyri. Everything was very expensive in Iceland and as an impecunious student we couldn't afford anything let alone buying alcohol, and I remember being quite impressed meeting a Brit who came into a café where we were having a cup of coffee and he was ordering alcohol. The fact was that he could pay for it. Anyway he was a naval officer in a visiting ship, a Type 14 frigate, called *HMS Malcolm* and we started talking and to cut a long story short I went onboard and that was my first taste of the Royal Navy. They were being paid enough for a run ashore. And the captain, when he wasn't driving his ship around, had been flying aeroplanes. It seemed to me this was the obvious thing that I should do.

As soon as I got home I actually wrote to their Lordships and said I was a volunteer and please when could I join? So their Lordships wrote back and said that I would have to go for interviews. I joined the Royal Navy in the January 1963, the middle of the very cold winter. I actually retired from the Royal Navy in 1996, so I did thirty-three and a half years. Somewhat to my surprise because I had actually joined the Royal Navy on a short career commission just to fly aeroplanes but I ended up transferring on to a general list commission.

I spent six months at Dartmouth learning how to salute and what to salute, and the rest of it and then went straight into flying training. I was very keen to fly fighters and so I ended up at Yeovilton in Somerset, which was the all-weather fighter school. I flew Sea Vixens and I was in a frontline squadron by the end of 1965. I joined my first ship HMS Victorious and we went out to the Far East and came back in 1967. That was flying Sea Vixens. It was during the Vietnam War and we came across the United States Navy quite a bit, particularly in the Philippines using their huge airfield at Subic Bay.

Then I became a flying instructor. I did a long course with the Royal Air force and the I went straight out to the naval base

Tim Gedge with Eleanor, a Beer Lugger

at Lossiemouth, in the north of Scotland where I was involved in the air warfare school. That was flying Hunters. Then at the end of the 1960s we bought the F4 Phantom from the United States and formed a squadron in 1969 at Yeovilton. That was 892 Squadron and then we embarked in 1970, in *HMS Ark Royal*. That was my life really for the next two or three years. I was there when we hit the Russian SAM Kotlin. I was actually up in Fly Co, Flying Control position watching it happen. It was gross error of judgement on the Russian's part, trying to cut across the bows of an aircraft carrier at the best part of 30 knots is not sensible. Several Russian sailors were killed.

Flying Phantoms… Take off was slightly out of your control because you were very much in the hands of the engineering side. If they produced enough steam and the catapult, you were airborne in something like 140 feet. That was the short stroke catapult which would accelerate you to 124 knots. It was what is termed 'eyeballs in.' You could just about hold your head forward if you wanted too. You had an observer in the back. The Phantom was a hugely capable aeroplane, it was a real challenge and exciting to fly. We did a lot of attack missions and it was nuclear capable, so it was a multi-role aeroplane. But the limitations on landing at sea were very real. It was a big aeroplane and it was landing quite fast, the ship was big enough but if the ship movement was great then there were very real limitations on flying. Of course we flew at night, as well. You had four wires to pick up. The target was always number three. It was almost entirely visual, you basically got the aircraft into the right attitude for landing and controlled your vertical descent with power. You got your left and right cues from the lights down the centre line and a vertical row of lights at the after end of the ship. And you got your 'up-down' cues from a projector sight which projected a horizontal row of lights and had a moving light in the centre and if the moving light in the centre was high relative to the horizontal lights you were high. Oh yes, 'a lot of elephants to stop' as people termed it. It didn't always work, but I was fortunate. It was an exciting time.

In the mid 70s I went off to the Naval College at Dartmouth. I was the aviator on the staff and I always joked that I had gone back to Dartmouth to do the two and a half years that I hadn't done as a short career aviator when I was originally there. After that I went to the Royal Marines as the aviator on the Brigade staff which was very interesting, operating at times embarked on *HMS Fearless* and *HMS Intrepid*.

Then we got the Sea Harrier into the Navy and I was very fortunate in being appointed in command of the first frontline Sea Harrier squadron, 800 Naval Air Squadron in the early part of 1980. And in the bizarre way that things work out, I had just handed that command over in 1982 when the Argentines invaded the Falkland Islands. So I was called back to Yeovilton to form another Sea Harrier squadron, 809 Squadron, specifically as a back up squadron for the Falklands war. We had an interesting 20 days of actually getting the squadron formed.

We eventually ended up with eight aircraft which were capable of war fighting but we were short of pilots. We had to train instantly two Royal Air Force pilots who hadn't flown the Sea Harrier before. We also brought the *Atlantic Conveyor* into naval service. I went down and did the first landings aboard the *Atlantic Conveyor* some seven days after we had first looked at her in Devonport dockyard. Huge sheets of steel were welded on to her deck and we left some containers to provide a bit of weather protection. There wasn't a proper flight deck and we were just doing vertical landings aboard the ship. I went down on a Saturday morning to Devonport dockyard and walked around the deck saying 'Cut this, leave that and let's do this.' It was half inch plate and the ship's beam was about 90 feet, and I remember saying 'Let's make it square.' So we made it 90 feet by 90 feet and that provided the landing platform for the Harriers.

I did three or four landings when the *Atlantic Conveyor* was in Plymouth Sound just to prove the system and then the *Atlantic Conveyor* sailed down to Ascension. About ten days later we actually flew to Ascension, landed onboard and then transited south to the Falklands war with all the aircraft cocooned in big bags apart from one, that we kept out just as a sort of air defence measure. The *Conveyor* was sunk and I was flying mainly from *Invincible*, and sometimes from *Hermes*. Yes there were five Chinooks, all of which were lost, then there were a number of Wessex helicopters, and also six Royal Air Force Harrier attack aircraft. All the Harriers got off, and one Chinook. The rest, and a lot of the Wessexes were lost and all the equipment that was on the ship. Better that she was sunk, rather than an aircraft carrier? Oh yes without any doubt. I mean there were far fewer people on board the *Atlantic Conveyor*, but very sad, a sad loss of life including Ian North who was the master of the ship. And I had actually had a camp bed in his day cabin during that voyage south. So that was an interesting period. Luckily none of my squadron were killed. We were fortunate in that respect.

The Argentinians had in the attack role, the Super Etendards with the Argentine Navy, the Argentine Air Force and the Navy had Sky Hawks as well A4s and the Argentine Air Force had the French Mirage 3s and Mirage 5s. There wasn't another single aircraft in the world that could have operated in those sort of conditions from ships. Conditions were appalling at times, huge seas, fog and high wind, very rapid changes in the weather. That's the nature of the environment down there off the Falklands and the versatility of the Harrier was of course that it

could essentially stop before landing, as opposed to the previous generation of hooked aircraft where you have to actually land and then stop.

If we hadn't had the Harriers down there I think we would have lost. It's as simple as that. We had eventually 28 Sea Harriers and we ended up with ten Royal Air Force Harriers, who were in an attack role. Some 1,500 missions were actually flown by the Sea Harriers, 400-odd attack missions carried out by Sea Harriers and about 1,000 defence missions. The end result was overwhelming in favour of the Sea Harriers. We shot down 27 of their aircraft with the loss of none ourselves.

It was due, purely in my view, to the huge benefit in training that we had, and I have made the point to many people that in the two years since starting the first frontline squadron, we'd actually fought in practice combat missions, the Sea Harrier virtually against every other aircraft in the western world, funnily enough with the exception of the Mirage 3 and the Mirage 5. Yes, over the fields of Somerset, around North America and the Mediterranean, all over the place. The colossal advantage was that we knew the strengths and in particular we knew the weaknesses of our system. We could avoid other people's missiles and press home our attacks with the system we had. The huge advantage of the Sea Harrier is that it was a very reliable and robust platform. We had been extremely well trained. They probably thought they were better than they were.

I think they were genuinely surprised that their aircraft were being shot down and that none of ours were because there is nothing wrong with the Mirage aircraft. You only have to ask the Israeli pilots… It was a well proven aircraft in combat.

After the *Sir Galahad* was bombed, I was sent ashore to sort out some problems in tasking some air force Harriers. At that stage I was earmarked to be going home as soon as the surrender was announced, to reform the squadron to go south and relieve the carriers that were down there. So I was actually inserted on a night time insertion, from the *RFA Sir Belvedere* via helicopter into the Falklands which was an interesting experience. Anyway this took me back to my time with the Royal Marines two or three years earlier and so I found myself actually on the side of Mount Kent, as the troops were moving forward and also down at Fitzroy when the *Galahad* had just been bombed. I was talking to 3 Brigade and also 5 Brigade and was actually in San Carlos water aboard *Fearless* when the surrender came on the 14th June. Then I went into Stanley a day or so later. No there weren't many bombs that actually hit the airfield. They had put dummy piles of earth on the runway, to make it look like there were craters and they swept them away for flying. Well over 200 bombs were dropped on the airfield and that was the time when we were looking at the airfield with a view to putting Harriers on it. I flew some 40-odd missions during the conflict and at the end of this period I was awarded the Air Force Cross, AFC.

So I came back, reformed 809 Squadron with 12 aeroplanes and went south for the rest of 1982 until the Royal Engineers had rebuilt the runway at Stanley to take the Royal Air Force Phantom aircraft to provide air defence. Now of course there's a huge new airfield that's been built in the Falklands. Funnily enough I was down there again for six months in 1983 as the Harbour Master.

So I was not allowed to talk about aircraft when I was down there for the third time. Harbour Master for Port Stanley, right down to South Georgia. It was a very extraordinary part of my life. The Falkland Islands government actually asked myself and my wife to go down for the 20th anniversary celebrations. It was fascinating to see the Islands again, five years ago. They were just totally different. Blossoming, yes, with a really ideal society.

Before the war there was a Falkland Island Company that was owned by Coalite, and yes, they lacked investment. It's the complete reverse now. There's absolutely no doubt in my mind that the Falkland Islands were very British, the people who live there were in many cases educated in England, they thought of themselves as British, and like many ex-pat communities, they were almost more English than the English. But by 1982 they were already teaching Spanish in the schools and there was a continuing build up, the Argentine airline flew into Stanley. There was an increasing relationship between Argentina and the Falklands and this was happening in a slow gradual way. The fact that Argentina invaded probably put the clock back by about a hundred years.

As Harbour Master I was there for six months and then I was back in the Ministry of Defence. I served for another 12 years after that. I was involved in the development of the next generation of Sea Harrier and the replacement, the joint strike fighter. Then I worked in the embassy in Washington for two and a half years. Christopher Meyer was the Ambassador when I was there, Reagan was the President and so that was an interesting time. And then I was at sea a bit and then back in the Ministry of Defence really until I retired in 1996 which is when I started on a totally different tack.

My parents in the 1960s had moved from Leamington Spa to Lymington in Hampshire and during my time at Yeovilton in the 1960s I was doing a lot of sailing at Lymington at weekends. I was very much into ocean racing, doing the Fastnet and a lot of the Channel races. When I was on the staff at Dartmouth in the 70s I ended up running the yachts there, teaching and examining sailing. So my intention had always been when I eventually left the Navy, to buy myself a boat.

Well to cut that story short, I ended up coming across this

building in Lyme Regis, which had been built by the Royal Air Force in 1938 as a base for marine craft. The RAF had run a four boat marine craft unit and they had barrack accommodation for about 50 people. These were based on 41 foot 6 inch sea plane tenders which were then re-classified as fast rescue launches. They went through various name changes, but essentially they provided air-sea rescue to pick up pilots during the war and after the war. A lot of the ranges in Lyme Bay were controlled from this building and the ranges were used for air to surface aircraft firings amongst other things. Then in 1965 the Royal Air Force left Lyme Regis and the RAF barracks, as it was known, was then handed over to the council, then the Rural District Council.

It was then run by the County Education Authority until 1993 as an adventure centre and then as an outdoor education centre. So generations of school children would have come here for the inside of a week, done trekking, sailing and canoeing. They had about 40 pupils here at any one time. So the building was then empty and I came across it in 1996. I took a lease on the building from the early part of 1997, then formed a company and we managed to buy the freehold of the premises.

Initially I formed a number of activities here, the core activities, being the school of boat building which we called the Lyme Regis International School of Boat Building. And then in 2003 we re-structured things and formed a second company which was known as the Boat Building Academy. The BBA is the training part and the other company owns the premises and effectively leases part to the BBA. The building was built as only the Air Ministry could build things. It was in the 1930s so it was built out of engineering brick, hugely solid with a lot of metal in the structure as well. Built to withstand anything.

Well I had done a lot of things with boats, but I had never actually built a boat myself, so the concept of having a school to teach boat building appealed to me. In particular I set it up to provide a new way of life or a training for people, for mature students, people who had a change in career, or were taking early retirement, whether through redundancy or getting fed up with what they were doing. So that was the concept and this drove the way we set the school up.

There was a parallel with John Makepeace at Parnham, and of course my home, since the late 70s, was in Beaminster. I got to know John very soon after we first went there. John Makepeace's course was a two-year course and I felt that we should run a course that lasted inside of a year. People changing careers need a training that is as short as we could make it, consistent with actually giving them the skills. So we devised a course which, having refined it, came out at 38 weeks.

We wanted to teach generic boat building, and one of the things I wanted to offer was the opportunity for people to build a boat for themselves. We are talking wood or glass fibre, but using wood in both traditional forms and in using modern wooden techniques in conjunction with glass and epoxy resin, also using glass fibre and polyester resin.

We were also trying to revive interest in wooden boat building, and keep the skills going but we didn't want to be just known as the old wooden boat building school, so we were trying to push the use of modern materials in conjunction with wood. We wanted to offer the opportunity for people to make a boat for themselves, which drove the size of the boats we were building down, if they were going to achieve it in the time scale. We are talking under 20 feet. Ideally, in fact, under about 14 feet for their own boats. And here we are ten years on.

The format of the course is similar. The qualification has changed slightly, we offer a City and Guilds qualification, which is recognised all over the English speaking world. It has stood the test of time and we start two courses a year, one in September and one in March. Each course runs for about ten months and they overlap by about three and a half months. When we are in the overlap phase we have up to 32 students here.

We have had people from all over the world, from Australia, New Zealand, South Africa, Argentina interestingly, Brazil, North America, Canada and quite a large number from Europe, several from Germany, Norway and Switzerland. The youngest was 16 and the oldest 71. The average age is middle to late thirties.

They don't decide what type of boat they are going to build until about week three or four of the course, when reality sets in. Some people come with the idea of building their mega yacht and during that first three weeks they can actually get a feel of how quickly they can work with their hands and they can also see what the previous course are producing and how they are getting on. Generally by the end of week three or week four of the course we have decided on the range of boats, and my aim is to have as large a range as we can so that we can move people around from one type of boat to another.

So for instance, starting this September, we are going to be building a 32 foot pilot gig, one of the rowing gigs that are along this coast from the Scillies to Swanage and we will be doing that as a school project. They will be working on it as well as their own boats. Sourcing timber is very important and getting the right sort of elm. In fact we have bought enough elm now for two boats and that is stored, air-dried, just outside Lyme Regis and we will bring that down in September.

There is one supplier of elm and this actually came from up in the midlands area. Gail McGarva, who was one of our students some while ago, is back on the staff, and she's the project manager for the gig building. We buy some oak from Yandles of Martock, but every gig is built mainly out of elm. Now what's going to happen in the long term when elm becomes more and more difficult to source I don't know. As far as I understand it all the gigs are now built according to the same specification. Six crew plus a cox and it's going to be an interesting project for us to do. So we are doing that at one end of the scale and at the other end of the scale we are about to embark on building an ocean rowing boat that one of my instructors wants to row from Newfoundland back to Beer in a race. The race is actually from Newfoundland back to Bishop Rock light vessel, but I think because he comes from Beer he wants to end it there. A team of four and so we may perhaps make the boat in the workshops here.

That will be probably a foam core with carbon fibre and epoxy, so it will be the other end of the scale. That will be done during 2008, I think, ready for the race in 2009. I think the race is set for summer 2009. My instructor Justin Adkin, built six of the boats in a race 18 months ago, over to Antigua and there were 26 boats in that race and he was in his team, four of them in the boat and they were ten days ahead of the next boat home. So the design is paramount and fitness of the crew essential.

Other boats? Well we have just built a Salcombe yawl and we built a X-Boat which is one of the Solent class designs. We've built a Folkboat, which was a nice project and a whole raft of smaller boats.

Lerrets? No not yet. We built a replica trow designed for use on the Fleet inside Chesil Beach, one that originally had been built in 1904 for the King to go shooting. In the event the King didn't go, but the boat was built. Ninety-five years later on it was in some disrepair, so we had a nice task of building a replica. It is now back on the Fleet and is actually in use. It was commissioned by the Swannery at Abbotsbury.

We are now running all the courses as full courses and the life changing experience seems to be what a lot of people come here for. The workshops are seldom closed, there are open evenings, weekends and bank holidays. We have fairy stringent rules about safety and security.

People come here knowing absolutely nothing about boat building let alone carpentry. So we have to teach them how to use woodworking tools. We also run a short course in sail making. It's not part of the long course at the moment, but we run short courses in a variety of subjects.

The vast majority of students go into the marine industry, this is the great success story I think. About two thirds are actually in the marine industry in one way or another. Some have run their own businesses before they come and do the course here, and use their new found skills to set up their own boat building, repair or related businesses. Some have gone into the industry and are working for other people.

The real strength of the course here is the fact it's a highly practical course so there is the minimum time in the classroom and the maximum time spent building boats or as a group doing the learning around the boat. This is our huge strength. My aim is to give people the competence to tackle most jobs, and also the confidence in their own ability. The fact that we have a range of different boats being built in the one main workshop means that even if people are not working on a particular type of boat they will have been in close proximity to different types of boat being built around them. So they will understand or they will at least know something about the intricacies of making the boat and the kind of problems if there are any that other people have.

The aim is that they sail their boats at the end of the course. We have a mass launching from the Cobb into the harbour in Lyme Regis. But actually finishing the boat within the time even for the small boats is quite a challenge, but it's nice to have something to aim for.

Instructors? We work on the basis of four boat building instructors and then I have got assistants, machinists, stores and administration people, so we have actually got quite a team here. Our instructor to student ratio is high. And that's what people are paying for, the instruction and the practical work that they do, so I hope that we are set for the future. We also do some repair work on boats. We are unique in the fact that a number of people can take boats away with them at the end of the course.

We have got people from all sorts of backgrounds. We even had a chap who was dead set on making a gondola. In the event he didn't make a full-sized one, but that was one of them. We have built a number of Norwegian design boats which would have been along the Nordic designs. We haven't built any coracles or curraghs here yet, but there is no reason why we shouldn't I suppose.

Women on the course? Well its probably approaching ten per cent, so it is not a male preserve at all. It would be nice to see more women on the course.

9. Gail McGarva – BBA Lyme Regis.
    Born Kilmacolm, Renfrewshire 1965.

*Gigs really have become very much my focal point.
I love working boats, I love open boats, I love
working with the skeletal part of the boat, the hull.
The sculpture of it. And after building Georgie, it
was very clear to me that was what I loved.*

I was born in Kilmacolm in Renfrewshire, Scotland and then moved down south when I was quite young to a little village called Eckington not far from the Malvern Hills. My father is a baker but prior to that there had been blacksmiths and carpenters in our family. After school I started a degree in psychology, but I decided that didn't want to pursue that after the first year. Preston Poly. I ended up being housed with all the fine art students and in many senses found it much more my home. Then I did a Certificate in Recreational Arts for the Community at Manchester Poly and got a job in Bristol. I was drawn to Bristol because of the docklands.

I was working at Windmill Hill City Farm as an education worker with children from the inner city who had very little concept of farming or horticulture. So we used to have a hilarious time with the kids milking the goats and building potato clamps. They would be astonished by the fact when you dug up a carrot, firstly you would see the leaves above ground, then the carrot would be unearthed below. They were used to having carrots in tins.

It was very rewarding work. Then the playgroup of the farm invited a Theatre in Education company to come and do a performance, focussing on environmental education. It was called The Travelling Light Theatre Company, which is Bristol based. They said they were looking for new recruits as actor-teachers. So I went for an audition, got the job and went on for about six or seven years, doing Theatre in Education, predominantly travelling around the South West.

In 1992 we decided to adapt a book by Alan Garner. The Stone Book set in the 1800s. There is a character in the book who's deaf and we wanted to research what kind of sign language would have been used in the 1840s. There is a school for deaf children in Bristol, so I talked to their drama teacher and other deaf members of staff as to what kind of sign language would have been used. I then decided to do some drama work with the deaf young children there. Then I was told about a course for sign language interpreters at Bristol University. The drama teacher I had been working with at the school said, 'You know, you would be a fantastic interpreter, why not go for the interview?' They offered me a place, so I took that leap. Our tutors were profoundly deaf linguists and so it was a complete immersion into British Sign Language. I did a two-year diploma then I went on to be a sign language interpreter for nine years.

But at the transition between Travelling Light and sign language interpreting, I came across a boat in Bristol docks, called *Minna*. She's an old, a very old, probably between 1910 and 1920s navy boat. She was lurking just along from what I call the 'cranes that look like giraffes.' This was in 1988, I spotted her and I always had an obsession for small spaces, living in small spaces. She had originally been a supply boat taking supplies and dignitaries to and from the shore out to the larger vessels. She would have had somebody standing, steering her on the stern deck with the tiller between their knees. The hull is made of Burma teak. *Minna* is carvel construction and then an inner skin of diagonal planking, real belt and braces. She will be quite dapper again one day, I keep promising her.

Gail McGarva with Freda the Friendship Boat

So that's where boats came in. She is 25 feet long with a 16 foot cabin which had been added on in the 1950s. She has just such immense character. Well I just absolutely fell in love with her. So I lived on *Minna* in the middle of Bristol, but with the most incredible sense of space all around with the tall ships and the dockyard warehouses.

I see boats as completely inter-bound with people. Boats are characters in there own right and they usually hold enormous stories in relation to people. In 2003 I came across an article in an American magazine which referred to the Lyme Regis International School of Boat Building, as it was called then. So I came down and spent the whole day here. It felt completely and utterly like home. The decision to be here, to be a boat builder was absolutely instantaneous. The qualification here is a City and Guilds so I sent off for the information about bursaries. I sent in an application form, was short listed and interviewed. Then I got a letter saying that they were going to award me a bursary which would cover all the fees and tools, which was fantastic.

I brought *Minna* with me down to live on land, so in turn I could restore her. I don't have very elaborate sorts of daily needs. Paraffin lamps, candles and there's a wood burner in the boat. From my perch on land there's a wonderful sea view and my daily walk to the boat building school is through the Undercliff. During my training I was in heaven, I still am.

At the start of my course I was inspired by an article in the Classic Boat magazine, about this gentleman, a boat builder who lived on Unst, which is the most northerly island of the Shetland Isles. The last boat builder on that island. He is called Willie Mouat, boat builder to the Boat Haven Museum on Unst, which houses all the remaining Shetland boats, from what they call Eela boats, which are the smallest of the range, to Foureens and then Sixareens, that are up to anything around 30 feet. Fishing boats yes, and historically each croft would have been allocated a boat. The museum is fantastic, if you are ever in Unst, do visit, it is just amazing. One boat per croft. The boat that I then went on to research more deeply was called the Gardie boat, that was the name of the croft. And that was the oldest boat in the museum. It was built in 1882. And from reading the article I just got this vision of building a daughter ship to that Gardie boat. I just thought it would be the most amazing thing to work with Willie and carry on the thread of history, to carry on those skills that he was fearing were going to be lost.

So I wrote to him and then spoke to him on the phone and I explained what my thoughts were. It was quite a nerve-racking moment. I had my speech prepared, I said about building a 'daughter ship' about working in conjunction with him, but was obviously very, very aware of being an outsider to that community. I am Scottish, but actually that made very little difference, because the Shetlanders don't consider themselves as being Scottish, they are Shetlanders. So that didn't really matter but I suppose it was a wee bit better than being English. So I asked Willie what he thought. There was a big pause and it felt like the longest pause ever and then he said 'We' and I think that the 'we' was very important because he meant the community, he said, 'We would be delighted.' I was euphoric, it was fantastic.

So in December I went up to Unst and met with Willie and we went into the Haven in the depth of winter, it was freezing, freezing weather. I went by boat from Aberdeen to the mainland of Shetland and two more ferries on from there. I met with him and basically scribbled reams and reams and took loads of photographs and took measurements of the boat. The Gardie boat is 18 foot by 5 foot 9 inch beam, she is clinker, she's a double ender, she has got very strong Norwegian lines. Used for working nets? Yes, and the lines of Shetland boats, they are beautiful, they are work boats, the lines are just stunning, I think. They just evolved from the waves haven't they? They look just like they have been scooped out of the sea, and I just fell in love with them. I love double enders, I think they are amazing in their shape. Willie then sent me by post, this amazingly weathered piece of cardboard which was the template of the central mould and then I lofted it, which is to draw the boat out full scale, with fairing battens.

Through the generations the craft of boat building would have been learnt by watching, a non-verbal thing, but here with Willie most of my learning was on the phone. It's a very difficult blend between something that's very technical and something that's very instinctive for Willie to express and for me to learn. All the boat terms in the Shetland Isles are in Norn, so I became very familiar with all those terms. It is Norwegian influenced. I became very conversant with *stammerons, hummlibands* and *haddabands*. *Hummlibands* are instead of a rowlock, you have a rope, and the *haddabands* are the main frames and the *stammerons* are an angled frame in the bow and stern of the boat. They were the most difficult thing to make on the boat.

They would use larch mainly. There is rarely a tree to be seen, and in fact I didn't see any on Unst. So yes all their wood is imported and that is very problematic for any builder there. You have to work with what you have got. Here obviously I had a little bit more leeway, the planking was larch and all the structural strength and the keel was oak. I had a heck of a job actually finding curved grain for the stems of the boat. So I went through this amazing learning curve building this boat with help from the tutors Roy Gollop, a local boat builder and fisherman, who builds by eye, and Jack Chippendale. Both were absolutely invaluable. Between the two of them they were just great.

The learning that the boat offered me was just incomparable to anything else. I built with just three moulds, three main frames. Quite early on in the process I decided I wanted to launch it from Unst, from the same slipway as the mother ship was launched. I decided its first water should be Unst. So I contacted Willie and we arranged to launch it in the following August. I finished the course in the June and carried on working on the boat for another month or so and then launched it the same day as the Unst Island Show.

I towed the boat with a series one Land Rover, which was an absolute star. Firstly I towed it all the way up to the west coast to show my mum and dad. I wanted to unveil the name first to my parents because I named the boat after my two grandmothers. Georgie was my father's mother, and McDonald was my mother's mother's name and so the boat was called Georgie McDonald. So I unveiled the name to them and from there I went up to Aberdeen. North Link Ferries, I wrote them a letter and said what I was doing. They gave the boat free passage.

Well it was quite extraordinary when we arrived on the mainland. Gales were a brewing and so they were about to cancel the smaller ferries across to the smaller islands. We managed to get the last one across to Unst from Yell. It was howling on arrival so I spoke to Willie on the phone and he said 'I so want to see the boat. If I could just come up and have a wee peep.' So we just pulled back the covers, he didn't see the full view and he could just see the shape. The whole thing about Shetland boats is that the second plank dictates the shape of the whole boat, and if you get that second plank wrong…

When I was building the boat, Willie would say on the phone, 'With that second plank, don't let it just sit exactly were it wants to sit, you have got to push it out a wee bit.' And I remember saying this to Jack and Roy and they were saying well 'what's a wee bit?' So we had to just go on instinct. So I breathed the most enormous sense of relief when he said that she was 'perfect.' I was really, really proud.

There was a few little finishing touches that I wanted to check with him in situ. We had a couple of days before the launch so it was lovely at last to actually work alongside him, in his workshop next to the boat museum. So we did some lovely work together in preparation for the launch and then local people came together on the slipway and we carried her into the water.

My vision was for Willie and I to row across the bay, each with an oar in hand, and that is exactly what we did, and it was amazing. This was August 2005. Yes it was a fantastic moment and a real honour to do that, an enormous privilege and a wonderful relationship to have created.

In the autumn of that year we launched her from Lyme, because I think double enders should have double launchings. It was like a carnival day really. I invited all my friends and everybody who was a current student at the school, local people and quite a few deaf friends as well. So it was a sort of bi-lingual ceremony, my friend offered to interpret, so I gave a speech of thanks from the boat and then the people who had been the main helpers on the boat were her bearers, and we carried her down through an aisle of people, a corridor of people. Everybody had sea salt taken from wooden bowls and they scattered that over her and we lowered her into the water. Jack and Roy came with me, and rowed out into the harbour.

In December 2005 I found out much to my great blushings, that the Boat Building Academy had secretly entered me for the British Marine Federation's Trainee of the Year Award, and that I'd won the award and that I was to go to the London Boat Show in the January to pick it up. What was amazing was that usually that award goes to people who are in the fibreglass industry. It did capture quite a few people's imaginations, and some of the boating press, because they saw it as being won by a traditionalist and that was very, very unusual. And a woman? Well, Yes.

I started researching gigs, Cornish pilot gigs and Bantry Bay gigs and arranged to go on a mini-apprenticeship in Ireland. A little hamlet near Dunmore East, County Waterford, working with a shipwright on an Atlantic Challenge gig of 38 feet long. Bigger than the Cornish Pilot gigs, which are 32 feet. Gigs really have become very much my focal point. I love working boats, I love open boats, I love working with the skeletal part of the boat, the hull. The sculpture side of it. And after building *Georgie*, it was very clear to me that was what I loved. I worked in Ireland for about six months.

Then I came back here and started to work on the idea of Lyme having a Cornish pilot gig, as there has been talk for a long while about Lyme Regis setting up a club and having a gig. For me to feel that I could have some involvement with the building of a gig would just be a dream come true. Whilst preparing for the gig project I embarked on my own project, the build of a 12 foot sailing boat. I call her *Freda the Friendship Boat*. She was designed by Frederick Goeller in 1915. She's a lovely clinker boat. She's gorgeous, I love her. All copper riveted. Yes, she is for sale. It will be hard to part with her.

It is now September and we have just laid down the keel for Lyme Regis's first gig. It's lovely because when I was researching my mini-apprenticeship I contacted a gentleman called Ralph Bird, who is a very established Cornish pilot gig builder and I went and talked to him. He was immensely encouraging and when I came back from Ireland, I reconnected with him. He's been really my key advisor with regard to the building of the gig for Lyme Regis. It is a fantastic project in terms of building bonds between the Boat Building Academy and the community and in terms of building bridges with master craftsmen and the passing on of boat building skills for many a decade.

The future? I have been having conversations with *Minna*, my navy boat and I have promised her that I will return her to the sea. She's been many a year on the river and obviously now she is on land. So I think it's only right and proper that she returns to the sea. My eventual image and thoughts for her is that she will be what I call *The Story Boat* instead of the story book. I think there are amazing stories to be told about Lyme Bay. I have a vision of her going out to sea with people on board her as a trip boat, and while they journey they hear stories of the local area, told by local people, stories of the local landscape, the waterscape, told on board *The Story Boat*. All boats have their story.

10. Justin Adkin – BBA Lyme Regis, Atlantic rower. Born Beer 1979.

Thirty-nine days we were at sea. The watches were an hour on and an hour off, 24 hours a day. Relentless… We were approaching the finishing line as the tail end of the hurricane came along. We were almost 900 miles ahead. No prize for winning. Cloud nine for about a year. Yes, it was fantastic.

My father's family moved to Beer in the early 1950s from Burnham-on-Crouch. Dad was in the Merchant Navy, cargo ships, the New Zealand Shipping Company and P&O. My grandfather was a pilot in the RAF and later on a passenger and commercial pilot.

I think growing up on Beer beach is what got me into boats. Beach fishermen are rare these days. I can remember going out on a boat with one of the old fishermen to pick up a landing stage that had floated off. We've got wooden ones that are pulled up and down the beach, but the tide had come in and it had floated off. We had to pick it up and drag it in. I was very young and could hardly see over the gunwale.

We have got the Newtons, they are the biggest fishing family in Beer, then you've got Bartletts, Aplins, Westlakes. They are still very active. It's slowly getting smaller. I have only been around a few years, but even in my time it's gone from 16 fishing boats down to eight or nine. They are all family owned, passed on down. Every boat has its own winch and site on the beach. Winches are all electrical now, they used to walk around a capstan. Sometimes the old fishermen used to leave bait for the guys that ran the small hire boats. And every day they chucked yesterday's and put in a couple fresh mackerel so they could take

a few slivers of the skin for bait. There is good mackerel fishing off the Head.

The biggest boat is 25 foot. Retrieving a boat when there is an onshore swell can be a bit tricky. I did some fishing when I was a teenager, half term and weekends, but I mainly grew up on the hire boats. Letting them out, launching the boats, showing the grocks what to do with them, making sure they knew their port from their starboard and rescuing them whenever they broke down as well.

My uncle had boats, all timber built. There were seven in the fleet but he has sold them now. Work carried on through the winter with scraping down, varnishing, reconditioning the engines. That's really where my first experience in boat work came in. The season would start at Easter. When I was 16 the newest boat we had was pretty much as old as me, but then there were boats that dated back to the late 1950s really. They can go on for years, maintenance is the key with all timber boats. Most of the beach boats are built in elm, especially the older ones, it's a very tough wood and salt water actually hardens elm as well, which makes it ideal for boats. Traditional for the gigs to be built in elm. It's quite stringy wood but it lends itself perfectly for beach use because they obviously take a lot more impact than harbour boats here in Lyme. There are a few landing stages along the beach in Beer, but when you got an exceptionally strong spring tide you couldn't use anywhere but the far eastern side of the beach just inside of the rocks.

When I left school at 16 I was trying desperately to get an apprenticeship in boat building. The boat building school here wasn't open then. Nothing in Exmouth, you had Lavis's and Rowsell's down there and Holmans. Dixons were working but they weren't taking apprentices. They were old families which were coming to the end and their sons didn't want to take on the

Justin Adkin in the lofting room, looking out to sea

business, it all seemed to be winding up down in Exmouth sadly. So I did a tool making apprenticeship for four years in a ceramics factory in Colyton. It was practical. I had to be making something, that's what I enjoy doing.

During that time my will to want to build a boat came through. I got a piece of paper and drew my boat roughly up to scale and bent rulers around and drew curves. I wanted to build myself my own rowing boat, that was my plan. I had always wanted my own wooden rowing boat but never really had the skills to build one to start with. I got my first rowing boat, a fibreglass shell, but all the timber on it was completely rotten and I got it quite cheap. I think I was 15 then but that was my first experience of steam, bending wood around gunwales and things. I learned on the job. Paul Mears in Seaton, H J Mears & Son Boat Builders. I was constantly pestering him when I was a teenager. How do you do this? How do you do that? I kept trying to build model boats when I was young and making a complete mess of it, but I kept plugging away. Eventually I said, 'Right let's have a go full scale.'

The first boat, I started building it in Beer and then had to move it halfway through to another shed in Seaton. I got really fortunate with the planking of the timber. Paul Mears found out that a couple of larch trees had blown down up at Rousden in a storm in January. He said, 'Do you want to come and look at these with me?' So we both came up and had a look. Then he shipped them out to a sawmill and had them sliced up. Quite good wood for boat building. It's very similar to elm in that respect because it's quite a stringy timber, quite forgiving on a beach. fourteen foot, the boat was. You have always got to work out which shape each plank is taking. Paul Mears was really good to me. Every Monday night he would come up after he'd finished working and give me an hour and a half of his time. My own evening school. I was very lucky and he didn't charge me anything. He helped me machine up all the timber as well. He was very helpful to me.

It took me a year and a half to make, I was about 20 when I finished, 1999, not long ago. At that time when I launched my boat I also finished my apprenticeship. I didn't make the oars, I got given a pair which was lucky, all with gunmetal rowlocks, tied on so they wouldn't fall over the side. I did quite a few long rows. Up to Lyme Regis and back again, Sidmouth and back. Picking the tide time right. That gave me a taste for going further afield. I had so enjoyed building my own boat that I was desperate to get into boat building. A friend of a friend mentioned to me that someone was leaving their job down in Exmouth at Rowsells, and he said, 'Oh come with me. I'll introduce you to Spud Rowsell.' I showed him all the photographs of my boat and told him what I'd done. He then offered me a weeks trial. Then a job at the end of it. I was very fortunate because he is a very good technical boat builder. Right place at the right time, one of those things. It wasn't a formal apprenticeship, they just took me on. Straight into building Salcombe yawls, which is nice. There were eight or nine on order when I got there. They needed someone that knew how to build a clinker built boat. Probably I learned more doing that one boat than I could have done any other way. It was good to be able to shadow someone like Spud who was in his mid to late fifties at the time and by the time I'd built two boats with him I was working on my own. I was with him from '99 until '03. He then retired and let me take on the shed, working for myself in Exmouth. I had a three-year lease and took over one of his orders for an ocean rowing boat which was in the early stages at the time. One of the first ocean rowing boats they made. It was a fibreglass hull with timber cabins and decks. We made a timber vessel originally, fibreglassed the outside of it, filled, faired and polished it up and took the mould from that. A prototype.

That one was rowed across by a chap solo on his own, quite a big boat for a solo 24 feet long. He actually broke the record at the time crossing the Atlantic to Barbados. He had a tracking beacon aboard his boat which we could look on the internet and find out how far he had gone every day. His name is Feydor Konyukhov. An adventurer, similar to Sir Ranulph Fiennes, really popular and famous in Russia. The very first ocean rowing race was back in 1997. Rowsell and Morrison who I was working for, built the prototype for that race, which was then taken away and made into a kit. Most of the competitors built the boats themselves for the race. Because that boat was so successful, they got orders and I was fortunate to come in at the right time.

When we were preparing for our Atlantic row we had to learn how to row with a sliding seats because none of us had done it before, like those that Steve Redgrave rows, it's all about technique, power and fitness. Once we got the hang of it, it was easier, about understanding the sea and being able to row with the boat rolling around. All of us, myself, brother, cousins had all grown up in Beer rowing tiny little boats around and capsizing them, just learning when we were young the hard way. I think we learned a lot in our upbringing in Beer, which far outweighed being able to row properly or not.

I was still in Exmouth in 2003. Peter Rowsell had retired and let me take on the yard. I then ran it for three years on my own, but in the middle of that we built our own ocean rowing boat. We had to get sponsorship, it was a £50,000 project. The labour costs were down. We built the boat almost half price really. Sometimes we would have to work on it during the day which obviously cost us. It was two-seater and two cabins, exactly the same boat as the solo rower had. We altered the layout of it so that we could get a berth forward, 2 rowing and 2 resting. The uncomfortable time came when we had a few storms and we all had to get down below, a bit cosy then.

I came across one of these ocean rowing boats training down in Exeter. They rowed down the Exe out of Exmouth and rowed along the coast here to Lyme Regis. A cousin of Roy Gollop's. He came up here met Roy had a few beers and rowed back the next day, but they rowed home via Beer and they came into Beer for lunch on the Sunday afternoon, and I rowed out in my little boat thinking 'What the hell is this?' I offered them a lift ashore because they had anchored off, and then when I took them out again, they offered me to go for a row with them in it. Of course I was at an impressionable age then, 18 years old and I thought this is a great idea to do.

Quite a lot of local firms gave us sponsorship and also when I started running the yard on my own you obviously build up a number of contacts. We managed to get quite a lot of materials for the boat in kind from companies. The boat is called *All Relative*. We started on the 30th November 2005 finished on the 8th January 2006. The start was an island called La Gomera in the Canaries which is just off Tenerife and we finished in Antigua. One of the shortest routes you can take. Thirty-nine days we were at sea. We had always thought we could be between five to six weeks, we thought if the winds were with us we might have been able to do it in under five weeks which would have been a world record. Not allowed to put up sails, we did dry our shorts on the aerial sometimes but that was as far as it got really. The boat was a shell on its own, two of us could pick it up, so it was less than 250kg, very light, a quarter of a ton, but then we had more than a quarter of a ton of food onboard, and the two batteries probably weighed 60 kilos between them.

Power for radio, lights and water maker, which was important. We had a 120 kilos of emergency water onboard which doubled up as our ballast tank. Then you've got safety equipment, first aid kit, wet weather gear, the life raft, survival bag.

The galley was a tiny little camping stove and one of our friends who I used to work with as an engineer, he made us a stainless steel pot that went around the cooker with a few slots in the bottom to get airflow up to it and we had a kettle that fitted perfectly inside this. It was gimballed so we didn't have to worry about the kettle falling off. There was very little danger of spilling boiling water on us. We had dehydrated arctic rations, Norwegian army ration packs. It was really tasty. We did take some wet ration packs as well, not quite as nice as the dry. It was wholesome, bits of meat in it. We had standard three meals a day. Porridge in the morning, biscuits and paté every day for lunch. Evening was one of the ration packs. We always ate two at a time but for Christmas Day or getting halfway we all stopped and ate together. The watches were an hour on and an hour off, 24 hours a day. Relentless. The worst part about the whole trip for me was you get that five minutes shout in the middle of the night after you have been asleep for 45-50 minutes and you have been dreaming about rowing and someone wakes you up and says, 'You've got to get up and start rowing.' And you go, 'Oh piss off!' But you knew you just had to get up and relieve your crewmate.

A tropical storm is slightly less than a hurricane. We got caught in three tropical storms and a couple of low pressure systems. The tail end of the hurricane didn't affect us, it was quite funny, but not in an amusing sort of way, we were approaching the finishing line as the tail end of the hurricane came along and it was tracking south easterly away from the Florida area and coming back down which is unusual. We were coming into Antigua and because we were quite a large distance away from 2nd, 3rd and 4th place boats, it went in between us and them and stopped them in their tracks. We were 600 to 700 miles ahead going into the last week and by the time we were finished we were almost 900 miles ahead.

We were one of three crews in the race that had been used to rowing on open water and we did have a particularly good boat, we got carbon fibre instead of fibreglass which normally we wouldn't have been able to afford. So we had a lighter boat than everybody else. The design itself wasn't any different, there were four or five boats exactly the same as ours in the race. There were four four-man crews in the race, 20 pairs and two solos.

Large waves? Once they got to a certain size you couldn't actually row up them and in the middle of the storm when they started breaking we just thought, 'No, this is a bit dangerous,' so we had to anchor up and batten down. We had a sea anchor a bit like a parachute which you deploy and it doesn't stop you dead but it certainly reduces your drift, instead of going backwards. You could probably average four or five knots going backwards if you are not careful in those sort of seas. We were averaging between half a knot and a knot. The worst we ever had was minus five miles in a day, because when the wind abated a bit we would always get up and row. We knew from the weather information we were getting that the eye of the storm was slightly to the north of us, so every time we could, although we couldn't row straight into it, we would row south, just to get further away from the eye of the storm. We had a satellite phone onboard and once a day we'd call our uncle in Beer and he was a navigator in the Merchant Navy and another uncle of mine is a weather forecaster for the RAF, so between the two of them we were getting some good information on what was going on around us. To start with he wasn't telling us anything like the strength of the conditions that we could expect. We rowed into it for much longer than we should have done really, because we didn't expect it to get as bad as it did. It was very warm. Once you drop down to 23 degrees north we were inside the tropics. Antigua was 17 degrees, so quite low.

We always found something pointless to talk about which was mildly interesting and kept us all amused. We are still talking to each other. We had quite a good rotation system on board. Every two days we would swap rowing partners and every six days we would actually swap cabins as well. Because all the cooking and cleaning and navigation went on in the aft cabin and the guy in the bow, all he had to do was concentrate when he was rowing and steering the boat in the right direction, that's where the foot steering pedal was for the rudder. We were normally constantly looking over our shoulder. Towards the end of the race when you are getting so tired it obviously slackened off a bit because we nearly had a head on collision with a tanker.

It was on the Wednesday before we finished on the Sunday, so five days out from Antigua. It was funny, I wasn't rowing at the time I was in the bow cabin, there was my brother and Martin my cousin rowing at the time, James happened to get up from the stern cabin and start brushing his teeth and looked over the bow and he said, ' **** me that's a big boat!' We spent a while, because it was right smack on our nose and he saw it about 400 yards away. They didn't see us. We had our radar reflector on, but it was you know… and we were straight on the VHS radio as soon as we saw him saying 'Can you see us?' ….. and no reply. Nobody on the bridge. We were working out which way was best to avoid it, because when you have something like that coming straight towards you, you can't tell whether it's going slightly north or slightly south of you. It's very difficult, because it's just one big wall of water coming off the bow. The conditions were slightly favouring south, so we decided to go

with the conditions and just rowed as fast as we could to get out of the way of it. Wrong decision and we could have ended up in front of it. It missed us by a couple of hundred yards I suppose. A quick dash out of the way.

We saw probably a dozen tankers on the way across. At night you could see their navigation lights and you could always tell which way they were going to pass you, but during the day you haven't got that luxury.

It felt fantastic to get to Antigua, best day of my life, easily. Hell of a sight. We approached land at night, Saturday night of the 7th January and the moon set on the horizon ahead of us and it goes red and orangey colour as it sets in the tropics, quite impressive. When it disappeared you had the little orange glow where it was. But you would go to sleep for an hour and get up, the moon is still there. That's what we thought to start with, then eventually we sussed out that that's where Antigua ought to be as well. The moon set smack on where Antigua was. As it turned out and we just kept looking at it and going: 'That orange glow isn't going away it's actually getting brighter,' Eventually we sussed out that that was actually Antigua. We sent a text message to our uncle saying: 'Land Ahoy.' We arrived at midday on a Sunday which is a pretty sociable time to arrive because we had family and friends who had flown out to see us all waiting for us. No prize for winning. Cloud nine for about a year. Yes, it was fantastic.

When we came home, I had the grim reality of going to work. I was still in Exmouth, this was January last year. The lease on my workshop was up in June. While we were out rowing life is really, really simple, all you've got to do is go through the daily routine there is no worries there is no this that and the other. I became slightly disheartened with being responsible for the workshop myself. I had a couple of people working for me, I wasn't enjoying the business side of it, so I kind of made up my mind out on the rowing boat basically, that it wasn't for me any more.

At the moment all I want to do is create things. I still had plenty of work to be getting on with, but I was always looking for something on the horizon. And Roy Gollop, because he served his trade down in Exmouth, Lavis's where he was working is two shops away from where I was, and so every other Friday or every third Friday he would come down with his wife Norma and pop his head into the workshop and say: 'How's it going, cor you should come up to Lyme Regis I reckon you'd be all right up there.' I was a bit dubious at first but I came up here and met Tim Gedge and had a tour around. As it turned out I gave it a crack. I started in July last year. I finished at the workshop on Friday afternoon and started here at the Boat Building Academy on the Monday.

It's very satisfying seeing people getting stuck in and wanting to do the job. I started midway through the March course which finished in December and then they took on the September course which have just recently left in the last couple of weeks and I'm on my second March course now. It's a combination of traditional craft and modern. I started off traditional, but when I moved to Exmouth I got more and more involved with the composite side of things. As much as I love doing the woodwork, I mean it's definitely the way I like to work, the composite side of things is just as fascinating as well.

I've designed my first proper boat, in my book, really. The first design that I did I sort of sketched it out and showed it to Paul Mears and he went: 'Yeah that will work, if it doesn't we'll make it work,' and that was his approach to it. This time around I've designed it all from scratch and I know it will work. So I'm happy to call this one my 'first' design.

I'd like to think I'd prototype it. We'll see how it goes. It's in its early stages at the moment. With regard to my boat, although I've designed it I used it as a teaching aid to actually go through the design process for the students here in the workshop. Also I've found since coming here that I'm doing less work than I was doing in Exmouth. But I'm doing work in the evenings in Beer for people on their boats.

In the future I would like to think that I would eventually start building properly again. BBA is a great interim. I thoroughly enjoy it here. But I do get a big itch to want to do another row. I would love to row another ocean. I would love to row from America or Canada and finish here in Beer. Gets me excited thinking about that.

For every Hundred feet of Dressed Freestone or Paving Stone, superficial measure or other dressed Stone. _ _ _ _ _ 1-0

For every Ton of rough Free Stone, Lime Stone or other Stone. _ _ _ _ _ 0-6

For every Trunk, Chest, Box or Bag per Barrel Bulk and so on in proportion. _ _ _ 0-4

For every Ton of Butter or Cheese. _ _ 1-0

For every Ton of Oil. _ _ _ _ _ 2-0

For every Barrel of Tar, Pitch, Pot or other ashes. 0-4

For every Ton of Cordage or Plaister Hair. _ 1-0

For every empty Pipe. _ _ _ _ 0-4

For every empty Hogshead. _ _ _ 0-2

For every empty Barrel. _ _ _ _ 0-1

For every Gross of Bottles. _ _ _ _ 0-6

For every Score of Hides or Skins. _ _ 1-0

For every Ton of Oil Cake. _ _ _ _ 1-0

For every Truss of Sail Cloth. _ _ _ 0-6

For every Ton of Sand taken within the Cobb or Harbour for Ballast. _ _ _ _ _ 0-2

For every Ton of Sand taken outside the Cobb or Harbour for Ballast. _ _ _ _ _ 0-2

All packages not ascertained as to size or weight to pay a sixth part of the Freight.

For all weighable goods not enumerated or particulary set forth in the above schedule to pay per Ton. _ 1-0

By Order of the Council
June 30th 1879

W. J. ATKINS
COBB CLERK

CHARMOUTH WEST BAY AND ABBOTSBURY

11. Richard Edmonds – Warden and Geologist Jurassic Coast *aka* Earth Science Manager. Born Oxford 1962.

My mum said that even at the age of five I had an uncharacteristic interest in these fossils.

My father did all sorts of things, he was a Spitfire pilot in the War. I only met him five times, I never knew him really. Great-great-grandfather on my mother's side was the captain of the *Cutty Sark* for a short period of time. My mother's side of the family comes from Liverpool. She is a Clark. I've lived everywhere from Inverness to St Ives, via London, Dartmoor for a brief time as well. I got interested in geology about 150 yards from here on the beach at Charmouth by a chance walk in the winter. It must have been in 1973, when I first came to Lyme Regis. We came for a walk on the beach and I picked up my first little fool's gold ammonite, and that was it. It was just a little one, about a centimetre across, small and absolutely perfect. Just lying on the beach. They're 195 million years old.

I had a very brief encounter with the fossils up on the Isle of Skye in Broadford Bay. My mum said that even at the age of five I had an uncharacteristic interest in these fossils. I started school in Monkton Wyld. I was the youngest there. It was very alternative and my mum was the matron. Then when she went off to train as a social worker she knew she was going to be travelling round all through my secondary education so I ended up in Woodroffe. It suited me better. I boarded. Mostly forces kids, it was hardly a posh boarding school, which was a good thing.

I was obsessed with fossils. In the winter time when there were storms I'd be out there every weekend, and I met all the collectors. Pete Langham, who's still collecting now, he's the guy who really first showed me what to look for. Barney must have been on the beach but I don't remember him, those were the main characters. Dave Costin who lives in Lyme now, cleans fossils, he doesn't collect any more.

I think there are some references to fossils, or curiosities, that pre-date Mary Anning, and an account somewhere of Charmouth and the Coach and Horses Hotel was a place you could stop off and buy curiosities on your way from Exeter to London. But what set Mary Anning aside was that she was the first person who had the local, hands-on knowledge and was able to communicate and talk to the great gentlemen scientists of the day. She lived partly in Devon before the family moved to Lyme. And it's just the same today, there are two or three people who will be remembered in the literature and they had the same skills, people who could talk to the scientists and the collectors. Samuel Clark found a fantastic *plesiosaur* in the 1860s, just down the beach from here.

After Woodroffe I went to the University of Hull to do geology. I was completely obsessed. That was just the right subject and the right course. They don't teach it like that any more, old-fashioned mapping, the broad based fundamental skills. Today you're much more likely to do an applied course, like geochemistry or geophysics. We did all of that but in various degrees and levels. The real drive with oil was micropalaeontology, but that included staring down a binocular microscope, I couldn't stand seeing double at the end of a two-hour session. Not my idea of fun. Micro-fossils evolved through time, they were the only fossils that survived being drilled, so if you can date them and age them, then you know where you are in the rock sequence. In the 1980s a lot of people wanted to do micropalaeontology. I finished university and had a year off. I'm

Richard Edmonds, Charmouth Beach, low tide

very glad I did it that way round, I don't think I'd have had the discipline to go back to studying after having a year off.

I just bummed around, it was great. We all shared a house in Hull, hitchhiking to the Yorkshire Dales or to Scotland to climb mountains. There was one trip to the Pyrenees which was fantastic. A whole bunch of us were really into mountaineering and winter climbing. At that time I didn't know what I wanted to do, but then after a year I thought I really ought to earn some money. Those were the days you could walk into the North Sea oil industry as a mud logger or 'shit bagger' as they used to call it. The first trip was fantastic, that was in June, 150 miles north of the Shetland Islands, so the sun set at 11 o'clock at night and came up at three in the morning. Sunsets and sunrises were the same thing. We had all the winter weather, big seas, snow. We found oil at one point, which was truly exciting, we were bottling it up and taking our own little samples. We were the ones who knocked the core out and the oil was fizzing out of the rock, it was extraordinary to see. I think that particular field went into production. And then the last time I was there I did eight hours work in two weeks, we didn't even have a hole to look after for five days, they were too tight to fly us off and on again, and at the end of it I just quit.

Then I volunteered with the National Trust of Scotland. I went to Arran for a winter because I knew I wanted to work outdoors at that stage. Arran was really nice because I had the mountaineering and I love Scotland. Cutting down rhododendrons, doing footpath work, a bit of education, it was the first time I did a talk which terrified me, and then this job came up. My friend from university said 'Have you seen this job advert for the first warden at the Charmouth Heritage Coast Centre?' And at that stage, 1987, I wasn't really thinking of moving back down to the namby-pamby South. But it was a fantastic opportunity, because being a geologist, there aren't many jobs that are about interpreting geology, it's a very specialist thing. The chance to come down to Charmouth where I learned my geology was too good to miss.

They were very reluctant to invite me to an interview all the way from Arran, but I got the job, so came back. It was a bare building, very simple displays, but the week before we opened, there was a truly massive landslide between Lyme and Charmouth. We still call it the 'New Slip,' 20 years on. And a friend of mine, Chris Moore had been along Stonebarrow, the other side, and they came along with these wide eyes. It had been a misty morning and the mist had lifted and there was this massive great black scar. I got down there in the end and the sort of stones that contain the fossils that you'd normally really struggle to find were everywhere. They were coming out like a conveyor belt, you could stand there, 'there's another one, another one,' for three days it moved, right through the very best beds of rock, and that was a great insight. Some of the blokes used an inflatable boat, but they filled it with so many fossils it sank.

In the summer it was six days a week which meant I had absolutely loads of time in the winter. If it was rough and stormy and the waves were coming across the car park at Charmouth, I could be out on the beach, and I think for the post of warden that's a real strength, because you can't be a non-collector. You've got to be really hands-on so when the summer comes you can say 'That section moved 25 metres last year,' and 'that's where a fish came out, and that's where this came out, etc,' and it's real to people. The schools are the most interesting. The really well-behaved kids, generally speaking, are the ones who want to go back when it's wet and stormy and rainy, and the kids that are a real teacher's nightmare are the last ones off the beach, all covered in mud, and they've really got down and found fossils.

I ran the centre for 11 years. And I do have to say it got to the point where I was over-tired at the end. There were very few surprises any more. The volunteers, who were largely retired people from Charmouth, were really interesting. We still have everything from a retired super-tanker captain to a guy who sold jets in South Africa, to school teachers, a guy who used to work at Aldermaston, a guy who helped strengthen the War Office in 1940 who was the head of the working party who did all the winter work. So a fantastic variety of people, who would invariably take a long time coming up with the most convoluted way of constructing something, and then do it that way. Really interesting people, people who had been prisoners of war in Burma, on the railway. That was great, that side of it, being involved with such a wealth and range of experience. The buzz is if people are interesting. The job was getting harder and harder.

So then, again, by pure chance, another job came up which was with Dorset County Council looking at the opportunities that World Heritage might bring to us. It was called the Jurassic Coast Project and I applied for that, and got it. The biggest role that I had was putting together the fossil collecting code for this area. I was in just the right position to be able to do that.

The worst thing about moving to County Hall in Dorchester was that gone were the days of that freedom in the wintertime, when it's rough and stormy. I couldn't figure out for the first six months why I was so frustrated, and then it just occurred to me,

Today is a spring tide, so it's high tide, there's a force seven or eight blowing ashore, there's been a landslide which I know is going to have fossils in it, and I've got to be in some tedious meeting in Dorchester, and that's the point. I decided I had to put the fossil collecting completely out of my mind. Forget about it, and just take it by chance at the weekend, or if there's a day when it's truly exceptional, just go for it. And that was a difficult thing to do.

But I knew the coast and the collectors and the fossils very, very well, and being a geologist and not unaware of the conservation issues we looked at the issue. This is the richest source of lower Jurassic reptiles, fish and insects anywhere in the world, but the process of erosion that uncovers these fossils is entirely unpredictable. You need to invest a huge amount of time down here if you want to find the fossils, in doing that however you gain an incredible amount of knowledge that's not academic.

The classic example is this dinosaur, *Scelidosaurus* which was found by Dave Sole, that was about six years ago down here. He found the first piece in a place you wouldn't normally look for fossils, there had also been a landslide, and he spent the next four months going back every single day, whether it was rough and stormy or not, and as a result he assembled about 13 or 14 blocks of stone which contained this complete *Scelidosaurus*, which is only known from Charmouth, and is probably the best specimen ever found.

But then you have expressions of concern from one or two academics that everything's hoovered up, things are being found and sold off and people can't do their science. We have one or two beds of rock which are phenomenally rich in fossils, the collectors were digging into those to extract them. So I put together a working group which included the National Trust, the principal landowner, the parish council, English Nature (now Natural England), the fossil collectors, museums and academics and for 18 months we kicked around all the issues and tried to come up with an agreed approach. We quickly agreed that the collectors do a good and essential job in fact.

If the collectors weren't down here, the fossils would be washed away and destroyed, we wouldn't have any fossils to argue about. But at the same time, certain specimens are important. It's essential that academics have access to those specimens, and that we know what's being found. At the same time, if the academics are looking for something in particular, they can convey that to the collectors, because the collectors are the eyes and ears.

Our view is that the science is important, but not exclusive. Just because you're a scientist, it doesn't give you any greater right than anybody else, because ultimately the finds are made by people, whether they're a milkman or an ex-boat builder or a lawyer, it's whoever is prepared to invest their time. Academics have had all the time in the world to come down to find fossils, but they don't because they're too busy. There's a guy called Chris Moore who lives in Charmouth, he's found two, possibly three new species of *ichthyosaur* in the last 12 years, all from Seatown. Chris has figured out how to extract these things from this extraordinarily difficult shale and clean them, and as a result he's found these new species, and I can't think of a better way to ensure that the fossils survive. In fact that's our priority. We want the fossils to be found, we want to know what's being found, and we want the scientifically important ones to be made available to the academics.

There's a recording scheme at the Charmouth Centre. The code is very simple. What we've said is we don't want people to dig in the cliffs and we want people to record their scientifically important specimens, and in exchange for that, the ownership will be transferred to those collectors. So there's a huge advantage for the collectors in doing that, the ownership is not contested. I should also say that nobody's ever stolen anything from this cliff because the landowners have never expressed their wish to retain all the fossils.

The parish council own the cliffs either side of Charmouth and the beach area westwards to Lyme. The National Trust own Black Ven and the cliffs to the east of Stonebarrow, but they also own part of the beach in places. But if the Trust said they didn't want people to collect they would still have the obligation to make sure the fossils are recovered, and the only way of doing that would be to pay someone to be the official collector. And you'd still have to police the beaches and stop people from stealing the fossils. It would be impossible. So the real issue is that the funding for the acquisition of fossils is appalling, compared to the arts. I sometimes go to the Tate Modern website and see what they've spent. Last year it was £1 million on one piece of artwork and £600,000 on another. Twenty thousand pounds would buy you a new species of *ichthyosaur*. It's absolutely nothing for a totally unique specimen. And the value, I think, is reflected in the time spent finding and cleaning the fossil. A lot of collectors want to see a world class exhibition here in Dorset.

The new fossil collecting code was part of the Jurassic Coast UNESCO bid. It was a very long process. The funding has come largely from Dorset and Devon County Councils, Natural England and the South West of England Regional Development Agency. What they like is that we have this very strategic approach, this very big picture of how the whole site works. The World Heritage Site itself is only from the cliff top to the low tide mark, but there is the idea of what's called the World Heritage Coast, and I think that is essentially everything that relates to the geology of the coastline and by that I mean if you look at Beaminster or Broadwindsor or Symondsbury or Bridport, the character of those towns and villages is entirely due to the local stone which comes out in the cliffs at Burton Bradstock. And there's a story there which links them together. The reason why the towns and villages of Purbeck look so different from west

Dorset is because the stone is changing, and I think that's the World Heritage Coast. I would suggest that the World Heritage Coast actually extends as far as London, through the Portland stone connection.

The World Heritage Site is not about mass tourism. We want people that come down here to have the best opportunity to learn about, understand and enjoy the coast. So that's about improving facilities, and in addition to that we'd like to see more people coming out of season. Something like 20 per cent of Dorset's economy is tourism based, but it's very seasonal. You have this big spike in the summertime, but some of the best times to explore are not in these six weeks but in the autumn and winter, particularly with fossil collecting.

The main aim of World Heritage is about conservation and education. Tourism is a spin off of doing those things really well. If people don't understand the site, they're not going to want to conserve it. The most extraordinary thing I find, is that about 60 or 70 per cent of the people I meet have the attitude that if the cliffs have fallen down, or there's erosion, it's a terrible thing. But if you think about it, the reason we have this extraordinarily beautiful coastline, which is internationally important and interesting, is because it's eroding. It's so blindingly obvious.

In reality the greatest threat to the site is the protection of towns and villages. That's the biggest conflict. And the word 'protection' is an interesting concept, because if you're a coastal engineer or someone who lives in a house on the cliff top then you're talking about wanting to protect the property, but if you're Natural England or a conservationist, protection actually means entirely the opposite, it means letting the coast fall into the sea. It's not just the geology, we've also got these fantastic sea cliff communities, all these cliff falls and landslides are fantastic habitats for plants and animals, particularly insects, which

specialise in colonising broken and disturbed ground and Black Ven behind us here is described as possibly the best example of that in Europe.

We're not saying coast defences shouldn't happen, because clearly in places they should, but it's getting the right balance. It's long term decisions. Can we really continue to protect a town like Lyme Regis? In the short term, 40, 50, 60 years, the answer probably is yes, but in the longer term, eventually we're going to have to walk back and abandon it. At the moment we're looking at the east side of Lyme Regis, the East Cliff, and here's a conflict. One of the highlights of the World Heritage Site. Black Ven is the largest coastal landslide in Europe, it's an absolute highlight in terms of the geomorphology, but at the same time, it's eating its way towards Lyme Regis. There are up to 170 houses at threat, including the main road through the town. When that main road goes there will be a lot of concern about the viability of the town as a tourist destination. I think it might be quite a good thing, it'll be a bit like Clovelly, but people aren't prepared to think that at the moment. There is a need to protect the eastern side of the town. There's already an existing sea wall there, that's reaching the end of its life, and we're now looking at what options are there to replace it. Currently the option is to advance the sea wall by ten metres across the foreshore which will obscure quite a lot of the geology and will mean you're not able to walk along the beach except at low tide. We think that's too much and there isn't a compromise being found there at the moment. So that's my job.

The reason we have a World Heritage Site is because between Exmouth in East Devon and Studland Bay in Dorset we have a record through 185 million years of the earth's history. The Triassic, the Jurassic and the Cretaceous periods of time. Overall the rocks dip or tilt very gently down towards the east, so we have the oldest rocks in East Devon. The Triassic is a whole series of soft mudstones and hard sandstones. At the Budleigh Salterton end you've got pebble beds which were laid down 240 million years ago by a huge river that once ran through a desert, then you've got the Otter sandstone around Ladram Bay and Sidmouth. Following along the undercliff you've got the Mercia mudstone and then the famous Jurassic rocks, the Blue Lias which you see around Lyme Regis.

At Black Ven, the very dark clay belongs to the Charmouth Mudstone Formation. Further east you get the Bridport sandstone which forms the fantastic cliffs around West Bay and Burton Bradstock. Above that is the thin but very famous bed, the Inferior Oolite which contains fantastic ammonites and which is also the building stone for Symondsbury and Bridport. As we move east, the rocks continue to get younger. The shores of the Fleet contain further clays, sandstones and limestone rocks and at the far end, the Kimmeridge clay has been eroded away to form the vast expanse of Portland Harbour. Across the water, towering cliffs of hard limestone form the Isle of Portland, which is of course famous for Portland Stone.

Moving into Purbeck things get a little more complex as in places the rocks have been folded into a near vertical orientation and then eroded into the extraordinary coast around Lulworth. Just beyond the Cove lies the fossil forest, a land surface that dates back a staggering 140 million years. Into the army ranges and we start to see rocks from the Cretaceous period including the Purbeck Beds and the Chalk. Hard rock layers form headlands while softer rocks have been eroded into bays. The Kimmeridge clay is named after Kimmeridge Bay but it runs eastwards to Chapmans Pool. The Portland limestone then takes control again, forming the towering cliffs from St Aldhelms Head to Durlston.

The rocks, and the fossils that they contain tell a story, or rather stories through time. The red rocks of East Devon formed in a desert. The Jurassic rocks formed under the sea, the fossil forest, well, it was a forest for a brief spell of time while the Purbeck Beds were salt flats across which the dinosaurs roamed.

The timescale? At Exmouth the rocks are 250 million years old, at Lyme Regis 200 million years, Portland 140 million years while the youngest rocks, the Chalk, is about 85 million years.

The fossils? We've got strange mammal-like reptiles called *Rhynchosaurs* in East Devon, they're not very well preserved, but around the world fossils from that age are really rare, so they are special. We've got the rocks around Charmouth and Lyme Regis, we've got the Kimmeridge clay which is phenomenally rich in marine reptiles, we've got the fossil forest which has its soil associated with it, then we've got the Purbeck Beds which are famous for dinosaur footprints but also for crocodiles and turtles, I was lucky enough to make a spectacular find back in April this year. I went down to a site meeting in Swanage, it was 11 o'clock, I had a couple of hours spare, thought I'd go down to Durlston Bay and found a fantastic crocodile skull, 60 centimetres long, perfectly preserved. And that's being cleaned at the moment. It's 130 million years old from the Purbeck Beds.

The UNESCO criteria we qualified under for World Heritage Site status, says is about major stages of the Earth's history, the record of life and geomorphological landforms. We have a record through 185 million years of geological time while the fossils chart virtually a third of the evolution of life, including the rise of the dinosaurs. And then the third element is active processes, and what we have on this coastline is what's been described as an open laboratory for geomorphology. We have superb examples of landslides, we have bays and headlands like Lulworth Cove, we have Chesil Beach, which is one of the finest barrier beaches with a lagoon behind it anywhere in the world and we have sea stacks like Ladram Bay or Old Harry Rocks.

Then we've got the history of science which reads like a Who's Who of the greatest names of geology, they developed the science on this coastline. The Anning family and most famously Mary Anning, who found the first marine reptiles to come to the attention of science, 1812, was the first *ichthyosaur*, 1823, the first *Plesiosaur* and 1828, the first flying reptile known to science. And those fossils spurred Henry De La Beche who was the founder of the British Geological Survey, he lived in Lyme in 1812 and knew Mary Anning. And from those fossils he was inspired to draw an amazing illustration in 1830 called 'Duria Antiquior, A More Ancient Dorsetshire,' and that was the first ever attempt to visualise what a past environment was like. This coastline provided the evidence. In addition to that we've got the educational value of the site, which is massive, and the landscape which is stunningly beautiful and varied because of the geology.

Pollution? The Napoli effect? In terms of the World Heritage Site, it might sound controversial to say that it has had little or no impact whatsoever on the core value of the World Heritage Site. It's not affected the rock sequence or the fossils or the geomorphology. The one pollution event that really could impact on the site is oil, and the way it would do that is not through a traditional sense of oil on beaches. Imagine this really heavy crude that comes from Russia. If this type of oil hit Chesil Beach, not only would it be very difficult to clean, it would lock the pebbles together and effect the dynamic nature of the beach and that could effect the behaviour of the pebbles, which could lead to a breach in the beach and flooding of the Fleet behind it. That would be a man-made, catastrophic impact on the World Heritage Site. That's where the concern comes with ship to ship transfer of oil. Lyme Bay is designated as one of the sites. The

trouble is that ships can transfer oil outside the 12-mile limit without any regulation whatever. At least the designated transfer area provides for the necessary pollution equipment to be on hand during regulated transfers.

Portland Gas is very interesting. I've been quite involved with it. If you went down to Branscombe and walked along the beach where the Napoli is today, you'll find this extraordinary rock, it's full of gypsum which is an evaporite mineral, and in the Triassic desert there were actually lakes. And those lakes evaporated and you got salts, rather like the salt flats in Utah and Death Valley. That's what it would have been like. But Branscombe was at the edge of the lake and so the evaporite deposits are very thin, but the centre of the lake was right underneath Weymouth and Portland, 2,500 metres down there's 400 feet of salt, and it's possible to drill down and dissolve caverns and pump gas into them. What concerns me is that I want to see this coastline as an exemplar of how we're going to deal with climate change. A lot of properties that are now at risk have been built in the last 30, 40 years. So my initial concern was should we be having such a massive development of infrastructure that clearly at some stage will require further coastal defence? But it's not that simple, the salt resource is only under Weymouth and Portland. The other big consideration is that if there were to be a catastrophic fire, you have to have a large area around the site where there's no people or property, and I think the site they've chosen probably is the best site. Our other concern is that it's built on a landslide that has been active at some stage, although I have to say that Portland Gas have spent a great deal of time and money working out what sort of a landslide it is, in an attempt to assess the risk of movement. They've done an incredible amount of work and the site they have chosen is now probably one of the most intensely studied coastal slopes in Britain.

The future? I came down from Scotland intending to do two or three years here, get some experience and go back, because I love mountains, but in fact I really love this place. The other thing I do is diving, a lot of scuba diving. I've got the best of both worlds, when it's rough and stormy I go fossilling, when it's flat and calm I go scuba diving. The only problem is that they both require weather conditions that you can't predict. I should really take up croquet or badminton. You could book a court and you know you're going to do it. There is nothing worse than a big spring tide and gale force winds and a diary fully of important meetings!

Dorset's got fantastic geology, fantastic diving, fantastic scenery, fantastic landscapes, fantastic wildlife, great people, super pubs and beer and I want to stay here. I would like to work abroad, helping to develop geo-tourism and geo-conservation initiatives, ideally through contract work as I would always want to be based here.

12. Tony Gill – Fossil hunter, Charmouth.
Born Honiton 1963.

It was about 300 yards past the tea van, so I saw this large vertebrae sticking out of this block, I suppose six inches… Yeah, I knew exactly what it was… We used a wheelbarrow… I came down at midnight and saw this lump of jaw, and that was the best bit.

My father's a farmer. And my grandfather, he was a farmer as well in Membury. A small farm, about 75 acres. Too much work for one, not enough money for two. Quite a struggle. Mother's side? They were farmers as well. School was Membury, which was a very small school. When I left school I became a mechanic.

Charmouth was our Sunday day out, back in the mid to late 1960s there were fossils scattered all over the beach. Even in the middle of summer you could sit on the beach and pick them up. There was very few people collecting here. Back then there was Barney who I'd never met, and there was a couple of chaps who used to come down from London at weekends. Other than that there was no one really collecting on the beach. If I'd known what I was doing you could have taken away carloads but we'd just pick up little iron pyrites ammonites that were loose on the sand and that's how it really started.

It's just that 'finding something' I think. I've always said if it wasn't fossils it would probably be gold, if we lived in Australia. I was an agricultural engineer with a firm in Axminster, Medland, Sanders & Twose. They were quite a big company. Repairing people's tractors? Yes and combines. Oh yes, we had our own van. We went out once and fixed the wrong baler, it was broken down but it wasn't the farm we were supposed to go to, it

was in a field, you drove up the lane, took the second right or the third right and you go in and find out what's wrong and you fix it, and then matey comes along and says 'What are you doing?'

I don't know who paid the bill. It's not our problem, we just did our job. It's changed in the last four or five years, it's really changed. You've got the big contractors, they're working 24 hours a day nearly.

Father's farm? Sart Farm. Rhymes with fart. It was dairy. Father's retired now. He's let the farm out. Now, he stays in the farmhouse and pretends to be a farmer. I did agricultural engineering for about six years I suppose. Then we went off to do cars and that lasted about five years, and then a quarry up in Scunthorpe, one of the old iron mines, they started digging that again and there were some stunning ammonites coming out, white calcite, really clear, so I went up there for six months, just collecting the fossils.

There was a break where you chase women and drink lots of beer and you forget all about it and then you get over that. Then when my daughter was born and my wife was in hospital and I was sat at home bored one day, I thought 'I'll go to the beach.' I went down and found some fossils and I thought 'This is fun, ain't it?' Mainly Charmouth, up to Whitby now and again. If there was a big storm you took it on chance but when you're working you might do the odd very early morning, get up at three o'clock in the morning and have a quick one before work, and weekends.

Competition? Yes. It's most of the time, the first one there will have nearly everything off the beach, so it's fairly fierce, the competition. Well after the Scunthorpe collecting I got back and I didn't know what to do really and just as I was driving down Lower Sea Lane I thought 'I'm going to go and ask in the car park if I can do a fossil stall in there,' which I did and they said

Tony Gill with the jaw of his tame Ichthyosaur, Mary

'Yes,' and it started from there really. The gravel car park up there. That was about 1990. We had that there for about a year or so, and then there was a complaint over something and the council came down and said 'You're not allowed to sell things in the car park,' so that finished that for a minute or two. So I approached the Parish Council about this place, because it was just full of bits of wood and the mill stones, and there were lots of tins of half-empty paint and so on, so I went to the Parish Council and they agreed. We were living in Colyford.

So I set up from here in 1991. It's grown exponentially. There's probably really only one good layer, the one they call the Flat Stones, where you find the beautifully preserved ammonites, large ammonites, from an inch up to, if you're really lucky, eight inches, the preservation is really stunning. There's several other beds, but you only get one ammonite in 100 that's any good. You've got the Crinoids bed, that's a relation to the starfish, it looks like a plant but it's actually an animal, and you've got half a dozen beds containing iron pyrite ammonites, and that's about it. The cliff might be 150 feet high, but there's probably only a foot in total of fossil-bearing rock… It's lower Jurassic. The iron pyrite ammonites tend to come out in the soft clay, the really nice ammonites, the asteroceras, come out in a big limestone lens, noduley sort of thing.

We get them out with a hammer. Break the stone down, we're not allowed to dig in the cliffs, quite often you see it sticking out of the mud slip and you dig the stone out. Only if it's fallen from the cliff. Yeah, the sea will erode the flat stones in the cliff where they drop down because the beds dip east. All the beds end up on the beach, so eventually the sea will erode the cliff and expose them but you're not supposed to take those out. If it's fallen out and the sea has washed it and it's sticking out, yes you're allowed to take them out. It's one of those things we

agreed to. So we have ownership so long as we stick within the code.

One or two big finds? Yeah, a large ichthyosaur. It was Easter bank holiday weekend 2000 and it had rained quite a lot, so I had a six o'clock start to see if there had been a cliff fall, and there was the cliff fall, walked up the beach, saw footprints, 'Oh no!' got there and there were lots of broken up stones, and there was this large lump of rock lying at the bottom of the beach, it was a big vertebrae. It was about 300 yards past the tea van, so I saw this large vertebrae sticking out of this block, I suppose six inches the vertebrae must have been, I looked down and there was lots of bone in it, quite often you find things like that and it's just rubbish, then found the next piece which fitted on to it.

Yeah, I knew exactly what it was, but quite often you can find these things but all the bones are scattered around, it's one of those things you might think isn't worth doing anything with, but I took them up the top of the beach just in case. We used a wheelbarrow but luckily enough it was bank holiday weekend and Richard Edmonds and a few other people were around with the day off so we had plenty of hands, one pulling it with a rope round the front and dragging it off, so it wasn't too bad.

I realised what we had when we found the first piece of jaw which was still set in the stone but all totally in order so you could see the top of the jaw bone and the teeth sticking down the side. I came down at midnight and saw this lump of jaw, and that was the best bit. I had a torch, and to come back with a foot of jaw which you could only just carry because of the weight, that must have been on the Sunday evening, that was the time you got really excited because you knew the rest was in there. You didn't know how long it was going to be and in total the head was six feet, I had about 18 inches of the eye socket and then the first bit of jaw, and you were imagining how long the jaw was going to be, you were dreaming it was going to be ten feet long. I spent many days up there, weeks actually, just digging into the slip looking for the rest of the jaw. You dig below, so you know you've definitely got down below where it would have come from. The only way to do it was to dig into the slip and dig through it. I'd go up there for two or three hours every day and just dig a hole, and I kept doing this for quite a few weeks, and eventually we did find the other two or three bits, strangely enough not at the bottom of the hole up right up the top, six inches below the surface.

Yeah. You don't get many of those. Large ones, there's the one that Mary Anning had, and one that came from Seatown about ten years ago, a bit smaller but still fairly impressive. So I've got the jaw. Yeah, the whole head. The whole beast would have been possibly about 35 feet. We've got quite a lot of the vertebrae column. On the day I found it, it was quite a rough sea, and every time a wave hit it there were millions of pieces of rib, finger size and all broke into one inch sections, every time the wave come up, you couldn't do anything about it, all you could do was pick out the big bits. I was there on my own, there was nothing anyone could have done, really.

It didn't need any preserving really, because it was in a stone nodule it's been chiselled down roughly, down just above the bone, then just prepared in acetic acid. It's not the strongest stuff but it slowly eats the stone away exposing the bone. Then you just seal the bone with a clear lacquer, something to stop the acid from attacking the newly exposed bone, and then put it back in the acid again, and this went on for about ten months. The rock is limestone. Effectively the bone has been replaced by calcite.

Has the *ichthyosaur* got a name? Mary. After Mary Anning. Other ones? Oh the *plesiosaur*, that was found sticking out of the cliff in Black Ven, just walked across one day and see a stone sticking out, touch it with a spade and you think 'That looks like a bit of bone,' then you have a bit of a poke around and you find a foot of vertebrae column, and you think 'Yes!' So a quick call to the National Trust, just get their permission, you are allowed to extract… They own down to mean low tide, then it's Crown Estates, and then they own, well I don't know who really owns the cliff over there, but the National Trust seem to, so they gave me the OK, and it was really exciting, I was expecting to find this whole plesiosaur and it was only about three feet long, which is a common thing to find, just chunks of them. Age? About 119 million. In those times it would have been a fairly shallow sea. Belemnites? Yep.

The shop? We started off as everyone does, saying we're only going to sell local fossils, and then you go, 'only British fossils,' then you have to have all of it because you cannot make a living out of local fossils. Your customers must come from all over the world. Yes. Chinese, Americans, Australians, New Zealand, plenty of Europeans, we had a chap from Mongolia in, a dinosaur expert. Kids love it, just to have a hammer and go and smack a couple of stones on the beach, and some of them do find the odd vertebrae or bit of rib. And if they can't find something they can buy it here. That's even better.

How it works in the shop is like the first day of the holiday 'What a rip off, we can get our own on the beach,' and then the second day, and this shows by the sales, they come in and buy the books, 'We're going to go and find one now, we've got the book.' And then Wednesday and Thursday the hammer hires go up, and by Friday you're not selling any books, you might hire one or two hammers, but you're selling loads of fossils because it's like 'Hm, they're not so expensive, they are hard to find!'

There's a definite pattern to sales in this shop.

The other fossil collectors round here? There's Chris Moore, Dave Sole and Rick Taylor, there's quite a few. If there's a really rough sea there might be six or seven people down here, and then there's a lot of people that will drive 200 miles. We've drove to Whitby for one, that was a 300-mile trip for us.

The cliffs are fairly dangerous. I mean stay away from the really sheer cliffs, there's been a fall this morning, and there's a block up there the size of a washing machine that's rolled from the top about halfway down the beach, if anyone had been stood there it wouldn't have done them a lot of good. If something big happened there isn't a safe spot on the beach. I think it's a case of just being sensible and looking up before you sit under the cliff.

Summer's our busiest selling time. People say 'What are our winter opening hours?' but if there's fossils to be collected we're not here. We're here sometimes.

In the workshop? When you walked in I was doing a bit of cutting, then we grind them and polish them on the buffing wheel, then we've got nice little air tools for preparing the ammonites. Helpers? We've got Rick and the lady there now, she's coming in doing a few hours, now it's getting busier. I've got the wife on the website. It's only been running since the end of November, the Christmas one was quite good, not as good as I'd dreamed but better than I expected. I think it's one of those things you're going to need now. You can buy things now in America. Some of them are easy to send, the other problem with rocks is the weight to value ratio.

We've got some Somerset ammonites. You don't find many fossils in Devon, you can find fossils right the way to London, shark's teeth, and Portland, you've got the fossils there, big ammonites, Burton Bradstock, Kimmeridge, there's fossils all through there. As soon as Dorset starts there's fossils right the way through, not much in Devon, you've got the dinosaurs at Sidmouth, I've never found a dinosaur down there but a friend of mine found one down there, a piece of jaw with three teeth, but I don't think it's been identified yet.

University people? No. They don't like professional fossil collectors, museums. It's got to be in a museum collection to be described, and if it's not in a museum collection they don't seem to be at all interested. They don't really find fossils, do they? They might know quite a bit about them.

It would be lovely to find a *tyrannosaurus* relative, an early one that preyed on the *scelidosaurus*, there's been one or two bones of a carnivorous dinosaur. Wherever there's something like a *scelidosaurus* there's a chance if that thing was stood in the wrong place there could be one turn up one day. When it was alive an *ichthyosaur* have been dolphin like I suppose with a longer nose and masses of teeth and it would have been a carnivore. Yeah.

Quite vicious? Hard to say, there's a fair set of teeth. Fins or flappers? Paddles. Which were mainly just for steering I think. They've been on Walking with Dinosaurs, so they have done computer generated images of them.

What's the future? Looking for more fossils? Yeah. And people? Yes, we've got them all. From the 'What a rip off, it's so expensive, I can't believe it,' to the next person walking in and going 'Wow, it's cheap in here, ain't it!' Some kids must have read every book on dinosaurs, they know so much on it. Then you get another kid come in and go 'Are you sure they're real? Did they really exist?' Sometimes that shop is packed through August, especially if it's not very nice, not if it's raining because they don't come down, but if it's a bit overcast and chilly that shop can be full, like sardines all day. I'll keep on doing this while they still let us. The Government's banned nearly everything else.

13. Lal Hitchcock – Beachcomber and sculptor. Born Woking 1956.

She had a jaunty hip stuck out, there was something quite sexual about her. She was blonde, probably dyed blonde, and she had a very confident expression, great lace-up purple boots, and I just thought 'You're the sort of woman that would break a man's heart, you're Sally Free and Easy.'

My father worked for Cable and Wireless, something to do with United Nations and satellite communications. He used to go off to places like Antigua and Canada, the United States, and Norway, but when he retired he became a full time naïve self-taught artist and cartoonist for Punch. My mother got a degree in history and she taught history part-time.

On my mother's side my grandfather designed boilers and made rubber tyres with latex from Malaya. He had an industry running in Lydney in Gloucestershire on the banks of the river Severn, and his wife was a mother of five children. On the other side, my father's father was a brigadier and very involved in Palestine during the war and post-war, and his wife, my paternal grandmother actually had an amazing contralto voice and used to love singing and playing the piano. If she'd been born 50 years later she'd have gone to music college.

My great-grandfather on my father's side was born in Portsmouth. He was called 'Painter' Hitchcock and he painted Royal Naval ships in Portsmouth harbour. He also went to the Battle of Ladysmith during the Boer War. My father didn't find out about him until he was well into his middle age. But my father was always a fantastic painter, he used to paint the outside of the house and the benches meticulously, he taught me to paint

and he used to say 'Don't overload your brush, and if you see any dribbles of paint you've got to scoop them up quickly.' He taught me how to prime and sand and undercoat and gloss, and it's funny to think that there was this gene, this painterly gene, and this connection with the sea.

At school, art was my favourite subject. Art and English, anything to do with writing and self-expression. I used to like pottery as well. When I was very little my dad taught me to cut lino, I've still got his lino cutting tools, and I think I was about six when I did my first lino cut. It was an old man with a bendy walking stick and a sign saying 'To Chobham,' I think, because we lived at a place called Chobham outside Woking, but it was all back to front because I didn't realise that with lino you had to write things in reverse before you print them.

I went to Winchester Art College to do my foundation. We moved to a water mill outside Winchester and I used to walk in every day to the art school. And then I decided to go in completely the other direction, which was Newcastle Polytechnic to do fine art. It was windy, with bitterly cold north-east winds, and the campus, I think, had one tree on it, and I pined for greenery and the South West. A lot of my art was idealising. I used to make things out of velvet and a lot of it was based on the countryside, a fictitious idealised version of the South West, bosomy hills and thick hedges.

As children my father used to take us to Dorset because he had this obsession with Romans, also with Celts. Dorset is full of hill forts. Also we went to the Isle of Wight because my father's great-uncle, Will Samson ran bathing machines and hot salt baths. His wife, Aunt Kate ran a tea shop and guest house in Shanklin on the Isle of Wight. So our seaside holidays were spent there, but the geology is almost exactly the same as Dorset and what we call Kimmeridge clay here, they call Blue Slipper. We

Lal Hitchcock on Eype Beach with her recycled family

would go looking for ammonites and all those kind of things. It might just as well have been Charmouth or Lyme.

Between leaving Newcastle and moving to Sydling St Nicholas, I got pregnant! And I also bought an etching press. My father had some friends who lived in Sherborne, I went to stay with them and I came across this house in Sydling St Nicholas which was 'closed.' It had no lavatory, I think it only had a cold water tap in the kitchen. It was right in the middle of the village in a derelict state, but it had this massive garden, about an acre behind. It was only a two up, two down. So I set up a printmaking studio there with my very young daughter who was then six months.

When she was two, we started walking over the hill from Sydling to Maiden Newton to catch the train. It was a good two and a half miles, up over chalky tracks, and then we would catch the train down to Weymouth, and we would spend the day on the beach. And then at the end of the day, completely exhausted we would catch the train back and walk over the hill again.

For a few years I then lived in Rampisham in an old farmhouse and started making one-off sculptures around the garden. I can't even remember quite how I picked up my first bit of rubbish off the beach, but something was happening that made me want to pick stuff up and make something out of it. I now live at Mapperton, and there was a person who lived here before me who used to do up old cars and the whole of my drive is covered in little tiny rivets and washers and then if I dig in the garden I find mileometers and speedometers, and broken glass and broken mirrors and reflectors and lights, and I think I put the two together. The very first pieces I made, two were faces, and two were people, and they involved driftwood bodies and stuff I found from my garden and drive.

I don't think I consciously had a motive. I had left my partner, I'd left my daughter, I was in therapy, I was in a bit of a state really and I wonder how much I was trying to work with lowly materials because I myself felt lowly. It was possible I was grunging around with very base things because I felt sort of base myself, it's also possible that I was working on a much more unconscious level, because I was in therapy. Printmaking is a very precise discipline where you have a blank piece of copper or steel or even just card, and there's something about knowing what you're going to do before you start out. At least that's the way I approached it. Changing from printmaking to beach combing was fundamental. Beachcombing is a very random act because what one person will pick up, someone else will leave and vice versa. I don't think I had any green issues, although I always recycled things at home. It was just emptying my mind and seeing what filled it, which, looking back was a change of gear for me.

I'm a magpie and I'm attracted by lovely bright colours, and I just started to see these beautiful bits of bright pink Frisbee or spade handles, or lollypop sticks on the beach. What I realised is that driftwood is beautiful and people love driftwood, but for me there is no humour in driftwood really. The humour comes from the objects that have had another life, be they paint brush handles, or washing up brush handles, or loo brush handles. They've had this previous life, and I'm giving them a new life in another context which has a tremendous potential for humour. The other thing is the colour, and by going for that grungy, awful recycled lavatory brush, I'm possibly picking up the thing that other people would walk away from.

If there are two pink plastic bottles on the beach, one is new and might have been left yesterday by somebody having a picnic, and the other might have been in the sea for eight months, I'd probably choose both, because the recent one would be pinker, because pink and red and orange are all very susceptible to ultra violet light, so they loose their colour much quicker than blue, for instance, which retains it and is rather beautiful. Red and pink are rather boring after a while. I'd pick up both because I'd pick up the bright one to use in a workshop with children, or even for myself, and the other one, with vestiges of pink, I would probably pick up, not for its colour, but for its texture and that sort of milky quality that plastic has when it's been around for a while.

I love really ambiguous pieces of rubbish, when you're not quite sure what they were in a previous life. It's amazing how many brushes I find. Paint brushes, hair brushes, tooth brushes, different types of paint brushes, for painting the undersides of boats. Brushes do have this beautiful way of weathering. If they're wooden brushes and the bristles have gone and you've got the holes still, maybe with just the stumps of bristles, or maybe the bristles have gone completely, and then the whole of the outside of the brush has been weathered and worn away and eaten away, you'll end up with the most extraordinary thing with just some punched holes in it that looks terribly precious. A really beautiful bit of rubbish actually becomes so beautiful that I can't use it in a piece of art because it's lovely as a thing in itself.

I particularly like foreign writing on plastic. I have found bottles with Cyrillic script on them, which I guess come from Greece or Bulgaria or Russia. It's a very strange thing, beachcombing, I only go down to two or three beaches on the Dorset coast, in that sense it's very parochial. I go to the same beaches, but what gets washed up is truly global, and there is that sense of connecting with the whole world. I have found a piece of wood with Chinese characters on it, I wondered if it came from the tsunami. I think things will turn up from the

tsunami because all the oceans of the world are joined and bit by bit things get through, so there is this sense of being connected to much greater things, and finding things that are just telling you a tiny bit of a story. I've been finding for many years clumps of coconut hair, I put it on my people and make it into hair, and I wondered where it came from, obviously from a coconut. But what was it being used for? And then the other day I found a very simple, beautiful little broom, the shaft was bamboo and all the little bits of coconut were bound on with pieces of wire. Just a very simple broom which I showed to someone, and he said 'I should think it comes from Africa.'

I go down to Chesil beach at Portland, I go to Chiswell, it's very, very good in the winter because of the tides there. Huge things get washed up, a lot of very ugly things, fridge freezers, dead dogs, there's been stuff from the Napoli lately, lots of dead birds, a lot of the stuff you really wouldn't want, oil canisters, some of them still have oil in them, really smelly, gunky, horrible stuff. I sometimes think I should be wearing rubber gloves and a mask. In fact I find a lot of rubber gloves there, which have presumably been worn by people who have been handling some kind of dangerous substance, so there's a kind of element of danger to it, and repulsion. But it's rich pickings. Eype is much nearer to me and I can top up on bits of wood but Portland is really my main treasure trove.

It is irritating when the beach gets cleaned. Yes, I have very mixed feelings. Ten, twenty years ago I'd have thought 'Oh how lovely, what a nice beach, it's beautiful, there's not a scrap of rubbish on it,' now I think 'Oh!' and I'm really disappointed. Equally I'm pleased for the people that are going to use the beach, but I kind of know that the stuff is only going to go into a landfill site. So all that's happened is that it's moved. I know it's always going to be washed up there, as long as there is traffic in the sea, and fishermen fishing, and people going for holidays, and stuff getting washed down sewers and sewers ultimately ending up in the sea. There will always be rubbish on the beach, so actually, in a way, it's a purely cosmetic thing. I can't get hold of that rubbish because somebody's put it in a landfill site, but unfortunately it's not going to rot or decompose.

I love combs, I'm very fond of wire brushes. If I found a wire brush that had a little bit of tar on it then fine, but if it's really gunky it has to be very, very special to take it home for cleaning. I've got something called Rhapsody, which is a rapeseed oil. It's brilliant because for years I was a printmaker and my hands have really dried out from using too much white spirit, and this stuff is oily, so when I de-tar things I reckon the rapeseed oil is doing my hands good. It's actually quite strong stuff. Sometimes I pick up things which have got layers and layers of paint, so I have to watch what I'm doing.

The sea sorts the rubbish. There was a wonderful programme on the radio all about the sea. The presenter interviewed various people, and one of them, an American, referred to the sea as a mischievous 'She,' a trickster or a kind of siren or goddess who actually sorts things. So a left-hand flip flop would turn up on one beach and right-hand one would turn up on another. Something to do with the way they were weighted, and it's true that you'll get stretches of beach where you'll find nothing but yellow bottle tops, and another bit of beach where you'll get hundreds of paint brush handles, and another bit where you'll get those ear buds for cleaning out your ears. The sea does have this enormous capacity for sorting things out.

Walking along the beach there's this noise, it's a lovely sound, it's great on a windswept spitty day. When it's pouring with rain I have been down to Portland and got so wet I've just sat in the car in these completely wet clothes and had a sandwich and had to drive home. Of course it's lovely when the sun is shining and it's early in the year or late October. When I'm on the beach I try to empty my mind of things I'm looking for. I've become rather set in my ways about what I pick up and what I leave. It would be very interesting for someone else to present me with a whole lot of rubbish and say 'Here, you have this and make something out of it,' it would be very different.

Other people give me things. I think the people who are most successful are my children because they know me very well. Children get great pleasure from giving me things. There is that lovely quality, which is that people feel they can present me with something that they feel I would like and there is something very delightful about that, being the recipient of other people's found objects. It's like treasure hunting. I think I'm very lucky that I can get excited about a bit of tubing, bright blue tubing, plastic, a little bit of wood that's shaped like a nose, a perfect eye, which is a shell with a hole in it. It's wonderful to be so easily satisfied and content with such lowly objects.

There's a woman I made in my house, she's called Rose with a String Bag, and she's made out of the outside of a thermos flask, blue plastic. Inside she would have had all the thermal stuff, metal, but she's blue plastic and ribbed, her face is made of driftwood with little washers and broken mirrors as eyes, with the broken mirror behind the washer, a nose made out of a rusty nail, lips made out of broken car light. I still use those pieces of car for faces. Her hair is, if you can imagine pulling off a plastic bag in a shop, you leave that stub behind. I quite often find stubs of all the plastic bags, whether they be white, transparent, it's green in this case. So she appears to have either a green torque or green hair, and her basket is made out of green criss-crossy plastic, that fruit would be wrapped in. Then she's got carved legs and arms, again made out of driftwood. I've painted her some boots which are laced with the inner core of electrical wiring, and the boot is very significant. I have little phases of doing things, and my latest one is women with high heeled boots.

Over the years I've become less strict about tampering. To begin with everything had a wonderful rawness which I really like. I can't go back to that, it's like lost innocence. The innocent days were about not tampering with things, hardly cutting things, certainly not painting things, not carving things, so the legs and arms didn't match. Now I'm becoming more particular about that, and in a way I don't like that. I'd love to go back to some rawness. I think that as I get older and my eyesight gets worse, and my ability to carry things and saw things and carve things gets less, I think I'll probably go back to that rawness. But for now they are more honed.

One favourite piece of rubbish I've got is a seed pod and it comes from the West Indies or Africa, it's shaped like a heart, a rounded heart, and it's dark red and slightly furry, and when you shake it you can hear the seeds rattling inside. That's my favourite natural thing, and my favourite man-made thing is a crumpled small tin that looks like it might have had powder paint or gold paint in it, but it's got very crunched up and concertinaed, and it's gone red and orange, oxidised, and there's something very pleasing about that. It's too good to make anything out of.

The sea is both alluring and terrifying, I respect it because it's very easy to drown, I swim out quite far and I'm scared to think what's underneath me. I have been in the water at night with phosphorescence off Burton, it was extraordinary. I didn't know you could get it in England. It was a thundery night, it started raining, and you could see all the lightning flashing out to sea and it was very warm. It would have been about ten o'clock and as I lifted my arms out of the water there was just this extraordinary, like blobs of jelly or frogspawn, illuminated, luminous particles dropping from my hands, and I realised that every time I moved in the water I would stir up these particles of luminosity. It was just water but something to do with the way it was illuminated made it seem somehow more solid. I've come across it a couple of times off the southern coast. I've also had shoals of mackerel swimming around me, it was kind of scary but to be swimming with these leaping fish is really thrilling, it must be very thrilling to swim with dolphins, so I think I find the water both alluring and terrifying.

The finished work ends up in galleries. I like them to be exhibited as a whole, as a family, because in a way so many of them are characters, they have much more impact if I show 20, 30, 40 of them together than if I show them in dribs and drabs. Quite a few teachers buy my work, the Mayor of Honiton bought a piece, he was an ex-policeman, he bought someone called 'Sally Free and Easy,' which was named after the folk song by Cyril Tawney, which is about a hard-hearted woman who breaks the sailor's heart, and it's all using sea metaphors, it's a beautiful, beautiful tune, and lovely words, very simple, very bitter. So I made 'Sally Free and Easy.' I name them after I've made them because the character emerges, and she had a jaunty hip stuck out, there was something quite sexual about her. She was blonde, probably dyed blonde, and she had a very confident expression, great lace-up purple boots, and I just thought 'You're the sort of woman that would break a man's heart, you're 'Sally Free and Easy.' So the Mayor of Honiton bought 'Sally Free and Easy.'

A Helen bought 'Helen in a High Wind,' she had a skirt made of plastic which was at a funny angle and it looked like it was blowing up and her hair was this sea grass, marram grass, blowing off her head. People do buy things when they share the name of that particular character, or the other thing is they just look like them, or they look like someone else, 'You've got to buy that, it's the spitting image of you!' and it is odd, they end up looking just like people I know. I think in a way they're all autobiographical, they're all bits of me, and I do tend to do more women than men. They wear more brightly coloured things, it's much more fun making a woman.

There are certain favourite characters that come to mind, like 'Princess Anne with a Clutch Bag,' because it did look just like Princess Anne. But it was in the days when I didn't put feet on my people and I didn't give them hands either, so she's got these extraordinary shapeless legs that end in stumps. They don't go down into elegant boots, but something about her jaw and her expression… sometimes I mourn them because their name and the person go so well together, sometimes I mourn the name more than the person.

I'd like to get into animation, I've started making sort of puppets out of threaded together, off white bits of plastic, starting with something that I feel comes out of a fridge, I don't know what it is but it looks like a bit of backbone or ribcage, and then I've threaded spoons and curlers, actually starting with bits of marine ply, which are very skull shaped. I found three and I've got one great big blue one lying on my workshop floor which will be a life-size skeleton, the others are quite little and I've threaded them together with wire and then I've hung them on fishing line. I'd quite like to just try making up stories for them, maybe I'll dress them and they'll be these little skeletal puppets that do things, but I have a friend who's an animator and he'd quite like to try, on my behalf, making something, just so I can see what I can do. I just can't think of anything better than making up your own stories, devising your puppets, maybe getting friends in to write music, maybe performing it yourself or getting friends to

do that. A home-grown puppet story would be great.

I do expect to find a body one day. I do. Maybe people who've tried to come into this country and who've been unsuccessful. In fact my little animation or story might involve that to some extent, the scenario, what would happen if I found three Africans who've made it up from the coast of Morocco and up through Spain. What would I do? Would I take them to the police? Would I keep it quiet, would I say 'come and live with me for a bit,' what would I do? At the moment none of the things that I pick up pose that kind of ethical dilemma. If it was a dead person, that wouldn't pose a dilemma, I'd just go and report it to the beach warden, it would be deeply shocking, but if it was a live person, what would it be my duty as another human being to do? Would I just silently smuggle them into Dorset and live with them for a few months and teach them English? I don't know.

I think as an artist you spend a lot of time philosophising. When you work on your own you can afford to do that, questioning all the time, 'Is what I'm doing valid, is there any point in it, there is so much art in the world, wouldn't it be better just to grow cabbages and potatoes and feed myself and feed some others?' And yes, I think that. But I think walking along the beach makes room for philosophy, because of the sound of the waves and the lack of interruption. I could just head off from Portland, back along Chesil Beach and not get off it until Abbotsbury or Burton or somewhere, so it's that sense of the rhythm of my feet on the pebbles, and the sun on one side of me and the sea on the other, you can't get lost. And that being alone with the elements, it is a wonderful thing. There is a sort of emptying of the brain that happens. There is time to ponder on life. 'What am I doing here and what is my part in this? Do I have a part?'

14. Geoffrey Good – Norman Good & Sons, Sand & gravel merchants. Born West Bay 1918.

We'd have probably five or six horses and at least eight to ten men, to look after them. There were two-wheeled putts, the wheels were nice and wide, not to sink in, and you backed it down and just with two or three of you around the putt with shovels. And then you bring it back up the beach, you'd have a string of horses you see.

I was born in 1918, just towards the end of the first war, October 20th. Actually. My father Norman was running the business, he looked after all the shipping in the war, and his father Henry before him. Our family has been involved in West Bay since 1828. The buildings are ours, the warehouses. We rented them because they belonged to the Pitt Rivers. Eventually they put it all up for sale and father bought this.

Earliest memories of West Bay? I think when we used to have the Designers, the sailing boats. They were about 16 foot, the Trevett family were very keen on that sort of thing you know in Bridport. They were hairdressers in Bridport and I used to watch them a lot and of course prawning on the pier. Still lots of sailing vessels coming in then. Mostly the timber, cement, oil cake for feeding cattle. Jute and hemp for the net and rope making company. Yes they used to bring that in as well and we used to store quite a lot of it in our premises.

Oh yes that big building there at the bottom, that used to be a drying place for the stone and aggregate. We used to dry it, grade it and wheel it out. There was a fire underneath it. Yes that's right, with steel plates on it. The horses used to get the gravel off the beach. Pea gravel that was for boats, we used to

load it into the ships, that all went to Scotland. Pebbledash. They loved it up there. I think it is because in the cities it was very dirty I believe, smokey in those days and of course you get a shower of rain and it washes it all off. Kept the north east wind out or something. Steam ships came in and schooners. And this photograph is the *Gisela Flint*. She made 50 voyages to Bridport. She used to come in with the timber. Baltic timber, the boats were German. Father was harbour master here during the war.

I went to school in Crewkerne, the grammar school. I was a boarder there, I didn't really like it but you get over it. The Designer boats were sailing, for pure pleasure. They used to have races and where the harbour master's office is over there, there used to be a bigger building than that and they would fire the guns to start them on their way from there.

This is the old account book, this is the book of all the ships that have been in here. Going back to about 1890. A very famous one who always used to be coming in here, now where is she? Yes we have got the cargos, yes. Where they were going? Grangemouth, these are all gravel. Padstow, quite a few different ones, *Helvettia* Padstow. Here we are, 1891 July, there's a cargo of oil cake from London, coal from Newcastle *Star of the North*. Timber, it's just foreign. Coal from Sunderland. Coal, coal, coal, timber. Stone yes. That says 1901, Gas coal was for the gas works. That was quite a business there, for then. Newcastle, Dartmouth, Hull, Lyme Regis. Yes we used to have Lyme Regis as well, often there was a part cargo you see, because it was a smaller port they couldn't take it all, so they'd take off the deck cargo in Lyme Regis and come back to Bridport and unload the rest of it.

Bradford and Sons, they'd buy our cargo, timber from Sweden or somewhere like that. There's Guernsey. Well yes we sent a lot of sand over there for their water filters but that's not

Geoff and John Good, Norman Good & Sons, West Bay

so long ago. West Bay sand was used for the stone cutting machinery. Yes that's right, what we call sawing sand. I see we have got old Henry Good here, and it is 1902. I think father owned a vessel, but it was only a very small one and he was in with somebody else.

Portsmouth, Hull, St David's, Goole, a lot of coal coming in. Quite a dirty cargo. Yes and it had to be shovelled in those days. Because they got these big buckets you know with the handle which they'd hooked on and hoist out but the chaps had to shovel it into these buckets in the hold. It was then tipped into lorries or carts. But a dirty job for the chaps loading it up. They were stevedores and Father, he'd pay them you see. We weren't the only warehouse. Where the flats are, that used to be Bradford & Sons, they were timber you see, and on the opposite side was Ralls & Sons, which are no longer of course.

The cargoes out were only stone, only our gravel. I can see Dieppe, Newcastle, Plymouth we used to send down to Plymouth they'd have it, it was mostly for the roads down there. Sunderland, grit to London, Torquay. There's a hemp from Konigsberg, Riga there's hemp there. Quite a few from Riga I believe. This is 1903. Falmouth, Dartmouth was that lime? Dartmouth and Falmouth. Manure from Falmouth that's interesting. Granite chippings from Guernsey.

These warehouses are listed. They are over 200 years old. Bit more that that I think. I started at the bottom. We had a concrete works where the church is now and I was put in there to make concrete, and we used to make posts, concrete fencing posts. You know. And a lot of the slabs, the concrete paving slabs for the council, in those days they used to have ours, but now, the machines that make them today, quite out of our league. We had a contract with the council. The cement would come in by boat. Those slabs were interesting in those days they always insisted

that we put lignite on the top you know that, little gritty stuff that shines. made it non-slip. I started when I was about 15. I suppose I did a couple of years there then they pushed me into the office.

We had horses. We'd have probably five or six horses and at least eight to ten men to look after them. Extraction from the beach with the horses. Quite hard work? There were two-wheeled putts, the wheels were nice and wide not to sink in, and you just sort of backed it back and just with two or three of you around the putt with shovels. And then you bring it back up the beach, you'd have a string of horses, you see. About four, like this picture. And this is quite interesting because you have got the wooden piling now on the pier which has changed a lot. The sea would go through the piers, yes it was all open really. They tended to do a lot more scouring in those days.

The council used to charge us so much a ton for the gravel. It's stopped now. Storms would it shift the sand around quite a bit. Oh yes very much so. Sometimes there wouldn't be any gravel it would be all sand, then it would be all gravel and no sand. We extracted both. The sand used to be put in the building to dry, until about 1970. I suppose they finished, the horses with the beach.

There seemed to be more to do then because the shipping was more if you take 25 ships in a year. Now there's a good year, 44 ships, 1927. The timber ships they used to take two to three days to discharge. We had cranes on the wharf to lift it out. Men in the hold to stack the timber. It was a council crane but before they had a crane of course it was done by the ship's derricks. Torquay, Salcombe, Christiana that's Oslo I think, Denmark, Hull, Antwerp, Parr, London. This was slag, oil cake and cement…

I caught TB in 1938, so that put me out. I went to a

sanatorium. Bournemouth I had to have an operation done there and they push air in, no that was Dorchester, they push air in to push the lung down and make it heal. Made you lie outside in the fresh air. And with all the windows open. Lucky to survive? Well yes it was just at the start when they put the air in the chest, before they used to inject gold into the body and the gold sealed the holes. Not very pleasant and they didn't always survive. They'd go on for years but it got them in the end.

During the war it was pretty hard going, most of the men gone you see, and it was only my brother, myself and one foreman and he was elderly and just drying sand for these huts that they were building where you chuck the sand on top of the tarmac, tarmac roofs you know.

The Navy used to have a couple of these little boats, you know these fast ones, MTB things. German aircraft? I saw one, I was just crossing over by the sluice gates there, and one came up through the piers and shot in over Bridport dropped his bomb and went on round and went off. I was in the fire brigade actually.

Very few vessels during the war. It picked up afterwards. Small trampers. They'd have their sail, but they would also have an engine.

Only about two or three hundred tons. Some only a hundred and fifty. The harbour freezes occasionally. Mostly timber vessels. Rotterdam, Plymouth, yes, granite chippings, Rotterdam again, Le Havre. Getting better in 1949. Rochester. Plymouth. Yes there are some quite interesting names of vessels aren't there. Is that *Lady Sophia? Coverack, Lady Sheila, Atlantic, Arch Glen.*

Dutch yes a lot of Dutch. Old harbour masters? Thompson. He was a navy man. He used to live over the coastguard's over here. We didn't get a lot of harbour masters really. My brother Reginald took over from Father. He was seven years older that me, he was well into it before I got in. There was fertiliser from abroad. Yes that's BASF. They were just bringing in nitro and phosphate. BASF had a lot of stuff around that time. That was the Dutch from Antwerp, and German vessels. The last vessel was 1989 fertiliser, there were a few in '87. Alderney, granite chippings. So we diversified into other gravels and the slabs for the garden. We used to get gravel from Cogden, of course that stopped, and the concrete, that faded eventually.

Now the gravel is all brought in, mixed up and then we bring it in and dry it and screen it. People use it for water filters. Aquariums yes a lot of that. No residual fungus or algae on it. It goes mostly to the Midlands. Here I'm late for my lunch...

John Good – West Bay. Born 1959.

The family have been Lloyds Agents for the port, since 1828.

I was born 4th June 1959 and started work in Father's yard in 1976, when I left school at 17. Uncle Reginald died a couple of years before I joined the firm. I worked on ships from the age of 14. I helped out on them. When we had a timber ship, you'd have a gang of six or eight, and the fertiliser ships you'd probably have about half a dozen in the hold and there would be others working on the quay. Originally it came in loose bags and then it came in palletised, obviously once it was palletised you only needed a couple of guys and they would steer the forks in and it became a less labour intensive in the last few years.

Originally the harbour had its own crane and then when the crane driver retired nobody else wanted to take the job on, so we had to bring in cranes from Portland. Yes we would know when the vessel was coming in and we would organise a crane to be there and hope to God that it didn't get blown away. The boats were never any longer than about 160 foot. Sometimes gravel went out. We used to buy in when we lost our extraction off the beach, 1984 we lost it. Basically, Wessex Water were spending a lot of money on flood alleviation and they turned round to the council and said 'Now look if you keep letting these guys dig the gravel off while we are spending millions to prevent floods, we are going to stop giving you any more money.' So they turned around and said, 'Sorry, this is the way it is, we will give you 12 months and that's the end of it.'

We buy from sources all around the country. It all comes in by lorry now, from Nottingham and from Kent. Alluvial river gravel? Yes we are trying to source actual rounded gravel, if it is sharp it's no use to us. We don't deal with sand any more. Mostly the plant that we have got here will grade into sizes anything from 3 mil up to about 20 mil, that's the normal sort of size. We do large pebbles as well but that's the normal range and it is used mostly for decorative and aquatic fish tank use. And also for water purification filter beds. Actual filtering of reservoir water for drinking, there is a complicated filtering system, many different layers of sand and carbons but it all has to sit on something that keeps it on the nozzles and they use our gravels because it is rounded and it doesn't compact, you want to keep air between the gravel to allow the water to freely run through it.

Garden ornaments? That's a relatively new thing, something that started about 15 years ago now and it's gone on from there.

Roman soldiers and a Buddhist monks. That's somebody who has provided us with some moulds, who wants these making, so he's supplied all the equipment and we are just filling them up for him. Yes we mix it up here and we have got a vibrating table and we vibrate them all down.

The heat treatment is actually because it's a very fine material. It stops the screen wires from blazing up, if you put it through wet they just clog. If it is dry it just runs over it nice and regularly and it screens it accurately and properly and also it saves what would be a lot of rusting as well, of course, of the plant up there. We have got an external one out here which we screen the larger sizes on. Yes trade is seasonal, it is more spring and autumn. Summer's generally speaking our quietest time and the middle of winter. Then people start to come to life in the spring and stockpile stuff for the water gardens and then in the autumn it's more.

I suppose we probably get through roughly about 5,000 tons a year. It sounds a lot but the major quarries are digging that a day, and that sort of thing so we are actually very, very small. I think what we can offer is the personal service rather than the bigger boys. We supply a lot of water garden centres and aquariums.

These buildings? I think we established that they were probably built around about 1780. A bit earlier 1760. That building was constructed roughly the same time as the harbour was, and it was used as a customs bonded warehouse. The family have also been Lloyds Agents for the port, since 1828.

15. Clifford Samways – Fisherman and Fishmonger, West Bay. Born Bridport 1932.

The reason people fish is because they love it, and they love being out on the sea.

I was born at 34 North Allington, Bridport, August 19th 1932. Coming up for 75. Sunday week I think. The day of the torch-light procession. My father was for most of his early life in the netting industry, an old firm called Houndsell. North Allington, it is long gone, it's somewhere in the region of the health centre that they have just vacated. He would have been too old for the Navy during the Second War. He was in the Navy in the First World War. He was on the *King George V* a battleship. He was a stoker. Then after the war my father finished in the netting industry and went on for the Borough Council. And that was actually as the war was on, because he had a retained employment, because in 1939 he was 39. So he was at the higher age and by the time the war finished he was 45. He ran the destructor in Bridport that burnt all the refuse. A hot job. At the bottom of the destructor yard was the mortuary. If it wasn't one thing it was t'other.

His father I know very little about, because my father was born when his mother was only 15. And she worked in what they called the manor house in service. And I don't believe there was much of a father, he was brought up by two very prominent people, his grandmother and grandfather. They were the Hardimans in Symondbury. And he was the sexton at the church, he worked for the then Reverend Maunsel. These are things I have been told. My father was brought up in Manor Cottages.

When I was a boy in the hay fields and the corn fields that was, just during the war, because I was just seven when the war started, I mean they were never in those fields without jugs of cider there, we were allowed an occasional sip. Not that it tasted very nice.

Mother's father? Oh yeah, he was in the netting industry all his life. His name was George Knight. They made all sorts but mainly, in those days, as far as I know it was fishing nets. He was an old man when I was a boy. They had these machines. Father used to call them jumpers because they used to have to jump on the thing, but the women were all skilled braiders. That's what they were. I mean the workforce of the factories in those days was every house wasn't it. I mean all the years I was brought up, as long as I can remember till I volunteered with the services when I was 17, there was never a time when there wasn't nets in the house, my mother had the fireplace with the crook stuck in here.

They were always busy. But she could come on the beach for me later on, years later, and mend my nets on the beach because I used to have a boat on the beach, which was a seine boat. All we had was a twelve-foot rowing boat. It was myself and a chap called Jack Barnes, his two brothers one whose name was Donald and a very old man, he was an old man when I was in my twenties and thirties, called Jessie Jacobs, he lived in a cottage that still exists down there now. I was doing it part-time.

National Service? I got on the bus and went to Exeter when I was 17, and volunteered for the services, to avoid National Service because it was a guinea a week more money as a regular. I volunteered and I signed on for 22 years. The Air Force. But during that time whilst I was in there they brought in some new ruling, but you could come out at the end of any three years, and I came out at the end of the first three years.

From 14 to 17 I did a three-year apprenticeship in baking

Clifford Samways at the sharp end, West Bay

and confectionery, and even though I volunteered for the services the people who I had my apprenticeship with had to retain a job for me if I came back. I came back and I went to see them and they said 'Well, you will be paid two and sixpence ha'penny an hour.' And that came to about £5/10s and I said I don't think it is going to be a lot of good to me, because by I'd had two stripes in the services for two years, so I had £8 a week pocket money. So I didn't take that job back. I went and saw the manager of Gundrys and got a job for two and eight pence ha'penny an hour.Yes netting. Netting was in my blood. Yes. So that was working Zay machines. There is still an old Zay in the museum somewhere. Anyway they got shuttles haven't they, and that was basically fishing nets and sports. But after I had been there a year they offered me a job as foreman, so I trained into that and when I was 29, eight years afterwards I decided that I was at an end product and wasn't getting anywhere. So I walked out of there with my holiday pay, £40, two weeks holiday pay, went down to Bonfield's garage and I paid all my money, £40 for an old brown van and decided to start. I needed a vehicle. I knew I had a boat here already. I had one small one called the *Kitty*, that was an inboard motorboat, but mainly what I used was a fourteen-foot clinker-built boat with a big outboard, not these modern, high speed outboards, Seagulls. And so then I had left my job and so I had to make it at sea. I had a guy working with me for a couple of years he still lives at the Bay, his health's not very good, Pat Day. They don't know quite what's wrong with him but he has difficulty in walking. He's now got an invalid chair but he came with me for my first year, and we used to go out there with pots and long lines and mackerel and in-between we had the boat on the beach which was an early morning or evening time in those days for the mackerel. And I don't know at the end of my first summer, during the summer I got a little bit disgruntled with my prices etc and I went to the local council. They charged me seven shillings and sixpence to sell my own fish on the quayside. And that was exactly how I started. That would have been in 1962. Things have grown a little bit since then.

Selling direct to the public? Yep. Sundays used to be so different then, all the farmers came to West Bay, thousands of them on a Sunday night, and I was on the quayside selling my mackerel, half a crown a dozen. But that was the best, first hand, they weren't worth very much at all. Not in huge quantities, then it got to the end of that first summer and you sort off think 'What the hell am I going to do now?' There is nobody coming to West Bay any more, and that is when I started in the October that year. I started my first market and I went to Sturminster Newton Monday. And on a Wednesday I went to Dorchester. Fridays I went into a car park in Yeovil, by what years later became the Bernie Inn, down the back there. And that's what it was all about. I was doing those market stalls myself, but I only lasted two years, then I employed someone else to do it, and I went off doing other things.

On the quayside that first year basically mackerel, yeah. In later years I used to go to London every Thursday and pick up London shellfish in Billingsgate. I'd drive to Billingsgate and be back on the Friday morning then you had it for the weekend. That is when I went from just putting boxes on the quay. I had a barrow and the health people were quite happy because I could put a canopy over the barrow. And I had it there for years and of course the council wouldn't let you leave anything on the quayside so I could wheel the barrow back. By then I had premises on the East Beach in Geoff Good's place. I had donkey's years there. I had four of the old Woolaway garages. I had refrigeration in three of them.

Dessie Gape from Burton, he worked for me for 40 years. And Bert Miller he worked for me for 40 years. Both have unfortunately died now. I was asked to speak at their funerals from the pulpit, because I had known them all their working lives, you can tell what sort of firm I ran. We were more like a family. Dessie I took him on as a driver, Dessie, actually. Yes. And he used to do the London run mainly. Oh yea we had big contracts at Lowestoft and West Mersea. You know on the coast.

Oh, there was plenty doing it. I was told that I was donkey's years too late. And that I would fail. I will never forget when I first asked to rent, originally, two of these garages on East Beach and nobody wanted garages, there wasn't any cars about. So I tried to get two of them, and I will never forget an old alderman, Alderman Gale said in the council meeting, 'You might as well let the man have them but he won't last very long.' I never forgot that and I'm still here. Yes they were all demolished.

I had thoughts that we would have liked to have stayed there, because my son has now absolutely transformed the business. Clive. Yes it's a totally different thing now. But he worked for me from just after he left school and that was an accident, he never had any intention of working for me. He wanted to go in the Royal Marines, and he was colour blind and they told him to come back when he was 18. This was when he was 16, so he came home and he took a job with cat's home, it is still there now, up towards what we know as Traveller's Rest. And one day he came home and told his mother, which of course was Arthur's sister, that he had lost his job, because the night before he had forgotten to feed the cats. And Mother, in this very room, it's been converted, in this very room said 'Well. You are not going to hang around here, you better go and work with your father.' So I started getting him up three o'clock in the morning and taking him to Brixham where I was going by then. Buying

fish in Brixham market? Yes but you have jumped on years now.

I first employed a man who used to come fishing with me, Archie Larcombe, he was an ex-service man who went through the Burma campaign. Sadly he developed a brain tumour. He worked for me for 18 years. He died. But in between that time I had Archie working for me, then I took on Bert Miller, then after that Dessie, but at one stage when I had a lot of county council contracts which was years later, I got up as far as 22 people. All to do with selling. Buying and selling.

The shop is Clive's, he started it off. We took that shop, the business took that shop when Clive married his present wife, Sarah, for her to manage, and when the family came, it was the end of that, that's Sarah dad that's there now. You got a gap of forty-odd years.

Well it just didn't seem to go quickly but it did. A man who became a great friend of mine called Harold Durrant at Topsham at Exeter, he took all the sprats all through the coast and he left Maranpro, and started his own which was Blackwater Bait up at West Mersea, and this was one fairly big step and he said to me 'I need someone to clear the sprats for me all winter from the West Country would you be prepared to do that for me Clifford?' and he said, 'I would pay you, I forget how many pence a stone now, to transport them from the West Country right up through to West Mersea.'

It was Devon, mainly Torquay and Paignton. And then my connections, there in Lyme Regis, John Wason, you've heard of him? That was my biggest fisherman. Well now you see there's a strange association between him and me. I think I bought his first mackerel. He was out fishing down here with a ruddy canoe of all things, catching mackerel in his lap. And we struck up a relationship there and I bought from him all the years he had his boats, till he had the big one, the *Barbarella*. Yes oh yes he is a big character. The whole of Lyme Regis Cobb area now is around the Wason family. You have got Chris and you've got Barry, yes the three boys, and they had a daughter but I don't know what happened to her.

Brixham, I started going to Brixham as they formed the first cooperative. Before I went it was Torbay Trawlers Limited. I wanted to go down there and buy, for my market and to take to London. Nothing much coming through West Bay. There is a lot more coming in now, in that type of fish, than ever there was. But I went down there and I saw this man who's name I shall never forget, Mr Muggeridge, he ran it all and he said 'If you come back in a little while, we are forming our first cooperative.' And that's when I started buying on that market.

It was in the 1960s. Yes. 1962 I started, '63 we had that horrible winter, good job I didn't have any employees then or I wouldn't have been here. The harbour froze over. Oh yes, it destroyed all the inshore fish, there was no lobsters left in there, no prawns, everything, when the spring came the sea, inshore, was dead. Absolutely dead. But yes, that was Brixham and of course we're now, probably the biggest buyer on Brixham market and Plymouth, and Looe and Newlyn. But of course the majority of the fish that Clive handles is exported.

West Bay Trawlers? I formed a small company with a man called Ralph Wilding, who was a Bristol man. Eventually he moved down here, but he was a Bristol man in a garage business, he had Hartcliffe Motors in Bristol, and he and myself and my wife at that time, we put a third each and we bought the *Valletta*, then a little later the *Red Wing*. Well that was Frank Butt's. Old Frank spent years for me after he retired you know.

He used to come to Brixham with me, particularly in the evenings. Yes I had those two, then I had another smaller one, and it's unusual for me, I can't remember the name of that one

but it was a fifteen-foot clinker, and the guy on the fifteen-foot clinker was Wilf Hallet, on the *Red Wing* was Spud Taylor, and on *the Valletta* was Eric Hamblet. In later years I was appointed as harbour master. Eric sadly died. You have heard of him, obviously.

That was all to do with pots, crabs. Because on the deck of the *Valletta*, we used to take tea chests, I used to buy a lorry load of tea chests, old wooden tea chests! Ply isn't it, thin ply, you didn't dare kick em. They used to line them with tin foil. That's right, but we used to take those on deck, because in those days the pots we had out were six miles south west of the Bill. I mean the hen crabs they were nearly climbing up the ropes, there were hoards of them. Today I limit myself to about a four-mile radius. But I didn't go to sea very much on any of those boats, I was too busy.

When I finished at 65, supposedly finished, even though I still go to work now, I wanted to keep a small boat and finish up where I started. Angie, my wife, she's 22 years younger than me, her brother comes out with me.

West Bay before the war? We didn't come to West Bay much, my mother and father by then, had moved from North Allington into Skilling, because I had a brother and a sister by then, and in later years another brother, there's four of us, and they moved to Skilling. And we always walked across the fields every Sunday to Eype. Eype beach was our place, you could go down to the beach and walk all the way up. We used to walk right out to what we called Oak Rocks, right out the end, right where nowadays in quiet times you can put pots now. Yes and you took your kettle with you and filled the kettle up with the water coming out of the cliff, it was great fun. That was the beach that we used.

My earliest memories of West Bay, really was during the war. All the barbed wire appeared and the first time the two

German Focke-wulfs came in over and strafed the town, there was casualties over that. They came in very low over the sea, straight up the valley and bang, bang, bang. I don't think they dropped anything in West Bay, it was the main street in Bridport. Because my father also belonged to the ARP, which you had to do. Well he was in the rescue and I know that he was involved with the removal of the dead. I can't remember how many but that is all well documented. There was another bad one, which I was stood outside the front door with my mother, and watched the German bomber. We always felt he was a bit wounded, he came in from the sea and circled over the town, we just watched his bombs come down, we never went indoors or anything. You didn't have fear during the war. It was something the Mr Churchill got right, we were going to win anyway, it didn't matter what these bloody Germans do, if you knew the real facts of it.

The beaches. They weren't open, no. I don't remember too much about how you got on them, but I know my father had a permit to take us on the beach occasionally. You used to have to show it to a soldier, because also there was mined areas.

Fishing during the war? Well the guy that taught me my job in Gundry's was a man called Wilf Burt. I bought his boat in the end, too, *The Flirt*, he was a man retiring, 65, when I went in the factory, as I was 22 when he trained me, so he was 40 years older, he had a permit to fish during the war, to trawl. I don't know how they worked that during the war, I really don't, but my two big memories of West Bay is those German aircraft coming in over. I don't remember why I was down there, whether I was on the beach or what it was, but I was certainly there when they came over. And the next big one, was the arrival of the Americans. Thousands of them, they came from everywhere, the place was overrun with them, overnight. Camps everywhere

then? That was West Bay, yes opposite the West Bay Hotel down there now, there's a concrete apron, as you drive in round there, they built a cook house there, because the Americans were all in Templemans store there. I don't know if it was late '43 or as late as '44. But there, those are my memories of West Bay.

And we were allowed to cycle anywhere, we used to cycle on the coast road a lot. I cycled to Weymouth a lot. Because believe it or not, you could buy a milkshake and beans on toast in Weymouth, you couldn't get anything in Bridport. All the way from Bridport, from West Bay, to Weymouth was vehicles parked. Vehicles, just waiting. yes. And that's the other memory, the morning of June 6th. It was all gone. There was no Americans left, no lorries left, no tanks left, no nothing, all gone. All the chewing gum gone. Yes and how they did that in one day, I don't think anyone will ever know. Oh they went from Weymouth, yes. Nothing went out of West Bay. No.

Working in Gundry's? Oh my God, ha ha. You were told that you could have two weeks off a year, the first two weeks in August, no other time. In those days I walked to work or cycled, because it was from Skilling to the Court Works, and I spent eight years there. I had to clock in every morning and every lunchtime, clock in and clock out. They were the main employer. Gundry's in the beginning, was just Gundry's. They were associated with others but they became Bridport Industries in later years. But Gundry's, working in there, well, I mean I did all the overtime I could, and for years I worked from six in the morning until six at night. And I have always been proud to say you were allowed to have three minutes to clock in, and in eight years I never lost a quarter of an hour, never. What made it worthwhile was the amount of overtime I did. My pay got better when I was given the foreman's job, yes.

And the nets were going all over the world. I go down the

West Bay for a walk when I can't go out to sea. Last week I went out for a walk and a guy I've seen walking about the Bay, turned to me and said 'Hello Cliff, how are you?' It is automatic, I said 'I'm fine thanks, how are you?' and we got talking. He was a high up sales rep when I was working there, he was doing Africa, Newfoundland, selling the nets that we were making. The cod nets was usually the Newfoundland's, yes. The machines that I was in control of were making, well three of them were all cod nets, and that was all done with this new product, nylon. It went from cotton, flax and hemp. The transition, I should say from about 1955 onwards. It was a gradual change.

Helicopter nets that was a later thing. During the war my father, in his spare time that he had very precious little of, in the evenings he used to make cargo nets, they were ropes. Nets for off loading? Yes, on the docks. And that was some of the best money I earned in my life, doing the knots between the meshes, they were spliced through and then bound round.

Boats being off loaded here, Oh yea the *Flint* ones. A German chap came, he had a whole fleet. Leckie is he still around? Still making nets is he, well I'm blowed. I knew him when he was fishing. I mean a lot of the mackerel we used to sell came from Abbotsbury, from the Huddy family.

Ash Huddy. I know the man who has just started to do a bit of fishing up there now and selling to my son, Alan Arnold, is a descendant of that family. He is starting to resurrect a little bit about what those people all those years ago was doing. They caught something like a hundred stone the other evening I was told. There's catching them, and there's catching them. And the time they pulled them up on the beach and found they didn't have boxes and no ice. I'm afraid the fishing industry is a different world now. In my early days I had no ice, Geoff Good used to let me put my mackerel down in that ruddy great

building at the back because it was the coldest. They're never going to be able to pull that down. Then I bought cold rooms in those garages. Those girls that used to work with Ash Huddy, they were as strong as any man. Yes right characters. The seine crews. Oh there is so much history, there at Chesil beach. There's that little book, The Knocker Up by Cyril Toms.

Export of fish? Yes but then you are dealing, in the West Country, you are dealing with quality fish, not quantity. The West Country is renowned for variety and quality. Particularly now, I mean Newlyn, it's all top quality. My favourite fish is whatever way I'm cooking it. I spend a lot of time in the kitchen. Clive started working for me and shortly he wanted to transform the business, so I let him. Then after a few years I suddenly changed it to being called C.T. Samways and Son, then we changed it into a partnership. And then I got out completely and three years ago he formed a limited company. He's supplying a lot of local restaurants. Tremendous, he's going further and further afield.

Crabs and lobsters? The furthest we went was six miles south west of the Bill. We didn't tread on the Lyme Regis and Devon people's toes. No. No. There is loads of ground to the east. And the less people come around the Bill, and a lot of them used to, crabbing, they came from around the Bill and fished this side. West Bay is quite unique actually, like Angie's brother who comes out with me, he spends a lot of time angling, and he will go to Weymouth and pay God knows how much money to go out of Weymouth. And I say 'Where have you been today then Ian?' and he will say 'We came out came around the Bill and around here fishing, because that's were the fish is.'

The changes in West Bay? Much safer coming in, in winter. I spent 22 years on the council and all we did was talk about the changes for West Bay, I never thought that I would see it. It was only the massive funding that came from government level. It was coast protection, sea defence in the end that's paid for it and MAFF put in a certain amount, which was a very, very good thing. There is MAFF money there because it's a recognised fishing port. It's more than doubled the boats there in the last two or three years.

Whelking has been good. We threw them away in our day. Now they are £600 a tonne. It's amazing how things have changed. In our day when you were seining and caught a squid or a cuttle fish or things like that you left them on the beach, they weren't any good. Now look at it! About the only thing left, that's not worth having is ruddy dogfish. Yes we have thrown them back for a pastime, loads of them this morning in the pots.

Quotas? Well they have affected us as fishermen more that it's affected us as fish merchants. Where it has affected us as fish merchants is watching out for things to be right because big brother is breathing down your neck. There is no way that you can fool those satellites. It's no good, a boat saying I have caught so and so somewhere and they weren't there, because eventually they will be told where they were.

Over quota? That's just something that they've never managed to solve. It's an absolutely bad set up they have got, the whole thing is bad, where you have got beamers out here now with quotas catching tons of sole and Jack Woolmington, 50 kilos a month. It's an absolute disgrace. A few years ago we had fantastic orders for mackerel in Greece and Turkey, it all went through Holland, but it finished up in Greece and Turkey, and about a fortnight before Christmas they stopped every boat in Looe, Mevagissey, down in Newlyn, all around the north coast because they had finished their quotas on hand lining, one at a time, and then if you watch this programme a fortnight ago, Trawlerman, a £7million, brand new one, goes out *The Peleagic*, puts a net around 500 tons in one go. Where is the sense? They only did that one year, they've reorganised themselves. But now they are doing the same things with these soles out here, I mean Jack Woolmington, that little boat of his he doesn't harm anything, conservation wise. And he's just on his own.

Yes and it's the same for all of them. Defra, well, when you think I have got exactly the same quotas with *Mavis*, as Jack Woolmington and I don't catch any. And last year when they stopped the sole totally, I kept a letter that I got from Defra, saying to compensate not being able to catch soles out here, I may catch three tons of cod a month out in the North Sea.

That's very handy isn't it? My mind went back to Ash Huddy at Abbotsbury, he used to put his boat on the back of a lorry and drive to Seatown. I supposed we were expected to put it on the back and go to bloody Grimsby or something, no, but that is bureaucratic nonsense.

Mavis? I have had her about 12 years. I already had her before I retired, when I was 63. The reason people fish is because they love it, and they love being out on the sea. Oh God yes, there's no other reason, I don't need it financially, so it speaks for itself.

The future, just more fishing ? Yes as long as I'm allowed to health-wise, I have got a job to get in and out of the boat now, but I manage.

16. Cecil Lexster – Netmaker, Abbotsbury.
   Born 1939.

I have sent nets to North Wales, Ireland, all the way round, North Norfolk, Channel Islands, the lot. The fishing industry is nothing compared to what it was years ago.

I was born just before the war. I can remember the Americans because Father had them in for Sunday lunch. They used to bring a joint of meat with them which was useful. Father was a swanherd. Great-grandfather and great-uncle they were the swanherds then. They only had four altogether. One down Chickerell, part-time and then Fred Lee at Cloud's Hill who was full-time and then Father and myself up here. Always the same number of swans, up to a thousand. We lost an awful lot in the 1963 winter. It was very, very cold. The fleet was frozen you could walk right across it. We were cut off here in the village for six weeks, completely cut off. They flew helicopters in with bread. Well there was tons of milk and they put up churns outside the school and people could help themselves and some of the farmers made butter and in the pub they had milk up on the bar and everyone was drinking rum and milk, just to get rid of it.

My great-grandfather he was a swanherd, but my grandfather he went to America and my father, who was also swanherd here, he was born in America, Vermont. He was a steam engineer to do with building the railways out there. And then he had TB and died out there. Granny Lexster sold up everything and came home when father was six months old. Alice, the grandmother, her side was Gregory Gill and he went down the swannery. They were already working there. Father did a year or so in the estate office, Strangways, and then he took on down the swannery. The Ilchester Estates.

Grandfather was Thomas Lloyd Lexster and great-grandfather was Gregory Gill. I am known as Leckie but my real name is Cecil. I am deeply rooted here. I don't want to live anywhere else. I worked down the swannery for 15 years in all. I had three years down there with Father then I went into the Army and signed on to get the money to buy a car. The estate agricultural wage was pretty poor, and I wanted a car, I ended up as three stripes, as sergeant within the two years and I had more money then than when I came back. I had to do my National Service in the Pioneer Corps. I was weapon training instructor. I won the Corps Championship at Bisley in 1961, ·762 SLR. I loved that SLR. I could knock a gnat's eye out with that. I used to love the snap. The target up, two three down. 48-49 out of 50 all the time. I shot at Chickerell, shot at quite a few different ranges all over the show. I enjoyed that, Bisley. I came out in 1962. I was in '59 '60 '61. I came out just in time for the bad winter. It was bad that was for sure.

I worked down the swannery for 15 years in all. We had thousands of birds here. We had 700-odd geese and they were in the field just outside the swannery gate and father had an old 10 bore, a duck gun and Father said 'Shall us have a goose to eat?' And I said 'No we didn't want to, leave the poor buggers alone.' They were starving and it was freezing. In the Fleet we have got the rivers running in and we used to turn the water on down through the decoy pipe, and we had half a dozen estate workers and we would go down in the morning and the idea is that once you break the ice, the birds come in on it and they keep it from freezing again, to keep it open to get fresh water to drink. So we would go down in the morning and come back after dinner and it was all froze again. 'Twas cold but 'twas beautiful weather, bright, real healthy.

Cecil Lexster afloat

The swans lived through the winter all right but when they were nesting, a lot of them started to die. They hadn't got the reserves. And we sent a lot away to the laboratory to find out what was wrong, because we thought they was being poisoned, but it was just over-strained hearts, they were absolutely knackered. We had birds right alongside the path nesting, hatched their young uns out and just walked round the corner and dropped dead. They were pushing it to the very limits. We had a lot of Hoopers and Bewicks. We had over 300 Bewicks and that. We usually get some here but we haven't had a cold winter for years. We had a good 300 here then.

The old boys, Father done it, when he was a young man, pecking for eels in the winter to earn a shilling. And with a spear, five prongs, I have never done it myself but the bloke who worked for the Ilchester estate down at Chickerell, Frank Rashley he used to do it and they always used to say he bought his house on the eels. Because they called his house on the corner in Chickerell, the eel box. That's what they called it, and he was a right rough old diamond, Frank Rashley. Hard as bloody nails. The eels get sluggish in the winter and the mud in the Fleet is ever so soft. Very, very soft like ooze, and basically he earned a lot of money. I mean I have caught eels in the Fleet and that was with little pots out of wire mesh, and we couldn't do that till they started seining some fish down here. Mackerel and horse mackerel, some scads, we used to put them in the pots for catching eels. Scad, boney old rubbish. When I was a boy I was part of the Abbotsbury seine crew. I was on with Leonard Toms and I was on his crew, soon as I got home from school then down on the bike to the beach as fast as you could get there. We used to like it. As boys we used to moan and groan and spy on each other with glasses. 'Oh how many?' 'Someone down Chickerell's having a shot, don't think we'll bother yet.' 'Oh come on.' There were two crews, Ash Huddy he had about six seine boats, and there was Bartlett's from Chickerell and a couple or more crews, here. Not so many as they had years and years ago. Ash Huddy had a big lerrett called the *Queen Mary*, we had the smallest lerrett of the lot called the *Maggie*, what Leonard Tom's had. Some soldiers came down the beach and pushed it off into the sea and it was gone and it was picked up by a French trawler and taken to France and he got it back. It had registration numbers on it, but how the hell they ever come back from France I never found out.

There was half a dozen or more in a crew. I used to row round, usually three or four of us rowing and one chucking the seine, and one or two on the lawn end, the shore end, and the crew done the ship end when we got round. You always shot on a full flood and in the evening, if you had a southern shot, when sun was speck high on Golden Cap, you used to get a lot of scads then on that southern shot and there was times when we was full up, half mackerel, half scads. We been down there till midnight sorting them out. I can remember one southern shot we had over 1,200 stone of mackerel and 1,200 stone of scads. We just left the scads in the gut of the sea. It's a lot of work sorting mackerel. Oh yeah, there was Cutty Thorner. Ray Laver, he took over from Cutty then there was Bartletts at Chickerell and then there was some didikois, they used to come, and they used to argue about what money you were having before the mackerel went on. And they'd say 'We'll give you 5 bob or 3/6d a stone.' and then eventually they would pay you there on what you had. Then they had to make the money up by taking the fish to Billingsgate. Now, they borrow your fish, then bid on the fish, make their money and you have what's left and that's the difference.

There is only part-time seining now. Old boys who have a

little play now and again, There is Chickerell, then there is Park Wall, then there's us, then there is Langton, then Swyre, then Burton. Good many years since a full-time crew. You want to see Alan Arnold, that is the last family that was full time seining and he has got a little boat and he has got a small seine and he goes down with his boys and has had a few the last couple of summers.

Other fishing? Well I'd had enough because when the last Lord Ilchester died and it was taken over with estate agents that come from London and they didn't know what the bloody hell they were talking about. I said 'I have had enough of this.' And I had an old friend in Weymouth who was a fisherman, he got cancer and died when he was 54 and I thought 'Well if I am going to die at 54, I want to do something I want to do.' So I went fishing and went trawling. I used to go from Weymouth and to Lyme Regis in winter, and go spratting with John Wason and pair up. Go spratting and sometimes we landed in Torquay. And there for a few nights in the 70s. I never went for mackerel, not trawling, we was on for skate and sole, and plaice.

I done a bit of potting out of West Bay, first part time when I was working down the swannery. The first boat I had, we built and fished out of West Bay. *Bonaventure*, that was a smuggler's boat from Moonfleet. And then the French boat I bought after that. I called it after the pub, the *Why Not?* I was fishing for about 15 years. Fine weather no fish. West Bay, they have buggered it up now, it is silting up. In the old days they could always wash it out but now they can't. They have buggered it up, honest they have. Originally when I was down West Bay there was a wooden gantry up the western side of the channel and that was originally there to walk the ships in. Sailing ships so they could walk them in with a rope, but the thing was when they done the scouring, it carried the water down a big chute. But that

fell down and it didn't scour as good as it used to, but they can't do it at all, because they have altered that entrance and instantly the bar now builds straight across the entrance. The sand comes in and Chesil beach, the drift is to the west and it keeps on building. They used to be able to flush it out for free, now it is going to cost them. More visiting boats coming up from Exmouth for the night.

After the fishing I was back on to net making, making trawls. Been doing it for 20 years. Never worked for Gundry's, always worked for myself. I was in-between buying boats and I had made a few nets up and all of a sudden I got enough business that I couldn't go back to sea really. I did it out the back for a start, then out mother's across the road, then now I am down on a farm by the swannery car park.

You buy bales of net, from Gundry's originally, then you cut it to shape to whatever patterns, you make up the rock hoppers, and foot ropes and over the years I know what size and sort of gear each boat needs. All I need to know is what horsepower they have got and what reduction gear and what they are catching. There is enormous pull on a net, the amount of horsepower in boats today it is tremendous, nets have got stronger and heavier built. Always trawl netting, the cod end to let them out. I am 68 coming up for 69. I don't want so much work and it is non stop, all the time. Basically I work in the mornings. I don't work in the afternoons much. My hands won't stick it, my hands and my elbows hurt and my right shoulder.

All my customers are pretty regular, the ones I got at least 20 perhaps more, all over the show. I have sent nets to North Wales, Ireland, all the way round, North Norfolk, Channel Islands, the lot. The fishing industry is nothing compared to what it was years ago. I remember when I worked down the swannery when I was a boy, Bridport had about five different factories down there in Bridport, Gundry's, Rendall and Coombs, Edwards ...

We had a mullet net made out of cotton. The estate had that up here and we used to take it back down there for the winter and they used to re-bark it and mend it and store it for us, for the estate. And we used to go down in the spring and pick it up. There was rooms there, and I can remember going in, there was all women sat there all doing herring nets. Loads and loads of herring drift nets they used to do. And then later on they done purse seines. John Gundry he went away to Iceland, took a lot of film and at the West Bay Fishermen's Association we had an evening they showed us loads of film. Before the cod wars, that was, and they had an Iceland fellah come down to show them how to rig purse nets in Gundry's and he was terrible trouble in the town because he was pissed up every night and he caused a lot of trouble. And I can remember Gundry's made a lot of purse nets for sardines for Africa, South Africa, sardine seines. I can remember because my mother-in-law worked in the factory and she used to be shutting snorkel netting, all inch and quarter nets for these sardine nets.

It was a big industry in Bridport in those days. I can remember a big purse seine net coming down on a lorry, bloody great thing. he was steaming and there was herrings stuck in it and they had it all on the fence outside and spread out to work on it. Originally it was cotton and hemp. You had to hang them up in the boat to keep them dry. All you've got to worry about today is sunlight, sunlight kills it now. It is so different, so totally different. Because of having the knowledge I have of trawling myself, I know near as dammit what size of trawl they want. They say what they want and we work it out between us. Polypropylene, it's all different different colours. You've got compacted twines now, a very hard round twine. I buy my nets now from Sicor that comes from Portugal. Most of my stuff

comes from Portugal. You buy a big bale of net and you cut out your patterns, and stitch it all back together. All done by hand. You can't do any of that type of work on a machine. They weigh quite a bit, and that's my problem. I've done my disc at the bottom of my back several years ago fishing. Fishing keeps you fit. A good thing. The fittest thing you will ever see is on Channel crabbers, they are as fit as fleas, time and motion, effort on them, that's why it is so dangerous. The Government don't want us, the fishing industry, persecuting fishermen now. They gave the rights away and they are jumping on them something rotten. Terrible. All the blokes want to do is go out there and earn a living. They haven't given them enough quota to earn a living.

Beamers, I had a chap working for me and he did his ticket down at Brixham and then he skippered a big beamer out of Portsmouth. She had 2,000 hp and that boat is tied up because they can't earn enough money to pay the fuel bill. They go to sea and earn twenty grand and fifteen will be the fuel bill and that only leaves £5,000 for all the rest of the crew the gear, the insurance and some of them work 8-10 days at sea and get £80. That isn't on.

It is most strange, I've got a mate down Plymouth who was fishing, then he went net making like me and he went to Portugal and back last summer and there's a hell of a fleet of small boats working a lot of trammel nets. And he said the market is full up with little fish, loads and loads of them but they still keep catching them. So in some respects they are like the French. The Frenchman I bought my boat from, he was interested in little fish not big fish. 'Little fish - plenty money.' The thing is this, we are wrong. We are taking the big spawners and they are taking heaps of little stuff, and leaving the big spawners. So maybe we are completely wrong in this country. Look over Canada and America, they have a top and bottom size for lobsters. So the big uns that are going to do a lot of spawning are left. We have got it all wrong, the Government and the local fisheries they don't do anything properly, in this country. They f . . k it up! Everybody says how bad the French are. Well OK, I have seen the tiniest little soles for sale. I been to France a few times, the thing is they have got conservation over there where they are not allowed to catch lobsters where they've released lots of lobsters.

And their scallop season, they have a proper closed season and I mean opposite there in Erquy Bay there are about 400 boats come fishing in there for the winter on scallops. They are allowed an hour and a half fishing three days a week. That's all they are allowed to do and in that hour and a half they will catch 500 dozen. They have police with planes and speed boats, so they are very well tracked, absolutely. The sizes and everything else. I was talking to a bloke there to buy his boat and he told me all about it. And they are so policed about it, and if they weren't, they'd kill the market. It is better to take a little bit every day. The amount of scallop that is there, because they have left them alone to spawn all summer and they are keeping them to a certain size, anything just under, a gnat's cock under the four inch, they got to go back. So it is more like ranching. Common sense and conservation.

Bad weather? We've had snotty days. In winter when we worked out of Lyme Regis you could go away from Lyme and have foul day but get back into the harbour easily enough. But to go round Portland Bill. No that's a killer, Portland Bill is. The amount of tide there on a spring tide, if you want to work days, you come away in the morning and you are against the flood, it is bloody ridiculous. From Bill Point to Pulpit Rock will take you 20 minutes to steam that. The boat's just going backwards, waste of time. I mean that's a normal trawling type boat that does seven knots. I mean we did a bit of bassing in the race, we

did a bit of that, but our boats were a bit slow. You need a fast boat, so you can nip up and have a drift down, then nip up and have another drift.

I been busy as hell since Christmas making sand eel trawls for bassers to catch their sand eels. Busiest I have ever been. There's a lot of bass boats in Weymouth and Channel Islands. Popular everywhere, and there's loads of bass. I mean they keep on about the French pair trawling, I mean they ain't going to stop. You will never stop them, they've got too much money invested in it. But the thing is this, there is loads of bass. I mean when I was trawling you hardly ever caught bass, rarish, but now our boats catch loads of it, amazing. Mostly work inside of 12 mile, some of the French can come in to six, and the Belgians.

The French rarely land here. Many of the Channel Islanders pop into Cherbourg. I deal with the Channel Islands quite a bit. Got some good friends over there. Doing some nets for Jersey now. Normal demersal trawling, 80mm for cod ends. It is only up the North Sea they are up to 120mm for cod. But down here you are always mixed fishery, squid and that. I mean you couldn't have big mesh you'd never catch them. Squid has become so important now, down here. Red Mullet, that has come on quite a bit. Warmer water I suppose and cuttlefish.

On the Fleet they practiced the bouncing bomb. I suppose it is just about still there where they build a dam out of canvas and metal work. I have shot a mullet net round there, but there was the framework of one of those bombs up on the beach at Langton Herring for years. But they have moved it now. A metal framework filled with concrete and people used to tie their trow up on it. They have actually got one of the high balls down the swannery, the other type, the one with dimples. I was too young to see the planes come in, but I can remember at the end of the war up at Cloud's Hill where our other keeper used to live, they did all the practising of rockets.

Reed cutting? We call it spear, I done spear cutting. Sixteen when I left school that was my job straight away. Thatching I forget how many thousands of bundles we used to cut, a lot more then than they do now, you got to cut it each year, you can't have last year's growth in it, you have to burn off last year's stubble. That was all cut by hand, we used to do the whole bed. All the fishermen were all took on and they called them strappers, there was a gang of 12 or 14 doing the spear. Cutting started end of January and we used to cut all the withies to make the bonds for tying the bundles up.

Lobster pots? I made mouths out of withies, not the complete pot. I made the Portland style of lobster pot, a round pot with a little wooden square mouth with a trap on it, like cat flap and a little lead weight. The lobster went in there and he couldn't get out. They were good pots they were. That was when I was working out of West Bay.

The trows are flat-bottomed boats, three planks high, but a trow is not perfectly flat-bottomed, you have got to have a bit of rocker in there otherwise you gets the suction and he won't row proper. And being such a low height on your gunwales and that you want your oars balanced right because you can't get them out of the water very far, as you are touching your knees, and when it is a bit sloppy in the Fleet… I took a lot of care making my oars for my trow, because I used catch mullet and eels in the Fleet. And when you are rowing around several miles a day you want your oars right. You don't have a rowlock, you got thole pins and copses. Far better because the oars balance, and you got to get the right amount of tipping on that oar, so that when he touches the water he will bite. With a copsed oar you got the balance with the copse, so you only just have to touch it and he will come up so you are not leaning on it. And when you pull, the amount of tipping is fixed so when he touches the water he will bite the right amount, not too deep. So little things like that are very, very important.

In the Fleet, mullet, bass and eels, little 'billy winters,' that's prawns but they are called 'billy winters' because they are only there in the winter. I have caught a little tiny sea trout but not a lot as it is very brackish water. And it can get quite stale up here. We get otters. In the pampas grass we always had nests down there and on a coot shoot once, Arnold was rowing me, and I was sat in the back with the gun, just to shoot across the water, and an otter swum under the boat, as close as my arse is to the floor.

Years and years ago they did punt gunning down Chickerell end. One of them, he got caught out on a mud bank and he got frostbite. The tide went down and he was stuck out there for hours and he got frostbite. Oh yeah there was a few shooting punts down there. Abbotsbury Estates own all the Fleet but the top two miles is bird sanctuary just above Langton Herring is the boundary, but they own the rights of it all the way to the Ferrybridge which was the railway bridge. They got the rights of the foreshore up to the high water mark.

The swans, they belong to the Ilchester family. In Queen Elizabeth I's reign there was over 300 owners, all with beak marks and ours was the only one on the foot. They ring them now, the mark on our foot, we just knick in the foot on the outside web, and that was supposedly an I for Ilchester, but it grows back into a V when they grow. You get used to it, handling swans, but if he hit you, you'd bloody know it. Strong? It could break your arm.

There was an old film years ago. Uncle Joe with a galvanised bucket and the swan smacked one side into the other. They can hurt. We used to fatten. You don't eat swan, you don't eat an old turkey do you? They are fattened in a pen, not killed before six months and not killed after twelve months, so they are fattened up just the same as you would do a turkey. We used to do half a dozen or so up at Cloud's Hill, they had the special pens there to do it for Lord Ilchester. We had a leg of one once. It is dark meat, very much like goose. I wouldn't fancy it at all to be honest. I think mallard and teal are far nicer. I was brought up on eating them. That's the only thing I really miss not being down swannery, is eating mallard and teal, because we had the duck decoys and we used to catch and ring the birds. And of course we caught mallard and teal as well. An ancient decoy pond but they couldn't work it now. Just for show now. I was the assistant swanherd and decoyman. I did a 15-year apprenticeship.

You can't make any noise, you can't whistle them in, and you got to watch where the wind is so they can't smell you. The old boys would burn a little bit of turf to take the smell away. We had a very posh bloke come down here and he wanted his son to see what we did, Major Miller Munday, friend of Lord Ilchester, he owned islands and God knows what up in Scotland. Thousands and thousand of acres. But he came to get his son interested in nature and birds and all that. So we had to show him how we worked the duck decoy and they came down in absolute silence and he came alongside of Father and all the bloody birds went out. He absolutely reeked of Turkish fags, and all the birds went. Yeah never forget it.

Father was well noted. He went on the television and the radio. In Town Tonight, he was known as Fred, Frederick Lloyd Lexster. He was well known all over the world. I don't expect anyone can remember anything about Ludwig Koch now he did all the bird recordings. He came over just before Hitler closed down everything in Germany. He came and stayed with us one winter and we did loads of recordings on to large gramophone disks. His son was in the London Philarmonic, played oboe or

something like that. Ludwig Koch's son. I can remember when he stayed with Mother out here singing opera of a night time. He was a character, he went to the Palace to teach our present Queen and Princess Margaret about birds. Ludwig Koch. Father and they was great friends.

Father knew Peter Scott when he was shooting. Father knew Billy Williams up at Peterborough. Burrough Fen Decoy was like ours only he had six or eight pipes and that was his living, catching ducks. That's where Peter Scott was with Billy Williams, shooting geese and that. Mother, she chucked so much of his stuff away when father died, we had a photograph of Peter Scott and Billy Williams alongside a shed with the geese hung up and a punt gun and holding up the cartridge. Now that would be interesting. I stayed there when I was 16. Father sent me up there for a fortnight and stayed up there at Slimbridge with Peter Scott. They had a decoy they had built and they had a big board up of how many ducks they were catching, but they were catching, time after time after time, the same birds, because they were all tame… When we caught our ducks we were getting our rings back from Russia and all over.

Once we caught a bittern in the middle pipe, and he bloody nearly had my eye out. *Whoof.* His neck and head came out and father held it 'Look at this bittern.' 'Oh shit' he nearly had me. And they are not small. Father was brilliant on bird song he knew instantly what birds were what. You can't work the pipe any more because you have done away with the paths. You can't work it today. It is all set up for visitors. The last time we worked the decoy was 1972, '73.

The Abbotsbury Garland. They still do it. Garland Day 13th May. Years and years ago there was umpteen seine boats and God knows how many garlands. They used to have a bit of shindig under the castle and have a party and the boats would row the garlands out and throw them on the sea, but they don't do that anymore. They just take it round the village and the kids collect a few shillings. There used to be a wildflower garland and a garden flowers one, but they are not allowed to do the wildflower one any more. The Arnold family used to do it as they were the last seine boat crew, then my missus took it on with somebody else for a few years. But it is only the one garland now and there is no seine boats. Just an old tradition to bless the sea and hope for a good harvest.

The biggest lerret I knew was 17 foot, the *Queen Mary*. Ash Huddy had that, and that was a cracking lerret that was. You run them down the beach on the back of the oars. Copses, turn them over grease them, for running the boats up, and one round piece of stick called a 'speck'. That high (3 foot) so when the sun is speck high on Golden Cap. That is the last shot you had. The seine net. You got your inners and outers, the bunce and the quarters, you got all your different seine stones. You had to get the weights right, he is leaded as well, to take it down quickly. And then he is on a little chain. He don't actually take the net down really tight. Venture seining is when you are shooting and shooting, not when the mackerel's straying. We all done that in the spring of the year.

We had thresher sharks, basking sharks, all bloody sorts, turtles, I remember Coronation Day, Ash Huddy, they used to have little flat bed lorry and they had a bloody great basking shark on the back, caught it that morning and Spot the dog, who used to sit in the basket in the bow of the seine boat, he was on top of this bloody great thing, twenty foot long it was, he had a little ruff round his neck. And somebody sat there with a little rod and a hook in his mouth. 'You should have seen the one that got away' and that was paraded all round the village on Coronation Day. I always remember that. Just one of those things, caught that morning. A very strong tradition here in Abbotsbury for seine fishing. But it has all sort of finished now.

17. Dick Dalley – Seine netter, coastguard and swanherd, Abbotsbury. Born Chickerell 1936.

You imagine, bouncing bombs and machine guns didn't do them a lot of good. The wildlife certainly wasn't bloody wild after that.

I was born in a little cottage in Chickerell, home delivery then. The old cottage is two cottages. We lived in one till we moved out to a council house out at Charlestown. I lived there for quite a number of years till I met my wife, who is an Abbotsbury girl. We got married, then a job came up on here in 1961. Vacancy, a little cottage on the shores of the Fleet on the estate and I was employed as a swan keeper.

My father, he was a labour master in a workhouse. That was at Portwey, it was a big place. Now it's a private residence. It was a hospital after the workhouse closed down. You get these old people there, never had no home of their own, and they used to go there for short spells, specially during the winter. Obviously during the summer they could rough it, you know, round about. That's where he met my mother. She was a cook there and they got married.

I know my mother's father, he was a railway man and her brothers used to work on the railway. But what my other grandfather done, he worked on a farm. He lived in Chickerell itself, they had quite large families in they days. Down Littlesea that used to be just ordinary foxholes, there used to be no holiday park down there like there is now, it's got quite large now. Breeding caravans.

When I was a boy I can remember being in Chickerell during the war years. The Americans came over to camp there. Obviously they was building up to go across for D Day. We didn't realise we was at war 'cause their lights lit up everywhere over the camp. We had blackout but both sides of us there was camp. Shrapnel came down knocking holes in the slates and that. The bridging camp was at a place called Australia Road. It was built during the First World War, named after the Australian troops what used to be based there. It's still used today by various regiments. They come down on summer, cadets mainly. They do exercises and that. Oh yeah the old rationing, you used to have to go to school Chickerell 'cross the fields. Now that's all built up.

Here at the Swannery we've got a replica of one of Barnes Wallace's bouncing bombs. For six weeks this gentlemen lodged with us. I used to bring my homework home. Obviously he was very good because I used to get ten out of ten for mine cause he used to do it for me see, the maths. When it come to it, he was one of the team of Barnes Wallace's, the bouncing bomb. But when that finished I went back to normal… I had to let them know then that somebody was assisting me. That's how it was done. They practiced the bouncing bomb here.

Well they also used to have silhouettes of enemy planes 'cause it was all visual with cannon on the planes and they used to have a set up above the beach area and have to come down to fire at these plywood planes they fired at them lots of times. The sunset blinded one or two of them and they hit the beach. These guys at 200 miles an hour, you can't just stop, can ee?

Disturbed the swans all through the war years. In fact the old swanherd said to me 'Do you know the swans come up here and laid and no young uns was hatched. All eggs was infertile.' You imagine bouncing bombs and machine guns didn't do them a lot of good. The wildlife certainly wasn't bloody wild after that. But after the war things settled down and slowly it built up again. I always mind him telling I that, the old swanherd.

Dick Dalley at the decoy pond

So I come down here. Cecil Lexster used to be here but he went fishing. Yeah so I used to stay and help the old man but the job was up there, you had to keep the swans up during the day. Winter time you would be fattening swans up for the table. That's the job that went on till the late 1960s. Just a few each year. About five or six months, they were quite big by then. They never been out on the Fleet or nothing so I should think they was quite tender. The gentry used to eat them. The old swanherd who used to live prior to I going there, his family lived in one cottage and next door was a shepherd and his father was a swan keeper. Obviously they got together and he married the girl next door and they lived there all their lives. He said the furthest he ever been on his bike, he rode to Chideock, he never been nowhere. He was a wise man. You know they put the phone in for them and some wag in the village said 'Whatever you do Fred when you hear the phone ring you must shout at the top of your voice so your voice do carry over the hill' He used to shout LIKE HELL.

I went to school in Chickerell then into Weymouth secondary. I started as an apprentice, painter decorator, then I thought 'this 'aint much good, I haven't earnt a lot of money.' Father was ill and I thought I better try and I went on to work for fruit and veg retail in Weymouth and sometimes help the wholesalers Digby's. I used to go as a fruit salesman and then I met my wife through fishing 'cause she used to do it full time as a living with her sister, brother and family. They was the last full-time seine net fisherman on Chesil Beach, Abbotsbury with her father Ash Huddy. My wife would be usually on the land, her older sister used to cast the net, her brother used to row round. I had a boat built by Bert Merrick in Ferrrybridge. He built one for my colleague who's long since gone, down Chickerell, a beautiful 12-foot mahogany trow. I said 'I could do with one of they.' He said 'I will make you one.' It took 12 months to build it. But the trouble was every season you take the old varnish and put new varnish on you took a little bit of wood off and the planks got a bit thin. So my boy made a model of fibreglass trow. So I got two fibreglass trows now. They are lighter and no maintenance. You just get the fibreglass and mend the holes.

Then there were lerrets. This one's Portland built. He's about 17 foot long, four-five foot in midships, pointed at both ends. Enables the boat to be launched from Chesil Beach as it's very shelving. It's very deep water, if you step in the water you might be up to your knees, your next step you're up to your head, so these can be launched or pulled in stern first according to conditions. They were used in Portland and various points all along the beach. They used to have bigger crews then. If you was out of work you had to earn a shilling so. They couldn't go in dole office cause they never existed in they days. You had to earn some money and you could go help catch the fish, you never got a great deal. At least it would put bread in your mouth and that. They are well built. The only people who have got one now and they do use it occasionally is the Langton crew. They got a boat exactly the same, 50-60 years old might be more than that.

They used a lot of them in rescue services. When the ships used to come ashore, these was the boats they used before lifeboats came into being. Some was six oars, some was eight. You have 'thole' pins, 'copses' are put on the oar. You could more or less balance with your finger on it. It had to be balanced 'cause if it was too heavy it was hard work but if it was balanced you could easy row them. It's the same as putting in the stern there the net which we cast out in a semi-circle using the rope. You shoot the semi-circle and as the tide was moving you shoot on the flood which will be moving from the west to the east. You slowly moved along so that they stayed level with the net and unlike today, slowly pulled it ashore. Hopefully you had fish in the middle.

See most of the trawlers they can look on the screen and see if there is any fish. Here we still traditionally shoot the net out and hope that you shot round some fish. We went over two nights ago. I suppose we were going over 4 o'clock, shoot the last on the ebb of the full flow there was only four - me, my boy, my cousin down Chickerell and a little grandson, four of us it was and two little girls. We never had to use ropes just chucked the net ashore. My little grandson managed to pull the boat around them and I think we had about couple hundred stone and we knew we had them.

But today see, unlike the olden days when you had all these hands to help, we had the little Fergie tractor, with double wheels on the back and the pulley on. Put a rope on the neck of the nose where the fish was to and then pull it so far. Even with all that weight, you pulled so it was tight and you could cut the net and tipped out so many. Tied off the other rope on to the tractor then slowly pulled them up. See in the olden days you had pots. Today you just box them up over there, load them on the platform back of the tractor. You would get 100 stone quite easily and bring them over put them in the boat and bring them across the Fleet.

We took 'em down locally, down Bridport. There is a wholesalers down there, Samways, we take them down. Obviously my boy had an ex-GPO van, he took on one, he had to ring for some help. It only took us about 10-15 minutes to catch the fish. It took then about three to four hours to get them all the way safely iced up down at the depot down at Bridport. That was two nights ago, we didn't bother yesterday, ain't bothered today, maybe Sunday we might go over again.

With a lerret you have someone in charge who owns the boat and owns the net. The one in charge he calls the tune because he put the time in making the net and the boat. Yeah, but when you got a lerret you need about eight to ten hands really to work a boat this size. You can't work it with four, impossible. The other end you've got to pull ashore, hand over hand. It's not too bad, it's all right you know, it's old tradition. I hope it never dies out but you never can tell. This is part-time work, in the evenings.

There's two little stones in the lerret. That's what they call lucky stones, most of the seine stones got holes in. Obviously you have heavier stones in the middle to hold the net down they got to be made right. There is a lot of work in making a seine net. So there is a lot of sewing you know.

My wife, Betty, used to do it for a living one time, specially logging in winter and fishing in summer. They finished a few years back now. When the old boy died they carried on for a bit and then they packed it in. Like I said my son's took it up again. but then obviously I took this job on. I still went fishing. When I first lived in the cottage there in the evenings I used to row across the beach, walk a couple of miles down and fish with the Langton crew. Then in the mornings I used to row over, walk up the beach, then fish with the Abbotsbury crew up here, it was about three miles. I used to start walking about three o'clock in the morning, get up there by daylight to shoot. Did it three mornings and I never woke up the fourth morning 'cause I was knackered. But it was nice, you meet different people specially the weekend when you get a lot of old farmers buying fish for their workers and theirselves. They come down Sundays meet up then back for a drink before they went on home again. Oh yeah the old farmers used to come down. I used to know a lot of them, they've all gone now though. It's all disappeared.

Swans? Yeah 1961, Well I was working with the Swannery, Fred Lexster was the swanherd then, Leckie as he liked to be known. I used to look out for the swans up t'other end. We never used to feed like we do today obviously. Where the children feed at dinner time and four o'clock we used to feed in the morning. It was wheat and chick crumbs. layer pellets now. Used to be kibbled maize. The herd, they do like staying up so after the nesting was over and the last of the cygnets was hatched, I used to have to round up the rest, maybe two or three miles down and gently persuade them they got to come up this end. They was getting into the moult and couldn't fly a lot. I used to go down with the boat and row up through. Obviously we used to have a dog or two with us. One I had was real old scruff bag, Heinz variety, she was faithful as the day is long, and she used to come with me in the boat. Used to shout at the swans and then I would start to sing and the dog would stand up at the front looking at the swans, howling her head off. The swans used to come on up then. So one day I was, I suppose, about a mile down through different little curves and that so I said 'Go on,' to Spider, so she went on down. I watched her, seen her jump over one hedge, then she jumped over another fence and went on and 'I wonder if she will.' Next thing I see is swans coming up, just about see them moving. I thought 'What's moved they swans? What's that little black thing swimming? This was the dog. When she got level with the house I went off and picked her up and gave her a little treat you know. Oh she was wagging her tail, I thought 'You clever little maid.'

Then every day after that I said 'Go on then' and away she did go in the morning bringing the swans up. Well then I used to row on up because if you did stay out of sight of the swannery, well the swans used to move off and nobody could see them. They pay their money to come in. Mind you they were only paying half a crown in they days. And then five o'clock I used to go on down and they used to follow I on down to where they was

that previous night.

This, the top three miles is strictly the bird sanctuary, then you go on the Broads before you come to the Boundary bends beach, marking the boundary of the estate. Then after that you come to Rodden Hive, Little Herbury, they call it 'island.' It is on real high tides, it is cut off, little peninsular sticks out. Then Moonfleet Hotel. And then on down in the Park Wall where the old church used to be. There is only the chancel of the church left when he had that great storm of 1824. Washed that away.

The last time I known it flood any distance was in 1987 I think. It was running in the cattle grid up there. When we got up here, it was up to our waists in sea water so we had a dingy here, We managed to get him bailed out and we rowed down the path to see what it was like down there. We rowed over the top of the rearing pens, looking down through the water and over the top of the reed beds which was nearly six-foot high to see where it was to. Then we looked to beach and saw these massive waters coming over, 'cause you know yourself the bank is 44 metres high 200 metres wide, sea was up by at least three metres, solid water. In the end we come to our senses and paddled as fast out over the fence and on. Don't go bide down there, we can't do nothing.

It was hell of a mess. The rubbish what been accumulated on the beach from passing ships up and down. Lots of these ships rather than pay harbour dues chuck it overboard. Took us a month to clear this place up to make it ready for the people to come in. Obviously the swans didn't mind 'cause they could move inland away from the water.

One year I went down and met a local gentlemen farmer, we had a farm manager, he lived in London. 'Oh' he says. 'Your swans is eating my winter barley.' 'Oh' I said, 'Two or three swans ain't going to hurt,' I said. He said 'You go down and see how your two or three swans are doing.' I said ' All right.' Got hell of a shock. There was about two or three hundred and the field was bare. I went on and went t'other way. I walked along, didn't speak no more of it. Well come harvesting in August that year I said after they finished up, I said to farm manager I said 'How did it go John?' 'The best crop we ever had.' 'They never cost you no artificial,' I said.' 'Tis recycled through my swans.'

We have about 600 swans during the season. 140 odd, they had this year breeding pairs. Unfortunately all the little ones don't survive regardless how much you look out to them. Obviously you can't be here 24 hours a day. So mother nature usually controls all who's going to live and going to die. We used to have little drives on the beach sometimes. You weren't allowed to say you were going to shoot a fox, 'cause this was a hunting country then. 'Go long tailing.' Nobody knew what the hell it was about.

The monastery themselves, they were the first ones to farm the swans. That was founded 11th century but the first record which was printed was 1393, that was when there was about 410 swans here and about 90 cygnets. There always used to be a swanherd. The first man, his name was Swiller he was like a monk and he was in charge of the swans and so it's been going down through different people all through the centuries, you know, keeping the swans. Well then the monastery was doing well, they built the little chapel late 13th century, same as the tithe barn which is just at the west end. He been repaired, that was last year, took quite a bit of reed. The reed from here.

I used to clean them out. They put 11,000 bundles on that roof so that meant I went through over 25,000 bundles to get them. I and a few more people, relations and that came to help. It took us a couple of years to get enough reed for the barn. If you going to cut it, you cut it annually. There is about 50 acres of reed beds altogether. four to five thousand bundles in a good season.

Hard work cutting reeds? It used to be 'cause when I joined you used to have to cut with a hook. My hook is still hung out there now, he's wore out, like I. We used to have a gang of us, eight cutting and four tying. Used to have eight right-handed men cutting. Doesn't matter if the man could cut, if he's left-handed he's not allowed to work with a right-handed man case you had accidents. One would start off and the next one there and he'd go on in stages. The left-handed ones used to come along and tie the bundles up and leave them. Come break time we used to stop and help carry and stook them up alongside the fence. Then they used to be hauled up to the barn and stored. Or if the thatchers come down and buy their own. Sometimes they bring their own trailer down. But there is not many thatchers use it. They use that foreign reed now.

Then there was dissolution of the monastery in 1539 and the gentlemen who was Sir Giles Strangways, he purchased the estate and was granted the right to keep the swans as well. And it's still in the family today. Fox Strangways. Obviously he was a commissioner or something to do with the King Henry VIII's entourage. He left the barn and little chapel on the hill but the main living quarters, there's is just a gable end left now. In 1993 we celebrated 600 years.

They had a stamp come out to commemorate the swannery's 600 years. They had quite a big do that year. In fact we had royal visitors, Prince Charles came here. Unfortunately I was the deputy swanherd and I was left with the royal menagerie, no that's not the right word, entourage… Anyway I had to take they round and answer their questions, my colleague took round his Royal Highness and he was very interested in the wildlife. His Royal Highness was. I had to meet him 'cause I was the oldest one, you know first one on the line, I was told I had to wear a tie and best shoes, I thought bloody hell best shoes? I work in a swannery not in town. Anyway he come there, the boss lady was here, she's 'Oh you do look smart,' 'Oh you look a picture too.' 'Now that's enough of that, we got royalty coming Dick.' I said 'All right that's OK.'

So he come and said 'How long have you worked here?' And I told him 'You know it all then?' 'I've yet to meet the man who does,' I said. 'I quite agree.' So he went on round. He asked a lot of questions. Then I met his father, the Duke of Edinburgh. Now he is totally different he was. I had to meet him down the centre down at Ferrybridge. He was doing a tour of the island and I was presented to him in the centre as the swanherd at Abbotsbury you see. His question to me was 'How do you call your swans?' I said, 'I don't Sir. I don't call the swans. Mother nature controls all who's going to live and all who's going to die in the world.' 'Well she's not making a very good job of it is she?' and turned round and walked out the door. I thought 'what a strange man.' Luckily the press was outside the door. I didn't know how to answer it.

The old flamingo he lasted a few years. I got fed up with people saying 'Why don't you find him a mate.' I said 'Here when I went a courting I made my own bloody mate, it's the same with the wildlife,' I said 'They'll find their mate if they are minded.' Well I don't know what, but this particular year he flew away. Instead of going on down the lagoon and staying with the swans down there and wintering on the molluscs and that, to keep his colours so well, he disappeared. He was gone for just over a month. The old keeper down there used to keep out for the swans down the lagoon. 'Can't make out where that flamingo is' he said. Next time he said 'Here there's two flamingos now.' I said 'I bet matey flew away took heed and gone and found a mate for hisself.' So next spring/summer time we come up. Swans are

nesting and we are open to the public the two flamingos are there. 'Oh he's got a mate,' 'Nothing to do with me' I said 'He went away last winter, one dark winter's night and come back with a mate.' He said 'Wouldn't it be nice if they got their act together and made a nest and produced youngsters,' I said 'Yes it would be see.' One Monday, it was one of they days when nothing seemed to go right, this gentlemen up there obviously knew about flamingos he came in, he worked in a wildlife park. He said 'I see you've got two flamingos.' How observant I thought. 'Well that's a Rosie flamingo and that's a Chilean.' I don't know 'cause it was bloody dark night when he flied away. 'Well yes' he says, 'That don't make no difference. Well yes,' he said, 'but if they do, you let us know.' With that I said 'What do you mean if they get their act together?' 'There must have been a terrible dark night' he said, 'not only has he bought back a different species but another male bird.'

Swans live on average 11-15 years. Well you can get some live up to 21. The oldest I know is not here but at Longleat, the late Lord Bath's place. Well this swan it's headstone said 27 years old. We feed in the morning, early in the morning, then the public are there at the twelve o'clock feed and the four o'clock feed. So obviously we got to feed the little families you can't put too much food down as it would go off, couple or three times a day.

In the winter you get a lot of swans from other places, like the Somerset Levels. They do come down from time to time. Some of the birds that have been ringed down here found their way up there. I've been up there in the spring time with the elvers on the Parrett and I made some friends up there and they took me to where these isolated pairs was nesting. I know that number. I'll check up when I go back down and found out that it was rung down here couple of seasons previous.

We try to ring them. We do get a lot which have not got rings on so obviously if they are fully grown birds you can usually tell, we usually put the orange rings on to denote that they are not ours. A metal ring one leg and plastic on the other as sometimes they do lose them. They never lose the metal ring so you just check up on the BTO ring, the metal ring, and normally once they find a partner they usually stick for life. Sometimes they start looking when they are about 12 months old, just when they are coming into the white plumage and usually they start breeding when they are about three or four years old. That's when they are classed as adults when they get the orange bills.

Sometimes they breed every year. It all depends on the conditions. If the winter's pretty bad well maybe they will miss a season. But usually once they find a partner they will sort of stick with that partner but by the ringing I found out that ain't quite true. There is one female here she had one marked down and six nice babies which she produced. The following year she came back to that spot and she had different cob with her. And I thought 'Ah.' Year after that she is back to the original one. I thought that she is playing the field and thought the first one was best after all. That's nature for you.

Occasionally you get Bewick and Hooper but very rarely, it's mainly Mute what's here. You get Canada geese down here, they do come here and help themselves, they are a bit of a menace. The grey geese they come in later on, they are down on the saltings down the far end, on the mud flats, they are usually down there, very rarely up here.

The tide? According to law it's not here, but it's bound to be. You get the sea percolate through that massive barrier of shingle and also you get spring tides. So you do get a lift of water but it takes a long time before a complete change. I think the scientists found its about six weeks for a complete change of water up this end. It's moving somewhere. You've got these springs running in from the hills behind this village. This particular spring rises in the village of Portesham.

Other waterfowl? Widgeon and teal, mallard. Obviously you get a lot of mallard breed here besides ones which come in. Lot of teal, that's the ones seem to go to northern Europe for a breeding 2,000 miles away from here. We're the oldest ringing station for wildfowl in Great Britain, we haven't for the past couple of year, because of that bird flu. The children wasn't even allowed to feed the swans. So worrying. The young pairs we had to take inland in case we had to put them all down. I am glad it never happened you know it would have been awful.

The only year I know when we did lose a lot was after the bad winter 1962/63, that was a bad one. Six weeks that lagoon was frozen. Helicopter station, he used to fly the bread into the cricket field. Soon as I see he coming I used to walk up on the ice, come up through, most of the hedges was bloody great snowdrifts, to the village get my bread and come on back again. So I used to get as many loaves as they would let me have so I didn't have to keep going every day. That was for myself. We had a lot of wheat brought up. Places on the Fleet never froze, underground springs. Swans used to congregate there and I used to put the food in, throw it in the water so they could have some. But once it froze tight on a neap tide then you had spring tide over the top and that froze again, 'twas about that thick you could have drove a tank over it.

Eventually it thawed and lifted when the next tide come, ripped the natural food up so the swans were suffering so they couldn't get on land because the snow was still holding on and couldn't get at the grass. Well I picked up one or two and buried them on the beach. Sometimes I buried ten. The most I ever buried was about 30. I was keeping count 200, 250, 300 died of pneumonia but could it be something like we've had recently, like flu? It didn't half go through them like wildfire. Leckie said about four pairs come back that season in the spring to nest and we built up again from there. We are up to over a 100 pairs now but it was really bad.

Retired? Well I haven't been doing much this year. I go round giving little talks at various WIs and such like. Just a few slides. I'm allowed out sometimes. Her indoors says I can come down to play. I don't do no work as such, I'm employed as a Swannery guide. Just to talk to the people and maybe take a group round occasionally, yeah. It's interesting you know.

I was talking to these ladies one day, a gang of them. 'You make us feel homesick.' 'Homesick?' I said 'What part of Dorset are you from?' I didn't know where they was from. 'Oh we are from Newfoundland.' 'Where's that?' 'No not here, over Canada way.' 'Oh' she says, 'the way you talk is the local language.' I said 'Is it?' Then I worked it out. Years and years ago they used to go out there catching the cod. Well when it was too rough to go fishing they went ashore and found other attractions. You can imagine what I am trying to say, that's how they got the local language there. And when they got back they sent me a letter thanking me you know. It's nice when you meet people like that.

Also I was a coastguard for 32 years. Based first at Langton then at Wyke. Once they even lowered me from a helicopter into a boat during a a training exercise. All we had was a trawler once and a couple at Abbotsbury with hypothermia and a bomb scare.

18. Dave Wheeler – Swanherd, Abbotsbury. Born Luton 1952.

The swannery is a truly wonderful place and I have a very unusual job.

The Barnes Wallis Bomb, the original bouncing bomb prototype spherical bomb is on display here at the Swannery. We have it by the gate. All the BBC archive films show the bombs bouncing along with Chesil in the background. There were several left behind in the Fleet. Over the years, I guess we have removed three or four. Some bounced over Chesil and ended up in the sea and some broke up on impact. It was top secret, but I'm told by a visitor who happened to be related to Barnes Wallis, that on his first visit to Chesil Beach he met the military bods on the beach and decided to check the agenda and the plans for the day but Barnes Wallis had left the paperwork on the train so it ended up in Plymouth. Top secret, but the papers were retrieved.

My name's David Wheeler, I was born in Luton but I never actually lived there. My parents moved from Bedfordshire to North Devon when I was five. Woolacombe at that time had only one or two hotels. It was quite remote then but it's changed dramatically over the years, now there's a good number of hotels and clubs. After school I went to teacher training college in Exeter, St Luke's. And then I took a teaching job in Sherborne. It was a good secondary modern school. After a few years I thought I should try something else. I took on a youth club in the village of Melbury Osmond and finally ended up marrying an eye-catching young lady from Melbury.

First of all we moved to North Devon, worked there for while but my wife really felt homesick. I came back to Melbury, approached the estate and applied for jobs. The first job that was on offer was a chauffeur's job and I thoroughly enjoyed it. After a time they offered me other jobs, I must have been so bad at driving. One of the jobs on offer was working at the swannery. I had previously visited the swannery, and had found it absolutely enthralling. My father was a country boy. He was brought up on a farm in Stewkley, Buckinghamshire, and later in life he enjoyed living in North Devon. We used to go over Exmoor an awful lot, and I guess the country was our love. On my mother's side, my great-grandfather worked for Lord Rosebery and lived in a beautiful little estate village, Mentmore, Buckinghamshire. He worked as a stonemason all his life on the estate. I guess my path has been determined by luck rather than by careful planning.

I started at the swannery in January 1982. I've been here 25 years now. We have a small working team. Between us we have to cope with the swannery as a visitor attraction, we have to manage the land and look after the wildlife. We flood water meadows in the winter to create additional habitats for wintering waterfowl. We coppice willow and harvest reeds but always leave borders and a few larger areas for wildlife. Some reed beds are cut regularly to supply good thatching material and we cut some rough reed to ensure the swans have enough nesting material. That's tradition here because spring tides can flood the nesting site.

The Fleet lagoon is almost eight miles long and it's open to the sea at the far Portland end. The normal rise and fall of the tide here is very small, but a spring tide with a good wind behind it can flood the entire site. It takes about three hours for an incoming tide to reach us at this end of the lagoon and so sea levels can be higher than the lagoon for a time. Sea water then percolates right through the beach. It runs over the clay core of Chesil, and pulls pebbles with it as it enters the Fleet. So craters appear all along Chesil where the water runs through. In a storm

Dave Wheeler on Fleet manoeuvres

a fair bit of sea water will crash over the top of the beach.

Cygnets don't do well without fresh water, in fact they are likely to suffer the effects of salt poisoning. One of the main reasons the swans nest colonially at this end of the Fleet, is that fresh water streams naturally run through the site into the lagoon. The swans are very accustomed to man's help and they take full advantage of that. They have been managed here for several centuries. We don't cosset them but we do everything we can to give them a reasonable chance of nesting and being successful.

The usual way for swans to nest is to become very aggressive at nesting time in order to clear out threats and create a safe territory. A good cob will command maybe half a mile of river. The cygnets remain protected by their parents within the territory and they have a large area in which they can safely roam for food. That explains male aggression to some extent, but here it's a very different situation, this kind of colonial nesting is fairly rare. It doesn't happen in many situations but there are long established colonies on the Volga Delta and in Denmark. They're not managed but they are studied. Cygnets hatching within colonies can so easily stray from the protection of their parents and become lost within the flock and lost cygnets are defenceless. So the colonial style of nesting is not the easiest of ways for swans to reproduce.

My belief is that the swans have used this lagoon for a few thousand years. It's common for swans to gather at moulting times, they are attracted to areas where food is plentiful. For a period during the moult they are flightless. They shed all their flight feathers at the same time. June/July. We normally time our round up towards the end of July. Most swans are usually flightless at that time but not all. The more we learn, the more we question. We know, for example, that nesting birds with

surviving cygnets virtually always take it in turns to moult. The female moults first. The male delays his moult by 30 days or more. So there's always one parent with a full set of feathers that can crash out a wing in defence of the family without damaging the new growth of feathers. Part of our study this last two years has been aimed at finding out what exactly triggers the moult.

Real animal behaviour research. Yes it is. We've been helped since the mid 1970s by Professor Chris Perrins from Oxford, the Queen's Swan Warden. He still directs our in-depth study of the Abbotsbury population. He introduced ringing here in the 70s. We have come a long way since then, and we've compiled lots of data. Every aspect that we can study, we are trying to study. We have histories on an awful lot of the birds here. We could use a quill pen but we tend to stick to computers nowadays. Every detail of the nesting is recorded, the date every egg is laid, the position of the nest and the ring numbers of the parents that are responsible for each and every nest. By knowing the egg dates we can predict the day clutches will hatch. Within 24 hours of a brood hatching we sex the cygnets and then apply a means of identifying the individual cygnets. They certainly don't like the disturbance, but it's over in a minute. We just move the cygnets a few yards away from the nest, we sex them, we apply temporary identification tags or expandable rings, and then we return them to the parents. By being able to identify the ringed adults and the cygnets we are able to reunite lost cygnets with their parents. It's a regular event. It's so difficult for cygnets to remain with their parents when the territories are small and other swans are nearby. They even take a little longer than usual to become imprinted here because many of our cygnets hear neighbouring birds calling to their young. It's a very confusing situation for our cygnets.

Adult swans are given large darvic rings, and metal rings

supplied by the British Trust for Ornithology. The metal rings are unique for each bird. Cygnets that hatch at Abbotsbury are recaptured when they are three months old, their temporary tags or expandable rings are removed and the adult darvic and BTO rings are applied. All swans known to have originated here are given white darvic rings. The swans are free to go anywhere, but in this area, any white-ringed swan is likely to have originated here. Our records would prove whether or not it did. Normally Mute swans don't readily form nesting colonies. Our colonial nesting situation is mainly due to the geography of the place.

The salinity particularly seems to suit the growth of aquatic weeds in the mid-Fleet but little grows at this end of the lagoon. Most of the swans feed on the beds of eelgrass for a good part of the year. Eelgrass is the common name for the main two types of *Zostra* that grow in the mid-Fleet but they also love *Ruppia* or 'Tasselweed,' and there's normally plenty to be found in the lagoon. They love sea lettuce and they love ordinary grass. The massive amount of natural plant food in the mid-Fleet and the very shallow water normally provides good feeding conditions for swans. So the lagoon may attract and support up to 1,400 swans in the winter. Normally we don't have to feed them in winter, but we do keep an eye on the situation. If the lagoon ices over or if they have any difficulty reaching an adequate quantity of weed we'll help out. In a bad freeze the birds can't reach weed, so they go to fields looking for grass, but then again the fields can be covered in snow. When conditions are really severe the swans are attracted to one or two places where freshwater streams continue to run into the lagoon and of course foxes are very clever and they will home in on those points. If swans lose condition the foxes are very successful. So we help. We'll tide them over these bad times. In fact they know full well that if it is difficult for them to find food down the lagoon its well worth

them taking a trip up here to Abbotsbury for a handout.

At the end of the winter any swans that are paired, of nesting age, and are in condition to nest, either leave completely or come here to the head of the lagoon where a constant supply of fresh water runs over the land. Good pairs, the more aggressive cobs get the good territories. They'll produce good cygnets year after year, the survival rate of their cygnets is high. The weaker pairs and the younger pairs can't compete for the better territories. Some of them nest in places where no fresh water is available to them so unless we provide food and water at the nest some pairs would have to run the gauntlet through other territories to get to the Fleet. Younger breeding pairs tend to lay late, they tend to lay smaller clutches and have less success. As they come into their middle years they are likely to lay earlier, bigger clutches and enjoy more success. As they get older it all tails back again. So there are definite patterns there. For safety reasons we do put a few carefully selected families into pens, purely to give them a better chance of rearing cygnets. We automatically copy all our data to Oxford University. The EGI-The Edward Grey Institute that have been helping us for so long, and the Slimbridge Wildfowl and Wetland Trust Centre. All our ringing data ultimately ends up with the British Trust for Ornithology.

The swans here are very approachable. To me the place has great scientific, and educational value. There is no better place for school parties to visit, children can safely stand close even when swans are hatching their eggs. Children can't see that anywhere else. Some schools come regularly year after year. Some spend all day with us and we take them around flower meadows and water meadows. We try to involve them in our work and they help us feed the swans. By the time we've toured the site and been through worksheets we've easily filled the day.

Mute swans are basically creatures of habit, they won't even move unless they need too. The general pattern is that their spring and summer nesting territory may not provide enough food to see them through the winter. So it's common for pairs to move with their cygnets to any large source of food. Lots of swans come into the Fleet for that reason. Our numbers go up prior to the moult and they go up again before the winter. At the end of the winter several hundreds return inland to nest, and some just to live on rivers.

My feeling is that if we packed it in completely the lagoon would still carry on attracting swans, particularly in the winter. They would still nest here but perhaps cygnet survival rates would fall and long term, well, who knows? We only help when they need it. We want to sustain a healthy colony. We are also very fortunate to have a group of specialist scientists who have been studying aspects of the reserve since the 1970s, the Fleet Study Group. Their archives are impressive, they have a website that's well worth looking at.

We have a very keen, experienced birder on the staff, Steve Groves, and he often gets excited about rare migrants. I don't think he misses very much. I get excited if I ever manage to see something unusual before Steve. I've got a very short list of such birds. One day on my way into work a hoopoe wandered across the track in front of my car then flew across to Horsepool Farm. You can't mistake them, but Steve was convinced I was pulling his leg all day. He couldn't rest until he eventually spotted the bird on a path in our reed bed. Ospreys? We're sometimes lucky enough to see an osprey or two. They fish in this lagoon. There is a lot of grey mullet, a lot of eels. In the winter a lot of waterfowl come to the Fleet and they also use the flooded meadows outside the reed beds. We get one or two avocets, but not many.

One of the most amazing sights I've seen was in the days when thousands of starlings would circle around before stooping down to roost in the reeds. Clouds and clouds of them would arrive from all directions and when I thought every starling in this part of the world was overhead, another belt come in. They would twist and turn like smoke in the wind then crash down into reeds often breaking the stems. Dick remembers the old swanherds using clapperboards to try to keep them out of the reed. It was an amazing sight. We haven't seen so many for a while.

Very slowly I worked my way up the ladder. It was a long apprenticeship. When I first came here I was cleaning toilets, digging ditches, cutting reed, helping school parties and working with swans, the variety was fantastic. I guess as time went on I did a little less of the real work and took on a bigger share of the paperwork. That's the way things go. But it's a very unusual job and a very special place.

There's no better place to study swans than here. We often employ students to help cover our busiest periods in the spring and summer. One boy from Kingston Maurward worked a summer here and returned the next. He moved on to Swansea University to study marine biology and after six consecutive summers at the swannery he moved off to America to study swans and waterfowl. He's still there and still travels all over America and Canada studying swans and he has contributed to several scientific papers.

We find for events like our round up, over 200 volunteers turn up. When swans moult their flight feathers they are grounded for five to six weeks. So late July's the very best time of year to catch swans en-mass. Our roundup is a wonderful two-day event, our version of Swan Upping. We start near the Portland end of the lagoon This year it involved 54 canoes.

I always write to the Commandant of the army camp at

Chickerell well in advance, and he always assures me we will be very welcome to launch from the hard and they promise not shoot on the Tidmoor firing range. I took the precaution of ringing ten days before the round up this year just to check, and I was told, 'It's OK you are in the diary.' The morning we arrived at the army camp we were told, 'We are shooting on Tidmoor so keep your heads down as you paddle through.' They kindly stopped, and waited. We involve canoe clubs and school children, there is a real good mix of people and ages. We slowly paddle the lagoon and any swans in the mid-Fleet move on ahead as the canoes approach. They have no other option. The older ones know all about it… We don't pressurise them, just slowly paddle along. We have to stretch into all the little hives and at the end of that 'drive day,' we stop just short of the actual swannery. We inflate and stretch an oil boom across the lagoon to prevent them travelling back down the Fleet overnight. But we know they will cheat if they get the chance so we have to camp there. On rotation volunteers watch the swans overnight to make sure they don't approach the barrier and follow it to the shore, then walk up the beach, and around the boom to make their escape. We have to watch them like a hawk.

Then at first light the canoes start to move around Shipmoor Point. More launch from the east side of this bay and more from the west and over 100 volunteers wade in the water to help the canoes persuade the swans to enter a holding pen to the west of the nest site. We sometimes catch over 900 swans.

As soon as we have them safely penned, we begin to remove them one by one, we firstly record their identity, their rings. We do have swan crooks but we don't use them unless absolutely necessary. It might sometimes be necessary to use a crook if a bird's on the water and not in easy reach, but my method of catching a swan is not to chase them, not to use crooks if at all possible. If I need to catch a single swan I can use food to crowd it with swans. It's then immobilised and it can be picked up. On rivers most swans know what bread is and just two pieces of bread will bring most swans to you, if you squeeze a third piece it'll sink, the swan's head follows it underwater and you can then pick up the bird. An aggressive nesting swan is easy to catch, they will come at you and they will sort of jump into your hands so it's no big deal. We've had fun and games sometimes though.

Going back to the roundup, after the ID rings are recorded we look at the actual condition of the rings and any damaged rings are replaced. Unringed birds are ringed for the first time. Swans newly ringed at our roundups are given yellow darvics to show they are incoming Crown birds. Swans originating at Abbotsbury carry our white darvics from the time they fledge. These are privately owned even though they are free to go anywhere. They are owned by the family that purchased this land from Henry VIII after the destruction of the Benedictine Monastery of St Peter's.

Every swan caught in the roundup is weighed and measured, we take blood samples to test for various things, partly for lead, and we know that traditionally here the lead levels are among the lowest in the country. We don't allow people to fish through most of the lagoon with rod and line and shooting has been carefully controlled over the years.

Nowadays we vaccinate every bird caught in the roundups to protect them from Duck Viral Enteritis. DVE can cause high mortality rates within a flock. There is the potential for all sorts of diseases but fortunately natural aspects of the site help to safeguard us. Salt water occasionally floods the site and I am sure that helps to cleanse the ground.

Swans are big birds they eat a lot and they create a lot of waste, everyday we rake and remove waste. We remove the droppings from the nest site every day and rake the rearing pens up to three times a day. We tried it on the garden, it didn't do a lot of good. We tend to put it topside of the reed bed. Reed beds have amazing properties they are a brilliant natural filter. They can even be used to treat sewage.

 I think the main reason the monks took interest in the swans here centuries ago was simply the value of the meat. They managed the birds in order to maximise the resource. Apparently swans counted as fish. They say monks could eat swans on Fridays if they got fed up with fish. They are still eaten now. I'm told it's a tradition at St John's College. There is an old rhyme that says, 'The Dons of St John's are very fond of swans.' And I believe swan meat is consumed at the Lord Mayor of London's feast day as well.

Quills for writing. We collect the best of the feathers throughout the moult and the primaries are sought after by calligraphers. They always want hard ends to the shaft. Primary feathers from the left wing are the most popular because most calligraphers are right-handed and feathers from the left wing bend away from the face when used by a right-hander. The Society of Calligraphers and Scribes use our quills and Lloyds Registry require them for recording shipping losses in the Doom Book. But there are lots and lots of uses for primaries. Many are supplied to a London company by the name of A S Handover. They take a short section from the shaft of the primary and fit sable hair in one end and a wooden handle in the other to make very fine paintbrushes for discerning artists. People who clean the workings of old clocks often use primaries. Beekeepers use them for sweeping bees off of honeycomb, fletchers use them for arrow flights. There are a 101 uses for primary feathers. There's one or two people that are very keen to get good quality secondaries and one artist in particular actually uses a feather as

his canvas. Ian Davie produces outstanding work. It's well worth looking at a website called 'Feather Art.' The only small feather we normally collect is a scapular, a fluffy feather from the base of the wing. They are sent to the Plumery in London where they are hand-sewn end to end and bound to form the plumes that adorn the helmets of the Queen's bodyguard, the Gentlemen at Arms.

The swannery pays for itself. But having said that we are very dependant on weather, some summers are better than others. We've tried over many years to develop the place in a sympathetic way. We want to maintain a peaceful refuge for birds. After all it's an ancient nest site, the last thing we want to do is spoil it. We even avoid using strimmers and any noisy machinery at the heart of the site.

The Estate's ownership of the beach ceases near the narrows, very near the army camp, it then becomes Crown property. The Crown seem happy for our wardens to manage their section of the beach in the same way we manage our own. So we have a warden stationed at Ferrybridge the other end of the Fleet. He is based at the Chesil Beach Centre, a wonderful information centre for visitors. It's fortunate we are at one end of the Fleet and he's at the other, between us we just about have it covered.

Taking off ? Swans are creatures of habit. They don't expend energy unless they need to. So whenever they take off, they will almost always face a head wind, they need to get up some speed if they are going to get any lift. If they have a strong head wind they can take off in a fairly short space. A lot of people think they always take off from water but they will take off from, and land, on land. On water they beat their wings, they race along to reach the airspeeds necessary to gain lift. If you look into the science of it, it's not actually the down-beat of the wings pressing on air that causes lift it's the reduced pressure immediately above the wings which causes lift. It's absolutely wonderful to see, and on occasions here, particularly in the October and November, there can be quite large numbers of swans taking to the air on a regular basis. On a breezy day visitors here are treated to quite an air display. It's wonderful to see.

Mute swans rarely travel long distances. Our ringing has proven it's fairly unusual for a Mute swan to travel 90 miles.

A lot will travel to Somerset. Very few travel to Hampshire from here. Having said all that, whatever rule you apply to swans, there are always a few that will break it. We have had a handful over the years that have ended up in central France. The last one found a sewage works and stayed there. I don't blame them for going to France but I would have thought the Fleet was a more attractive place to be. They all seem to know where the Fleet is and most return eventually.

Swans mating for life? The majority will stick to their mates and will nest on the same spot, that's the usual thing. We have known on the other hand, one swan have three mates in consecutive years. That's not unique to this place. We know that similar things happen on the Thames and other rivers. They are not all perfect. But its uncanny the number of times someone will ring up to tell us that one of a longstanding pair has died and then a month later will ring to say the other one has also died.

Our own records clearly show that swans tend to choose a mate of their own age. We've got one or two swans here now that are in their early to mid twenties. Nationally the average age has been calculated at between 11 and 12 years. The majority stick with their mate for life but they display to one another every year. They are forever bonding and courting. Their body language is easy to read. Schoolchildren that come here soon pick it up. If you see a big cob hissing at you, you know it's not a very happy bird. Here the birds accept people. They are unbelievably tolerant. I remember just a year or two ago, I was

watching very closely because it worried me a touch, there were two very tiny girls with their parents not very far away. They were standing close to a female swan incubating eggs on the nest. One little girl picked up a piece of reed, handed it to the pen, and the swan accepted it with her bill and tucked it in. So the girls busied themselves finding reed to hand to the swan. They moved slowly, and the swan was happy to take every piece as it was offered. Eventually there was no more reed to be picked up and the swan virtually said 'Well come on, pass the reed.' It was amazing.

In May and June you can stand beside nests as eggs hatch, but you will very likely see cobs facing up to their feathered neighbours. You could say at nesting time they're 'neighbours from hell.' The nesting season is an exciting and very special time of year.

We all get to know the old timers, the characters, some are very well known to us. It's sad when you eventually lose birds like that. There was one up here, Niddy his ring ID happened to be N.I.D. so we affectionately called him Niddy, he nested for many years in the stream here. About five years ago his mate died and he just wasn't interested in swans for a long time but he still kept his territory. Then this year he suddenly took a liking to a bird further down the stream but she already had a mate and was already on eggs. Every time her mate was at the far end of his territory, Niddy would visit her at the nest. We wondered what on earth was going to happen, then one night there must have been a serious fight between Niddy and his rival. The body of the rival was found in the morning and sadly Niddy died very shortly after.

We experience some sad times, but they are easily outweighed by the good. The swannery is a truly wonderful place and I have a very unusual job. It's a privilege to be here.

WEYMOUTH AND PORTLAND

19. Ken Lynham — Fisherman and local historian. Born 1937 Easton, Portland.

The thing about the sea is you haven't got to be frightened of it, you've got to respect it 100 per cent. I've had some hairy things out there, you're bound to. It is the only job that has absolute freedom.

I was born in Victoria Place. The Lynhams came to Portland in the 1820s and there were two first cousins. They came from Bridgwater in Somerset for the building of the prison. One was the chief warder and the other was an engineer. The convicts built their own prison. They commandeered the Admiralty quarries, the Grove, then they went on to build the first part of the Portland breakwater. My father Edward, was born in 1911, the youngest of six, two older brothers were also quarrymen.

The quarries really took off in Wren's time. We've got history back to that. It was the Lowmans, grandmother's side that were the quarrymen. One of her brothers was a fisherman and had a pier on Portland, and her father was the general foreman at the United Stone Company. There were boats all around the island, but the main place at Tophill was Church Ope Cove, but they were clever, the fishermen adapted cranes to launch their boats round the island. I started full-time fishing from the cranes out the Bill in 1960. My mother's father Walter Slade, was also a quarryman, he quarried the stone for the Cenotaph in London.

My early recollections of the war were in an indoor shelter in 1943, a bomb hit Crown Farm just up the road, and all the windows and doors were blown in. The Germans dropped three across the island. One hit the churchyard, one hit the farm and one hit the borstal. It was still a borstal then, all boys. There were daylight raids, a few bombs landing on the island, quite a few people killed. I started school in 1942 and we had air raid shelters in the playground, we had tracer bullets. The interesting thing that sticks in my mind was D Day, obviously the harbour full of ships, but the Portland lighthouse was the navigation point for all the Yankee bombers going over, and we used to count them going out in the morning and see how many were missing when they came back at teatime. We had a big American camp at Wakeham Field and one at Portland football ground. The majority of the incumbents were coloured.

I spent hours at night in the air raid shelters, we were unceremoniously grabbed out of bed, and all the kids were jammed in when the air raid siren sounded. You never saw a banana or an orange. There were no toys but I remember I had a go-cart made out of odd wood and pram wheels.

Exposed? Well I suppose we were, we had machine guns and heavy batteries all round the island, and out the Bill they dug trenches and put mounds, so's there couldn't be a landing by glider. These were the defences all round the island. You'd have a hell of a job to land a boat because the boat would have to come in to Portland Harbour or to Church Ope Cove which was mined.

I've got photos of the VE Day street party. We had two parties because we had VJ Day as well. There were many conscripts who did not return from the war. I went to school with quite a few of the orphans. When the war broke out my father volunteered for the Navy and of all things found himself with others on Bernard Docker's yacht, *Shermara*. They were sent from Portland, they were a Special Branch and wore full Navy uniform. They went to Scotland and they were doing ASDIC patrols. Father was up there when the *Hood* was sunk and then they got transferred on to tugs because of all the activity in the

Ken Lynham at Red Crane

Channel. The rest of the war he was on the tug pilot working between Portsmouth, Southampton and Portland, standby for damaged vessels. There was an incident when he was away. Some Yanks had missed their navigation and about three or four of them had got stranded on the Shambles Bank. That was a major operation because they were vulnerable to air attack.

The Lyme Bay tragedy, that was part of the excuse, wasn't it? They thought it was a mock raid. They didn't realise it was German E Boats, they thought it was operational. It's a very interesting story. It was hushed up for obvious reasons. The kids that were going to school at Underhill, the school is right on the cliff and they were all telling us 'You've never seen anything like it,' this was 1944, and the Yanks landed their LCTs on Chiswell Beach and the dead were taken straight to Bournemouth. They did what they could for the wounded, but it was all hush hush.

I didn't know anything of this until about six months ago but I'm a Liveryman and Freeman of London, from the fishing industry, and of course you meet all sorts of people. One gentleman I've had a lot to do with is Lord Strathcona, he owns the Isle of Colonsay in Scotland. He was based in Portland on an MTB during the war and his wife was in the Wrens on Portland. About six months ago he said to me that they'd formed a coastal trust for coastal forces and did I know that Portland was one of the main bases where all the small boats were trained and set up and they landed the agents into France? *HMS Attack* was based on Portland. I believe a lot of the training for St Nazaire was done here.

He said 'We're forming this trust and we'd like to put a plaque to commemorate it because there's very few of us left now, somewhere prominent on Portland.' So I said 'Yeah, the obvious place to put it is on the lighthouse wall at the Bill.' I said 'Thousands of people visit every year and you overlook both

bays, 'cause you were involved in the Lyme Bay tragedy, and course Weymouth Bay for all the other activity that was going the other way.' So I arranged a meeting, the council, the local RNA, everybody was over the moon, and the one who's objected and stopped it, is Crown Estates…

Portland was always a Royal Manor. You've got the Crown agent put on Portland by Crown Estates. I don't think he's paid a great deal of money, but this is how antiquated it is. He summons 22 good men and women and true, so there's nothing democratic about it, it's the sole appointment of one man. The Court Leet. They're sworn as a jury, they're summoned to attend what they call the encroachments and all that, I mean I'm not a member, so I only know what I've read, and from people I know that have served. There's the Chief Constable, and Constables of the villages, Reeve, Haywood and Bailiff. It's only what's termed as Crown Lands. The sole task of the Court Leet was to look after the commoners' interests against the Crown Estates. Of course the Crown Estates then was the Royal Family and now it's a government department. It's only really a token body.

My father was brought out of retirement to open Albion Stone. He would have been 66. My father for the last 15 years of his life was working for the Bath & Portland Stone Company as the Foreman Selector, and if you were an architect, my father would show you around the island explaining what stone was what. His claim was that he could walk round London and tell you which stone came from which quarry.

In the 1950s a young girl called Jane Lang at Oxford University did her PhD called '*The rebuilding of St Paul's after the Great Fire.*' She came to meet my father and he showed her around the quarries and explained where the stone came from. What her book explains was that the man who really put Portland on the map was Inigo Jones (1573-1652) and that St

Paul's wasn't destroyed in the Great Fire, it had been destroyed in 1620 by lightning. Inigo Jones, because he'd built the Banqueting Hall with Portland stone, was then commissioned to rebuild St Paul's Cathedral also with Portland stone. This was in the 1620s, and he had a pier built, called Girt Pier in Church Ope Cove at his own personal cost of £500 which was a fortune. So the stone came from the Church Ope area, the area we called Chyne, and it was transported by horse and cart and shipped to London in coastal barges, the biggest load being about 180 ton. When you think the stone had to be got down the cliff, into barges. The incline railways didn't come until years after Wren's time. It wasn't until the 1670s, after Inigo Jones had died, that Wren was commissioned to rebuild, and that's when he discovered Portland stone. There was enough stone on site for the first two years of reconstruction. Inigo Jones must have come to Portland and discovered the stone in a landslip and that was the start of the stone trade to London.

There was hundreds of quarrymen and at school all your house teams were named after quarries. So you had Courtlands, Kingbarrow, Broadcroft and Perryfield. Kingbarrow is the one that Wren really exploited and it's the one where all the stone came from for St Paul's, at the top of the island. The stones were moved with Portland jacks. All it was, was a square block with a cog wheel inside with a lift up. If you had a two inch gap, you could lift five ton. During the First World War, the fishing industry took the stone companies to court for tipping the stone into the sea and ruining the beach where they launched their boats from in Church Ope. The fishermen won the case and the stone industry had to build the pier. They could shift a piece of stone that was 70 ton only by hand. I can prove it.

When I was 13 I went to Weymouth Technical College. I was one of the last ones to use the train. The station here was just down the road in Easton. It was beautiful. The train came right round the cliff and through the dockyard, it was absolutely brilliant. When I left school I passed the dockyard exam, did a five-year apprenticeship as an electrician, then National Service on the Isle of Wight, REME, and when I was there I had pots and was fishing out of Freshwater Bay. When I was demobbed my mother had a small business, just a little shop selling pretty well everything, so I helped her out with that and did fishing. And then when my wife came along, she had it. We sold fish as well.

Father was still working as a quarryman. He was made foreman in the 1950s and was working in Broadcroft. He quarried the stone for the Roosevelt Memorial. Everything big on Portland was called 'girt,' so you had 'girt kibbles' and 'girt sledges'. The metal they used was wrought iron slabs. Half a pig was half a hundredweight, and a pig was a hundredweight. They had 'rubbling gangs' and 'cap gangs'. Now the rubbling gang used to take all the overburden off and they were paid by yardage, and the cap gangs were the ones that took the freshwater tier which is now the Purbeck tier off, and that was the first stone that was crushed because it was pure and they had a big crushing machine. Then the quarrymen did the rest.

There was a blacksmith's up the road and when you went in as a boy, that was your first job, to carry the tools to the blacksmith because the kibbles had to be sharpened regularly and he'd put new tips in. My father when he was 14, actually worked under a hand crane. I can remember hand cranes working because there was one independent guy who owned a bit of land and I can vividly remember that. Of course we used the hand cranes for the boats. I used a hand crane dozens of times. If they had a big, what they call 'task,' which was the big area of stone and they had to get out the Whit Bed, they had to all help each other. It was a combined thing. But the other thing was that quarrymen were paid piecework, and they used to draw a minimum amount per week.

At one time the Square Mile was only allowed to be built with Portland Stone. I remember going up to the Festival of Britain and the big thing was the Shell Building, they actually put in a stone yard just to deal with it and it was called the Shell Yard. And of course all the war graves. That was a huge trade. The sad thing is now that they've gone right down to the blue clay. They're actually mining under houses now on the west side of the island. But since father died, he died '89, I've had very little to do with the stone trade.

Somebody came to Portland in the 1800s writing for a magazine, and he said he was astounded because the population up until the prison come was only about 2,000, and being an island you either had to walk from Abbotsbury to get here or come across by ferry, and he said what was amazing was how long lived they were and the size of the Portlanders. They attributed it to the lime being pure. The average age nationally wasn't more than 45. Here the majority were living to 65 and the vast majority of the men were over six foot.

When I started fishing I had just a 14-foot boat, crab and lobster pots, netting in the winter and then I went full-time. In 1968 I had an 18-foot boat built with a winch in. We worked about 112 pots with that. I was the first one commercially to use the Race, bass fishing. When you were potting you get all sorts of things come up with the gear and we had a board which was one of these diving boards and we saw these birds working and I said to my mate 'we'll chuck it over one day and see if it does work,' and we had an artificial red gill and we threw it in and immediately started catching bass. You could work several off the stern of a boat that size, and it's genius. You tie it and you have it 30 foot off the boat with a long 30-foot trace on to your

bait, and depending on where you put the hole in the board is the depth it dives to. It's a lazy way of fishing because when the fish gets on, the board comes to the surface. I still use them today.

Somebody had been using it down the Westcountry prior to that. You obviously had to have propulsion to keep it down. It would go down to 30, 40 foot if you want it, depends how you set it. We started doing that in the 70s. It was jumping about a bit, and when we were working that one we still kept the 14-foot boat out the Bill under the crane, because that was what we used wintertime. I then moved fishing to Castletown. And then in '72 I had a 30-foot crabber built called *Anne* and we kept that one until my sons left school, I had four children, two boys, two girls. Stella, Paul, Mark and Anne. I've been fishing ever since.

I've still got a mooring down Castletown, still got a hut. What altered my way of life was in '72 I had a 30-foot boat built and went fishing properly. We were working 300 pots and fishing up to six miles because we still only had a compass, there was no navigation aids. We were lucky on Portland because we had the Shambles Bank, which was a lightship on one end and a buoy the other, so when you were fishing outside of that you had the perfect landmark. South of the Bill up to the Shambles, that's where our main fishing grounds were.

When I first started there were seine crews working from the beach. I started out of Red Crane. That was a funny story because there's always been a bit of rivalry between the Underhill fishermen and the Tophill fishermen and yet the day I started one of the well known characters, a bloke by the name of Joey Stone, he come alongside, and bear in mind it was only a 14-foot boat and we were rowing, he had a Seagull outboard on, and he said 'I hear you going full time.' I said 'Ar.' He said 'Well done, I don't mind helping you now.' And he looked and said 'What you got there then?' I had a bag with all my food and a

Thermos flask in, and he said 'You'd better start chewin,' my son. I'm out here 12 hours a day, and as long as I've got a wad to chew, I don't need to eat or drink.' And the same knife he used to cut the bait, he used to cut off the wad. He kept it in the peak of his cap, and he'd never spit over the side, he'd always spit in the boat. He reckoned it done the wood good.

Seine crews? There's still two young lads down there on Chesil, I've encouraged it. Several people have tried out the Bill and there's still one or two trying, but the crane out the Bill now is mainly used by divers. When my sons left school they came fishing with me, and we realised we had to get bigger and we went to Falmouth and had a modern 12 metre Vivier crabber. You only have one skipper on the boat, my eldest son, Paul, was obviously going to be a brilliant fisherman. So we said 'Right, we'll see if the younger son come on, see what he's going to be like,' so I stayed on with them for a few years.

I then got involved with the politics of fishing. In the 70s, I had taken a leading scientist to sea tagging crabs by the name of Dr Eric Edwards. We're still very great friends, and when he realised that Paul was capable of running the boat, he said 'I want you to go in.' So I went in first of all on the Sea Fisheries Committee, where I met Dave Sales, but then Eric Edwards was offered a top job with a fishmongers company in London as their consultant, which was as big as you could get, with the prestige and that, and he said 'Within six months I want you up there, I want you on one of the committees in the Fishmongers.' I said 'Ar.' So anyway, 'There's no reason now, Paul can go to sea,' he said. 'You come into the other side and put something back.' So that's how my involvement come with the Shellfish Association, but I had already been put on the Sea Fisheries Committee. I went on there in 1972. But that was interesting because going to London opened new horizons. You met all the leading lights in the industry and then politicians and then you realise the political influence these livery companies have got.

So why did we give our fishing away? That was Ted Heath. It was political. All it was, was entry into Europe. France said 'We want exclusive fishing rights,' and they came out with everything they wanted to let us in. What people don't realise is that we're at a greater risk now than we were then because all we had to stop them fishing inside our limits was a derogation. He signed up to equal access to a common resource, so it's only got five years to run, and if it's not renewed, the biggest Spanish, French, any boats in the EU, can fish right up to Chesil Beach. Right up to our shores.

The best conservation byelaw we ever brought in, is that no vessel in this district over 12 metres can fish within six miles. That was brought in 20 years ago. Either side of us is 15-metre byelaws, Devon got 15 metres and Sussex is 15. Now that's a vast difference. Now if Sea Fisheries Committees are brought down in number, which they're on about, we could lose that 12-metre byelaw. We're saying there should be more local control, not less. We've got the support of the conservationists on this one, they can see that you want to be strengthening Sea Fisheries Committees make them more local than they are now.

Lobster size? There again, if you'd said to me ten years ago there'd be lobsters aplenty, crabs aplenty, we'd have said 'Rubbish.' This year has been the best year. Now funny enough I was talking to a leading scientist on Monday, he said 'What's your theory?' I said 'It's bound to be global warming, there's a vast change, it's not the conservation changes that we've brought in, increasing the minimum size, because we've only been doing that for the last ten years that it's been stringent.' I said 'These animals are 20 or 30 years old. It's something else.' He said 'Oh trust you, Lynham, to come up with something else.'

Eric Edwards discovered that when the crabs release their berries here the tidal stream sets them eastwards and they settled on the sandbanks between the Isle of Wight and St Alban's Head, even up as far as Nab Tower, and then the crabs migrated westward, so they came back. Dave Sales and I have always agreed that things have altered, because the French came right into six miles and hammered the lobsters. The lobster fishery went down. No doubt about it, but why has it all altered now? Doesn't make sense, does it?

The other thing where we sell ourselves down the line is that every other industry gives their value as the total value, whereas the only statistics ever given for fishing is first-hand sales. Crabs have been down to £1 a kilo, lobsters have been down to £6 a kilo. So if you say Weymouth and Portland first-hand sales is £5 million, if you went to the total value you'd probably be trebling that.

We had an Italian bloke come here that started processing crab. He realised there was a huge market if you could get top quality crab meat to hotels in London that wasn't frozen. So he was buying crab, cooking it, processing it and delivering it to London two or three times a week, fresh. I heard last week that now he's probably cooking three-quarters of a tonne of crab a day. He's got local women hand picking it. I've always been a big believer in value added.

It's funny, when I first started bass was just bass, someone had the brainwave to call it 'sea bass' and the price trebled overnight. The other sad thing is that the way the press operate, there's no shortage of cod, for all they're saying, and there again the EU rules on cod is the most ridiculous thing there is. The public think about these greedy fishermen, but you put your net in the water and you can't say 'No cod today, thank you.' But on Red Nose Day last year a trawler off Cornwall estimated he had

£3,000-worth of prime cod. He called up the MAFF office and said 'I've got these cod, it's Red Nose Day, can I put it on the market and donate it to charity?' And they wouldn't allow it, he had to dump it. Half the world's starving. Bradshaw went to sea in a crabber, and the first pot that came back in, he said 'What's the hole in the top of that pot for?' I was a bit rude to him.

Sadly we had a tragedy in the family, I lost my grandson Peter. He was 20. That was potting. Rough weather. But son Paul is one of the top skippers and it was the last trip of the day and he thought to himself 'Oh thank Christ, it's finished,' and he done something he never ought to have done, it was the very last act of the day. Peter was a wonderful grandson. He never smoked or drank in his short life, very conscientious, it was a terrible loss to the whole family. Over 700 people attended a memorial service in his honour. Another one was lost the next day. Always conscious of the danger. Yeah, well the thing about the sea is you haven't got to be frightened of it, you've got to respect it 100 per cent. I've had some hairy things out there, you're bound to. You're out there and the weather deteriorates, but that's it, but you had to do whatever you had to do every day. It is the only job that has absolute freedom.

The furthest we went off with just a compass was six miles. Two sons and a grandson are still fishing. We've got quite a few on Portland now. We've got two full-time boats off Chesil Beach, Castletown we've got about ten boats but of course we've got several Portland families with bigger boats who've got to fish out of Weymouth. It's surprising how many registered boats there are on Portland. More than you think.

There's a lot of gilt head bream in Portland Harbour, and we're saying nowthere's a lot of bream and funnily enough, cod have showed up again this week. No shortage of cod, that's due to global warming, no doubt. Everything was a month early this year, spider crabs come a month early. We were the first ones to sell spider crabs to Spain, here on Portland. We fished pots. Started when the weather broke in March, and we fished right through to what we called Fair Day. Portland Fair was always the 5th November. When the weather broke we brought the gear ashore, we went netting, and we had big mullet nets. We used to get the shoals of mullet round and if you had the odd cold spell we used to do well. We used to shoot this big net and drive them in, because the only ones you got were that size, the small and the big went through. We used to buy the net and make our own, and all our own pots in those days. The whole thing has altered out of all recognition. Bass and spider crabs, we were on the northern limit of both in the channel. Now you've got a bass area in Liverpool Bay, you've got one in the Thames, and you've got spiders in Liverpool Bay, right up as far as Whitby.

Mackerel? We used feathers. The healthiest food in the world. All the nutritionists know it. If you have three mackerel a week, you practically do away with heart problems. Funny enough now, lobster is coming along the same lines. Herrings? Yes, the last I knew a bloke at Burton Bradstock was putting out nets for herring at certain times of the year. And course down there in Cornwall, they've started the pilchard fishery now.

The Fishmongers and Livery Company? I was put on the Shellfish Association with Eric Edwards in '81, and then I was rapidly made chairman of the Crustacea Committee. The Fishmonger's Company sponsors the Shellfish Association and the Salmon and Trout Association. You're asked to give a speech at a major dinner at Fishmonger's Hall, and if you do that, you've got to become a Freeman of London, to become a liveryman. I was the first ordinary fisherman to be made Freeman for ages.

Superstitions on Portland ? You can't mention them long eared things, not on the island or on boats as well. Oh yeah. The other thing, a lot of people on boats. If you talk to the infamous Nantes brothers at Ferrybridge, they was going to have a load of boats built and they did a deal with Volvo for the engines, and all Volvo engines were green, and they said 'If you want to sell six engines, they got to be blue not bloody green,' and Volvo actually altered their production line!

Kimberlins is our foreigners. Don't matter if you come from Weymouth, you're a foreigner. Then you have Tophill and Underhill. Oh there's hundreds of Portland terms. Ope is the interesting one, they always say it's an opening, which makes sense for Church Ope and Big Ope and all that. The other thing was, when we were fishing, the fishermen used to say 'We had Bill Ope,' what that meant was if you went from Durdle and you sailed east, Bill Ope was when you could see the lighthouse free of Blacknor Point.

The other thing I've never, ever understood, if you put pots strung together on one rope, you always called them a triangle. And when you were shooting, now you've got a navigator. But in our days, they would say 'Where's your top end?' and you'd give them a landmark, and they'd say 'Will you shoot up hill or down hill from that?' Now either side of the Bill was north or south, so it was always up hill or down hill.

I can name all the rocks from Balaclava to Bill Point. Balaclava, King's Pier, Queen's Pier, Folly Pier, there's a rock there a lot of people call Shag Rock, it's not, it's Old Gardener, you go Little Beach, Ballet's Wall, Durdle Pier, Rod's Weir, Harry Hillier's Ope, Steamer, Church Ope, Chyne, Freshwater Bay, we call that Neddyfield, Tank Rock, Breston Point, Sand Holes, God Nore Point, Way's End, Broad Ope, River, Butts, Long Points, Coller's Ledge, Pom Pom, San Patten's Pier, Red Crane, Mugleys Plain, Bill Point. I'm probably the last one that can walk round them and say 'That's that.'

Smuggling? Oh yeah, I was involved in smuggling. The last bloke who smuggled on Portland died about two years ago. In them days all it was, was fags and booze, and we were down there. I had a young family and we were struggling and we had an engine broke down, and this old boy was the general dogsbody for everything, and we knew that he'd bring in bottles and all that. Anyway, to cut a long story short, our engine broke down and he said 'Oh there's a winch on my boat, you lads take my boat on, I ain't got nothing on for a few days until your engine's done.' So he lent us his boat, and when our boat was done we said 'How much do we owe you?' 'No,' he said, 'you can do me a good turn one day.' And the good turn, I shall never forget as long as I live, come the last weekend in November, just prior to Christmas, knocked on the door, ten o'clock at night. 'Want you, get your mate.' Went down across Portland Harbour, got out through the northern entrance, put the lights out, sailed up to Lulworth and there was a Dutch coaster, went alongside the Dutch coaster. That was the first time I'd ever seen litres of spirits, it was 1969, all the litre bottles, dozen bottles in a box, was put all down through the deck, and all the fags was put in his little fore peak for'ard. We sailed into Castletown Pier, unloaded it on custom house steps in front of customs. I said 'What the bloody hell are you doing?' He said 'They won't suspect nothing if you unload stuff here.' Anyway, that was the only time I was ever involved, but it was a lot of whisky and a lot of fags that was brought in. He was raided not long after, he wasn't caught, he was too clever to get caught, but I reckon the last smuggling took place on that scale in about 1969.

The lerret? When they started putting lifeboats around the coast, Portland was an obvious place to put one, so the Crown Estates owned all the land at Church Ope Cove, and they gave the Lifeboat Institution land to build a hut. This was in the 1820s. They built the hut, and Portland's famous for its lerret, which was launched and could be rowed with either four or six oars, no engines about in those days, and we used what is called a copse oar, and the beauty of that is it balances the oar so you can row it all day, you haven't got that weight. And when you come ashore in a rough sea you can just let the oar go, it'll swing back. So when they came, the lifeboat said 'rowlocks,' and they said 'No, copse oar or nothing,' and the fishermen wouldn't give in, so the lifeboat never ever come to Portland. But the fishermen said 'We'll put a lerret in there.' So when the epic accident happened off the Bill, the collision of the *Forest* and the *Avalanche*, the fishermen launched the boat, that was 1877, and that's why Avalanche church was built, in memory of all those drowned. But where our family came in, my wife's great-great-grandfather, Tom White, was the last fisherman to die that was in the rescue boat. So my sons got even more into the fishing side than I have.

20. Judith Frost – Artist, Chiswell, Portland. Born Leicester 1956.

The quarry has eaten cliffs out of the hills, and it's steeped with history, and all the time you've got this vast expanse of sea, which at night of course, becomes this sort of black hole where there isn't anyone… So you very much feel on the edge, you're on the boundary.

When I was young, I went to primary school on the Braunstone Estate on the edge of Leicester which is quite rough, but I left there when I was ten or eleven and went to Loughborough, to a convent school until I was 18.

My mother was a nurse and my father was a mechanical engineer who worked in Leicester. My grandparents on one side were farmers from Cornwall, arable I think, they came from Bude. They went bankrupt in the war, I think. They'd moved up from Cornwall to Leicestershire. They'd amassed quite a lot of farms but then something went wrong and money was called in. My other grandparents were also from the land, they were threshers. They came from Northampton. My grandmother was rather ambitious and my grandfather bought businesses, he had a bus company and a shoe company and they went bankrupt in the war as well, and then the business that was in her name was a boating business on the river Soar in Leicester. They had a café and I remember the bread slicing machine that sliced extremely fine white bread which you had for your cucumber sandwiches, and they hired out boats.

After the convent I went to art college. I remember the headmistress saying, when I asked for her reference she said 'I hope you won't have to use this. You should be a nurse.' So I ignored that and went to art college.

I did fine art. Painting. Landscape. I was totally dominated by landscape. I remember in Newcastle I rented a cottage by a reservoir and did works about that. We did go to the sea in Newcastle, we went to Whitley Bay and things. And then I moved to London to go to the Slade, and I did paintings there. My working space was so small in the Slade, and I was such a mouse. I started to do installation. My final piece was a sort of river made of canvas running through rocks and I covered it all with slate, I took ground slate and put it onto canvas and then ripped it up, it was an extremely laborious thing to do. In Newcastle, I'd put peat onto canvas, so there was a desire to be so honest to materials that you cease to allude to anything and just put it on there. It was a very rich brown.

I got some criminal compensation because I'd been attacked, and I can remember my tutor originally saying 'Every cloud has a silver lining, so you must apply for this money.' So I did get, I think £2,000, and so when I was at The Slade that came through and I thought 'What can I do with this?' And I looked in Time Out and there was an advert saying 'Boat for Sale', for about the same amount of money and so I went off, phoned up, had an appointment and bought it. I went to a dinner party the same evening and I just announced that I'd bought a boat and the first question was 'What's it made of?' and I had to admit that I didn't know, and the dinner party went sort of quiet, and obviously they just thought here was a total nutcase who's just bought a boat without knowing anything.

It was 28 foot I think, it had been a lifeboat on a liner that had come over from America during the war, so it was about 1940s and it had a tiny little bedroom and a living room and things, all squeezed in, and it was at Kew Bridge. I was sandwiched in between Betty Marsden and her son. Betty always

Judith Frost with sea defences, Chesil Beach

used to say 'I've given up a house in Hampstead to live here. Darling, come and have a drink.' And she used to have a magnificent 100-foot box on a barge. It was hilarious. It was a real community with everything going on. Somebody's boat sank because it snowed one day and somebody's son was a pyromaniac and everyone was frightened of them. Somebody walking along the footpath looking for a shaving point because they'd got to go to the House of Lords and had to shave. That sort of thing.

I had to maintain it myself, and I had no money. At Kew the boat sinks down on to the mud every time the tide goes out, and I used to tip it over and paint the bottom, what I could reach. I had a little garden with tomatoes and artichokes, they were quite successful. Eventually I sold it to a man who arrived in a Morris Minor and a bowler hat. It was extraordinary, I'd given up trying to sell it, and then he arrived and he was a diplomat who felt he'd been overlooked for promotion, so he'd decided to live in London.

I left the Slade and moved to Dorset in 1984. I had a friend who had come to live in Bradford Peverell, so I rented a room in this big house. Strangely I only stayed a year and a half. My hand was forced because they had to sell the house. So I went back to London. So that was my first taste of Dorset and I didn't come back again for some time.

Then I met Margaret Somerville and I bumped into her in a pub. In London I'd had a job working in a prison, and they said 'Oh I know someone who lives in Dorset, perhaps you'll meet them, she married a farmer.' And I said 'Ooh I doubt it,' but lo and behold I bumped into her in a pub, and by chance she said 'I'm going to Portland to look at buying a studio.' She's a painter, so I went with her and she bought the studio, and that was the first time I'd been to Portland, and because of that she then opened it as a gallery, and I'd come down. I had a show there, I

did the opening show with her in 1986, so I was in London but I'd got this connection in Portland, and that went on for some time.

The gallery was on Chesil Beach, right on the beach, tucked into the beach. A guy had run it, he'd been in the navy and was an amateur painter and so he built a gallery to show his own work in and he was going to sell it, so it was an obvious thing for it to continue as a gallery.

My life has been by chance, chance meetings or friends getting me jobs. A friend was teaching in Pentonville prison, she couldn't do the evening classes and so I took them over. Then I worked at the women's prison at Holloway. I taught painting. It was good fun at the beginning. In Pentonville, at that time, it was petty thieving and things and my group was quite light hearted. I can remember somebody saying, when I was showing them a Rembrandt, 'Oh I've got one of those!' He said he'd stolen it from Norway. In fact he hadn't been caught for that, he'd been caught for stealing paint to decorate his flat. Whether it was fantasy or not, I've no idea, it sounds to me, retelling the story, that it is fantasy, but at the time I was mildly curious about this. And there was a guy who said he was the drinking partner of Francis Bacon, and whether or not he was, I don't know. He could have been. It was all fairly light hearted. Working in the women's prison was less light hearted, it was working with the women with psychological problems, and that was scary.

In fact there were never wardens in the class. At Pentonville when I first started there were wardens outside the door, but as the drive to save money increased, one dealt with the whole thing on one's own, and there weren't any wardens anywhere near the place. Certainly with the women who had psychological problems, you felt it was a lifeline for them, because things were so dreadful all the rest of the time, and in a sense the painting allowed people to go in on themselves and to be able to achieve something that they hadn't been able to achieve in their lives to date.

How did Portland strike me? One immediately saw the sea and it seemed wonderful. People from the rest of the county told you that Portland was a bit strange, and one liked it. What I didn't like was coming over on the causeway, it's like an umbilical cord, you feel that maybe that's Portland's view of things because maybe they'd like to be cut off from the mainland, but I didn't particularly like getting here, but as soon as I was here, in this tiny little area, that somebody described as 'the armpit of the coast,' I liked the atmosphere. There was a boat builder's, and a car repairer's, and a fish shop, people were doing things. People making a little business, just doing it, there was a feeling of freedom.

There are no trees in the landscape. The strange thing is that what happened when I lived here was different to what happened when I visited. When I visited I did lots of paintings of the coast, and there are photos of me drawing rocks and things, but that changed when I actually lived here. I realised that the landscape isn't about a view, it's about change, and I would say that has influenced all my work after that. And that was to do with going out on to the beach and seeing that it had changed. Twice a day the tide shifts it, so the whole thing is in flux, and that's the difference between visiting somewhere periodically and living there, and this is pounded into you really, so that influenced my work. But I loved it. I loved walking round, and if you visit Portland by car you might think 'This is a very strange place,' but if you walk round it on the coast path, it is magnificent in parts, and very changeable and varied. The cliffs are both natural and man made, because the quarry has eaten cliffs out of the hills, and it's steeped with history, and all the time you've got this vast expanse of sea, which at night of course, becomes this sort of black hole where there isn't anyone. So you very much feel on the edge, you're on the boundary, and that again is very interesting, and then that of course reflects back to women, particularly, in the Victorian age, who were picking up seaweeds and finding their freedom on the edge of things.

When Margaret first bought the Chesil gallery, which must have been about 1984 or '85, there were other derelict properties around and I asked the council if I could buy one and the council said 'No.' They weren't selling them, they had plans for the area. Then in something like 1991 I got a phone call to say that these places were for sale and was I still interested? This was at the point when I was in London and property had become so expensive.

This place is called Ranter's Lodge and The Dead House. That's the address. I think it was possibly made up by a journalist, they were trying to list these buildings because the council, I think, would have liked to have knocked them down, so there was a groundswell in the area to try and get them listed, so the names refer to their histories, really. Ranter's Lodge, I think was a sort of chapel for only about two years, around 1850 and I think that the Ranters were dissenters from Methodism, and the name just refers to the fact that they ranted. The Dead House, which is the other building, which is later, was used to put the dead bodies in after shipwrecks, of which there were several on Chesil Beach. But again, when you actually ask people about this, it all gets mixed up in rumour, nobody really knows, and then they say the bodies were put in the basement of the pub, which is actually very cold and would make sense.

The *Madeleine Tristan* is the one wreck that was left, there are a lot of photographs of that, it was 1930, but I don't think anyone died on that. There are stories that people died drinking the liquor from the cargo, and they drank so much that they died, but I'd have to research that. But there's a lot of rumour and myth and it all gets lost and forgotten and mixed up.

I've put skylights in it, and it's light and airy now, rather than sombre. But it causes a lot of problems when I say my address. When I went to the doctor's and said I live at the Dead House, the woman got very cross and said 'Write that address properly.' And I said 'It is the proper address.' But that was because the doctor's had been refurbished in the mortuary and they thought I was making reference to it. I found that out later.

The locals were trying to list it. And they did list it, and that's why the council wanted to sell it, because they certainly didn't want to do up a listed building. And so I bid for it and got it, nobody else wanted it. They said 'Oh, a foreigner bought that place down at the bottom, it'll get flooded.' Because at that time we'd already had floods in 1979 and in '89 and the sea defences had been built in between, so that's why the council didn't want it. They knew the sea defences were good and the flooding wasn't in any way as bad, but the sea still comes over the top if it wants to. I think they had wanted to knock it down and build a housing estate on this land but I think they realised they couldn't do that. So I got it to run as two studios, and to rent one of them out. It was derelict and I got a local builder that I worked with and we did it up in a very basic way. That was done in '91 and '92.

When I first saw it, I can remember coming here when it was totally misty, and it was full of pebbles in both buildings, and it was very slimy and green, mildew and stuff growing everywhere. It was damp and dank, like a pit really. It is in the beach but it's also in the pub car park, you might even say it's below sea level, it's certainly at sea level, which is a little difficult when you come to insure it, but I've put skylights into both sides, and the floor in one side was rotten so I've taken that out, and so they're both

light, which was important to me. You do get fantastic light in here. People seem to like coming to them. It's very good in terms of a studio, and people find it very good to write here, because you sense the weather because it comes in through the skylights, but you're totally focussed on what you're doing, whereas with a view you're attracted out and that means you're not focussed. I'm not sure if that changes as you get older, that desire for a view. Anyway, there isn't one. Although a lot of time was spent thinking about how you could try and get one, and mad fantasies about viewing platforms or periscopes.

There were a lot of things which happened which were actually accidental, because the place had been used by kids and they'd seen it as their sort of den. One time after it was done up I came back and my window was smashed and they'd been sitting on the gabions using my two lights on the beam in the middle of the top floor as firing practise, and so there were about 50 stones and a broken window, but that was explainable really, they were just playing and that stopped.

I was young, relaxed and unconcerned. And then, once I had the brake cables cut on my car. I noticed there was fluid and a smell and a stain where something had happened, something had dripped out of somewhere, and in fact what had happened was someone who was a bit mad had gone round the island and cut several people's brake cables, and I thought it could have been a personal attack and actually it wasn't. My neighbour, who is the beach warden, Derek, who lives in the hut opposite, we were always on cordial relations, and he was always very helpful and nice, and it was fine really. There is a group of old men who are often out on the benches, and over the years one has got to know them in a neighbourly way, they're very helpful. Bert comes and helps me with lots of odd jobs. He says 'Well, I'm not doing anything else,' so we set about doing house maintenance.

Portland has changed since I first came here in 1985, there have been a lot of incomers. The Navy have now left and it has been advertised as a tourist place now. I keep to my little world down here. I don't get involved in the politics because I think actually they're so extreme, both on the top hill with the quarries which they're extending, and with the Navy leaving and the submarines coming and the Olympics. I came here because I wanted space. I wanted space.

The sea is a great leveller. Talking to people, it's not like living in rural Dorset, which is very dominated by the rural. This is dominated by the sea, this enormous presence, which can go from being extremely frightening, and unbelievable, unbelievable in the sense that I have been flooded here, and when you sit here most days you cannot believe that water has come into both houses. And it can also be like a duck pond. You can go out on to the esplanade and it looks like a lake, just totally still. I think one thing you realise when you live here is you're totally in tune with the weather. That may be about living in the country as opposed to the town, you know where the wind is coming from.

The weather is very changeable. You don't get too depressed if the weather's not great because it doesn't stay. It can change two or three times in a day. I'd say it has a pretty good climate. On the top of Portland, like yesterday, they were in mist and we were in relative sunshine. It can be that the mainland is in mist and we're not because we stick out.

The beach is stunning. And the sunsets are unbelievable. In a way the emptiness, the still of it, even though the tourists come and see the sunset and things, because the beach is made of pebbles, and although you can swim there, which is great, it isn't for everybody, because it's quite difficult to get in and you can only really swim in the corner when it's calm. There's this undertow which is magical when you hear it, the pebbles being

sucked out, and you don't want to be going in there swimming unless you're a very good swimmer and know what the weather's going to do. So given all that, it is the opposite of Weymouth in a sense, even on a hot day there won't be that many people there, because there's also oil. Not all the time but little pockets of it sometimes, and it is, of course, called Dead Man's Bay. Everything does gravitate there from the whole of Lyme Bay, so things do turn up there eventually.

Portland is limestone. I can remember it being described by somebody who had been born on Portland and had something to do with space exploration. Originally he had started off investigating dust in space and he talked about the difference between dust in space and dust on Portland. He described Portland as a place where everything on it was alive once, made of living organisms, which is so obvious, but when it's said like that you think differently about it. Everything here is in flux, and that has changed my work. I try to evoke that, and I create temporary work. In fact, I came to work with dust because I was flooded.

The first piece of work I made in relation to that was a table, I'd actually been given some money to make three dimensional work by South West Arts and I'd got myself in a bit of a pickle, I was trying to make things with plaster and that sort of thing. And then I suddenly was flooded. I wasn't here, and when I came back the entire two buildings were covered with this mud. I just didn't know what to do so I just put wellingtons on and sort of existed with this mud. The garden had been totally ripped out and all the bits of stuff that I'd been collecting were smashed all over the place, and it was a mud bath out there, and a mud bath in here. And then I had to get something to dry it out, and then I was left with what in the end I called sea dust. It's like a very fine grey sand. And so I then started to think about all the other sands on the island, and I made a table which is a metre square, and on it I piled up all the different Portland stone dusts, including this sea dust, and then other different types of stone dust. In a way it was summing up an area, and I then suppressed them with plates so they became sort of burial mounds so there was a further reference both to death and the landscape, and the pre-history. I realise the work references time.

As soon as you start using stone, I suppose, it has these amazing time spans. So that was one piece of work that the sea just dumped on my doorstep, and then another piece of work which was slightly different was one time I came out of here and the beach was entirely white, it was covered in globules of palm oil. Lumps of fat about a foot across, sometimes smaller. What had happened was a tanker called the *Allegra* had been in a collision and its tanks had been pierced and this palm oil had seeped out into the channel and it had solidified on this beach, and there it was, white. Everybody was amazed. I just started to gather it up and then exhibited it.

It did smell of palm oil I suppose. Sweetish. In fact they were going to get it cleared up but it took so long that by that time the seagulls had eaten it. I'd collected some, there was loads of it, and the seagulls loved it. And because the beach changes it gets covered up, so in fact I don't think they did clear it up in the end. And as soon as the hot weather came it melted and seeped into the sea. I exhibited that for quite a long time. I realised that it floated a bit like an iceberg, and so I put it into the bath and exhibited that with a photograph of an iceberg. That was one piece I was quite pleased with. But you would never have any idea of doing anything with palm oil unless it was dumped on your doorstep. And I've recently done a piece with sea dust in London. I've still got the same dust. I just put it into a bucket and it's up there, dried out like a great stone. I used it to do a table

top piece in London in the Matthew Bown Gallery, that was just a white and a grey table top referencing, just the idea of dust I suppose. And he wrote about it in terms of 9/11.

The problem with living in Dorset, or living outside London, not just for artists but I would think for anyone, is making money. And in the end it's always been a problem that I've had to move out of the county often to make money and one's always grabbing bits of time to be here and to make work, and then *The Weare* prison ship arrived on Portland, and because of my history of working in prisons I got a job there for a year. It actually prompted me to apply for other things, and in fact I got a scholarship to Rome so it meant I didn't have to teach on the prison ship any more. I'm glad I'm not doing it now. I'm too old, I think. I think what happened was, in the end when someone comes back into your class for the fourth time in a year you realise there is something going seriously wrong with this system, and that you're propping up this failing system, and that you should probably go into prison reform, which is far too enormous. And I don't have the skills to do that or whatever, either that or artists are selfish and in the end they don't want to do it. But I'm glad that it prompted me to go off to Rome and do things with dust in Rome.

My garden was savaged to the point of eradication by the flood. It coated everything and killed everything, and I had the idea that I would put my plants in pots, so that I would be ready when the next flood came. It did take a while for things to get growing again, but now what's happened is we haven't been flooded since about 1995, so the plants have now grown out of their pots. You get this incredible salt burn, this fine spray over this area, and if I was a proper gardener I would be hosing it off, but I forget. Even my tamarisk is stunted. My honeysuckle has one flower and it's about 15 years old. It's all about timing. The plants that do well are the ones that disappear into the ground and then come up about May time and don't have to take on this savage weather, but it can happen anytime. It burns. Bay trees, lavenders, they all get savaged. Hebes are very good. They've done me well in 15 years.

Chesil beach changes enormously. Sometimes you get sand up in the corner because all the stones are pulled out by the sea, and then it can deposit them back so that they're almost vertical, a 20-foot or so wall of stones, and then it can be stepped. And then there's all the rubbish. Well apart from the palm oil, I've built things in the house from wood I've found, but because I got flooded in here and all my spare wood store was smashed, I've become a bit slow at gathering things that I don't have an immediate use for. Otherwise you find that you're living in a sea of things that might be useful but then take over your life.

The fear of being flooded is a fear you have to live with. You just think 'I'm not going to do this again. I'm not going to spend three weeks wading through rubbish because I've collected it.' I realise that I'm going to be one of the only people living down here at the moment who's actually experienced it. The beach warden, Derek, has given up his hut which is a shame, he's now 75 and the Environment Agency has taken over and is now giving out these flood warnings which are useless because they're all at the wrong time. Whereas before I felt quite secure because Derek would say 'It's going to come over,' now, although it's all research and the trip buttons are tripped and the woman phones you up and says 'Put your sea defences out,' it's not accurate enough.

My sea defences consist of a board on the gate! Which, as it comes over the wall, probably isn't too good. But the houses have existed since 1850 or whatever, I don't feel too vulnerable. In the past I think they were used to flooding. You just knew it was going to happen. There are people here like Derek who watch the sea every day. They are so experienced, and that experience is going I think. Another experience is coming, I'd say it's not quite tuned in enough yet. It's slightly scary. But I moved here when it was flooded. I built the place with its plugs above water level, except the builder went and put the actual electricity meter on the floor. I was on the ball but not totally on the ball.

We've got a new beach warden, he's one of the only fishermen left, there are two and neither of them can make a living, but they're totally in love with the sea and on the millennium I was here with some friends and we went out on the beach and Steve was in his boat on the millennium with a drink. It was very poignant that. And fishing, Derek said they used to catch 400 crabs a day when he had his business, and now it's four if you're lucky. I don't know what's happening there.

I rent out Ranter's Lodge, that's back again to an artist making money, it's working well and I really enjoy having people renting. A lot of people enjoy coming, maybe it's like recreating my holidays on the sea in Barmouth, rented houses in 1950, there's a touch of that, but I've got stainless steel saucepans! Not aluminium. But not much else. I've still got a Baby Belling.

I think I'll always be here. I like it here.

21. Clem Carter – Fisherman, Weymouth. Born Weymouth 1969.

You've always got your favourite skipper you want to work for and your favourite boat. You can get on with him and you know he's going to earn you a good bit of money.

I was born Portwey Hospital just up by the harbour in Weymouth, 1969. Dad's a sign writer and mother's a greengrocer. He's been a sign writer since he was a boy. He's coming up 70 but he still does about one job a week to pay the bills. He's not full time but he still does it. He does it all by eye. He turned up to paint the back of my boat, and he just paints it straight on, no computer or drawing. He did the sign for Weyfish. He's got a sailing boat, he's had a sailing boat since he was a boy, so we were brought up on sailing boats, pleasure boats. And when we were still in prams he'd set off to Cherbourg or the Channel Islands with the three children and his wife, we'd be gone for five, six weeks, spend our summer holiday roaming around on the breakwater at Cherbourg, collecting the wine bottles out of the rocks. If they had stars around the top you could get a deposit back on the bottle.

His grandfather was a sailor on a cargo ship, his father was an engineer. Papa Knowle, his grandfather was. Mother's family, her parents were from Birmingham. Her father, he was in the Navy for years and then he left the Navy and became an archaeologist. He was doing a book and when he died somebody else finished it and it's now been published. It was about North Dorset, he had a dig up there. Up by the Clay Pigeon. Mum used to crew on the *Winston Churchill* before she had children.

Nan, her family was from Jersey, she came over when the Germans invaded. I think she had three or four sisters and a couple of them ended up in America, one of them lives two doors up, she's always lived two doors up. Grandad hid away on a coal barge to get a lift to Weymouth just as the Germans were invading. That was with his son. They later had a daughter but she was born when they were living in Weymouth.

Some of the family that was left over there. I think there's one still alive now. I went over as a boy and stayed with them, a couple called Sid and Maude. They lived in Rozel on the top of the hill and I remember staying there was a small dog, they had a springer spaniel dog and he had a little fishing boat down in the cove and he took us out to pull his lobster pots up. Have you been to Alderney? Everywhere you look there's German bunkers. When I was in my twenties I worked on a few crabbing boats and the nearest port at night was Alderney, so every night we'd go into Alderney, and in the summer they used to have a carnival week and all the youngsters from the island that had moved away would come back and they'd have parties and barbecues, but some of these parties were in underground bunkers, and you could imagine what used to go on in there!

I grew up in Weymouth. We lived just up from the harbour. The harbour has changed. There's not a fishing community down there any more. There used to be a lot of fishing boats and everybody knew each other and you could park your car and you had a stack of lobster pots or crab pots or nets on the harbour and you could leave them there overnight, but now the traffic warden would ask you to move on. There's less boats, you can't leave your fishing gear and you can't park anywhere, it's just not what it was.

I got a dinghy with a little single cylinder Lister in it when I was about 13, and before and after school we used to go and pull our lobster pots up and put our nets out to catch spider crabs. We

Clem Carter, Skipper and Emma Gorrell aboard Wild Frontier

used to cycle home from school, straight down to the harbour and go and get your nets in. You could do a couple of hundred pounds in a week on spider crabs. When we left school and went to Scotland, we used to bunk off school and the school teachers knew where you were, but they didn't seem to give us too much hassle as long as it was all right with your parents. I used to take the tutor crabs and lobsters, this was at Westham Secondary School, just as you come into Weymouth.

There was about six of us all the same age, all keen to get a job on a crab fishing boat. When we were kids we would set our pots just in Newton's Cove. But in them days you could go down the pier with a bicycle wheel and catch 100 spider crabs in an afternoon. You wouldn't catch them now. You wouldn't catch anything there now. A boat used to come in from Guernsey, and he'd come over to Weymouth, pick up all the spider crabs in Weymouth, nip down to Dartmouth, pick up all the spider crabs and crab down there, then he'd go over to France and make a good profit.

When I left school I got a little boat, bigger than what I had, the little one was 16 foot, then I got a little bit bigger one, but my mates were going to work for other people further afield, up in Scotland and they were coming home saying 'We've earned this' and it sounded like they were having a real good time. I needed to get some more experience and they were earning such good money that I left my boat tied up in Weymouth and went with this guy from Guernsey who went up just near Lewis, Stornoway and back down again. It's just a loch, and to go to the pub was about an hour's walk.

French boats that the French were updating to more modern boats. They had more funding than us I think. The Guernseymen were buying up all the French boats. We were only catching crab. We were on a crabber. She was about 60 foot. She carried ten

tonne of crab live. The skipper was a Guernseyman, a guy called Peter, we were on shares.

Yeah, the first place we went, there were two boats from Guernsey and the other guy had been there before, he knew a bit more about the area than we did, and he says 'We'll go this way and you go the other way.' There was a radio we used to have on board, they used to call it the Big Set and at a certain time he'd call the other guy, he was probably going 100 miles north, and he went to Rona, North Rona, and we called him up this night and he said 'Yeah, we shot the gear away at midnight and hauled it up this morning and it was full up.' He had six tonne. We were getting two tonne a day, so we shot off to an island next to that called *Sula Sgeir*, and we shot all the gear round *Sula Sgeir* and by the time we'd got all the gear off the deck, we got a couple of hours kip and it was time to haul again and the crabs, crab pots, you couldn't get another crab in them. To swing them over the side you had to put two hands on them. We were using skate and gurnard as bait. Nobody had gone up there with crab pots.

We were doing 120, 130 bongos a day. Bongos are those big blue pots you see on the harbour. It was all going to a processing plant in Inverness I think, we could only carry ten tonne live and from Ullapool to *Sula Sgeir* was a ten-hour jaunt for us, and so by the time you've wasted a whole day going in and a whole day going out, and we'd fish for three days, so one and a half days we'd be able to keep live, the rest we couldn't keep live. So it was dying, so you're not going to get such a good price for that. It needs to go somewhere that it can be processed straight away. We were getting about 40p a kilo, which now you wouldn't bother for that, but in those days it wasn't so bad. Nowadays the boats are a lot bigger and better and they can stay there all year round now, but you had to be on your way home by the beginning of September. We came down through the Irish Sea on a 60-foot boat, we'd carry all the pots on board, and you had to be really careful the way you load the boat up, all the weight's got to be in the right place. 700 plastic pots is, I mean just the rope is ten tonne. It's a hell of a lot of weight. You can't have them shifting.

I was up there for two or three months. I went back the following year with a different skipper, it was a company with a crab factory on Paignton Harbour, big crabbing family, Browse, and I got a job with them, because when these two Guernsey boats came back and news travelled, the next year everyone was there, and this company just had a brand new steel shelter deck, state-of-the-art boat built, so I thought I'd go on that one, because that's luxury. Bunk, shower, heated oilskin locker, there was a cook on there. Cooking in bad weather? Well up there it's not so bad because whatever way the wind is, you can go round the other side of the island, but sometimes if you're in the channel, you're out all night, cooking normally, the skipper would run downwind whilst you're cooking or whilst you're eating. Bad seas? Yeah. Seen some good seas on the way back down. The worst ones was down off of the Scilly Isles, you get a real good swell down there. A 40-foot wave sounds big, but it's not much really. Sometimes if you walk down to Portland Bill you see some big waves down there. But if you were in a boat they'd really look big, wouldn't they?

We'd get in first thing in the morning, unload the crabs, shower, and a pint, and you'd leave at tea time so you were back hauling again first thing in the morning. We spent a lot of time at Kinlochbervie, some interesting nights out there. We seen whales, I seen shoals and shoals of whale here before, ten mile off the Bill. If you did ten days and you got £1,500, you'd had a good trip. The boat would go to sea non stop, and if you wanted a week off you had to arrange cover, car hire and not many people drive on their own. It's 14 hours to Paignton.

How many crew? The first one was four crew and the skipper, five altogether, but 'cause the first trip we didn't expect, we didn't even think it was possible to catch that amount of crab in one day, so we were totally not prepared for it, and we could have done with a couple more hands. I can remember, we were so tired after six weeks of catching all this crab, you know the old payphones where you put your fingers in? Well I had to go and phone my mum, and I remember going into this phone box after unloading one morning, and putting my fingers into the thing, and they were so fat and swollen and sore, after that first trip on the old wooden boat, the *Vagabond de Mer*. It's still going, my mate owns it now, a lad from Teignmouth.

The Scottish fishermen? Well it was only two seasons and the Scotchmen thought 'Shit, why aren't we doing this?' Most of the people catching crab were all down south. The Guernseymen were doing it before we were. I remember as a little kid sitting on the pier seeing these Guernsey crabbing boats coming in, and then you saw people in Weymouth who were running angling boats changing to crab fishing. Same as what happened in Scotland. In August, in the summer when we were in *Sula Sgeir*, the lobsters, we went down to the Flannans and filled up with lobsters, and the lobsters were so big and old, they all died in the boat. They all died because they were past their sell-by date. Nobody had ever fished them. That was good fishing there. One of the boats went right to the west there, Rockall. They were chasing a different breed of crab, they called them king crab, and they heard that you could catch them out there. They were from Paignton but the boats were based in Scotland. Trevor Bartlett, the owner of this boat, they designed these pots and they went down there and they did catch a few but the water was so deep.

That water up there is no different to the English Channel. All the buoy lines, the crew don't spend any time in the wheelhouse, you went in there to give the skipper a cup of tea and that was it. I remember measuring out the buoy lines and it was no different to the English Channel. The only time we used longer buoy lines was south west of the Scillies in that big swell. You need longer buoy lines there. You don't get a very good slack tide.

The second boat was called *Kingfisher*. That's still there now. We'd fuel up in Kinlochbervie, the closest, or Ullapool. We did really well on those sort of trips, but it's hard work and you'd try and do two or three weeks and then get back for a couple of days, and then go back for another two or three weeks, but I used to try not to do too much in the same place, I'd have a good few months on one boat and then join another boat, and try the best of everything. You've always got your favourite skipper you want to work for and your favourite boat. You can get on with him and you know he's going to earn you a good bit of money. There's a couple that you know they're going to earn you the best money, but he's going to treat you like shit.

Shares? They were all different but I used to get about ten per cent each, so half for the crew. The skippers owners? Yeah. Most of them, apart from that *Kingfisher* one. The best one we ever worked on was the *Kael Coz* but she ran aground at Padstow. I quit about two weeks before to do another trip to Scotland. I quit because she was going for a refit and was going to be out of action for six months, so I went off and when they went back to sea with this new shelter deck and new wheel house, they were fishing up at Lundy and they were steaming into Padstow one night and he ended up steaming up the rocks. He'd just spent about fifty grand on the boat and he hadn't told the insurance company so he only got what it would have been, I think.

We went to Grimsby as well, did a couple of months there.

There was just as much crab there as there was in Scotland, but it was all smaller. We went to Dartmouth and got a job on a crabber. I had a girlfriend who was living down that way and I got a job down at Kingswear. It was good fishing as well. We had one lad who came to work with us, this is on that *Kael Coz*, and we was chucking the pots back over, it was a summer's day, it was quite calm, but a rope had lassoed him round the neck and dragged him over the side, and nearly killed him. It went right through his windpipe. It was horrible. But he's still around.

Spider crabs? You don't see them much any more. Nobody really wants them. Yeah. I had a bad year one winter so I got a job filleting fish at Paignton Harbour, a place called Brixham Sea Fare. Nigel Bloxham, I worked for him one year just filleting plaice. It was cold on the hands.

With crabs there's no guts. Every crab's got to have both claws clipped, and in the English Channel now, you catch two bongos per string, that's good, but when we were in Scotland it was 25 bongos per string, and every crab's got to have its claws clubbed, but after that experience up there, we were real fast at doing the claws. You could still do that, it's like riding a bike.

We've been working on that scallop boat you seen us come in on, and it's unbelievable what you see smashed up. When the dredgers come up and they empty out on the deck, there's crabs, lobsters, starfish, loads of life all smashed to pieces. There's talk of a scalloping ban in Lyme bay within six miles or something. it would make a hell of a difference.

I dive for them, I enjoy that, and I don't see there's any harm in that. There's no shortage of scallops, but those dredgers, to catch one basket of scallops, if we go diving over a patch of scallops that somebody's been dredging on, I can swim along the channel in the sand and I can count how many dredges he's got on each side because you can see the lines in the sea bed.

Smashes it to pieces. And the worst ones are those beam trawlers. The whole belly is just a massive chain, and that's just smashing everything up. Hopefully the fuel is slowing them down. There's quite a few people turned over to line caught fishing. My mate's got a line caught bass and scallop business. He gets more for his fish. When a restaurant buys scallops that have been caught by a dredger, they're all gritty, but the scallops a diver gets are all nice and clean.

I worked from Kingswear, then we spent a whole summer at St Mary's, that was really nice. Whilst we were down there, once a week we had to go down to Penzance to unload, so we'd go there once a week, and the more you're catching the more frequent you have to go backwards and forwards. Then St Peter Port, we done a few weeks, a couple of months out of there, I suppose. Then Stornoway, Breasclete, Ullapool, Kinlochbervie, Grimsby, nowhere really up the east. Alderney. We still go to Alderney now. It's nice there.

So I came back from travelling around and working on other people's boats, and I was working on a northern clipper down in Dartmouth, and it was the end of the season and I had a bit of money saved up, and I thought 'If I don't spend this on something, I'm going to blow this in the winter.' So I bought a fibreglass hull and put it in my mate's field, who's a farmer, down in Devon, and every time I had a bit more money I'd buy the wheelhouse, or the engine, and then the girlfriend I was with down there, that all went wrong, and I missed Weymouth, so I put the boat on a trailer and brought it back to Weymouth and put it down by the quay. She was called *Giselle*, she's in Ireland now, she was 20 foot, I sold that one and bought another one, I had a wife and a baby on the way, and that was a 26 foot, and I bought that from a guy called Gerald Driver. I went whelking and crabbing with that one, did really well with that one, and

then somebody on Portland who owned this one died, so I bought that one off of the widow, got a really good deal on that. I worked that one for two seasons crabbing, she was the *Royal Manor*, but every time you paid the crew, the next day they were drunk, and you'd get outside their house at five o'clock in the morning and no lights were on, and then the girlfriend would say 'He didn't come home last night,' and I thought 'Why am I bothering doing this?' And I should have stayed with that one because I could have worked it single handed, but instead I borrowed a bit of money from the bank to get this one.

Then I had so much hassle with crew, and at the time, a nagging wife with two little kids, it was a nightmare, so somebody just happened to be walking along the harbour one day, and that day the crew had let me down, and this person happened to be walking along the harbour and said 'Is it for sale?' and I said 'Yeah,' And I said a stupid price and they came the following week and they took it, which allowed me to buy the next boat, the one I've got now, cash, all paid for.

Wild Frontier, and I only go to sea on my own. I don't need a crew and I can take eight or nine people out fishing, and I'm paid before I leave the harbour. Daewoo 350, but it's de-rated from 500. I still fish in the winter. I like to keep working, and you don't get a lot of exercise with this, you're just strolling around talking to people, undoing tangles and that sort of stuff, so you need to get a bit of exercise now and again. That was about six years ago. We've got about 25, 30 angling skippers down there now. We're the busiest port in the country for angling. They pay whether they catch or not. They pay 45 quid to go out fishing for the day. The cheaper trips can be 40, sometimes 35, but if they want to go out and try and get the big stuff it's normally about 45 quid, and if you try and you don't want to take out any less than nine. There's some reefs and some sand banks out in the channel. One of them's called the Penis Bank. We just make names up for most of the stuff.

There used to be a Decca navigator, you couldn't buy them, you could only rent them, and the display was a box the size of a portable TV, and then the electric box to go with it was the size of another portable TV, and the wiring and the aerials, and now it's all in that. Favourite wrecks? People have been going to a wreck called the *Salsette*, the beginning of May you normally get a shoal of bass turning up there, then there's pollock on the HMS *Delight*. There's so many wrecks. If you saw some of our track plotters, it's just wrecks everywhere. They're after the bigger fish. Bass, pollock, cod, ling, some people like turbot fishing. Last week we were supposed to be on a five day trip to Alderney. 80 per cent of that trip would have been fishing for turbot. You get a lot of that over there. There's a lot of sand banks around the Channel Islands. Anglers aren't interested in catching conger.

You get to the Channel Islands on a Monday night and get rid of the customers, they all go ashore to a B&B, then we go back to a mooring where we've got a mate who leaves us a dinghy out, we go back to the boat, gut the fish, wash it, pack it in ice and then either go ashore for a meal or make something on the boat. The fish they've caught go into a cold store on my boat. We've got an insulated fish room which keeps stuff up to a week, we take half a tonne of ice with us in the summer. We get that from Weyfish. If they're not catching it's not fun for anyone. Most of us get our business from the internet these days. People come from everywhere. We've had them from all over. They're good trips if you've got a group of workmates, we go for a week and they have a good time. If we're on a wreck and there's lots and lots of fish there, when everybody's had two or three we'll drift a little way further from the wreck and they'll say 'Oh we've stopped catching,' because we want to keep it for the next day

and the next day. Whereas if you were commercial you'd catch it all in one day, wouldn't you? Just wipe it out.

Trawler races used to be fun, but now all the characters have gone, to keep Weymouth Trawler Race going the people who organise it have to call up all the other harbours to get them to come down, because there ain't enough trawlers in Weymouth. I think the last Weymouth Trawler Race there were two boats from Weymouth, there were three from Guernsey, two from Brixham, it's just a con for the council to make a load of money and the pub owners.

Living on Portland? I like it. I never thought I'd live on Portland but I'd have moved here ten years ago. We were living in the town centre in Weymouth and it was mad. The things we used to see out the window in the middle of the night. You get the fog. I suppose it's because you're higher up.

A lad went over the side recently, didn't he? Yeah. That was the second one to go over, they made these ramps on the crabbing boats so that when you're throwing the pots back over, you don't have to physically throw them back over, they get pulled off the ramp. In the space of just over a year two boys have been washed over the ramp. Two boys the same age. Both Portland lads. One on one boat, one on the other.

NOTES

The P& O liner *Salsette* was on her way from London to Bombay when she was torpedoed by UB-40 on 20 July, 1917. She was 440 ft long, had 600 portholes in her white hull and had yellow funnels. She held the Blue Riband for the fastest crossing of the Atlantic and was described as 'one of the most beautiful steamers ever built'.15 crew were killed. Some say she is one of the best wreck dives in the UK.

HMS *Delight*: She was a D class destroyer sunk by German aircaft off Portland on 29th July 1940. Six ratings and three officers were killed including the ship's captain, Cdr Fogg Elliott. 57 were wounded.

22. Emma Gorrell – Café owner and caterer, Weymouth & Portland. Born Plymouth 1973.

People say that island life is very inward looking but I think it's an outward looking place. Because our life is based around the sea for Clem and the weather for what we both do, we're constantly looking out.

My father's a chef and my mother's a nurse. Naval on my father's side, and mother's side, well, mixed bag really. They travelled around the world and my grandfather's somewhere in Australia and my grandmother enjoyed that life. We were schooled mostly in Africa, we left Dorset when I was three. Where in Africa? Round the south mostly, but we moved all over the place. With my dad being a chef he dragged us round most parts of the south, my brother was born in Swaziland, right in the middle of the pocket there.

Father was employed by the Holiday Inns, and they tossed a coin when they were young, my mum and dad, would they go to Oz or would they go to Africa, and they got to go to Africa. I think that's where my love of the wilderness comes from.

Happy childhood? Yes, absolutely amazing. I have no regrets about being dragged around the place. Didn't stay anywhere longer than two years and it was a nice way to be. Those big open spaces are what I crave for now sometimes. Educated in English schools? Yes. We first went to school in Uplyme, and then came across to Dorchester, so I did my GCSEs in Dorch and then did a degree in Plymouth in environmental science. I enjoyed it.

Catering? We've always cooked really, we haven't had much choice. My dad's mother used to keep a really good healthy farmhouse kitchen alive while we spent all our childhood holidays there. We had a grocer deliver to the house on a push bike and grew a lot of veg, so we learnt an awful lot then. I've always enjoyed cooking. Learned from my dad? Yeah, and now I'm always ringing him to ask him things, like today I had to ring him, we've got a big function on this coming Saturday and I sometimes need reassurance. So I rang Dad quickly, 'How much pork will I need for 97 people? It's a casserole,' and he tells me. Yeah he still works and he's a good chef, he's very relaxed, nothing fazes him. No shouting? No effing and blinding? Oh yeah, there's plenty of that, I've worked for him in kitchens and it was an eye opener! Lots of effing and blinding, but I think that's a chef's perogative, isn't it? Lets off all the steam.

I used to work in the holidays in Dad's pubs and I don't think there's a café in Weymouth I haven't worked in at some point, so I know a lot of people around the town, and I do enjoy it. I love feeding people. It's a good feeling.

My own café? The café came our way in, oh, it wasn't so long ago, maybe five years ago, and it was up on the seafront, it still is, going great guns. Café Blue, it's a great little place, very small, and we opened all year, it was a real thing of mine, I wanted to make sure that locals were looked after as much as holidaymakers.

Winter? Yeah. It's a great time, I really like it. About April time you get the optimism of summer and that vibrancy, and everyone's a little bit nervous of what's around the corner and will it be peeing down all summer? Is it going to be a bumper season? Dependent on the weather ? Oh, almost entirely. Weymouth Bay is majestic and sweeps around in a huge gigantic curve, but if you get an onshore wind those seafront cafes really struggle because nobody wants to go up there, the sand's blowing a hooley. There are some nice cosy cafés nestled in town, so you've no need to go and expose yourself to the wilds!

We would stay open the whole winter. Myself and one other, and he was great, a really good chap, a real bohemian he was. He was into it, had the same passion for it as I did, and we loved him. Finding staff? They tended to find us more than we went looking for them, which was really nice. Most of them were customers or kids from town. Dan, my right hand man was somebody I'd spotted ages ago and I thought he'd be just great, he's got punky hair, crazy tattoos and make up, but a real gentle manner. He's six foot seven, a real character, and all the old ladies at first were slightly shocked. It'd be OK in London, you'd expect it, but Weymouth's a little bit more reserved I suppose. He gauged every person through the door and pitched himself on their level. He cared about people and and was proud of his creations - his coffee cakes were works of art. In the café he tapped into something he was really good at.

Regulars? Oh yeah, every day, and I really miss them. I really miss them. Oh crumbs, there were so many, there were some really nice people, we had one guy who would come in every single day, and it's a merit of how well your coffee shop's doing, whether you've got this chap drinking there or not. He's an eccentric ex-school teacher from Cologne, and he has a massive shopping bag with not much in it apart from an international newspaper, and weather reports. Absolutely integral to how you function each day is whether you've spoken to him about the weather. He'd predict the fronts and whether we'd be busy on this day or that day, it was great. Always right, a believer in St Swithuns. If it rains on St Swithun's day you'd have a really wet summer. I do miss that guy. Espresso Man.

It was a coffee shop, so really good coffee, lovingly prepared sandwiches, homemade cake, coffee and walnut, Victoria sandwich, scones, plenty of clotted cream, that kind of stuff.

Traditional seaside grub really. We didn't do night times. We didn't want to work too hard! We opened very early and served breakfast to mostly families, ferry passengers, Weymouth is a Channel Island port, and old folk who have always risen early. We liked our evenings off! Well we sold it last summer, 2006, so this will be my first summer not there. It's Easter now and I'm thinking 'Gor, it'd be nice to be up there, feeling summer creeping up.'

In some ways, the wintertime was the most interesting time on the seafront. All the local characters would come out of the woodwork and whilst making money is harder, you've more chance to learn about folk. Everyone is known by their favourite drink or by some funny mannerisms: *Backwards Forwards Man, The Incredible Floating Girl*, all the curly perms and coach trips, hen parties and drunkards mostly. I miss them. We also looked after the beach workers, the Punch and Judy man, the dishy Pedalo boys, Beach Control and all the lifeguards. A real community and not a bad view.

I do outside catering now. We do a range of different events, weddings, a lot of corporate events, anniversary dos. I'm hoping to do more on the boat with Clem, cater for more boat trips which I think will be fun, picnics, garden parties, that kind of thing, and I love it because each one's so very different. I don't have a formula that I can take round to people, each person's different, their requirements are different and it's nice chatting to people and letting my brain fizz away as to what they actually want. It's nice to be cooking and looking after people.

How did I meet Clem? He kept coming into the coffee shop. Well he's so handsome! The girls would just drop everything they were doing and run to his table and it was embarrassing really, I tried to be really cool but I fancied him like mad. He went out to sea and one day phoned and said 'Would I like to meet him for a drink?' And I thought 'Oh my goodness! I'd love to.' But I've since learnt that it wasn't him, it was his friend that phoned because he's so desperately shy, he put his friend up to it, and I wouldn't know his voice, he'd only ever asked for coffee, so we went out. It's great. We went to the pub on the harbourside, and then he said 'I've got to go and collect a crew member for work tomorrow, I've got to go now.' So that was fine, I thought he was just driving to Portland but he was driving to Exeter to pick them up!

We've been together a couple of years, not terribly long but it's great. I've been on Portland for a while on and off, in-between trips overseas, I've been there, I don't know, going on ten years I suppose, but we bought our house last year. It's just near Church Ope which is a little cove just below the museum along from Portland Bill. There's so much here, but Portland still feels a bit secret. Weymouth and Portland are a borough, but they've both got different characters and that's the really nice thing about living on the island, Weymouth as a busy centre, but it has got all these amazing places on its doorstep. I like driving home across the causeway and putting all the chaos of Weymouth behind, it's really peaceful.

But to be a Portlander you need to be born here. I love it and hopefully we'll spend the rest of our lives here, it feels good. All the old school people are very keen to be identified as Portlanders, yeah. People say that island life is very inward looking but I think it's an outward looking place. Because our life is based around the sea for Clem and the weather for what we both do, we're constantly looking out. I think a lot of people would be like that, weather dependent, facing the elements.

Traditions and superstitions? You can't say the R word! No, you can't say it. And there was a thing recently, a woman was in a competition on the television, she was a Portlander, it was a

Saturday night show and the question was about *The Curse of the Were-Rabbit*. To win the money she said that word, and something really bad happened on the island because she'd said it and she was a Portlander. I can't remember the incident entirely now. The holes in Portland's centre were blamed on the bunnies but the real cause was probably the quarrying.

I hope to spend more time on boats this year because I'm going to have more time, I'm not tied to the café. Yeah. I would like to learn a bit more about it really. Do I fish? I don't, no. It's not that I don't, it's just that I haven't had time. I'd like to learn a bit more. I'd like to cook fish, it's exciting to try new ways of preparing stuff Clem brings home. We are spoilt really. You feel really smug knowing how fresh everything is. When I learn more I can be of more help to Clem then. He does these amazing trips across to Alderney, across to Guernsey, he's always looking for good crew. He helps me so much with the catering. He's so silent, he quietly gets on with it, and he knows me, so knows what needs doing, and I want to be of equal help to him really, so I need to learn my ropes. I think that's the way it's going to go eventually, we'll definitely work more together.

He supplies fish? Yeah sometimes for my catering. In fact we've got a big celebration coming up in May where we've to do a big splendid display on ice, he's going to supply the fish for that, yeah. Local suppliers? Yeah, I think you have to. To sleep at night you need to know that what you're doing's proper really. We're really lucky, Clem's mum is a greengrocer in Dorchester. She's much more than a greengrocer, she supplies most of Dorset with its fruit and veg and homemade cakes. She had a shop and the business got too big for the shop, so now they have a distribution centre, and we supply most of the harbourside restaurants here. We go down as far west as Exeter, right the way up north Dorset, Swanage to the east. She's a very hard working person, but it's all food related. We all speak the same language.

Polish workers? Yeah, we've got heaps. They're great. I don't know if they're indicative of Poland in general but they're such grafters. They're young, they're not studying language, but what we pay them here in fruit and veg is the same as what a general practitioner goes back home, and that's why they're willing to do the hours. They're a good team. A little bit secretive. They don't want to tell too many people too many things, and a selective knowledge of English! Weymouth now has a shop selling Polish food and the sausages are fantastic.

The Olympics? 2012? It's a mixed bag really. At first it was mass hysteria, it was a great collective hooray, it was great news for the area, and a real buzz, a lot of people had worked really hard to get it to happen, but you know how people are, they think 'Ooh yes, but, have you thought of this?' And I don't know about the sustainability of the investment that's being made. Probably the money would have been better spent in the hospitals or somewhere on a project for something more sustainable, although we haven't seen a massive investment yet. A lot of lip service but not a lot of action right now. I can't help thinking it's got to be fun. We've got to celebrate the coast and the resources that we've got, so I can't help thinking that, but I'm not going to think I'll be a millionaire or anything. We have been using the boat to help with sea trials and competitions at the Sailing Academy. The sport is so exciting for youngsters, really exhilarating and involves a real sense of pride in competitors. It would be nice to think of all these spin offs from the Olympics generating local work and optimism.

Other characters in the café? Simon Eastwood? Oh crumbs! Is he still alive? I didn't even know his name. I liked him an awful lot because he is an eccentric and you give him an inch and he'd be really grateful because he'd rock into town, and he lives in a hole in the ground, doesn't he? With his cider press, he lives in a hole so he's always a bit grubby and he insists on wearing a bowler hat, and he's always very well dressed, carries a flagon of cider, but you don't worry too much about that, and he'd always come in on that Burton Bradstock bus so he'd always get here really early, and our café was the only one open in the winter on the seafront. So he'd get off the bus and he'd always reek of cider, but living with his press… and he'd tell me he was off to court that day, and I didn't know the guy but he is famous locally, you read about him in the paper and he's upset some neighbour. I can imagine he's an aggressive sort, he's always upset somebody, but he'd go off to court and he'd come back at the end of the afternoon and he'd tell me how he'd got on, and sometimes he wouldn't come back, but I'd see him get on the bus later on in the day, he's a great guy. I always worried if he didn't come back that he hadn't been good in court. He was one of those grateful for some kindness but I don't think many tolerated him.

Other characters? Well there's the Portland twins. James calls them modern-day recyclers. They must be in their sixties now, maybe not that old, and they've lived on Portland all their life, shared a bed, shared everything, still do, and they come down to harbour side and collect anything and keep it in tubs. It's all really well organised in their house, so they'd have a corner for stacked newspapers, and a corner for combs, plastic combs, tin cans and carrier bags. Clem had to go in there one day and help them read a meter for the electricity and he couldn't believe it, it was bulging at the seams this house, full of junk. They stand in their window from dawn until dusk, looking out, just abusing people that walk past, shouting obscenities. They recently had to move house, they've moved into Weymouth, got a smaller house. They live just on the outskirts, I don't think they'd be allowed in the town, they don't adhere to the rules, that's why they're interesting. And this one guy carries a paper takeaway cup everywhere that he goes, he must be fit, he walks for miles and he'd come into the café and he'd only want to spend 50p, that's all. And he'd say to us 'I've had me breakfast' every morning, 'What have you had for breakfast?' 'I had lasagne. I had lasagne for breakfast today.' And he was 'Lasagne Man' of course. I'd never seen him eat, he was tiny, had very long fingernails and always wanted to spend 50p. Yeah, he could buy a cup of tea for that and sometimes and I'd give him a scone or a slab of cake. And he'd smoke a cigarette. I'm surprised we haven't seen him now, he's always around.

Are there any that are sadly missed? Oh yeah. Loads of 'em. There was, one of them, Johnny he was called, this going back a good ten years, he had a dog called Zappa, and when he went it was a really sad case because he was young, he'd chosen not to take part. And he really looked after his dog. He passed away. I don't think his lifestyle helped… There are 'good eggs' and 'bad eggs' and Weymouth attracts them all. A very transient population, if you are down on your luck you may as well be by the seaside.

Clem, he works on the harbour so he was constantly meeting customers and things. But we spend hours down there just watching people go by, and if we go to any other town we always have to go and find the boats!

23. Rupert Best – Submariner, Non-executive Director of Portland Port and West Dorset fruit farmer. Born London 1943.

One of the only VCs awarded in this country in the Second World War was won on the Foylebank in Portland Harbour by Leading Seaman Jack Mantle when the ship was attacked by Stukas on the 4th July 1940. She sank but not before Jack Mantle won fame for fighting his gun when fatally wounded. He is a local hero and is buried on Portland in the Naval Cemetery.

My earliest memories are of living with my mother in houses owned by relations and family friends, first at Maiden Newton and then Dorchester, whilst my father was at sea. My grandfather had gone out to India as a forester, and when he came back in 1921 he bought a farm, Hincknowle, in Melplash. He remained interested in trees – he advised the County Council - and he planted up orchards. He was the youngest son of Lord Wynford at Wynford Eagle, which takes us back a couple of hundred years. The first Lord Wynford was a friend of the Prince Regent and his solicitor, who later became Attorney General and eventually Chief Justice of the Court of Common Pleas. He was also MP for Bridport. He went to Crewkerne Grammar and was a close contemporary there of Captain Hardy of Trafalgar and *Victory* fame. He represented him in a court case and one of his sons joined the Navy and was a midshipman with Hardy onboard HMS *Ramillies* in the War of 1812.

My father was the eldest son of six children. He joined the Royal Navy as a 13-year-old cadet at Dartmouth. In the late 1930s he was serving in the New Zealand Division in HMS *Leander* and met my mother in Auckland. She came over to England at the height of the U-boat war to marry him. He qualified as a gunnery officer during the war, and was much involved in a whole series of amphibious landings, Salerno, Walcheren and Normandy on D-Day, where he was the Force Gunnery Officer for Juno Beach. He trained up a lot of landing craft, and I think particularly the rocket ships and vessels like that. His role at the time of the landings was coordinating Naval Gunfire Support for the Army ashore. His last job in the Navy was as Flag Officer, Gibraltar, which he left in 1966. By coincidence, although it eventually came to nothing, he then did some work for the Bath & Portland Group on a proposed container port at Portland.

I joined Dartmouth in 1961. My early recollection was spending an awful lot of time rushing around. Very exhilarating and I have never been so fit in my life but it was only later that one felt 'It's all very well rushing around, but which direction are we rushing in?' My midshipman's time was spent in HMS *Chawton* a minesweeper, when we became involved in the Brunei Rebellion in 1962, and then in HMS *Hermes*, an aircraft carrier.

I eventually went to submarines in 1966. I spent the first three years in various diesel submarines, including 18 months out in Australia. Then came back and did my nuclear training. I was a seaman, so I had a couple of commands. HMS *Ocelot* was a diesel boat and HMS *Courageous* a nuclear Fleet Submarine. As it happens they're both museum ships now. In *Ocelot*, I think we probably had the only home port visit to Bridport ever made by a submarine. We anchored off West Bay and the Mayor and various dignitaries came onboard. We had a jolly run ashore and the only problem we had was that the tide was still out when the pubs shut in the evening and it took a bit of time for the fishing boat to get us back to the ship.

Rupert Best comes up for air, inner breakwater, Portland Port

Being captain of any Queen's ship is an enormous privilege and pleasure, to which nothing else can compare. The qualifying course for command was, and is still, called 'The Perisher'. It was an intensive six months and about two thirds of the students made it to the end. In those days, the seven weeks at sea was mostly spent attacking warships using short range torpedoes in close proximity to the targets, in which we were taught how to go to the limits of safety in order to achieve the operational objective. It was a commonplace to claim that 'attacking is better than sex'. It was certainly exciting, mentally and physically demanding, with the adrenaline flowing, and deeply satisfying when all went well.

Contact with Russian submarines? Yes. I think most of us got involved in one way or another, at different times in our careers. There is much talk nowadays about the Cold War, but at the time one didn't really think of it in quite those terms, though certainly there was a perceived threat from the Soviets. HMS *Courageous* went down to the Falklands. The boat arrived back in Scotland on the day of the invasion, after six months in California, where she had been conducting the final acceptance trials of RN Sub-Harpoon, the Navy's first submarine launched anti-ship missile. We had it down south but didn't use it.

The deterrent submarines, what was then Polaris and is now Trident, stay out for two months or more. In other nuclear submarines, our longest patrols, because it took about two weeks to get down to the Falklands, tended to be about 90 to 110 days. Crew? About 120. Personal space is very limited on a submarine. For some people it's limited to a bunk secured in a torpedo rack. Most people had their own bunks but some shared by hot bunking. If you could draw the curtain, that was your personal space.

Navigation? In the older conventional boats, we spent quite a lot of time working out of Portland where, if you were deep for three or four hours and unable to take a fix, the strong tides in the Channel could carry the submarine quite a way from the dead reckoning position. Making use of a tidal atlas, we used to work on a system of a pool of errors, so that we could stay safe by knowing we were somewhere inside an ever expanding circle…

The job of submarines at Portland was to act as the loyal opposition for the destroyers and frigates working up and we used to spend a week or so at a time down there. Normal shipping? You always had that, in peace time. The time you had to be most careful was when returning to periscope depth, having been deep, because when you're deep you're safe from collision with surface ships. There were one or two accidents in the Channel over the years.

Portland used to host nuclear submarines pretty regularly. The first port visit outside the USA by USS *Nautilus*, the world's first nuclear vessel, was to Portland in 1957. Years later, I visited there in a boat, when we spent two weeks alongside working with the scientists, and the intention is that it should happen again. We hope that we'll be getting one this year for the first time since Portland Port took over.

Quietness was key to everything we did. Acoustic tiles? All those sorts of things. Yes, you can hear them pinging you. Detecting ships is not so bad in the Channel, but in places like the Mediterranean, you get various bathymetric layers, where different layers of water can block out noise, just as you get refraction with light, and longer at a safe depth, that is below the hull of the deepest draught ships. We would listen for propeller cavitation, and then, as ships became quieter, we were looking for the narrow band frequencies of machinery noise. One was always concerned about what technology the Russians had to detect submarines but on the whole, once you were down, you were not detectible.

Torpedoes? We carried between 25 and 30. They were essentially of two types. One was the Mark 8, which was a straight running torpedo with a big bang and fired in salvos. It was a development of Whitehead's original, with a maximum effective range of some 4-5,000 yards, although the ideal firing position was 1,150 yards just abaft the beam of the target. Wire-guided, electric-driven torpedoes were used initially as anti-submarine weapons. Submarine against submarine was not easy and required much more control over the weapon. Those torpedoes have now developed into the Spearfish, which is used against both ships and submarines. The submarines are now fitted with Tomahawk, so they are into land attack and bombing from long range.

Although the Commanding Officer has ultimate responsibilit, in the Royal Navy, management of the nuclear power plant is in the hands of professional engineers. The reactor is a kettle. It produces steam to drive the turbines. It is very well protected and one gets used to sleeping within 50 feet of it. All the accommodation in those boats was for'ard of the reactor.

The food in the older boats could be quite good, but we had a limited capacity for fresh vegetables and so on. Cooking in diesel submarines had its own skills. I remember, when I was second-in-command, coming home from service in Australia, I said that I was fed up with the scrambled eggs and that I could do better and would cook breakfast for the ship's company. I quickly found that cooking scrambled eggs from egg powder for about 60 people was rather different from having to cook with fresh eggs for oneself at home and before long gave way to the chef. This was an old wartime boat where water was limited and facilities fairly basic. Submarines were sometimes kept out at sea

unexpectedly for operational reasons. In one case, I remember the submarine's First Lieutenant telling me that the main problem was running out of toothpaste. On another occasion, when I was in an American boat, the coca cola and ice cream stocks got a bit low.

On British submarines there's alcohol on board, though many people didn't drink at sea at all. The tot of rum went out in 1970, but prior to that there was a rum issue at the same time every day. Senior rates were entitled to it neat, and junior rates had it mixed.

Arctic waters? I never went under the ice. Recently, the press reported that a submarine had a fire when they were under the ice. In a smoke-filled boat, with everyone breathing out of masks, they would have had to find a polynya - a patch of open water — in order to surface or snort so as to clear the air. Fires in submarines are not much fun and that event must have been exceptionally well handled.

Everyone did regular escape training, and you had to be in date to qualify for submarine pay. The training tank went to 100 feet. In trials at sea, the team went down to, I think, 600 feet. That was free ascent. Nowadays the principle rescue system uses mini-submarines. Traditionally there were two ways of escaping. You either flooded up the whole compartment until the pressure equalised inside and out, and then you could open the hatch, take a quick gulp, fill up your lungs, duck your head under and go out of the hatch and away, breathing out rapidly all the way up. The other method, tower escape, was similar but involved flooding a small compartment which could just take one or two people at a time, while the others remained in the dry.

When I left the Navy in 1989, I went to the London Business School. About a year after that I was contacted by a couple of people who were looking at establishing a new port on the south coast. Portland was a possible option and they knew of my Naval and Dorset connections. When the Government announced the closure of the Naval Base, we focused on that and formed Portland Development Partners. It took some time for the Ministry of Defence and the Crown Estate to work out who would be the seller, because under the deeds of 1849 or thereabouts, although the Admiralty had absolute ownership of the land, there was a clause giving the Crown Estate reversionary rights should the site not be required for defence purposes. Our concern, and that of other potential purchasers, was that the buildings would deteriorate very quickly if the new owners could not move in as soon as the Navy had left. It took the help of two MPs, Jim Spicer and Ian Bruce, to set up a meeting with the then junior defence minister, Lord Cranborne, who had himself been the MP for South Dorset, and it was he who, in his own words, cut the Gordian Knot. Within a few days the Crown Estate had renounced their rights and the Ministry of Defence started the process that led to competitive tenders by several different groups. Throughout the tendering process, the Navy at Portland were very even-handed and went out of their way to accommodate anyone who might have proposals that would create new jobs.

Most of the tunnels and underground spaces are under the Verne and not in the Port. We do have four 10,000 cubic metre tanks, which the Navy had looked after very well. They were built just before the last war and are in full use.

The senior member of our team of three was Norman Thompson, who lived in Burton Bradstock and had been a radio officer on Liberty ships during the War. He had become deputy chairman of Swan Hunter and had sorted out the privatised Malta Dockyard before being invited by Lee Kuan Yew to privatise Singapore Dockyard. He then set up the mass transit system in Hong Kong and had also been Chairman of the Poole Harbour Commissioners. We needed someone to fund the purchase and that person was John Langham. From his company headquarters outside Dorchester, John had built up the family company, Langham Industries, after starting with the management buyout of Stone Manganese, the propeller makers. By 1994 it was a group of about 20 companies, including Appledore Shipbuilders. The situation at Portland was very similar to the sort of thing that the company had taken on before so, in December 1994, we formed Portland Port Ltd as a subsidiary of Langham Industries, specifically to bid for the Naval Base. We faced some keen competition but eventually were selected, as the preferred purchaser, in April 1995.

We immediately moved into a portacabin on the Base. Flag Officer Sea Training continued to operate there until July, so I'd be working in the evening in the portacabin with a whole lot of blanks being fired around me as the ships were being exercised in facing an attack by terrorists. And then, on 25th July, the Navy sailed away, leaving a reduced team to shut the place down. We took possession at the beginning in March '96, and finally completed the purchase in December '96.

The only remaining naval presence was the Queen's Harbour Master. Portland was a Dockyard Port, which was run under different legislation to commercial ports, so we had to go through the process of promoting a Harbour Revision Order in order to change the legal structure. The Queen's Harbour Master finally left when the HRO came into force on January 1st 1998. We had had a Public Inquiry into our proposals, with over 300 objections, the majority from windsurfers who had been led to believe that we were trying to keep them out of the harbour. That was completely untrue. In fact, our aim was to make as few changes to the well established practices as possible. I was in the witness box every day for two weeks. In the event, the Inspector ruled in our favour on practically every count and we emerged with the most up-to-date and, arguably, the most effective harbour constitution in the country.

The breakwaters, including the Breakwater Fort, were part of the deal as were a whole lot of listed buildings. We took over about 350 acres in all, of which perhaps 60 or 70 were useable. We had to buy a couple of Mulberry Harbour Phoenix units, which were also listed. It was a period of great uncertainty on the island. For 150 years - in fact, longer, if you go back to the quarries and Christopher Wren - the economy had been based on government funding and then, quite suddenly, that security vanished. This had various effects. There was a perception of a power vacuum, and a lot of individuals and groups, local authorities and national organisations all wanted to get in on the act. We were also constantly faced with proposals of how we should run the harbour, so we were having to respond to these additional pressures whilst trying to get a business going from scratch, with no customers and substantial overhead costs.

The port functions through two parallel but separate companies, Portland Harbour Authority Ltd, and Portland Port Ltd, with the same shareholding and the same board members. Portland Port Ltd is the commercial port operator and Portland Harbour Authority Ltd is the legislative authority for running the harbour. The Harbour Authority is a statutory authority, responsible to Parliament though the Secretary of State. It has the power to make byelaws and has its own police force.

We began with six lines of business in mind, of which all but one were started in the first year or so. We have handled various dry cargos, such as timber, steel, peat, agricultural products and a service to the smaller Channel Islands, some of which proved to be insufficiently profitable to continue. As we have become better known, there are some encouraging prospects for the future. We handle a few containers and, although we will never be a significant container port, there is some more of that traffic that could come our way.

The Mere Tank Farm has been the basis of an inland fuel distribution business with Conoco. The tanks have now been bought by the Regional Development Agency and will soon all be dismantled to make space for boat storage during the Olympic Games, so we are looking at an alternative tank site within the port. The tanks under the hill are used by Greek-owned, Portland Bunkers International Limited. Portland is well placed geographically to fuel ships passing up and down the English Channel. A bunker barge, actually a 5,000 tonne tanker operated by BP Marine, supplies the ships at anchor, either in the outer harbour or, more usually in winter, inside breakwaters.

Dictated, in part by the limited port infrastructure we inherited and Dorset's present road system, we have particularly focused on marine services, providing home port and other services to vessels that do not require to transfer cargo or passengers. Our first marine service customers were cable ships, initially BT Marine, subsequently taken over by Cable & Wireless Marine, who established a cable store and brought in their cable ships. They moved their bases at Southampton and Middlesborough down to Portland at a time when a lot of submarine cables were being laid across the Atlantic and around the world. Cable & Wireless were then taken over by Global Marine. We are the UK cable ship centre, with the biggest facility of its kind in the world. We have two large ships based here, a lot of storage and an ROV servicing centre. Many millions of pounds of investment went into Portland.

Marine services also include warships. Although, for understandable reasons of political sensitivity, we did not get many naval ships for several years, the Navy never really went away because QinetiQ, formerly the Defence Evaluation and Research Agency, has three test ranges in the area, two inside our harbour limits, that are regularly used by warships and naval auxiliaries. Time has moved on and the Fleet is currently one of our largest customers, particularly for ships of the Royal Fleet Auxiliary, which need the deep water we can provide and for whom, as warships become bigger, there has been a shortage of berthing space in Portsmouth and Devonport.

The fourth line of business was cruise ships. We have a dedicated passenger terminal and ships have been coming, either to visit or embark and disembark passengers, since 1998. It has taken time to get going but that is changing. We are now part of a regional grouping called Destination South West and, with Poole, we hosted the biennial Seatrade UK Cruise Forum in April this year. This was a very successful two days attended by the leading lights of the international cruise industry. It will take about three years to see the results, because these companies plan a long way ahead. The 2012 Olympic Games will attract ships and we're particularly well placed in the South West because, other than Falmouth, there really is nowhere deep enough and with the facilities to provide turn-around capabilities for the larger vessels now coming into service. The cargo-passenger ship RMS *St Helena*, serving the South Atlantic, is a cruise ship of a slightly different kind. Portland is the terminal for her twice yearly visits to the UK and we expect to see her until the island of St Helena gets its airport sometime after 2012.

I suppose you could say that Her Majesty's Prison *The Weare* was a marine service of a sort. The arrival of HMP *The Weare* in 1997 was not part of our business plan but it was a very good customer. The decision to close it was made very shortly before the last general election and the final prisoners left in August 2005. The ship is being converted for use in the offshore oil industry and is with us for another month or so. I think it did work and was effective. It certainly provided employment at a difficult time. It was a Category C and D prison, so inmates rarely stayed there more than six months. Apparently, its disadvantage was that there weren't enough training facilities. On the other hand, the great thing about a prison ship is that you can move it to where you want and can also put another ship alongside it with all the training facilities you might need. I think one of the problems was that most of the inmates came from London and further north and it was a long way for families to visit. On one occasion, I went on board for a carol service, which was a cheerful affair and not unlike other ships company events I've been to. The Governor sat amongst the inmates and we all had coffee and buns afterwards. The only complaints I heard were about the food and that there was not enough sport, both of which will be familiar to sailors the world over.

Fifth in our target business was ship repair. Manor Marine, a local company, rent the former MoD repair and small vessel building facilities and there are several engineering and underwater operations companies providing services to vessels of all types.

We thought that ferries would be early customers but for various reasons that has not happened yet. They will come in time. We're the closest point to France west of Newhaven and we are well positioned for Iberia. You'd take an awful lot of traffic off the road in France and Spain, and France has a lot of rules on HGVs on the roads at weekends and so on. We are looking at roll-on roll-off ferries, particularly freight, with passengers coming in on the back of it. Various things have happened since the early 90s to slow ferry traffic growth. There was the ship lost in the Baltic, leading to new safety rules and additional costs, the opening of the Channel Tunnel and the loss of duty free between EU ports, all of which have cut ferry profitability.

At the moment the place is jammed full of containers from MSC *Napoli*. One problem is some of the perishable foodstuffs are beginning to smell a bit. In addition, many of the containers are full of water and are extremely heavy, making them difficult to handle and damaging our road system. It'll go on for a few months yet. Having sprung a leak, *Napoli* was due to come into Portland, but she then started breaking up, and that was when the decision was made to beach her. When the analysis is done I think it'll prove to be a textbook operation of how a problem like that should be handled. No lives were lost and, given the filthy weather at the time, that in itself was a remarkable achievement. Very little oil was lost. If it had broken up or been sunk in much deeper water, the problems could have been much worse. The recommendations made by Lord Donaldson would appear to have established a very robust, well prepared organisation. The UK doesn't have ports of refuge, it has a coastline, and says 'Depending on the circumstances, we'll go for the best possible place'. In the meantime the whole operation is being conducted from Portland.

The *Napoli* barrels? I am told by a cidermaker friend, who bought some, legally, on e-Bay that they're fantastic barrels. They were apparently destined for a South African vineyard, best Allier oak.

Portland Harbour is large. There are about 2,000 acres inside the Breakwaters and, within our harbour limits, there are another 2,500 acres outside. The original pair of breakwaters, the Inner and the Outer are important to us as a commercial port. They are the ones that were built between 1849 and 1872. The other two, which were completed in the early years of the 20th century, are lighter in construction and they're important in the protection they provide for dinghy sailing. They're also important in terms of prevention of coastal erosion and flooding. In the days of the MoD, the Government used to spend about a million pounds on breakwater maintenance every three years. They were England's biggest marine-related, civil engineering project of the nineteenth century and the Duke of Edinburgh came in 1999 to commemorate the 150th Anniversary of the laying of the first stone by Prince Albert, the Prince Consort.

The Northern Arm is leased to QinetiQ. The breakwaters are industrial structures and are not safe for public use. We also have to think about security, not just in connection with warships and submarines but also with cruise ships. The port as a whole is an industrial site and, as such, it is potentially a dangerous place for the casual visitor. Like any other commercial port, we don't encourage untrammelled public access within our boundaries and, recent government legislation on port safety forbids it.

After 10 years, we now have a pretty good idea of what Portland's markets are likely to be. The Naval berths and infrastructure are getting old and do not really meet the needs of a commercial port, so we have submitted a Harbour Revision Order with proposals to reclaim about 35 acres of land for new deep water, coastal shipping and ferry berths, together with a floating dock. We are looking at a construction period over 30 to 50 years and are hoping for early approval so that we can complete the first phase, which will provide a new cruise ship berth, in time for the Sailing Olympics.

All the sailing, including the windsurfing, will take place in Portland Harbour and Weymouth Bay and this is the only venue outside London where there will be medal ceremonies. My own view is that this is a pretty special opportunity for Dorset which occurs only once in a generation.

History? One of the only VCs awarded in this country in the Second World War was won on HMS *Foylebank* in Portland Harbour by Leading Seaman Jack Mantle. *Foylebank* was a merchant ship that had been converted to an anti-aircraft ship and was doing training in Portland Harbour when she was attacked by Stukas on the morning of 4th July 1940. She sank but not before Jack Mantle won fame for fighting his gun when fatally wounded. He is a local hero and is buried in the Naval cemetery. Those killed in that attack, and indeed in accidents or in war, are buried in the cemetery, which is within our land holding but isn't owned by us. There's a public footpath to it.

I'm well aware of HMS *Sidon* because the 50th anniversary of her loss was two years ago, when the Dorset branch of the Submariner's Association, set up a memorial and organised a ceremony of commemoration. The submarine sank after an explosion in a high test peroxide torpedo and 13 people were killed. She was lying alongside the depot ship, just about to go to sea to conduct firing trials. I believe the Russian *Kursk* was lost for very similar reasons. The difference between *Kursk* and *Sidon* was that *Sidon* was on the surface with some of the hatches open, so the blast vented out, whereas *Kursk* was dived. The waters around Portland are littered with the graves of ships. The aircraft-carrying *M2* is another sunken submarine close by. *Sidon* herself was raised and eventually sunk as a submarine target.

HMS *Osprey*, the naval establishment, ceased to exist when the air station closed in 1999. The original buildings have now been razed to the ground. They were on the upper level of our estate and some of the area is the site of the proposed gas storage proposed by Egdon Resources and their Portland Gas subsidiary. I understand it will store up to about five per cent of the nation's reserves. The intention is that the gas should come from the main line at Maperton, via a new line to Ringstead and thence across the Weymouth Bay to Portland. Again that wasn't something we planned. We had had the area in mind for a car import-export base.

At my home at Melplash we have about 45 acres of cider orchards. They're mostly the well known varieties. The original bush orchard, planted by my father in 1972 had Dabinett, Yarlington, Michelin and Chisel Jersey. Since then we have planted more, including one solely containing Kingston Black, the doyen amongst cider apples. When he moved here, my grandfather took over some traditional Dorset orchards and then planted two more with standard trees before the war. He was much involved with Long Ashton and the Bath and West, and he made cider in conjunction with a couple of cider makers in Stoke Abbott and another one in Netherbury, which they sold under the brand name *Linden Lea*. My hope is to make cider once again at Hincknowle.

24. Liisa Wallace – Diver and Entrepreneur: Aqua Hotel, Dive Dorset, Underwater Explorers: Castletown, Portland. Born Helsinki 1964.

You almost have this dreamlike state when you are underwater.

I was born in Finland. My father used to import products from Japan and the Far East. My mother worked in the Foreign Office, she actually worked in the MI6 and was posted to Helsinki during the 1950s during the cold war and she met my father and got married.

My Finnish grandfather was also a trader, he had a margarine factory in Vyborg in the eastern part of Finland, but he died when my father was very small and after the Second World War, Finland had to cede that part of the territory to Russia and my father and his family, in line with all the other Finnish people of the town, left almost overnight. And in fact my grandmother told me they all left and had a suitcase and a teddy bear each and this always sounded quite evocative to me. It happened around 1939.

My parents got divorced when I was five, but I saw my father fairly regularly. My mother was English and was born on a farm in Hertfordshire although the family came originally from Ayrshire in Scotland, both her parents were of Scottish origin and they were farmers.

My mother, we discovered that she worked for MI6 by total accident, and even until her death her close family didn't realise that's what she did. She was a secretary and told me a few things like when she was still working in England in London she would be sent to aerodromes with great bundles of money to give to people and when all the Blunt spy affair came out, we were watching it on TV, and she said 'Now I realise why all the spies we trained to infiltrate back into eastern Europe got caught,' because she knew these people were her bosses. I suppose the information was all passed on. I don't know what she was doing in Finland and once she got married she had to leave the Foreign Office which was her cover. I was 13 when we left Finland.

I think Helsinki was a great city to grow up in, very human scale and very safe. Even at five or six I could wander and travel on the public transport system quite safely by myself, if not with my father's approval. My father was a very good linguist, fluent in Japanese and he had the foresight to speak in English at home. Even after my parents divorced, when I visited my father, we spoke pure English and at home with my mother we spoke a mixture of Finnish and English.

I landed in Norfolk in England and went to boarding school. Very interesting for a foreigner, but I didn't totally integrate. The main thing that struck me was that you could leave school in England without a single piece of paper which outlined your educational achievements. In Finland education is without exception appreciated and realising that there were people that thought that schooling didn't necessarily deliver any value, was quite a shock.

I did well at school and went to university to study economics first at Coventry and then at Manchester. I worked for BT in Swindon in the purchasing division IT department and in London I was involved in redesigning the forecasting processes. Then I came back to Swindon and became a buyer myself and used to buy private digital networks. It was a great company to work for.

After university I went on holiday to Larnaca in Cyprus and saw a 'Try Dive' advertised and just thought it was a fantastic

Underwater Explorer: Liisa Wallace in reflective mood, Castletown 'Strip'

experience. It wasn't just the things you saw but the sense of weightlessness and you almost have this dreamlike state when you are underwater. I came back to England, found the local dive club in Swindon and I took up diving. We used to come down to Portland a lot. Chesil was a great place for shore diving. Just get your wetsuit on and walk out into the waves. Right in the cove is best, there is a little reef out of Burton Bradstock, but Chesil Cove is great.

You always see flatfish. Cuttlefish, they are my favourite underwater animals. Fish are dumb they just look at you. Cuttlefish, sometimes they say that people can have a sensation of someone watching them in a crowded room. Same with cuttlefish. You can be diving and feel that someone is looking at you and you turn around and a metre away is a cuttlefish, just following you out of sheer curiosity. They are not dumb like fish. There is a form of intelligence and you can connect with them. They look like tabby cats and they change their colour. You can sometimes get to stroke them. They are fascinating.

It was a BSAC Club that I joined and I worked through all the levels. I like being underwater and I'm not too discriminating about what I'm diving on, it's just the whole sensation of being there and the silence. It's not totally silent because you can hear these echoes, but it's the fact that everything above the surface goes out of my head for that time I'm underwater. And you do hear sounds. I remember once diving off Chesil when it was quite rough, a bit too rough to go in really and I went in with my buddy. There wasn't much to see and we were in about nine metres. I heard this noise and it sounded like a noise from children's playground in the distance. What it was, was the stones tumbling on each other and it really just sounded like a playground in the distance. They call it 'grinding'.

We say in our advertising that Portland is Northern Europe's premier diving destination and I think that's true because you have got so much to see. Apart from a big choice of wrecks you have also got a lot of sheltered sites for people who want to learn to train and you can just do shore diving. You have got all the wrecks on the breakwaters which are sheltered and shallow and you have got ledges on the west side which are called the Aerials when there used to be aerials on the cliffs there. We still call them the Aerials because we drift that part of Portland and these limestone ledges are like big steps and they are so full of life and you get lot of crustaceans, all sorts of crabs. Mussels grow there and you get crabs feeding on them and flatfish feeding on the mussels and it's almost like the fish counter at the supermarket. Then you've got Lulworth Banks famous for scallop diving. There are great gullies and ledges.

My favourite wrecks? There is a wreck called the *Warrior* which is a sailing ship. It had been requisitioned during the war, it's quite broken up so it's not often dived but it's quite far out, so you get good visibility there even at that sort of depth. There are loads of big conger eels that live in the hold. This yacht has a swimming pool and depending on whether it is covered or uncovered by sand you can see the mosaic floor of the swimming pool. So congers have taste. The wreck is at low 60 metre depth so it's a mixed gas dive. The *M2* is quite a nice wreck because it's completely intact and small enough you can see it in one dive. So you can go round the whole wreck and dive and you can get the sense of this submarine. There was another submarine I think it was *HMS Sidon* that did actually have the same fuel supply as the *Kursk*. (hydrogen peroxide, see notes p.165)

I gave up my job when I was about 30 and spent a year going through Europe and Asia and got as far as Indonesia, then came back. A delayed gap year. There was this opportunity and I knew diving around Portland. The Navy had just pulled out and

Portland was very depressed and the building where we now run the business from, the hotel, was known as 'Aggie Weston's' - Dame Agnes Weston's Royal Sailors Rests. It was a charity, they ran hostels for Christian seamen, but I think they were more like Christian hostels for seamen, started in Devonport. They no longer needed the building, a very sturdy building. I knew somebody who'd just left the Navy and started a diving business with RIBs in Castletown and there was this opportunity to expand and provide accommodation for the divers because the diving business was doing all the marketing to bring the customers down and half the revenue was being spent in the 'Strip' as they call Castletown. He needed a business partner and I came in at that point. We first got a lease on the property and then managed to buy it a few years later from Aggie Weston's. It was built in the late in 1880s. A large place and quite a lot of sailors could sleep there. Pretty much set out as a hostel, so over the last 12 years there has been a lot of money spent converting it to more of a mainstream hotel.

The sailors would drink in the pubs on the Strip and then come across late at night to sleep in the hostel. Sometimes the sailors were between ships and they had no home to go to literally. They had some family rooms as well so I guess families did come down and spend time with their husbands.

I started running the business in 1996. The diving business had started a year before. There are three enterprises there, the diving business, the hotel and a shop. We had the RIBs and then there was the opportunity to start a diving shop, because all these divers coming down would need to buy some equipment and then Parry's of Portland closed down and sold up. I bought the business including the pontoon in Castletown beach, which enabled us to run hard boats, because before that we were just running RIBs off the beach. That's how we moved into running hard boats. Customers' expectations had been going up and RIBs are quite cheap to start off with but they get quite costly in terms of age and repair. You still have the same pay costs but you can't get as many people on them. I am an instructor, but when I decided to open the shop I also started the school, and the people I employ run it. I employ 12 to 15 people depending on the time of year.

We came across some diving equipment that wasn't available in the UK, it's called Halcyon and we started importing it and then I realized there was quite a lot of demand for it. It's something different. It is kind of the BMW of dive gear. It's strong and rugged and fairly simple. They do mainly wings, the floatation devices and various accessories and I realised that we could sell more if we distributed it through the UK rather than selling it through one outlet. That's how I started the import company and now we have been picking up other products that we import as well.

We named the hotel, *Hotel Aqua*, we have 18 rooms now and they are quite large rooms. We can sleep about 47 I think. It has always been pretty much full at weekends and through the summer it's reasonably full during the week, but it can be very quiet weekdays. We have our own bar and café. The café does quite well because the divers want somewhere quick and convenient to eat. We've got quite a lot of non-diving customers as well and that's what we are doing now in the hotel. We want to diversify so hopefully we get commercial people in the week and the divers at the weekend.

When I used to instruct, the absolutely nicest thing to do it was take someone on their first dive and it doesn't matter how boring or miserable the dive appeared or uninteresting, they would come out eyes the size of a dinner plates. 'Did you see that starfish?' I remember my first dive in the sea in the UK it was the same, it is a different world as they say.

On the wrecks you can only dive them at slack tide and the slack water period moves depending on neaps or springs or whether it's the 'before or after tide' – before or after high water. If you are doing shore diving especially off Portland Bill it's quite easy to get into trouble, you have to make sure that you can actually get back.

When I first started coming around here, fishermen used to complain of all these divers robbing their lobster pots, but I've never actually seen that happen and I don't think you get that. Mind you we have so few fishermen left, the fishing industry has taken a terrible hit.

We can't walk on the breakwater, I expect some people sneak on to the Chequered Fort and have a look around. We dive off the edge of the breakwater, lots of the wrecks are placed on the breakwater on the inside. Some have drifted off while they were anchored or off their moorings and broken up against the wall, settled along there. There are three or four. The *Countess* is the most intact one and makes a really good training platform, it's got this deck at six metres, there's another one called The *Spaniard*, but I think it was 1997 we had those huge gales and the oil rig in the harbour broke away from its moorings and actually it bumped into that as it was wandering around the harbour. We were scared it would actually make its way out into the bay.

Very, very few divers really do any wreck penetration most of them would stay on the outside. We used to be allowed to dive The *Hood*, which is on the southern entrance, and that was quite interesting. It's nice if you see a glimmer of light at the other end, but I never felt totally comfortable or that interested unless there was a purpose. If you can navigate through and get to the other side like you can on The *Hood*, that's quite interesting. I would like to do some cave diving in those huge caverns that are abroad, but potholing in the dark doesn't really grab me. Congers are only a problem if you disturb them, probably actually quite timid. I've come across some congers at very close range quite unexpectedly but they've never done anything. I think you have to do something radical to get them going...

When you do the training course, we supply all the training equipment. You have to have your own mask and boots and a snorkel. Apart from that we provide a suit. Then you need some sort of a wing or BCD inflation device, a regulator and a cylinder, which quite a lot of people just hire, they don't necessarily buy them. People also have to learn the underwater signals as well.

A test, which we do, is all part of the four-day course, then they can dive with another person with the same level of qualification, the lowest level of underwater qualification. There is no law stopping anybody going into a shop to buy all the gear and going diving but the training assists a vast majority of people to get qualified. I don't think anybody just goes diving without training. If you don't understand the effects of pressure which can give you the bends, or the effects of oxygen becoming toxic at depth, then you can just have a convulsion underwater and die from oxygen poisoning, or you can get the bends on the ascent or if you come up too quickly and hold your breath your lungs can burst.

You control the ascent. You are weighted to be neutrally buoyant underwater and then the importance of the inflation device, the wing, is of course giving you support when you are on the surface waiting for the boat, but you also adjust your buoyancy by putting more air in there or less. So as you come up the air in the wing is expanding so you have to release it gradually and that's part of your training, you learn to control your ascend rate by controlling your buoyancy.

We go as far as Swanage, we have done the *Kyarra* a few times. It's quite a long trip for us, that's interesting it's probably had a million dives on it over the years and you can still find a little bit of crockery or a little perfume bottle somewhere in the bilges. She had a fair bit of freight on her when she sank. *Earl of Abergavenny*. What's left of that is under the seabed and that's been excavated quite extensively, a long on-going archaeological project.

One of the things that makes Portland such a good place is that we have got the protection of the Bill so the prevalent weather used to come from the west so we could dive in the shelter of the east side, but if you have easterly weather but you've managed to get around the Bill you can dive on the west in shelter. If it's really bad you can find somewhere along the breakwater inside the harbour or just on the other side to dive.

Diving clubs are one of our main customer bases. Traditionally a club would book a whole boat for the day, but we find our edge in the market is that we take bookings from individuals and we also run shuttles. Our boats are quite fast so we come back between dives, which means we can get four dives into a day as opposed to a typical day charter. They go out, dive, hang around for a couple of hours and then do a second dive.

I quite enjoy lots of things on land as well, but it doesn't matter where I am or how long it is since I last dived I still enjoy it. To me it's the fact that I don't recollect anything, you know the whole 'above the surface world' just disappears. Almost like a dream world, similar sensation as being in a dream, gives you time to ponder, bit like underwater meditation. You have a buddy. Underwater communication? It's interesting you get different people, some people you can have a really good rapport with, and you understand what they mean, then there are other people that can't communicate as well. That's a nice thing about diving when you can have a buddy and you can easily communicate. You can listen to taped music underwater only if you got a full helmet, but I know some people who do very long deep dives, with very long decompression, decompression is really boring. There is a recompression chamber if you have an accident, the nearest one is in Poole. If you have a very long deep dive you have to take stops as you are coming up and they call that decompression. Sometimes there are very long decompression stops if you've had a long dive. I would be happy diving 65/75 metres, about 30 fathoms. People don't take ipods down but I know people take paperbacks for these long decompressions, it's not typical to have these long decompressions. I have heard of people taking paperbacks down and they tear a page off as they read it. This is probably more like some cheap thrillers, I don't know too many divers who would read Dostoyevsky. We make it work because of the hotel and the shop. We are probably unique.

Sometimes we get what's called 'May Water' and you get these algae blooms, it depends on how much sunshine there has been and how warm it has been. Last year when there was a really cold spring right until June we had 14 degrees of water in June which is cold and we hardly had a bloom, so we had lovely clear water. We had a bloom this year so that cut down the visibility, but also the storms cut down visibility. The clearest time is February providing there hasn't been a storm, so it's balancing the storm against the bloom. I've never seen a dolphin underwater, but you do get them around Portland and occasionally a seal. There used to be a dog seal, I haven't seen it for a few years. It lived in the harbour. When we used to keep our boats in the port sometimes early in the morning you'd find the seal sleeping on the pontoon, where the boat was tied up. If you dived The *Hood* off slack when there was nobody else there, you could see this seal underwater and it used to give quite a few divers a fright.

I haven't seen torpedoes but I have seen lots of spent shells and sometimes you can pick up nose cones and things like that. If you come across something on the seabed and it's not part of a wreck you can just pick it up. In theory anything you take you are supposed to report to the Receiver of the Wreck, doesn't mean you have to give it up, but you have to report it.

There is no such thing as a diving museum, but David Carter who runs the *Abergavenny* archaeological project is really keen to start one. He wants to find a home for all his *Abergavenny* artefacts. Quite a few people would like to start one. I think it would be good to have one. There are quite a lot of evocative stories about the wrecks.

I don't think Aggie Weston would approve that we have got a bar in the place. The woman pirate in the bar, we were going to have a competition to name her. I got her. I think it was an impulse purchase, some of my staff are not totally keen on her. She comes from a dive show, there is an artist who makes pirates and life-size diving cartoon figures as shop displays I suppose, and I just saw that, end of the show, good price, you know. Look what I've got! We still have a bible in every room.

Sometimes we get people who were based in Portland and they come around and they are in the café, 50-60-year-old chaps with their wife and they ask you, 'Is the Navy still here?' Then they start telling you about their days here. The place must have been something of a legend. The Strip, even The Greasy Spoon, it was closed down when I came here but it still had the sign which said: 'We serve all serving nations.'

On the prison ship visiting days we get quite a few people in. When people were let out, they would usually come. Apparently there was no bacon allowed on the prison ship, so the first thing they do is come for a bacon buttie at the Café. You would always recognise them because they would have all their goods in a clear plastic bag.

When I am older, when I retire, I would like to go back and live in Finland for a year or so. That would be nice…

Vyborg: During the Finnish civil war which followed the Russian Revolution of 1917 *Vyborg* was first held by Red Russians and then captured by the White Russians. In between the wars it was Finnish and changed its name to Viipuri. During the Second War there were many bitter struggles against the Russians and the small Finnish army inflicted very severe losses on the Red Army. First there was the Winter War Nov 1939-1940 then the War of Continuation June 1941-Sept 1944. Vyborg changed hands several times. Since Sept 1944 it has been in Russian hands.

Warrior 2: A once beautiful steam yacht built with no expense spared. She was requisitioned in both wars but her luck ran out in 1940 when she was attacked from the air. Her bow is a fantastic site and she still retains many of her very heavy brass fittings.

M2 : An enormous 2,000 ton submarine that had an aircraft hanger at the stern for a seaplane which could be used for spotting. On the morning of the 26th January 1932 the *M2* was taking part in a submarine exercise in the eastern region of Lyme bay. She dived and was never seen again. She was lost with all hands. It is thought that the hanger flooded. Her sister ship *M1* was sunk after a collision off Start Point in 1925. Also lost with all hands.

HMS Sidon: Hydrogen peroxide in the torpedoes. One exploded on June 16th 1955. *HMS Sidon* sank in Portland harbour. 13 men died. Two years later she was refloated and sunk as an ASDIC target.

Dame 'Aggie' Weston was born in London in 1840 the daughter of a barrister. She had a good education but decided that her missionary zeal was of better use in Devonport than in darkest Africa. She started writing to soldiers and then sailors. So successful was her campaign to get them off the bottle that she was eventually asked to set up a temperance house close to the dockyard entrance. That was in 1874. Later Sailors Rests were set up in Portsmouth, Portland and Sheerness. When she died she was given full Naval honours. In 1941 there was a frigate called Weston-super-Mare. This was nicknamed Aggie on Horseback..

The Countess of Erne was a paddle steamer, but was used in later life as a coal hulk in Portland harbour. She sank in 1935 after her moorings broke lose.

HMS Hood was an old 14,000 ton battleship built in 1891 and at the outbreak of war was deliberately sunk across the southern entrance to Portland harbour to prevent U-boats from entering.

The Spaniard was a 3,000 ton Spanish steamship that sank in 1900.

SS Kyarra is an Australian steamer that was sunk by UB 57 with a torpedo on 26th May 1918 and now lies upright in 30 metres of water off Swanage. Bottles of champagne, wine and perfume still turn up and the odd gold and silver pocket watches. Six people lost their lives.

The Earl of Abergavenny. On 5th/6th February 1805 this massive East Indiaman was caught in a storm and sank a mile and a half from the safety of Weymouth Harbour. She was captained by John Wordsworth, the poet William Wordsworth's younger brother. At 1440 tons *The Earl of Abergavenny* was the finest ship in the fleet. This was her fifth voyage. She was destined for Bengal and China and carried a very valuable cargo of coin, silver dollars, tin, lead and iron, as well as much cloth and glass, military stores, 40,000 gun flints, harnesses and saddles, Wedgewood ceramics, clay pipes and wines which would have been eagerly desired in the Calcutta. This cargo was estimated to be worth around £200,000 but it never got to India. It is said that the Wordsworth family had invested heavily in the voyage so that they could finance William's work. The next leg to China would have been the most profitable with the trade in opium from India being particularly lucrative.

The Earl of Abergavenny was caught on the Shambles sandbank for a few hours and badly damaged below the water line. Pilot error is the general consensus for their demise, 'Oh Pilot, pilot you have ruined me' Wordsworth's own words apparently. The pilot had no great knowledge of the coast it seems. John Wordsworth brought her into deeper water and tried to run for Weymouth sands. But he was unsuccessful, the leak was too great and the great ship became waterlogged and began to drift then sink. There were over 400 people on board, 160 crew, 160 soldiers and 30 Chinamen, the rest were passengers. Realising that they were doomed a number of sailors attacked the ship's spirit room but were held back by the officers. John Wordsworth was last seen clinging to the quarter brail of the mizzen but refused the offer of the mate Mr Gilpin to be taken off. Some say he did not want to be rescued but evidence in Bodleian Library seems to indicate that the rescue was simply unsuccessful.

Despite rescue boats being sent out some 250 people, including the captain, John Wordsworth eventually lost their lives. His body was not recovered until a month later, his sword was also washed up. They were buried in unmarked graves in Wyke Regis and Radipole churchyards. William Wordsworth and his sister Dorothy were much saddened at this loss. William wrote about the loss in the Elegiacs. It was the same year that William finished the Prelude.

The Earl of Abergavenny lies in 8 fathoms well within sight of Weymouth beach and Esplanade. The masts remained visible for many months and she became a tourist attraction. Nothing was saved at the time except the dispatches and some valuable prints being sent out to General Lake.

Interestingly much of the cargo was salvaged in 1806 by a diving bell operated by Mr Braithwaite. In 1921 the navy blew the vessel up as she was hazard to shipping. Today there are still several rows of wooden posts sticking out of the sand. Careful excavations have been done and she is a registered archaeological site. They have even found one gold cufflink with the initials JW engraved on it.

All vanished in a single word,
A breath, a sound and scarcely heard
Sea – Ship – drowned - Shipwreck- so it came.
The meek, the brave, the good was gone,
He who had been our living John
Was nothing but a name.

From Elegiac Verses by William Wordsworth

25. John Tweed – Development Director for the Weymouth & Portland National Sailing Academy Osprey Quay, Portland. Born Colchester 1950.

Sailing has a reputation as an elite activity and we want to overcome that. We want to show people that actually it's for the whole of the community. At the same time we want this facility to be a substantial and lasting legacy of the Olympic Games and Paralympic Games.

Yes it is a good day today because there is a lot of different things going on, there's people learning to sail and there's a very large fleet of Optimists about to go racing. It's a National Championship and over 380 youngsters will be competing. The children are between eight and fifteen. It is very important to them, and it is a breeding ground for future champions. People like Ben Ainslie started on Optimists.

The Optimists are small, lightweight, very stable boats for young people to learn to sail in single handed. Today they are in three large fleets. There is a junior, a senior and a regatta fleet. They race against each other. There is a committee boat out there, the two masted boat by the naval vessel. The start line is always into the wind. They have time signals so you know you have five minutes to go. So they have to sail around behind the line and try and cross the line at just the right moment. If they are ahead of the line they might get called back. Races are normally started with a gun, or an air horn.

In Portland Harbour and Weymouth Bay, the sailing waters are some of the best small boat sailing waters in the world. It's a combination of factors. Portland is a large enclosed harbour, the second largest man-made harbour in the world, 2,500 acres of water with good clean winds across the Chesil Beach, predominantly from the south west or west. The wind comes across the beach not too turbulent and so you have got relatively flat water in the harbour. The breakwaters stop the swell coming in. For the larger competitions we would use Weymouth Bay. The other great advantage is that our tidal range is just about the lowest tidal range anywhere on the UK coastal mainland. It's between 1.9 metres and 2.4 metres. That means we have very weak tidal currents within the harbour itself. The tides are generally quite weak in Weymouth Bay until you get towards the east, towards Lulworth. The breakwaters certainly have an effect on the circulation. You have got a gentle anti-clockwise flow in the harbour but it's only a quarter of a knot.

I was born in Colchester in Essex, in 1950. It was a Roman port, but it's not actually on the coast, it's on the River Colne. Colchester native oysters have had a very good reputation from Roman times when they were a staple food of the population, rather than being a specialist dish as they tend to be now. There is a Colchester oyster festival each year to celebrate the first dredge of the year. Its only when they get scarce that they suddenly get expensive.

My father was a structural and mechanical engineer. My grandfather was a baker. I started to sail when I was at college. I then returned to Essex and lived at Brightlingsea which is on the coast, and started sailing dinghies with Brightlingsea Sailing Club and larger boats with the Colne Yacht Club. And then the family moved down to Dorset in 1989.

I'm a chartered surveyor and I was appointed County Valuer for Dorset in 1989. The job of County Valuer is to look after the property interests of the County Council - in relation to purchasing land for schools, police stations, fire stations,

John Tweed, Osprey Quay

everything that the local authority needs. Dorset also has a substantial number of small farms to encourage young people into the farming industry and to give the council a stake in one of the major industries in the county.

I'm now Development Director for the Sailing academy, so my role has been to oversee the development of the Academy from its start through to what it is now and looking forward to 2012. The main sailing event in the Olympic Games is two weeks and then of course the Paralympic Games are for a further week in the beginning of September. In 1997 my role changed and I started to do a series of special projects reporting directly to the Chief Executive of Dorset County Council. These special projects were an attempt to ensure that Dorset got a fair share of Lottery money, this included major projects like the redevelopment of the Tank Museum and smaller projects including village halls, play groups etc. The Sailing Academy was one of those special projects. The Royal Yachting Association had been looking for a base for the National Centre of Excellence in Weymouth or Portland for about 30 years.

In 1995 the Navy started withdrawing from Portland with the closure of the main naval base. The Royal Navy Air Station, HMS Osprey closed in 1999, which is where we are now. There were a lot of helicopters based here at the height of its operation, I think there were up to 105. It was a big operation, a continual buzz.

In 1999 a not-for-profit company was set up to try and secure a National Sailing Academy on this site. It doesn't have charitable status but it doesn't distribute any profits. Any surpluses that we make we plough back into the enterprise. So the not for profit company was established, with no assets and no money, but just a vision of what could be achieved here. So with the support of the Royal Yachting Association we persuaded the Ministry of Defence to let us into this site in March 2000. The opportunity to operate the centre was advertised nationally and a local company called Sail Force Ltd, run by the Gollop family, was appointed. They had been running a sailing school and an event centre on the far side of Portland Harbour. They had a lot of experience of running events and training in the local waters and they were outgrowing their site.

In 2000 the Academy started to occupy one of the squadron buildings, a hangar, and a slipway, which had been built by the Navy when they were experimenting with hovercraft. It is a nice slipway, but it doesn't go to the low water mark. We got a short-term lease at a relatively cheap rent. The freehold was then sold to the Regional Development Agency who continued to lease us the site on a reasonable basis.

About 4,500 jobs were lost when the Navy went and there were economic studies showing the area would have a 16 per cent unemployment rate. Currently it's 1.6 per cent in Weymouth and Portland. So it's pretty good going. I was still working for the County Council but in early 2002 it became clear that I was spending almost 100 per cent of my time on the Sailing Academy project. So in April 2002 it was decided that I should transfer full time to the Sailing Academy. The County Council gave financial support to the Academy but so did Weymouth and Portland Borough Council and West Dorset District Council. Quite far-sighted of West Dorset because it's not their area but it is on their doorstep and of course the benefits spread out.

So in 2003 we submitted a detailed planning application for this development and our funding applications. We were successful in getting a £3 million grant from the Sport England Lottery Fund, and a £4.3 million grant from the Regional Development Agency. We then had to raise £500,000 in partnership funding. To complete the development for which we had planning permission we needed £9 million so we decided not to carry out all the marine works. We had permission for a second slipway which would have gone into deep water, so we put that on hold as well as more pontoons.

We also did a very rigorous engineering exercise on the main building to cut the costs down. So we were in a position in September 2003 to award a construction contract, which we did, to Dean and Dyball Construction. Part of the academy building is an old hangar, which we have refurbished and recycled. Part of the site was tarmaced, it was a fire training ground for the fire crews to learn on, and so there was some contamination that had to be dealt with. We also reclaimed part of the harbour.

We were officially opened by The Princess Royal in June 2005. In July 2005 the London bid was successful in Singapore, so we had moved from a not-for-profit company with no assets in 1999 to an Olympic venue in six years. It's pretty remarkable.

Sail Force Ltd had been appointed to manage the Sailing Academy. At that time I was the only employee of the not-for-profit company. But then we developed a partnership with Laser, who are the world's largest manufacturer of small boats. We've got them here at the site. So they have got 35 boats available for sailing instruction, which are replaced approximately every six months. So they always have brand new boats. They then sell them on, it's a bit like car demonstrators. So they are slightly used but it does mean there is a constantly up-dated set of boats. So that's the way in which the sailing school works.

At the peak of activity in the summer quite a lot of those instructors will be university students who have got the appropriate RYA qualifications. Up to 20 instructors. There's also a big community and education element linking in with Dorset and other schools. One thing that we are very strong on is that sailing has got a bit of a reputation as an elite activity, we want to overcome that and to show people that actually it's for the whole of the community. And so, through Laser, we liase with local schools. They have a community sailing club here one evening a week were they take the youngsters on the water.

We also have an associated charity called the Chesil Trust which is set up to overcome the barriers to people participating in sailing, whether that's low income or some form of disadvantage or disability. And so earlier this year we did a 'Sail for a Fiver' week where every year six pupil in the Dorset schools in the whole of the county was given the opportunity of coming here and sailing for a fiver. We had nearly 500 in the first week. Each of those sessions costs about £25 to put on, and so the children contributed a fiver themselves because we felt that we if we gave it free it wouldn't be valued. Laser put in £5 and the Chesil Trust put in £15.

It was very successful, got some good publicity so we ran a second week. We hope that we identified those who show a particular enthusiasm or aptitude and that we can offer them the opportunity of pursuing it.

Yes we are talent spotting. If only 10 per cent of the young people get the opportunity of sailing then we are missing out on 90 per cent of the talent. And if we want to keep our pre-eminent position in world sailing then we need to find them. Last year we ran the World Youth Sailing Championships here for 16 and 17 year olds and they very much have their eyes on 2012. They were representing their countries in what was a full-on world championship and we had 63 nations taking part. In the last Olympic Games and Paralympic Games in Athens there were 61 nations. There were representatives from all around the world in that event, even from places like Myanmar, formerly Burma. It was great to see those. And we had a parade in Weymouth with the country flags and banners. It was just fantastic.

We have also hosted children from Chernobyl. That's something that's done by the community in Portland on an annual basis. That was great. They enjoy sailing. There is a strong Ukrainian sailing team.

The reduction in the naval activity has really opened up the area for recreational sailing. When the Navy were here there were about 17,000 ship movements in a typical year. Currently there are about 600. That's the scale of the difference and even if this activity doubles then it wouldn't be a problem. The area has a rich maritime history, there was even a torpedo works at Ferrybridge. But traditionally there has been quite a lot of recreational sailing, Castle Cove Sailing Club, Weymouth Sailing Club, the Royal Dorset Yacht Club and so on, but not on the scale that it currently is.

In addition to the Optimists racing there are Laser Picos used as starter boats in the sailing school, these can be sailed single handed or with two youngsters. When Dorset schools' sailing regatta was held here, earlier this summer, it was actually blowing very hard and so a lot of them spent quite a lot of time in the water, but we had a lot of safety boats out so they were never in any danger.

We have another company called Windtek who do the windsurfing tuition, that takes place here as well. You might also see youngsters raft building, in canoes or in Dragon boats, that's through PGL which is a company that's over at Osmington. They bring thousands of people here each year to do those water sport activities. So we are getting lots of young people on the water, some of whom haven't really been had the opportunity before. For sailing they do have to be able to swim so that they do not panic if they do go into the water.

Some schools come and spend an activity week, here both in and out of county. Milton Abbey School has a fleet of boats that they keep here. In the Olympics there will be a conference later this year in which the number of classes will be discussed in 2012, so there could be some changes. Currently there are 11 classes, which include two keel boat classes, Yngling, in which our girls won a gold medal in Athens and the Star and then you have got fast dinghies like the 49er class, and there is a few 49ers down there, 470s, Lasers and coming all the way down to the windsurfing and there are two surfboarders in the Olympics.

Optimum conditions? Well at the lowest end is six knots of wind up to about 25 knots. It's getting fairly extreme by the time you get up to 25 knots but that's the envelope. In China the Olympic sailing is going to be in Qingdao, a relatively low-wind area in August and there are some strong tides so there is a bit of concern. If you've got a lighter crew you do better in light conditions whereas you need more weight for heavier conditions. So that's a factor. Going around buoys is watched pretty carefully. And the attention is to try and sort out any disputes on the water as far is possible rather than to resolve them later.

The International Sailing Federation nominate who the judges are and so they will have International judges. We are providing the main venue but the London Organising Committee of the Olympic Games and Paralympic Games will be responsible for putting on the show and they will work with the International Sailing Federation.

With regard to accommodation for the Olympic Games, the current intention as far as the competitors are concerned is to bring in a cruise liner and to have it moored alongside in Portland Port. Hopefully HMP *Weare* will have gone by then. Yes we will be right in the middle of it in five years time.

There will be spring tides in the first week of the Olympic Games in 2012 so we will have exceptionally low and high tides. The current slipway is 35 metres wide, the specification for the

Games is for a 150-metre slipway. So the Olympic Delivery Authority (ODA) are letting a contract for substantial works to be undertaken here including more reclamation of the harbour, adjacent to the Sailing Academy. These works will double the size of our dinghy park and provide two slipways almost at 90 degrees to each other each 75 metres wide. So if the wind directly is directly on one slipway then the other can be used. The ODA will also be providing marina berths for 125 boats. These will provide moorings for the keel boats used in both the Olympic Games and the Paralympic Games.

The frontage to the water is changing substantially and there is going to be a commercial marina built to the east of the Sailing Academy with 600 berths. This is being provided by Dean and Reddyhoff marinas who will be injecting private money which is also going to help provide for the Olympic facilities. Work started on the marina in October 2007. The Sailing Academy works will start in January 2008 and be complete by October 2008. So while the focus is on the Olympic and Paralympic Games in China and the elite sailors are away, the works will be done here. The venue for the Olympic Games and Paralympic Games will include both the Sailing Academy and the Dean and Reddyhoff marinas.

With regard to medal prospects in China, sailing is a very successful Olympic sport for Team GBR, and so we have got girls in the Yngling class, Sarah Ayton, Sarah Webb and Pippa Wilson, and we have Nick Dempsey in the Windsurfing class. Paul Goodison is a good prospect in the Laser. At this level it's a young person's sport. In the top squads it is very intense, they have meteorologists on site giving them a briefing each day on what is likely to happen with the weather, they have further experts providing advice on strength and conditioning, nutrition, etc.

At the top level some of the other sports regard the sailing squad as a model of preparation for athletes, given their success in the last few Olympic Games. At the last Olympic Games out of eleven main sailing events Team GBR got five medals, that was two golds, one silver and two bronzes. It's a fantastic result. We could very well see some good performances and medals being won out here in 2012, so that might mean that quite a lot of people turn up to watch it.

For the Olympic Games five courses are planned, one will be in Portland Harbour, the other four will be out in Weymouth Bay. Probably the best place to watch it will be somewhere in Weymouth. It is a natural amphitheatre with high ground around Weymouth Bay, lots of places people can get to, but it is also intended that there will be grandstands with big screens on the beaches and a 'carnival' atmosphere will be created.

Sailing is unique in having two test events and so the first of those test events is in 2010. In previous Olympic Games, each country has been allowed to put two boats into that event. So potentially that's twice as many people and twice as many boats as the Olympics themselves. And then in 2011 there will be a further test event which will be the same number of competitors as the Olympics themselves. The European nations are pretty keen as are America, Australia and New Zealand, So there's very strong competition.

In terms of the Olympic class boats there's one class with three crew, which is the ladies Yngling class. The 49er class is two, the Star is two, the Tornados are two, the 470s are two, the Lasers are single-handed, the Finn is single-handed, and the Windsurfers are obviously single-handed. The Tornado is a catamaran.

We want the works at the Sailing Academy to be a substantial and lasting legacy. We want young people and the community to come and enjoy the facility we also want to hold world class events here. So that will give us a very substantial profile.

We've also got some very interesting ideas about running academic courses here and we are starting an association with Weymouth College to run tuition here, to try and supply young people with skills for the burgeoning marine leisure industry. In the South West, there are estimated to be 32,000 companies actually involved in marine leisure. Most are very small companies with two or three men. Weymouth has got quite a few micro businesses, but the majority of people employed in that industry are 45 or over, so there is a pressing need to provide the skills for the next generation in that industry.

Sailing is a very benign sport. We have powered boats obviously, for safety boats and so on, but we make sure that they are all properly maintained and that they are not putting hydrocarbons into water because we are operating within a very sensitive environmental area here. Portland harbour is a refuge for over-wintering birds and so noisy construction works in the winter like pile driving don't take place between November and March. We have entered into an agreement not to use certain parts of the harbour in the winter months, so we have exclusion zones which are sanctuaries for the birds. Most of them are waders. Generally the birds favour the shallower areas, on the Hamm beach and on the Northern Shore so that we don't go into those areas in the winter months. We have also got some

interesting terrestrial ecology here. We have got Portland sea lavender growing on part of the site, we have got some scaly crickets, which are found generally on the Chesil Beach but they are also here. In the sediment at the bottom of Portland harbour lives a microscopic worm, which is unique to Portland harbour in the UK and is an internationally protected species. It is called *Armandia Cirrhosa*. There is also a mussel farm on the inside of the northern breakwater and scallops are farmed within the harbour.

Sail making has changed a lot. Canvas is quite a heavy material and it is used on vessels such as sailing barges. Modern sails are made of laminate materials such as mylar or kevlar, both really modern lightweight strong materials. Sail making is a very specialist area and there are a number of very good sailmakers around. All the sails have to conform to a very rigorous measurement to ensure that nobody is given an unfair advantage. Just like Formula One racing everybody is trying to push the envelope all the time, trying to find a way of getting a little bit more speed. Modern materials do help in today's very competitive world.

Whilst we have been concentrating on modern or new boats, there are many older boats still being sailed very competitively. These classes are still very important, there are some classic classes and we have a number of traditional class boats, for example the *Sharpies*, where there is still considerable interest and enthusiasm in wooden boats.

26. Nigel Bloxham – The Crab House Café Ferrybridge & The Fleet Oyster Farm, Wyke Regis. Born Gloucester 1958.

We opened in the last weekend in April 2005, to what we thought was a horrendously busy night of seventeen people. The rest is history.

I was born in Gloucester 1958. We all used to go and watch the Severn Bore when we were kids. In those days the lakes at Stroud froze and we walked on the ice. Father was a commercial artist, a sign writer. He was from Birmingham, West Bromwich and Great Barr I think. My mother was a Cheltenham girl and that was it, they had a fruit and veg shop, my grandfather had done the same. I was aware of kitchen food at that early age. My grandmother was the cook at the convent school, Charlton Park, Charlton Kings. My grandfather was the gardener. When I was about six and we went down to Devon, to Torquay. I used to stay with them in the school holidays. You were either in the kitchen or in the garden there was no other choice. If you did well and behaved yourself you went pigeon shooting as a treat. The real things, yes of course.

My parents are still in Torbay today. My mother had a florists and a greengrocers to bring in a bit of cash for my father's business. He ended up painting scenery for stage shows most of his life. All over the country. Dealing mainly with amateur operatics who employed professional producers, directors and scenery painters. He sold that business and retired at 64 but he's still doing it now and he's 75. He says 'I can't believe people want to pay me to do what I love doing.'

We always messed around in the sea, scuba diving or sailing, and a lot of sea angling off the rocks. I went to school in Newton Abbot. So all the lakes there are ex-clay pits. I loved the cider bar at Newton Abbot. With my other business at Paignton, if I get foreign guests I always take them to the cider bar. I tell them it is part of their English education. They love it, they all get 'Totally Jack Assed.'

There used to be a Polish camp up there after the war. Yes that's Stover. They used to process the fish because Young's had a factory there. I can remember going to school with Polish people but then their grandparents couldn't speak English. It was quite fascinating in the 1970s. They must have been there 30 years. They had their own shop inside and everything.

I did a little bit of work in the hotels, dishwashing and that sort of thing then I went to college at Torquay to do the chef's course. A great friend of mine also did it, his last job was the executive chef at the Sheraton Doha, before that he was in Cairo for ten years. He likes it warm. He's worked around the world. Head chef in the Mandarins, the whole lot.

Two-year course. The old City and Guilds. It was actually really very good. After college I went straight into a chef's job. We did one of the first carveries, The Hare and Hounds at Kingskerswell. It's still a carvery. A very successful one. Then I worked for local nightclub and pub owners, restaurant owners, then I went to London with the Hilton Group. The staff kitchen got done for 'health'. That's not really what I thought the Hilton was all about in those days. While I was waiting for that job to come up I worked for a local fishmonger who was supplying me in Torbay. I did two months work experience and I really enjoyed it, so I ended up going back and working for him for nine months. Then I got involved in a fish business myself, supplying fish to chefs around the Reading, Windsor and Basingstoke area. Fish from Brixham. I used to fill up a van and come home when it was sold. Seafare Products, that was the start of wet fish and

Nigel Bloxham sizing up the menu

wet fish processing. They just couldn't get hold of really good fresh fish. I could also see the potential.

It was 1981. One of my customers was this chap in Bristol, I had to deliver to this one little restaurant which was like a little disused corner shop. You had to walk through the kitchen to get to the dining room behind. All the herbs were hanging up and that guy couldn't wait to dive into the back of the van and talk to me about things. It was the Greek bedsit area, and that guy was Keith Floyd. And I can remember him saying to me one day 'Nigel, I need some fish,' I said 'We've had storms, I've got sprats and nothing else.' He said 'need some fish I have got to cook for HTV at lunchtime.' And that was his first TV cooking thing. I said 'What did you do last week?' And he said 'I did carp in tomato sauce,' because I couldn't sell him any sea fish. The housewives are really going to do that aren't they? I used to have to get him out of bed to pay the bills. Three o'clock in the afternoon. He had a mate down the road who had a restaurant called *Bon Auberge* and his mate used to walk around in Gary Glitter suits and high heels. He was an ex-band manager anyway. Floyd he used the Stranglers music didn't he on his first series, there was a big tie up because this guy used to be something to do with the Stranglers.

That was '81 I reckon. There was another place in Park Street, I used to pick up fish and deliver fish there, then come up the motorway to Basingstoke see, but it worked. It was learning and having a lot of fun. I just enjoyed myself as a young man. I'd buy in Brixham Market. I'd buy it one day, take it up the next, and come back the third day. It evolved and changed.

Three years on it became very aggressive. A national company got involved, they started to distribute every day. I couldn't compete. So I started to supply them. That made sense. So then I had a nice fish processing business and we started exporting fresh fish to Switzerland and all sorts of places. We'd do a lot of plaice fillets. We used to send on a Monday and a Friday to Switzerland by road. The Friday lot would arrive there Monday and the Monday ones would arrive by Thursday for their weekend fish. They used to like the little plaice fillets. They were very good. They were Swiss Germans and they did it extremely correctly. Once you dealt with them, they feel that you must deal with them for life.

I had the pickle business as well. The pickle marinade business for seafood products, which is doing very well at the moment. We are going into local line caught mackerel, particularly the line caught mackerel that started up in Cornwall. Well that's Nathan Rosarieux. They've done really well with it. Dorset have clicked on to it, they've just had a grant for them to start it up and Devon will follow. Waitrose. It's because of the story they are buying it, not because of the price, like Nick Howell and the pilchards.

I started the pickles and marinades to utilise cuttlefish in Brixham. It was on the quayside rotting and they didn't know what to do with it, so I started to do mock fish, tried to sell it as squid bait. Eventually I saw what the Italians did with it and I thought we should do that. Sadly I can't afford to buy the cuttlefish in Brixham, its now the black gold of Brixham, the saviour. Brixham wouldn't be there today if it wasn't for the cuttlefish. Forget grants and expanding businesses and money, it's cuttle. The cuttle is now a huge industry. It goes to France and Italy, Japan takes an awful lot. And they want the big ones, so I have to buy mine from the Far East now cleaned and ready to go. That's ironic isn't it? Yes. Like these whelks going to Korea? I've got some in there caught by my friend on his boat, canned in Liverpool, Korean whelks.

So the pickle business evolved out of the van business. What happened was M and J Seafoods. I thought I can use the cuttle fish and we made some up and took it there. They said 'That's good, that's brilliant.' And they said 'We'll have ten cases next week please.' And that's where it started. It's now a three-quarter of a million pound business. From ten cases. Seafare Products based at Paignton Harbour.

Boats? I've just bought a boat and registered it for fishing and diving. I'll be catching fish for here, which hopefully will be great fun as well. I wanted to get back into cooking. The oysters came with this restaurant. It wasn't completely alien to me, because while I was down at Paignton harbour there used to be an oyster and mussel purification business in one of the units, that I still own. He wanted to go back to America, so he sold it to me. So for a couple of years I was processing mussels and oysters. The mussels were from the Teign, Exe and Dart. Then the EU regulations changed drastically and the farmers were going to get grants to do their own purification so I felt I was going to get squeezed out. I desperately needed the space for the pickle business so that's what happened. We closed that down and the pickle business opened up. Then this restaurant came up. A friend of mine had it for ten years, didn't really do anything successful with it. We opened in the last weekend in April 2005, to what we thought was a horrendously busy night of 17 people. The rest is history.

Oysters? A man called Neville Copperthwaite started the Abbotsbury oyster farm here in 1989. He wrote a piece about the history of oysters on the Fleet and how the Saxons had them and they belonged to the abbey till the abbey got the chop. In the 1740s a chap called Captain Lysle goes and buys 30 tons of oysters from France. Then there's the fever hospital at Ferrybridge. He goes on about them having diseases in the 17th and 18th cent, also the Romans coming here for them.

Well Neville came in '89, the Abbotsbury Estates came to him and said 'Find something to grow in the Fleet.' And he came up with oysters. The oysters grew like rockets then but they put too many out there and they didn't grow. Peter Hoare came when David Jarred had it. David never really did anything with it and he said 'Nigel I want you to have because I know you will do it.' So we came to a deal and I took it on. Peter Hoare had come back from Australia and became the general manager for David. Then I came in. I liked Peter's new system of hanging baskets and getting rid of the old racks. We are the only northern hemisphere farm to go over to this system. They grow quicker, they are a better shape and much better meat. Less hassle, yes. We don't get mud worm, we don't get disease. We have just tried to get a grant to do an expansion on that system. Peter Hoare is now the consultant. I got to be different and I could see the potential of marketing. That's why we have got this new oyster. It's the same species but we call it the *Portland Royal* and it has started to take off. This next winter we have got a contract indirectly with Caviar House for them to sell *Portland Royals* in-between natives and the normal Pacifics. It's a very good niche market. A quality product and Harrods want a small one and they are going to call them *Portland Princesses*. I mean Jersey Royal potatoes worked didn't they?

We have got them on wooden posts to which we then attach a rail and then we hang these baskets on the rails. They rock in the sea therefore the oysters are turned over and the sharp edges get knocked off, so they don't concentrate on shell growth, they concentrate on meat growth. They love the temperature because there is more food in the water and they work harder and move harder, it's a bit like us really. We slow down in the cold don't we, shrivel up and disappear.

The salinity varies at different times of the year and different weather conditions. At the moment we have got a lot of fresh water coming down because of the rain. All the food comes with the salt water from Portland harbour and all the nice minerals comes from the chalk streams which makes a good shell.

Oysters feed on the micro-organisms in the water, the plankton. We get the blooms, they feed on the blooms. We don't get the bad ones although the local health guys do monitor it. The one thing we do have on our doorstep is the UK's regulatory body in Cefas. The UK's body on oyster farming. We are run by regulations and it's sat on our doorstep so we tend to think we probably get kicked hardest. On the other hand they do buy oysters off us for trials, so it's not all bad.

Actually Chesil Beach isn't impervious, I mean the sea gets through, it seeps up. It's like a big filter bed. Of course most of it does come in through Portland Harbour, you know we watched this Napoli thing, we were glad it went where it did and didn't come here because to have oil on our oyster beds would have been disastrous.

The beds? At the moment we go just up around the corner here with oysters but we have to go beyond the narrows and there is an area there that's on the lease but it's not being currently used. I'd like to use it in the future but we've only got certain days we can get up there and work it which is a problem because they shoot some days. And of course we can only do it on the spring tides. In the 1970s MAFF were doing trials there secretly on the bridging camp, which I thought was quite nice of them to turn a blind eye. Saying that oysters grew very well. Yes like rockets, they described them, didn't they, in the report?

We are aiming to do 350,000 a year as a limited edition oyster, like a good wine. A chateau? That's exactly how we are operating. I employ my father-in-law. Dave Scott as the oysterman. He used to work in a silver mine in Sierra Leone. We have seasonal staff in to help. The seed oysters we are buying them in from Jersey. They are a nice oyster. They have done the best of the lot.

Staff? In the restaurant we go up to about 14. Some of them are casual staff, and we have got four permanent that work right through the winter. Chefs? I think I've found it in a local lad who then went to work away and has now come back to work. He came down here and cooked for me and he was very good. So I am going to executive chef it and he's going to do the day to day cheffing, and my son's going to commis for him. Hopefully it will work out. It will be an interesting time.

The menu? We have had a bit of weather just recently so it's not as wide as it sometimes is. I have quite often got conger eel on the menu. Yes, everything that we put on the menu is caught by English fishermen on English boats. Most of them I have known for the last 25 years between Poole and Looe. So it really is the most local fish we get. Customers come in and say 'Is it fresh fish? Is it local fish?'. And I say 'You ain't gonna get it like you get it here. Oh and sometimes it is flapping.' I get crabbers who land to me who get congers and bull huss in their pots and I mean he just puts in his vivier tank and lifts it out live and says 'Here you are Nige' and throws them to us like a rugby ball.

We have got live tanks with crabs and lobsters in and the oysters. We have had congers swim around there just to give the heebie geebies to the staff. Some people do smoke conger, yes hot smoking. Yes it's all right. The first people to smoke conger was Jackson's in Newton Abbot. I know that because I was the first person to take a conger there and ask them to hot smoke it. It was good. Smoked eel goes for a premium price, this is why we thought, conger, there's plenty of them let's try and use them. We put conger on the menu now. Normally we do it as blackened eel, Cajun spices and a bit of chocolate in it and blacken it in the pan.

If I put conger eel it wouldn't sell, if I put blackened eel, it sells.

The only thing that's on the menu that doesn't come from that area is the prawns. Unfortunately non-fish eaters eat prawns in my opinion, so they have to go on because the public demand it. At least we buy them in raw but frozen, therefore we control the cooking. We only put them on the menu when we are short of fish. Yes I have got soused mackerel with local cider, I've got pan fried butterfly fillet of red mullet, we got a ginger Jake smoked herrings, smoked in Newton Abbot. We have got Thai fishcakes, in which we use all our trimmings, fish off-cuts. If it's cold miserable weather we'll do a chowder to use up the odds and ends and the mackerel mousse, you know the local mackerel smoked and made into mousse with beetroot salsa, whole local beetroot done with a bit of balsamic vinegar to sweeten it and horseradish. Horseradish is very good with beetroot and mackerel, so it goes very well.

Dogfish normally goes to London as rock salmon. Rock and chips. We do it with red wine and bacon and thyme, it's like a meat sauce because it's a meaty fish, if you have got a meat eater who walks in and wants to try a bit of fish it's excellent. We get a lot of people like that who want us to help them, so I will talk them into trying a huss or a skate because it's only got a bone in the middle it won't bite them and it's a meaty texture fish. Its like swordfish, shark family, like tender pork, so that works really well with the red wine and bacon, it's not an alien sauce to them either, it gives them their gravy. So that works quite well, large plaice fillet. We have some super large plaice fillet coming in at this time of the year.

Skate, we sell lots of skate, skate with chorizo, the spicy oil comes out of the chorizo, with paprika and spring onions it goes really. You see lots of people using chorizo with fish now. Perhaps it's time for us to change. It got written about a couple of times saying how good it was, so it became almost a house signature dish. Red mullet with sun-dried tomato sauce, that's literally sun-dried tomatoes and olives and whizzed up together and away we go. The red mullets are starting to come in now and they run quite heavily late August and September and we also grill them with pesto.

I don't know what's going to happen this year because this year's weather is so different, but last year we got the mullets and the dorys early, lots of dorys came in last year. Squid nearly all through the summer whereas it normally used to be September onwards. Cod fillet, line caught is beautiful. This is called summer cod down here. It comes down and it feeds on the wrecks, it eats a lot of sand eel and it's got a lot of oil in it. It eats very well, it flakes, making a gap in the fillets but it doesn't have the shelf life. You need to use it.

Brill it's a great channel fish, you get lots of it over on the Channel Islands. We've got it with wild mushrooms today. Which is nice you just put the wild mushrooms on the top, mix wild mushrooms with some butter and some parsley and a bit of mushroom ketchup and away we go, it's as simple as that, it's quick and easy to do and brill fillet needs very little cooking – my favourite at the moment. I'm not a great sea bass fan, there is too much sea bass farmed, all the pubs around are selling it. Ours is wild, I wouldn't deal with anything else and I insist we buy the bigger fish and fillet it a lot of the time. We've done it pan fried with citrus fruits, I just enjoy cooking that one and it looks great coming out on the plate and the customers receive it well and that's good news. That's probably my favourite at the moment.

I like gurnards and conger, pollack, we haven't got any pollack on we use loads and loads of pollack we use loads of gurnards when we can get them. Whole grey mullet, that is a fantastic fish. That is a great eating fish. I know it scavenges and it goes around harbours and things like that, it's a great fish. We are baking it whole in fennel salt and serving it at the table. So we can crack the salt, stuffing the belly with fennel and lemon. Sometimes we do the grey mullet Singapore-style, citrus fruits, and Singapore spices. We also have to cater for vegetarians.

Crab and oysters, well that's what we are good at. We insist on nice big crabs and full ones. We do the Chinese crab. It's not a Chinese crab, as most people ask, it is crab done the Chinese way. The crabs are good, and we serve them whole or halved. Well everyone wants to eat them in May when they are at their worst. As soon as the sunshine arrives they think let's go and have a nice crab. Wrong time of the year to get nice crab, they are just getting good now, the best time of all is Christmas, just before Christmas. Spider crabs. When we do get them, we serve them up the same way.

Oysters? We think we have virtually cracked it all year round. We have got some that won't breed, they don't spawn. And this will be the first year, so it's quite exciting stuff again.

The location where we are, here, this was the oyster sheds. It was tanks, then they started opening up to sell a few oysters, then oyster bars with bring your own wine and with a table and chair outside, then they started doing cokes for walkers, then it progressed into a sea food café and wet fish shop. And we now get a lot of people asking to buy our fish but we don't really do that because we are just too busy. I'd love to open a shop in the shed next door a sea food deli and sea food art, something cranky like sea food art and sea food deli and do books and something like that, have a bit of a coffee bar with a slice of cake in the afternoon and that sort of thing. Course I'd only do fish books and seaside books.

Ferrybridge where we are is actually a very interesting place because it was the ferry into Portland wasn't it? And this ground we are on, when they built the new bridge, they dug it out and this became reclaimed land, and so because the Estate owned the bottom of the Fleet it became theirs by default. Abbotsbury Estate? Yes it's Stangways, it's now the Ilchester Estate with Charlotte Townsend. Yes she's a lovely lady I like her. The torpedo works was over there wasn't it? Yes that was the other side. Todd's was this side and the torpedo works was the other side.

Good reviews for the restaurant ? Yes brilliant. Oh God we haven't scratched the surface, not really I mean, do we do another one, restaurant? I don't know, I'd love to do another one back home in Torbay.

Well the crabbing industry started out of Paignton harbour. So much has come out of the Paignton area with crabbers and crab boats the Browses and Dartmouth. My friend from Paignton has got three boats, now it's all crewed with Paignton and Dartmouth crews. And they are now fishing off the top of Denmark. Unbelievable, so it's a world story, it's almost like the Newfoundland cod. I'd love to open a crab house at Paignton harbour to the crabbing industry and have the museum to it and to tell the story, it's a real bit of history. It's modern history really because it's all happened in the last 50 years but it must be remembered, it can't be lost.

27. Heddon Johnson – Weymouth Rowing Club and conservation builder. Born Karachi 1952.

They came around one evening and we sat around the kitchen table and they said 'We'd like to build a Cornish pilot gig.' And that's how it all started and we were both very touched and we said 'Of course, we'd love that.'

My father was in oil exploration and he spent his time before the war in the Far East exploring Borneo and Sarawak, mostly for Shell, but he was working for Burmah Oil after the war in Pakistan. He had during the war, gone into photo-reconnaissance and he used those skills for geological exploration, stereo photographs. He mapped for BP, something like three-quarters of a million square miles. Most of that was in South America but when he was in Borneo before the war he discovered those oil fields that made the Sultan of Brunei so rich. He had a degree in geology from Durham and on his first job did a lot of exploration on his own. He used to live with the Dayaks in Borneo. Yes with a bit of head hunting and pig sticking.

I left Pakistan for the last time when I was about four. We had a beach house in Karachi, the monsoon must have come in and the car ran out of petrol. My dad had to get petrol and I have got this vivid image of him in a white shirt turning flesh coloured as it got wet stomping through puddles rather crossly. He was a great gardener. Then he came back here, we went to Northumberland for a bit. Then he moved to London where he took a job with BP in photo-reconnaissance. He became head of department and that was just before it all started going computerised. He did everything by hand. I grew up in Woking, he commuted.

I went to university at Keele when I met my wife Tor. She worked in the Northcott Theatre in Exeter with a very good friend of mine. I studied geology and chemistry and then got thoroughly cheesed off with both of those. I'm a very practical person. If I see someone do something I always feel I can do it myself and with a bit of practice I can do it quite well. Tor's mum later on moved to Dorset. I came down to visit and there was a fish farm at Winterbourne Houghton. They were in deep trouble. It was summer of 1976. I stopped and said 'You need a hand?' and they said 'Yeah, got some wellies?' I started work that day. The water had heated up and there was no oxygen. They had to clear it and aerate it. They weren't very good on pumps. With siphoning you get movement of water for free. So I helped them out and stayed there for several years. It was eventually bought by a chap called Sam Holland who had a trout fishery on the Itchen and we turned Houghton into a brood farm. We were responsible for eight million eggs or live fish a year. Nearly all rainbow trout but Sam was an interested breeder and he used to cross-breed with char, arctic char and brown trout. Some of them were great sports fish. We would sell eyed-up eggs or fry from quite small to three or four inches and we built the farm at Iwerne Minster. The eggs and fry really want crystal clear water and plenty of it. I ended up managing that place for him.

Tor's mother married again. She had a house in the south of France. It was a communal hamlet so all the houses were based around communal bread ovens and wine presses. Her new husband bought a ruin and asked if I would project manage its redevelopment. Tor speaks fluent French so we moved to France. I was out there for about two and a half years. Hands on work really attracts me. This was 1982. We had vines that I looked after and took the grapes to the commune. My eldest son Hadrian, went to school in St Tropez. Tristan was about six

Heddon Johnson with Sir Tristan and the ladies of the Weymouth Rowing Club

months when we went out there.

But I had a house here, in Milborne St Andrew and I made the decision to come back and concentrated on conservation building. I like old buildings. I was drawn towards the real nitty-gritty of deconstructing houses and then reconstructing them. Carpentry and joinery. Yes I can turn my hand to most trades. Conservation builder. Yes I would like to think I am. That's my speciality. I do it for other people. I also design.

Boats? Well it was my son Tristan who worked in Weymouth at Kingfisher Marine. He started because a friend of his worked there and they used to go pressure washing, it's a vile winter job. Kingfisher Marine is based on the corner of the harbour before the bridge. They must have done a 100-150 boats over winter. Owned by Dave Caddy, he's also a chandler and does various boat repairs. Tristan first of all started washing these boats. It was a way of getting money at the time. He was early teens and he then started to enjoy it. To cut a long story short he ended up as an apprentice marine engineer. Dave Caddy liked him, he worked hard. So Tristan was working there and he went to boat shows with Dave Caddy. They went to Southampton, which is where he had an accident and was killed.

It was a complete mess. Kingfisher Marine were agents for a firm called Sowester. They were on their stand at Southampton. Tristan was just down there for a day trip. This was 2000 and Tristan had gone down with the firm's secretary and they had arranged to go out on a boat that Sowester were selling with another Sowester agent. They had gone out for a demonstration on this RIB and the girl had asked if she could have a go. The agent who had spoken to this girl an awful lot on the phone wrongly assumed that she was familiar with boats. So he gave her control and she didn't have a clue what she was doing.

It was a very pokey, a real sports car of a RIB and she pushed the handle of the throttle down and turned at the same time and just lost control completely and threw all three of them into the drink. And when the agent had given control to this girl she hadn't put on the 'kill cord.' If you are attached physically to the key it will cut the engine out when detached and anyway she hadn't put it on and so this boat was left whizzing around. It was a rigid hull with inflatable bags around the side. So they were all in the water and they had got separated and some people, very brave people came into rescue them.

This was September, so the water was quite warm and they managed to get to the other two. Meanwhile this boat had done another circle, come across and hit another boat, out of control and started to go piggy back on this other boat and the guy just pushed it over and it went off again. And because it was locked in a tight turn and because it was hitting it's own wake, it would then jump and its turns weren't predictable. So it was all over the place. Unfortunately it went over the top of Tristan and he died on the way back to the stand.

It turned out that there was an awful lot wrong with this boat not only was it bloody powerful and it was stupid that they hadn't attached the 'kill chord.' They had tested the boat and found fault with it and various technical things with it. I don't actually think that Sowester had paid the invoice for it because it was a demonstration boat. They were only going to be paying a percentage and so everyone in court was fighting over it. It was a grey area. They found there was a fault with the hull, it had a tendency to chine when taking turns, skipping sideways. There's a little blade on the back of an outboard motor that has a little fin on it just above the propeller. The propeller produces two forces, one pushing the water out the back and the other one trying to pull it sideways. Torque tab, yes. They'd set the torque tab out the wrong way so it was making things worse. In this case the accident was fatal. Certainly it was a contributory factor. With fatal accidents like that there is a chain of events in which each link has to be in place and if any one link is not there, it might never have happened.

Well I'm sort of furious with Sowester, Simpson & Lawrence. They had gone into liquidation. No they didn't build the boat but they tested it and ignored the advice of the chief of the sales staff who refused to get in the boat. He thought it was too dangerous and they took it for demonstration at the Boat Show. If they could get a new boat quickly on the market, so much the better.

An inquest? There was a trial of the agent who took the boat out. The case was that as master of a ship he had failed to carry out his duty of care, masters responsibilities etc. That case failed because the judge dismissed it after about five days because he said the prosecution hadn't proved that this RIB was a ship. Now a legal definition of a ship is a vessel which is capable of being navigated. Well as a layman I just can't see what the problem is. Navigation is by moving from one point to another either by sight or by instrument, well it's capable of that. I actually think that the judge had decided that the guy in the dock wasn't the right person in the dock. It should have been the company directors and I think he used that as an excuse.

Tristan was 20 when this happened. A young lad with everything in front of him and a job he liked. Also he had gone through a bad period, a friend of his died the Christmas before. Those two used to do pressure washing. He drowned in the Swannery in Weymouth in mysterious circumstances. He had left a nightclub. I knew him, he was a loveable rogue and nothing really added up. He drowned having left this club. Someone said they had seen him asleep on a bench and that was the last sighting of him. He was found in the water ten days afterwards. To skip forward, the two boats that we have at the rowing club

are Sir Tristan and Penny and the chap who died was called Simon Penny but known as Penny by all his friends. Lots of people see the boat think its after a girl but in fact it's Simon.

Whilst Tristan was working for Dave Caddy, a chap built a boat and Tristan helped him. There were three of them, Andrew, Alan and Tristan. Traditional boat building. Alan had served his apprenticeship at Dave Caddy's some 40 years earlier. A wonderful boat called *Megan*, she's gaff rigged she must be 40 feet long. She was cedar plank, little cedar plank tongue and grooved and then fibreglassed in and out and on top. At Tristan's funeral there was Andrew, a chap called Bill Noble and Dave Caddy. They came up to me and said 'We've got an idea can we come and talk to you about a memorial?' And I said 'Fine.' And they came around one evening and we sat around the kitchen table and they said 'We'd like to build a Cornish pilot gig.' And that's how it all started and we were both very touched and we said 'Of course, we'd love that.'

And at that very first meeting they said to us 'We must think of a name and also think about colours for this boat.' Tor and I said his bedroom is painted in Rasta colours being of that age and they all sort of coughed and spluttered and said 'Yes well we'll think about that.' And then we had a meeting in the Royal Dorset Yacht Club in Weymouth to see what local support we had and it turned out there was a lady there who was heavily into coastal rowing from Chichester - sliding seat rowing. She said she would be more than happy to coach. So that sounded promising and there were other people who thought it was a good idea and people who were prepared to put a bit of money in.

Well if you buy a pilot gig off the shelf it's going to cost about £18,000, so we decided so build one from scratch. An oak keel which is laid first with a bow and stern both coming up in oak and then the planks are English elm on oak ribs and when we built that, that was all we were allowed to use. The boats are scrutineered by the Cornish Pilot Gig Association and they send along a team of three guys three or four times during construction to measure up. You have ribs, these frames along the length of the boat that you set up and you build to these. They're called moulds, eight points along the length of the boat and in-between follows naturally. You then take the moulds away.

Pilot gigs. Swanage has one. Lyme and West Bay are toying with the idea. The boats are 32 ft long and with four foot nine inches across. Six rowing, one cox. When shipping came in under sail the pilots would row out from small Cornish ports to pop a pilot on board and gain a pilot fee. That's where the competitive element came from because if you could beat your neighbour, you would get the job. They would pilot ships up to Bristol, Liverpool or London. So they were very knowledgeable, these pilots. Our two were probably the first Cornish pilot gigs built in Dorset. They go as far east as Holland and there's one in Australia. They are very stable, very forgiving boats to row. You can take out a crew of relatively inexperienced people and still have fun.

Alan Hanger, who had served his apprenticeship in the loft upstairs, agreed to build the boat. He was semi-retired then. Andrew and Bill Noble found the wood and and all three of them built the gig. Yes it was very exciting. I used to go along. It was a thing of outstanding beauty, especially in its raw wood state as it was taking form. Beautiful curves, it was stunning.

I wrote letters to Tristan's friends and family. Their donations probably represented the lion's share of the money, with lots of people making very generous donations, anything from twenty quid to five hundred. But the gig all told only cost us about four and a half grand because of everything being donated. The elm was seasoned, cut quite thin. In a normal year they build over the winter to stop the elm cracking. There are still a few elms around. On the Scillies they're completely unaffected. There's plenty of elm growing but they're not big trees.

The rowing club was set up at that meeting in the Royal Dorset Yacht Club. We have a membership of about 100. We have a huge membership on the ladies side. I'm very keen on the vets crew. We have vets and super vets and super super vets as well. Vets in gig terms is over 40 which is in my opinion too young. We have the odd super vet event which is over 50 and super super vets are over 60. They are great. There's no holding back and they are healthy. It gets people out on the water.

Originally the boats were kept in a cage on site, enclosures, like they use around building sites. We had a compound like that near the slipway opposite Debenhams and we kept the boats there. We had two of them there for a while and then we wanted to build a shed opposite Debenhams. The council weren't keen on that so they suggested a site on the other side of the harbour underneath Nothe Fort, just up a bit from the lifeboat station where there's another slipway and its there that we built a shed. The first one we built using a big old concrete panelled garage and we adapted that by putting bits of wood between the concrete panels. We extended that last year with the help of Dorset Works who took us on as their charity of the year. It helps financially being a charity and sponsors look at you more seriously. Our charitable aims are to help the disadvantaged, the young and provide a healthy occupation outside.

So we've got two boats and commissioning a third one. That will be built by Dave Curragh who is a boat builder of some renown who's been building boats for the clubs that are at present the most successful clubs. The idea is that this will be a racing boat not to be used for everyday use. That's being built in Cornwall.

Well the trailer that was the next thing we needed to go racing. A chap who knew Tristan used to own the firm that provided the big cranes that lifted the boats out of the water for pressure washing. Richard had an engineering workshop. Dave Caddy said to him one day 'We need a trailer.' And he said 'Oh I'll build you a trailer,' and lo and behold he did. They're specially designed. So that was built and we go racing. We went to Rame and Cawsand. That was the first event we ever went to and of course came last in everything. Later that summer we had our first success. Our vets team, of which I was a member, came in fifth out of about ten. We were so pleased with ourselves.

Pilot gigs are incredibly stable. On the Scillies three years ago there were huge seas when we were racing. You wouldn't dream of going out in it unless out for a purpose. Not an incident in sight. The races went on and the boat along side you would just disappear. You'd be up and they'd be down. That's what they were built for wasn't it? Yes 2002 we went to the Scilly's because Tristan was killed on 22nd September 2000. We had Sir Tristan in May that year and Penny I think April the year after. So we went to the Scillies in 2002.

What I didn't tell you was how the name came about. It was sort of obvious but it was just trying to find a connection between Tristan and Cornish pilot gigs and the Arthurian legends and Celtic history. I like the name Sir Tristan, it's noble, grand, it's good. And so that's how it got its name. As for its colours my son Tristan had a book which had illustrations in it from a French manuscript of the story of Tristan and Isolde and Sir Tristan's colours in this book were this livid green with the three gold crowns and so I suggested then that those would be suitable colours for the boat this bright, bright green. So these colours were adopted and the paint was donated by Blakes a paint company. They hadn't got the green I wanted, so I they let me have a couple of sample pots and I played around by mixing in yellow until I got the green that I was after and they kindly mixed up a batch of that. We give it a new coat each year.

In Scilly this year it topped a hundred gigs. The buzz! It starts on the ferry crossing from Penzance. The big mass migration is on the Friday morning where there are hundreds of people queuing to get on to the boat. It is the Scillonian and she's weighed under and you wonder if everyone stood on one side whether you wouldn't all topple over. The boats are craned on. They take two or three boats at a time. So the boats have been going over for a month or more. On that Friday morning the last three boats will be going over and this great mob of people. Everyone is very excited and we all know each other by sight so there's lots of chatting going on. I tend to go earlier now and it's a more select mob that goes out earlier, but there's still that feeling of camaraderie. The first race if everything goes according to plan will be on Friday evening.

The way it works now is that they have the vets races on the Friday and then the heat racing will be on the Saturday and Sunday. The way they work the heats out, is that they have a long race which is from St Agnes into St Mary's which is about 1.7 miles. Starting can be fun. You can imagine a line of a 100-odd gigs in one race that looks like it's a mile long and they say it's only half a mile long, but I don't believe them and you have got two start boats at either end. They are in radio contact and originally that was it. Now they have a series of RIBs, safety boats dotted along in front of all the gigs, so they now create a line using these RIBs and everybody else is held back. The start you will hear on the radio and then the RIBs get out of the way. That's how it starts but the noise is unbelievable because the oars on the gigs are held between wooden thole pins, and the oars rattle between the pins. It sounds like some primeval drumbeat going on. It's just pandemonium, coxes screaming. A bit like what an ancient galley would have sounded like.

They have heats of 12 in the second, third and fourth round. If you win in that heat or come second in that heat you will go up in the next round and two will go down. It's quite a fair system. Two races a day, a long race and one short race, 1.1 mile. They go from Nut Rock off Tresco, which is opposite Hugh Town on St Mary's straight across and that's spectacular too. The islands are low lying and look like they should be in the Caribbean especially on a fine sunny day. The wonderful beautiful clear water. If it's wet and windy it can be quite miserable.

This year we won our first trophy ever on the Scillies. We were 25th out of a hundred. That's pretty good. To row the long course, the 1.7 miles, in a following wind you would get it down to about 12-13 minutes, as against wind, 20 minutes. Our ladies came in 27th so they did well too. Occupations of the rowers? Everything. We really are all-inclusive, we have solicitors, fishermen, carpenters, all sorts, teachers. Out of Portland Harbour we tend to row either along the beach towards Preston and Bowleaze Cove or we go up the other way which is towards Portland and row out to Chequered Fort and back.

It's now become a very important part of my life. I am chairman. I'm also head coach. We were lucky enough to have one member who had come up from Cornwall who actually has the pasty shop in Dorchester, where he imports pasties made in Cornwall. He can then cook them here on site and it turned out that he had been a gig rower and loved it. And when he moved to Dorset he thought that was the end of his gig rowing but it wasn't to be.

So he was our coach at first. His real name is John Hardwick or Pasty John so he coached for a while and we kept getting hints from other clubs what we were doing wrong and all the rest of it. Eventually I said I'll take on the job of coaching so that I unify everything whether I'm right or wrong. I'll get you all doing the same which is actually the art of gig rowing, it's a real team event like any rowing. Synchronised, balanced got to be doing the same, timing. Yes the stroke rower, the rower nearest the stern, nearest the cox actually sets the rate but the cox can tell him to increase. Women members are better organised than men. We do mixed rowing but we don't train together. The women have always been better at turning up and sorting themselves out, who's going to row, in what boat, what time. So newcomers find it very easy to slot in with them. Men are far more haphazard…

We also took advice from guys who rowed for a club called Caradon which is in Saltash. At the World Championships on the Scilly Isles they were the world champions for 11 out of the last 12 years. They adopted that name very early on when there were probably only 20 or 30 gigs.

Hopefully our club will grow. All the current gigs are based on a gig that was built by William Peters who came from St Mawes and he reckoned that the finest gig that he built was a boat called the *Trefry*. Newquay were the starters of the modern era of gig racing, they found the ruin of the *Trefry* and restored it. She then became the spec from which all other gigs have been built and that was done by a chap called Ralph Bird. Must have been 30 years ago if not 35. Now they are being computerised, the drawings, so that anywhere in the world can make them.

28. Mark Poulton – Punch & Judy Professor, Weymouth. Born Gloucester 1972.

Once Punch is in your blood there's no getting him out. I say to people 'What sort of Punch and Judy do you want? Do you want an old fashioned traditional Punch and Judy, do you want a modern politically correct Punch and Judy?' And of course they all say 'No' to that one. 'Or do you want a stupid violent show?' And they all say 'Yeah.' That's what they want.

Mum was a teacher and Dad worked for British Telecom, as it's now known, in Stroud. My grandfather had several jobs, he was a gardener. My gran cleaned the bank, me other grandmother was a cleaner. I've got a sister, she's in St Albans and works, I think, for the German tourist board.

While I'm in Weymouth I'm living temporarily in a caravan on Bagwell Farm, that's a campsite the other side of Chickerell. I'm based in Paignton, got the house down there. I come back up in May, work all the way through.

I went to school in Gloucestershire. Not that I spent much time at school. I was doing summer seasons. My parents were getting letters asking why I wasn't turning up for GCSEs and I was up in Llandudno doing the Punch and Judy, so they got grief about that, then I left school a year later, May 1989, a week after passing my driving test and moved down to Devon and was doing Punch and Judy down there for a living at 17.

Saw Punch and Judy on this very spot when I was four years old and knew there and then that it was what I was going to do. Everything captivated me. Just the look of the show. That was a good show that I saw. Just the atmosphere, the puppets, the

voices were clear, the theatre was lovely, so everything, it was just magical. You become a Punch and Judy Professor by reading up, watching as many different shows as you can, different performers. I was told at an early age that if I was going to do this as a profession, to try and learn every aspect from woodwork to carving to sewing the costumes, publicity, book keeping, so I've tried to master every aspect of it.

I did a summer season up in Llandudno, that was for the Codman family, it had been in their family for generations. It's a couple of hundred years up there on the seafront, and then when I left school I started my own business which was really difficult. In debt for the first few years because I had to buy a car, and buy some puppets because I was very limited with what I could make, just sort of learning then. I was doing the full performance. I was 16 years old. It was hard work because you don't get a day off. In the school holidays you're working every day for six weeks doing three shows a day, and you get knackered out.

You don't get paid, it's what you collect, so it should be the better the show, the better the contributions coming in. When you're on the beach you have to get the same people to come back and if your show is weak people will not contribute. You get a lot that don't contribute anyway, they will say 'No, it's not up to scratch,' and it really puts you on the spot. You do the show as best you can to get the same people, and working the beach and busking the show when you're not paid, it does sharpen you up something chronic.

Down in Devon there's a lot of leisure parks and that kind of thing. It was nice to do, and when I was working Goodrington which I was doing for nine years, I was down there seven days a week and then I was down there five days and doing the leisure park two days so I got that guaranteed money. But the reason I

Mark Poulton, Punch and Judy Professor

quit on the beach was that the council were charging me so much money and the people were refusing point blank to put anything in because they said it was a public beach and they didn't have to pay and all the rest of it. It was the something for nothing mentality, and I couldn't survive and I ended up quitting.

Once Punch is in your blood there's no getting him out. But my predecessor here at Weymouth, the one that I saw, he had to retire due to ill health and he asked if I wanted to take over. That was 2005. So he asked me if I was interested in taking over and my wife was about to have our first baby, so our daughter was born and a month after that I moved up here and was doing the show full time, and haven't looked back since really.

I bought some of the puppets. I made as many as I could, but without having any money I could get the wood but then I had to get the carving tools, so it was really, really difficult. There's Mr Punch and Judy. You can have the basic set with the policeman, the baby, Joey the clown who came from Joseph Grimaldi, the crocodile, devil, ghost, then you can have the additional ones like the boxers, plate spinners, the doctor, the horse, endless really, you can put so many in.

The show itself is an evolving tradition, and that's something I really try to put across to people. If it stayed the same as it was 100, 200 years ago it would stagnate because back then it wasn't relevant to children. It was not a child's show. And nowadays it has been watered down to a certain degree but when you're working the beach you have to make it relevant to everybody watching. So I've taken it back and there'll be a line for the adults and then a line for the kids. But Joey the clown was taken from Joseph Grimaldi who was a real clown and his act contained a string of seven sausages, so that was a modern character to the time, and in his act was this string of sausages. Also you have the crocodile which originated with the dragon,

and we think with the birth of Peter Pan, and they had the crocodile with that, that's how he came to be in the Punch and Judy. There's the hangman, Jack Ketch, who was a real London hangman, he came to be in Punch and Judy. So you let new characters into the show but you don't let them take over. There's one that keeps on making a repeat appearance. In the traditional show Mr Punch had a mistress called Pretty Polly.

The first record of a show we've got is May 9th, 1662. Back then it was the string puppet marionettes, Punchinello. When Samuel Pepys went to Covent Garden to buy a painting he saw the Italians performing Punchinello. Some time after that people stopped going into the marionette theatres, so the puppeteers cut the strings, turned them into glove puppets and took them to the people. But we've got no date for when that was. But with the Punch's mistress, first of all when I made her it was back in the 1980s and that was Samantha Fox, a few years later, exactly the same puppet, it was Pamela Anderson, and a few years later it was Jordan, so you can have the same character and keep on bringing her back. She'll be in the main summer season when I'll bring all the extra puppets up. It's only me in the booth.

This is one of the last Punch and Judy shows still operating on Weymouth beach. You get the families that come down and want to keep the tradition alive and will put in a contribution, but I'm afraid there are people who you're not going to get anything out of but they're the first people to complain when it's not here. The Llandudno show is still there throughout the summer on and off. It's gone from everywhere really. Margate, the Smith family was there for many years, Weston-Super-Mare, they pay a performer now to work in the park a couple of days a week, Broadstairs in Kent, the council pay a performer to do a couple of days a week in the school holidays, Teignmouth, Dawlish, Dawlish Warren they pay a performer to work once a week in the school holidays, and that's the way it's gone.

I'm a puppeteer as opposed to a children's entertainer, so I'm interested in all types of puppet making. The puppets that I make are all hand carved out of lime wood. The old shows always used to have a live dog, Toby to start the show, and the puppeteer in me starts the show with a puppet dog. The one that I've got at the moment is a wooden puppet, but I'm in the process of making a lot of lightweight ones which are made along the same lines as the Muppets. I'm experimenting with different types of foam, and I've just ordered a load of antron fleece from America which has a two-way stretch which was used on the Muppets. The actual fleece comes over like skin, it covers the foam. The wooden ones are more authentic without a doubt. But when you're doing a lot of shows the lighter the puppet the better.

I make them for other people. They go all over the world. I also make booths to order, everything from the wooden ones to the ones like I'm using today which is a portable one. Sew all the canvas, paint all the front, paint the scenery, everything. I do have a workshop at the back of the house in Paignton. Sometimes I mend puppets on the beach in the big booth, sometimes in me van, sometimes in the caravan.

I think the term 'Professor' comes from Victorian times when you profess to excel in your chosen profession, there is absolutely no academic thing there or else I wouldn't have got it. Simple as that. I'm in a group called the College of Professors, which is a bit tongue-in-cheek. It's mainly men. But I have recently got to know a couple of female professors.

I did Easter 2005 in Weymouth, it was nerve wracking taking over from Professor Guy Higgins, he was here for 29 years and I think he was 71 when he gave up. He did a good few years here. I took over from him and then we had a big handing over ceremony in May that year, and that was a nice little event.

We had the mayor and a few of the local councillors come down, television and all that malarkey. They presented Guy with a plaque and said 'Thank You' to him, which was really nice, more than I got in Torbay. I bought the theatre off him and one or two other items. That was it really.

Obviously we use our own puppets. My style of show and look of show is very, very different. My show, it's a cross between the Carry on Films and The Simpsons. There's gotta be lots of double entendres. You also make it relevant to that audience. The audience in my show totally dictates how the performance will go. You make it special, you pick on people. My predecessor didn't really go down that line, but there again the busker in me, the puppeteer, I do that side of things. I think it makes it special and you can get people coming back because they don't know what's going to be in the show, but nor do I.

Within a week of me being here there was a complaint that it wasn't basically Guy's show. They said it was very camp. It was quite amusing the letter that I got because they said 'The Punch and Judy shouldn't be camp, it should be traditional.' Now if I did a traditional Punch and Judy the person would have a lot more to complain about. Well it was all for adults, it was a reflection of society at the time. The origins of Punch and Judy is slapstick comedy, so what we do is slapstick, but back then it was violent, sadistic, sexist, it was everything to the extreme, but that was what they wanted. Because you only give the audience what they want at the end of the day, and I say to people now 'What sort of Punch and Judy do you want? Do you want an old fashioned traditional Punch and Judy, do you want a modern politically correct Punch and Judy?' And of course they all say 'No' to that one. 'Or do you want a stupid violent show?' And they all say 'Yeah.' That's what they want.

Domestic violence? I wouldn't say Punch beats Judy up. I

think the most trouble we've had as Punch and Judy performers is the media pumping out what they think of Punch and Judy. I had policeman from the Metropolitan Police come on an internet Punch and Judy message board saying how it should be stopped and all the rest of it, and I said 'When was the last time you actually saw Punch and Judy?' And he said 'I haven't seen one for years and years.' I said 'Well before you start making accusations, come down and watch the show.' And he did and I could tell he was in the audience because he laughed and laughed and laughed. The media don't do their research properly. They insist it's the same script from 150-odd years ago which is rubbish. I always say in the show that the term politically correct is a contradiction. If it's political it's not going to be correct.

I like Mr Punch. I'd say he's got a bit of everybody. The nearest character to Mr Punch, is Basil Fawlty. In the way he does the things that people would like to do, but know they can't. If people have complained in the past, you have to say 'if it was a real baby Mr Punch threw down the stairs then it would be violent, but it's not, it's a block of wood, it's a puppet.' After all he's just a wooden actor. It's a lot tamer than television. Concentration spans have got shorter. In the past children have thought it's just a giant television screen. Television has been an influence because you can use stuff that has been on there, turn it around. Politicians are a good influence on Punch and Judy because you can just take the mickey out of them so much. But the quicker you make the puppets, the quicker they go out of favour. I always say my puppets are far superior to politicians.

When you're doing the busking side, people's attention spans are 20-30 minutes. It's very rare to go over 30 minutes. Years ago performances used to be 45 minutes to an hour, I never did that. I do 45 minutes occasionally but 20 minutes is about right.

Inside the booth it's very small. In the summer it can get up to 109 degrees. The booth should work for you as a performer. You shouldn't have to look down. I stand up. The backdrop is the same as a two-way mirror. The old fashioned way of working is hands above your head, there's a way that I can move the scenery back, step down through a trap door and work hands above head which is good for if I'm doing a couple of puppets that are juggling, or plate spinning or something like that.

It's really bad for the blood circulation. I like to see the audience, it's also better if you're stood behind the puppets for the eye line. I've seen so many bad shows where Mr Punch is talking to Judy with his head looking up at the sky. If Punch is talking to Judy then make him look at her. If he's talking to the audience then make him look at the audience. My workshop is full of monkeys at the moment. A monkey that plays the tambourine, a monkey that comes up with mops and then two juggling monkeys that juggle with beanbags.

I get charged for this pitch. It's a fair rent that I have to pay, it's a business.. The season is about three months. The rest of the year I rely on private bookings and I can do the puppet making.

Normally the crocodile's in every single performance. We got to the end of a couple of shows over the weekend and I said 'Oh nobody's noticed that we didn't have a crocodile in the show.' And of course they all want the crocodile then.

You collect the money before, during and after. You've got to really. Rene the bottler does that. She worked with my predecessor. She used to collect money off of me when I used to watch the show as a little boy. It's quite strange. With the voices it's just the same as doing impressions. Punch's voice you use a traditional instrument to make that voice, which we try and keep a trade secret. The main problem is that otherwise children would go and put squeakers in their mouth. So we've always said

'Don't put anything in your mouth.' Originally, you see we didn't have the internet back then, with all the information and so I only got given one when my voice broke. Punch doesn't sound right without it. It's called a swazzle but without that it's a puppet show, it's not Punch and Judy. Some puppeteers will do a terrific show, call it Punch and Judy, and it's got the traditional characters in but it's slightly too polished. Punch has always got to have that bit of rough and ready, it can't be too slick and polished and perfect because of his origins. He comes from the street.

You've got to have a microphone nowadays. My voice is croaky at the moment anyway. You've always got to keep your voice above the audience, they've always got to hear you, and especially here with the road as well you'd end up with no voice at all otherwise.

This is the traditional pitch. There's been one here since at least the 1940s. I've got footage of a show here in the 1940s. There's been a show on Weymouth beach since the 1880s. He had three pitches, one up by the Jubilee clock, one by the swing boats and another one here. I've built a replica Victorian show with the hand cart which was the same as Professor Murray would have used, he wheeled it up and down. Instead of people coming to the show, he'd literally take the show to the people in the three pitches.

I performed in the Millennium Dome. The Living Island I think it was called, and they invited various Punch and Judy performers to go up and do a slot in there, so I did a few days in there which was nice. I did the 'After Show' for the Brit Awards,

and launch of a website called Icons which was for the Ministry of Culture I think. It's definitely still in demand. But now that I'm here at Weymouth I'll stay here all summer.

Being biased, I'd say this is the best pitch in the UK. It's just that you've got a nice big clean safe beach. You've got the tourism and leisure team which are very pro-tourism here, you've got the support, you've got the beach crew which will come up and if you need assistance they'll be there, you've got the lifeguards, you've got lost children's, you've got the PA system. It works. Everybody pulls together. And on other beaches you may have some of those elements but not all of them. And people have a certain remembrance of the show here that's been built up over the years so business has built up and people expect to see Punch and Judy. So I think it's the best. I don't think there's any other beaches that you can work this long a season, from May to the end of September. Most of them you've got the six-week school holiday, that's it. Maybe the odd weekend. I live two minutes away from the beach in Paignton, and for me to come to a different resort, that says something.

The seaside is in me blood. I've got salt water running through me blood, I'm sure of it. I couldn't live inland any more. There's no way I could live anywhere else. If I could I wouldn't choose to live in a busy coastal resort. If I had my way I'd live in a little tiny farmhouse on the Devon coast in the middle of nowhere away from everybody, but I think that's because I work with people in the summer, so I like to stay away from everybody in the winter. A holiday? What's that? I don't really go on holiday any more.

29. Mark Anderson – Sand sculptor, Weymouth. Born Walton on Thames 1965.

The sand comes from the beach. This is definitely one of the finest sands I've ever worked with or walked upon.

I know very little of the history of sand sculpting. My grandfather never spoke of anyone apart from Jack Hayward. My mother trained as a chef and my father, after doing National Service, I don't know, we lost track of him. My grandmother was a working housewife and my grandfather was a electrician/handyman and sand sculptor. They lived in Esher in Surrey. Gramp would come back down to Weymouth in the summertime from about 1965 onwards after he retired, and he would do the sand sculpting pretty much full time from then on. He said that when he started what they used to is something called scratching, which was when the tide came up and then went out again it would leave a really quite solid flat area where they would scratch designs in the sand and passers by would throw them pennies into the water which was still close by and they would dive in for the pennies, that was how it started for him.

He said there were some people doing three-dimensional stuff as well, so he got involved in that, he said he was a little bit older than some of his friends and colleagues and his work was always a little bit better, so he'd earn that much more money. It sort of went from a game to becoming a way of supporting himself on top of doing other jobs. He would do this and have his younger brothers look after it for him. That was back in the twenties, things have changed a little since then.

Gramp was born in Andover, his family moved down here when he was four in 1914, his father, Thomas Arthur Darrington, ('TAD') had a shop in St Thomas Street selling all sorts. He also gave horse racing tips as a sideline and after a good win you would see a sign in the shop window reading 'TAD'S RIGHT AGAIN!.' The First World War was raging and British Empire troops were all over the place, especially in Weymouth and Portland. By the end of the war in 1918 there was masses of military equipment going cheap, so being a resourceful chap 'TAD' turned his shop into an army surplus store. They used to have this stuff called blanco which was a white paste used by the Royal Navy and Royal Marines to put on their belts and webbing to make them look ultra smart and very fancy. Gramp was a bit of an inventor always trying his own way out, at the time he was working on a ten-foot high King Kong, the film had just come out, it was 1933, so he would have been 23 years old. He thought it would be really good to give it some colour, so he tried some watered down blanco round the mouth and then applied red powder paint on to the teeth to give it a bloody look, It was really effective. So that was how he kind of discovered how you could paint sand. Blanco which is some kind of calcium carbonate or chalk, mixed with water to the right consistency can be painted over the damp sand, after leaving it to dry for a while you have an ideal base for painting your powder colours over, and the great thing about it all is it just crushes back into dust, and we've been using the same sand now for 80 years.

Sometimes when I'm making a Tutankhamen mask or a kid's animated character, something that really needs a bit of a gloss to it, I'll use an acrylic paint, which I peel off at the end of the sculpture's life and dispose of.

The sand comes from the beach. This is definitely one of the finest sands I've ever worked with or walked upon. A geologist friend of mine took a sample of it for me, measured it through the

Mark Anderson with his own Dorset coast

various sieving processes and it turns out that it's a grain size of .015 of a millimetre. His boss said, it was quite extraordinary that 97 per cent of the kilogram test bag was so uniform. I think it's made up from Chesil beach, which is 18 miles long, in some places 45 feet high shingle beach with stones ranging from pea size at Burton Bradstock to hen egg size and bigger at the Portland end. Billions of pebbles knocking together for thousands of years causing a very regular sized grain. It is very close to being a silt. The classifications are: clay, up to 0.002mm, silt, up to 0.06mm, sand, up to 2mm and then gravel up to 60mm, so it is 0.09mm above coarse silt which is naturally cohesive.

What we do is mix the sand with water, sometimes we hand pack it, which is a two-person process, one of us, typically a friend or brother-in-law, will roll the wet sand into a big ball, throw me up the ball and I'll pack it into place. It's a time consuming process but it's OK if you're doing something small. If we want to do something bigger then we use forms, which we discovered after Gramp and I had been invited to the world championships in Harrison Hot Springs in Canada back in 1992. The forms we use are typically two feet high strengthened planks of wood, bolted together, made into whatever box size necessary and then filled. We put in a few inches of sand and a load of water, pack it down with a road tamper, and then a few more inches, keep on going like that until you've filled up the box. Then you can put another box on top, make whatever configuration you want, take the forms off, unbolt them, unscrew them, and you're left with a really good, solid block of sand. That's the idea.

Weymouth sand does require a large amount of water to help the bonding process, so if, for example, I go to a shopping centre or somewhere where I haven't got easy access to water, or if there's no drainage, I use a screened unwashed, silty quarry sand which bonds really well with very little water.

In the 1920s Len Clifford and his younger sister Violet would come down from the east end of London on the train and stay in a boarding house along East Street for the whole summer. Their parents were butchers up in London, so it was like 'There's some money, go and have a lovely summer,' and they did, it was fantastic for them, but that was the age of innocence when you didn't have all the social problems we've got nowadays, they came down for a number of years with 'Vi' eventually meeting Fred in about 1934, she was 17, he was about 24, and they fell in love, he moved up to London to be near her. He would still come down in the summer and put up a show which his younger brothers would look after for him, he worked for Rolls Royce at that time as an electrician, They married in 1940, and over the next ten years had three girls, Mum and her two sisters Toni and Jeanne.

In 1939 the war came along so all of this area here was barbed wired and mined to repel any invading forces, so sand carving was put on hold. He was working with the Americans up in Bushey for a number of years as a civilian electrical engineer. After the war he continued to work with electrical appliances but he would still come down and do as much as he could on the beach given that he had a family and a job to keep up.

He loved sand sculpture. He absolutely loved it, there was never much money involved. He would say 'There aren't many things in life which are free, but this is one of them!' He enjoyed being able to do his thing and for people to walk past in wonderment and throw in some coins to show their appreciation. He would create a sculpture in about a week which would last for about three weeks and then he would change it. I make things a lot more sturdy, just by my way of compaction, and when I finish them I spray them with a windproof solution which stops erosion or paint them which has the same effect as a windproofer. He didn't bother so much with that side of things, if something was wind damaged he would repair or change it. He definitely had favourites, as did the visitors and he would do the same things quite often, starting the season with the seahorses then go on to do about four other sculptures throughout the six-month period. Back in his day there was a problem I believe with the corporation. They weren't too keen on any kind of structures on the beach so before 1965 I think it was, he would always just do his work on the open beach, there was a bit of chicken wire around it, fingers crossed, hopefully you wouldn't get too many drunken sailors taking a walk across the work at night, but that was it. The fencing was just there to stop the dogs and the idiots really. But what happened was, in, I think it was 1967 or 68, he was asked by the Daily Express to go up to the Ideal Home Exhibition, take 10 or 15 tons of Weymouth sand and do a display up there. It was a major success with a lot of press and television coverage, which is obviously very good news for the Weymouth and Portland tourist economy. After that he became much more appreciated within the corporation, and they were happy for him to build a structure here and have it protected because it proved on a national level to be so popular. It showed Weymouth in a very positive light, and they started to look after him from that point on really.

He did retire in the late 60s which freed him to come down here, lodge in a guest house and work all summer. We moved down from Walton in '69, that was my mother and my sister and myself, and so Gramp would stay with us from that point on with Nana visiting occasionally. Every year he'd be down here ready for Easter and crack on until September when everything disappeared off the beach, so a good five or six months.

Mum would help operate the trampolines. When I was five I used to run around the beach all summer, jump on the trampolines, pick up the pennies for my grandad, just being a beach kid. It was fantastic. I went to school in Weymouth. I was never very good at school, In the summer from when I was 11 to 15, I worked for my grandfather making the tea, picking up the money, keeping the place nice and tidy and fetching the water. I used to wheel a large blue cistern 500 yards or so over to the sea wall, throw down a bucket on a rope, pull it up, and fill the cistern which he would then use to make the sculptures with.

I think when I was 11 I did do one small sculpture and people did throw money down. I think it was Goofy or Pluto but whatever it was, it wasn't bad at all. I didn't get any pictures unfortunately. But I never followed it up with anything until I was 22, when I just decided I needed to do something that was more compatible with me as an individual. After I left school aged 15 I went to catering college and then worked within that industry in Weymouth and then up in London for four or five years, I then tried a few different things for a year, temping, office work, but again that didn't really agree with me too much.

When I was 22, I said to myself 'Right I really need to take some time out and see what I want to do for the rest of my life.' So I set down… 'I want to be creative, independent, I'd like to work outside, I'd like to travel, I'd like to earn an income based on the merit of my work and freedom from too many constraints. And one day I thought 'Hmm. My grandfather seems like a very content man and he's ticked all of those boxes.' And I went downstairs and said 'Gramp, I'd like to be your apprentice,' and he was like 'Urr, OK, trying something else, eh?' And I said 'I'd really like to.' So he said 'OK, come down,' that was in February, March of 1988.

To start with I wasn't very good at all because I hadn't done anything sculptural since being at school which was six years before and even then the sum total of my school art work would fit in a small shoe box. But I watched him and asked him questions, he would never force feed me which was so essential for me. As it was, he'd let me get on with something and I'd say 'Gramp, what am I doing wrong?' or 'how would I do this?' And he'd say 'Try this,' 'try that.' And I'd say 'Ok, thank you,' so it was a really natural process.

But what happened here was because you've got probably half a million people walking past on a good season, minimum, I think we have a million and a half visitors to the area throughout the year, so because of that, and you've got kids who can be the most honest of critics, there were too many comments like 'What is that?' or 'That's rubbish!' I always hated being on stage at school, I was always the one doing the curtains or something behind the scenes, so being out here, I was really conscious for a long time, so I knew if I was going to have any chance of surviving this I was going to have to improve quickly or grow very thick skin. Sure enough one day after about three months working with Gramp there was a sign at the back saying 'Sand Sculpture by FG Darrington,' and underneath he'd tacked on 'And grandson Mark,' which was lovely.

We always had a different modus operandi. He would get down here at seven o'clock in the morning, typically, fry himself up a bit of breakfast in the hut there and then crack on. I'd get down about ten, being a young man and liking going out and enjoying a few beers etc. He'd always have a bit of a groan at me, but hopefully secretly he would remember what it was like to be that age. Normally I work with a picture of the subject right next to me to use as reference. If it's a person, I'll have photographs from a number of angles giving me as much information as possible to try and achieve that likeness, whereas he wouldn't.

He'd look at the picture back in the shed then go down into the 'pit' and do his thing, he'd capture some part of it and he'd have an essence there. He was more of an impressionist I think. I'm trying for perfection. Fortunately I know that I've got a way to go yet, which is a driving force, to try and get it just so, but there is a negative aspect to that, and that's the time it takes me to achieve a particular sculpture. It's a balance really.

Sometimes I don't use much reference material, I had a job last year where a TV company approached me and asked me to do St George's Dragon. It was for Art Attack, a kids' programme and as they wanted it in such a short time, we had to work very quickly, which proved to be quite liberating as there were no constraints on the final image. I could see why Gramp worked the way he did! When I get a commission for a festival event or shopping centre, sometimes the client will say, for instance, we want an underwater scene, then it's pretty much made up on the spot. It's a loosely based format, we know we need a helmeted diver, treasure chest, corals, fish, octopus, these kind of things. I also really enjoy architectural commissions, one of my favourite pieces was the Cityscape we did for Citi Bank and last year one of the jobs we completed was a 1:100 scale replica of the Canary Wharf development, about 25 buildings, it was striking.

Do I like the ephemeral nature of the work that I do? That's a good question. It's natural. It's part of being alive. Everything has a life cycle and a span. One of its special qualities is that it's only there for a moment, people witness the work being created as they stand watching, it is something which captivates the onlookers, they are amazed at what we do with a seemingly unworkable material, it does live on in peoples memories and photographs, although some sculptures have gone unphotographed. Typically it's been when I've been waiting to finish the sculpture, and we have some idiot come down in the night and destroy the work before I get a chance to photograph it, which is a bit of a shame. A great shame in fact. It's hard. As I'm getting older I'm finding it more physically exerting and demanding, there's a lot of bending over, a lot of back and knee work. I've got knee pads on but at the end of the day, I'm standing up now going 'Ouch.' It's pretty tough.

My grandfather was 85 when he stopped, which was amazing. He had a stroke in June '95, it was very soon after somebody had come down and destroyed a lot of our work. That was it for him really, he lived for a further seven years, up until that point he was really, very active and he rarely suffered from rheumatic aches, he put it down to using salt water and always being physically active, he would lift a shovel like, I wouldn't say a young man but he was certainly very keen always to 'get on with it.' We went to the World Championship Sand Sculpting Competition in Harrison Hot Springs, Canada in 1993 and 1994, he was so appreciated by the 100 or so carvers at the event, many were inspired by his passion and hard work and told him so, which made him feel very proud, it was a most fitting way for him to end his career. I hope I am as fit, active and capable as him when I'm 84 years old. Yes of course I'd love to have him here. I have very fond memories of my time with my grandfather.

I don't really enter competitions any more, too much work for too little reward. I did them for maybe four or five years, I now concentrate on paid commissions and a couple of top events where I get to work with some of the best sand sculptors in the world. We get together and work on some big (2-4000 tons) and very fine work twice a year, aside from that and the dozen or so other jobs, I'm down here pretty much from April to late September.

Last year 2006 was a bit hectic, I didn't get as much done as I would have liked to due to there being a lot of work away from the beach, also after it was knocked down, I really do lose heart, obviously, because there's so much effort getting a sculpture completed in the first place. The last few years have been a lot better because of the CCTV, but even so last year they got down and destroyed what I was working on, 'The Pirates of the Caribbean.' Unfortunately, I have this fear in the back of my mind, 'How much time and effort do I put into this?' Because I know the more effort and time I put into it, if that sort of thing is going to happen, the more it'll pain me, and the less time and effort I'm going to want to put into it again, which is rubbish.

Right now, I'm going through the process of getting a new compound, it will be in the same location, a completely secure area, much more attractive, wave proof and slightly larger which means I will be able to accommodate friends from other countries as guest sculptors and we can do some amazing stuff in there. That's what I would like to achieve. It's all with the planning department and the council at the moment but the timing is perfect due to the beachfront regeneration project and the 2012 Olympic sailing events being held here, things will be really moving forward over the next few years.

This year's theme was suggested and sponsored by the managers of a national holiday park campsite company, Haven. They have two local sites, Weymouth Bay and Bluewater. We worked on the ideas together and came up with Dorset landmarks, including Durdle Door, the White Horse, the Olympic rings which may become a landmark, Corfe Castle before it was destroyed, Portland lighthouse, and a few other things, some Jurassic stuff, skeletons of underwater creatures, and a couple of characters, Rory and Bradley from the campsite.

I made the seahorses a couple of years ago, 20 feet long and 8 feet high, it was one of the sculptures Fred loved to do and people loved to see, 7 white horses striding through the waves, he took the image from a beautiful 1950s painting which was on his dining room wall. My sister Karen inherited the painting which I borrowed and had next to me while I recreated the whole thing, you can see that on my website. When I was seven Gramp made the Jungle Book which will always be my favourite, I never thought for a moment, 25 years later I would be doing one of my own. Another of my favourites was his George and the Dragon, I tried that one too about 15 years ago but his was really excellent, it's probably one of the finest ones, that he ever did.

In the last few years I have netted off all of the sculptures, even though it's a fine netting it slightly diffracts the light somehow and you can't see as clearly as you once could which is quite frustrating being a visual art. It's a shrimp netting, and it's very tough and will stop most things. Once upon a time we would only net it at night to stop these idiots that seem to do anything the moment they aren't being monitored. Over the past 10 years these morons have been getting more brazen, I'd be working away and a coin would whiz past my head and strike the sculpture. With no proof to who the thrower was, there is nothing I could do, after this had happened a few times, I made the decision to work behind netting, Once again a tiny minority gets to spoil the pleasure of the majority because they are allowed to get away with it. I have been to events in Italy which are completely open to the viewers, no damage, no touching, no throwing things, just respect!

Weymouth along with most towns in the UK went through quite a bleak period where the economy was starting to base out, supermarkets were effecting traditional town centre businesses and a number of shops were turning into very cheap 'goods' stores and charity shops, but in the last few years it's really started to come up again and it's getting better. Definitely getting better. People are much more positive, which is great. I love it here, I really do. I live on Portland, which is beautiful. I've been to many places around the world but I always come back here. I just wish that some people would be a bit more respectful and some people could manage to pick up their crap after being on the beach all day. In Australia you have a $50 fine for littering. People Do Not Litter!

In the winter months I used to just put on a backpack, stick a pin in the map, and go and see what was there, but that was before I got a mortgage. The weird thing was that when I didn't have a mortgage and I was doing whatever I could to get by, whether that was fruit picking, or extras work, just anything at all, always having a bit of an adventure, I used to think 'It'd be so nice to come back to a little cottage or somewhere that I could call my own?' So I managed to do that seven or eight years ago, and since then having a mortgage has tied me up so I don't go travelling any more. But I do go away a couple of times a year to Italy, visit a load of friends who happen to be sand sculptors.

In terms of the history, Professor Mark Poulton, the Punch and Judy man who collects beach ephemera, showed me a postcard with a chap, 'Swift' Vincent, in front of an excellent sand sculpture of an artillery man and his dying compatriots next to their howitzer, entitled 'The Last Shell' which I guess is either, just after the Boer War, 1901, or after the First World War around 1918. I would like to introduce a photo gallery as part of the new compound featuring as much early work and as much history as I can get on the subject of sand sculpting on Weymouth beach, and possibly some other places as I can find, which is sadly very little to date. I recently discovered in some boxes from his attic, photos of my Grandfather and his work from 1934 which are wonderful.

So after 'Swift' Vincent my grandfather was here, and there was also a chap called Jack Hayward, a local man who's still got a lot of family left in the area, he used to do amazing cathedrals, really beautiful. They were probably eight, ten feet high and 15 feet across, superb detail. He was here up until about 1970. A lot of people still come along and say 'We were here in the fifties and your grandfather used to do these amazing cathedrals,' And I say 'That was Jack Hayward, my grandfather was the one doing the lion getting ready to pounce on the deer and the Loch Ness monster,' that kind of thing. They must have worked alongside each other, but I don't think they were friends because Gramp never talked about him. I guess they just put up with each other. Apart from that I've seen a picture of a chap in Atlantic City, New Jersey, in 1896 or thereabouts, a guy called Mr Taylor, he was working on or under what they called the boardwalk doing sand sculpting from that period. Apparently it got quite big and there were a quite a few people doing it, so many so that the local council decided it was a bit of a hazard and they stopped it all.

But it's quite funny because I was out in Australia about ten years ago in a place called Manley, I tried the sand out and it was some of the best I tried in Australia, not as good as Weymouth. They have a Victorian crescent shaped beach area, reminded me of Weymouth absolutely ideal, it's a great tourist venue, very close to Sydney. Someone mentioned that Manley had a 'Sandman' along time ago so I went to the library and did some research, sure enough there was an ex British Navy Captain, Captain J. Smith who retired to Manley in 1908. The article stated, when he wasn't chasing pirates around the South China Seas he used to do scrimshaw, which is whale bone carvings and on his retirement he became the sand sculptor there until about 1927. Then after him another chap came along whose work was some of the best I've ever seen, he was superb, he was Ukrainian. He got there in about 1927, he was a stoker who jumped ship and eventually landed in Australia and somehow became a sand sculptor. He came over to England in the 1930s and he set up on Bournemouth beach, and again, if you ever see any postcards of his work it was really, really beautiful. Most of the works which I have seen were either religious or socially inspired as this was in the time of the depression, one part of the scene would be an overweight family, obviously very wealthy, and then the back half of the scene would be an underweight family, obviously on the breadline. There would be a message there. John Sucumlo or Surcomlin was his name. Amazing.

The future? Well I'm 42 this year, my grandad was 85, for me that's a whole lifetime away. Whether or not I last that long I don't know. I'd like to think I'll go on until I'm in my grave, which is who knows when.

LULWORTH TO SWANAGE VIA WORTH MATRAVERS

30. Jim Miller – Fisherman and minesweeping, Lulworth Cove. Born 1922.

'Through the teeth, over the gums, look out guts, here it comes!' We were Churchill's Pirates...

I was born 1922. We lived up Sunnyside. Straight up the road on the right. They call it Bindon Road now, why I don't know. Father was a fisherman and grandfather. Oh Christ, yeah. We've traced them back 500 years so far. Couldn't get any further. All down here and at Tyneham and Worbarrow. That photograph, that's my grandfather Ned, and that's his boat, *Dauntless*, she had red sails. Crabbing and lobsters. That's a little lugger. Boats were built in Weymouth. That's my grandfather and those two are Bob and Bill Williams. The other one's my father's uncle.

In the summer months we'd go four or five mile along the coast. That's me in the boat years ago, with the old lobsters. Lindon Gibson, that's the market we used to send them up to in Southampton and they'd take them out to the liners. We'd make our own inkwell pots. Willow. Bait was any fish. We chiefly used to buy gurnard from Milford Haven or else cod from Grimsby.

School was boring, wasn't it? I joined up in 1940, and when I came out I fished for me father for four or five years. Seventeen I was when I joined up. Joined the Navy at Portsmouth barracks on 14th October, 1940, and then within a week I was down at Portland. Then I went to Lowestoft in the old trawlers. Went up there, see? Patrol Service they called us, but we were minesweeping. East Coast and then three years in the Med.

I can remember some of the vessels. *Peter Carey*, the *Satsa* and the *Sarka*, whalers from South Georgia and South Africa, and then two or three motor launches, MLs. They had four numbers. *1047* was one, can't remember the others. You swept all the time because the worst place was on the mouth of the Thames, Harwich, up to Lowestoft, round Dover, that was the worst place of the lot round this way. These mines they dropped, they all go off from the bottom. They're not a moored mine. Magnetic mines and acoustic mines. Magnetic goes off with the metal in the ship and the acoustic go off with the vibration. They tick over and tick over, they might wait for ten ships to go over. You'd be sweeping all day, nothing… 15, 20, 30 fathom. But in deeper water they'd have moored mines. Magnetic mines would be dropped by German aircraft. They also used to drop them off the old E-boats. But a lot of these mines, see, they'd tick over until about 10, 20, 30 boats passed over them, and you'd think you'd got em all, and then up would come a convoy and up would go some of the ships. We saw some of the ships go up.

On a trawler we had about 25 crew. With magnetic mines, you towed over the stern, a big heavy cable, and with acoustic mines you had a frame that went over the bow, and all inside there was a jackhammer. He'd be belting away on a plate the whole time and that would set the acoustic mines off.

We had a steel boat but you used to take the ship in to be degaussed. The mines, they'd go on the bottom. The only ones that would come to the surface was these moored mines, but you swept them with a wire and a paravane. At the end of sweep was jaws, the mine wire would come along the sweep wire and be cut. Then he'd pop to the surface and we'd try to detonate him. Hell of a mess when a mine goes up.

You had trouble from German aircraft, bloody sure you did. Heinkels and E boats on the east coast. We had the oerlikon gun on there, the 20mm. 12 pounder on the bow and a couple of Lewis guns, but then again, we was fighting a modern war with First War weapons. The old Hodgkiss and Lewis, they was First War ones, and point fives, all First War weapons. These were big

Jim Miller with this year's harvest

trawlers. Going up to the White Sea, the old fashioned skippers, they was all right. There was a bloody great heap of yer. Swept in rotations and all that. One lot would be sweeping all night, then another lot would come over and sweep the same ground.

You didn't have to go out far in they channels to run aground in the Thames. They had other various things for very shallow water. I always remember the first mine I saw go up when I joined the old *Peter Carey*, t'was getting dark and it went up, all the mud and shit, you could smell the mud. Right from the bottom. Of course E-boats were a problem. All down the Thames. The last buoy at Harwich that we used to go to was called B8. I remember all these things, and that was the last buoy, that was as far as we used to go, B8 buoy, then we'd turn round, go t'other way to Dover. Bloody great buoys they were, those buoys, they'd tie up there, the buggers, at night time. You wouldn't see them. First thing you knew was a load of bullets flying around, mate. Oh ar. You didn't see 'em did yer? Sometimes you'd have about 60, 70 boats in a convoy. Quite a tempting target for a German. Oh yeah. Lot of bloody boats sank in a convoy. No radar, nothing at all. Radio contact, that's all.

There was a chap living in the village, he was in one of these gun boats. They had a turret, four guns, controlled by one man with a joystick, like an aircraft, and they could fire thousands of bullets a minute. Thousands. Cut the bottom right out, they'd fire along the waterline and they'd cut the bottom right out of a ship, them buggers could. I met him up in the Adriatic.

I was in an Eytie ship, up in the Adriatic, and we went in this little port there one morning, no one about and not one boat. I heard a familiar voice, it was Pat O'Hare I went to school with him. We were based around Malta, Alex, and all round them islands. I volunteered to go foreign. They lifted two of us from an ML in Milford Haven aboard a boat, the *Welsh Trader* and they

took us out to the Med. We went to Turkey, Alexandretta, and we'd go round the Dodecanese islands. But I left that ship somewhere in the Med, and ended up in hospital up in the mountains up in Syria near Beirut and the Jordanian border. A New Zealand hospital. But all the boats in the Dodecanese, they lost the lot. Every one got killed. I was lucky, wasn't I. Someone up there was looking after me. These *caiques* or *kayaks*, they'd tie 'em up under the cliffs, put a few nets over em, a bit of green stuff, and no bugger could see 'em, could they? That's what we were supposed to do, but old Jerry had heard of all that. They got chamfered up.

We done a bit of minesweeping out there. I remember we went to sea once, sweeping up round towards Italy, and all of a sudden we saw sodding great battleships coming towards us, we didn't know they'd just give in. We were sweeping up there, and they put the fear of God in us when they come along. Didn't know nothing about it. They'd just surrendered. The poor buggers were starving, the old Eyties. They hadn't seen sugar or spuds for 12 months, but as soon as we appeared they had everything. We give them everything.

We used to be up round Split. Camisa and Split, from Barletta, or Brindisi. No fishing but I had a game of football. And the Albanians mined the bloody football pitch, they did. When they got there they found the pitch was mined. Went to Gracie Fields' island, She married an Eytie didn't she? Capri. I'm certain it was. I went there. It was foggy. The skipper didn't know where the hell he was. All of a sudden we heard a cockerel crowing and the old man said we must be near land or something, and of course when the fog lifted there was a old boat alongside of us, he had chickens on board.

Malta, They wouldn't take the old Eyties there, they wouldn't. They'd have slaughtered 'em wouldn't they? The *Ohio* was there. We was tied alongside that bugger. O H TEN that's what I always called her, OH10.

A massive tanker, she survived dive bombing and torpedoes and was towed into Valetta harbour. When she come in she was tied alongside the jetty and just rested on the bottom. We used to go alongside, and other boats, to get fuel. OH10 they used to call her. She was bombed to buggery. Bloody great tanker, the *Ohio* was, I think one of the biggest.

We used to take 'em from Barletta up to Split, a few of these, I suppose they were secret service buggers, the quiet ones, the silent ones. We used to go up to Split or Camisa, you couldn't get there until it was dark, 'cause if you had one flag up they'd fire at you, you pulled he down and put up another flag and then you were all right. Partisans, old Tito. I got his badge somewhere, Tito's badge with a star on. We'd see kids up there with their bloody hands cut off. They'd put tin cans on the stumps with a hook so that they could eat and drink. We used to bring back all sorts. The Levant schooner squadron. Yeah I heard of they, and then we used to do convoys up to Tripoli a week up there and then back to Alexandria. Sometimes you had a barrage balloon that you towed above you to stop the aircraft coming in low.

Tattoos? Ha ha. Bloody daft twat, wasn't I, to get tattoos? Marked for life. She was naked, this one, Mum played up, so when I went back I had to get her dressed. I always remember that. Daftest thing you could ever do. How the hell could you be in decent company and roll your sleeves up?

We never slept in hammocks, on the old trawlers you had bunks. Food was bloody good always. We had a cook aboard one trawler, he was a baker, he could bake a cake, he'd come down the mess and say 'Lads, what do you want tomorrow? Liver stew?' We used to say 'No, we'll have a cake.' He'd make a cake. Or he'd make a jelly in a bucket, but he couldn't cook a bit of

meat. He was a baker. A Geordie. He'd make a bloody good cake, 'cause you could have all the currants and fruit you wanted, couldn't you, in the services? We had plenty of meat. There weren't any Wrens. No bloody fear.

Those photographs on the wall, them boats, that's *Sarka*, that one. That's a whaler. Used them for mine sweeping, they were very fast boats. *Laurana* was the one I was on in the Adriatic. An Eytie boat. *Europa,* that was a depot ship up Lowestoft. Only a holiday camp, that's what it was. I was lowest of the low. Able seaman. Our mob was only a branch of the Navy. They wouldn't recognise us as proper sailors. We were Churchill's Pirates. It was through him that we had a medal. That was a silver badge that you wore on your cuff. Solid silver. *Patrol Service. Sweep and destroy*. The Navy didn't like us having that, they didn't. Especially that one there. Solid silver. That's the fifth one they issued and we used to wear it on the cuff. I got demobbed in 1945 I think.

I've got medals, North Africa, Italy, The Atlantic Star. The last one there is one the Kent government give every serviceman that served in Kent. I was based in the Isle of Sheppey at one time. That's in Kent, see. It was thruppence a day if you never had the tot on board. Our mob was on for bloody years after the war, minesweeping. It was dangerous work, bloody sure it was, no bugger knew where they were, did they? Half of them was covered up with silt. I'm talking about abroad, Holland, when they were on the mud flats.

Cheers you old bugger. 'Through the teeth, over the gums, look out guts, here it comes!' We've had some bloody good piss ups in here, mate.

Lulworth? When I was growing up there, was nine fishermen here. I suppose three parts of them was Millers. Half to three parts. My grandfather was one of seven boys. We didn't have winches then. We have now though. We used to only persecute lobsters and crabs. We never sold them locally, 'cause they'd want them for next to nothing. You'd work with the dealers all the time. They'd pick them up in a truck and give you a big handful of white five pound notes. Big white ones. We'd keep them alive in the water in big boxes. They'd come down generally once a week, sometimes twice. And they'd go into Poole. What they do now is you take them in yourself. There are Spaniards in Poole and they put them on a lorry. They'll take anything that comes out of the sea.

When I was young, sometimes we had to have a day home from school to go out and pull an oar, that was me and my brother, we was under 14 then. That was me and my father and me older brother. We used to pull an oar each. No engine. Three or four miles up and down the coast. We used to row all the time. I had sodding great blisters on me hands. You don't go to sea in real bad weather. The only time when it's bad is when you're caught out there. Then you've got to come back in, and that's easy enough, isn't it?

People talk about smugglers and that. I'm the only one left now who knows anything about down the beach here in the olden times. I've got pictures of all the old men and that. There's Michael Miller, he was the last of the old smugglers and he lived in a small one up, one down cottage in the garden of the Chief Coastguard on the end here. He was blind but the Chief Coastguard, Rowsell he still liked to keep an eye on him. The old sailing boats would be about 22 foot. That's what they were. When you bought the boat you had the sails. They were always red. You had to do them yourself to stop them rotting. You had a mizzen and a main mast and a foresail.

Tyneham was a lovely little place before the war. My father had three uncles that lived there, Tom, Jack and Charlie. They moved them in 1943, old Charlie was 80-odd, he died the first day they turfed him out of Worbarrow, the first day he died. I think t'was Jack, he went to live in a house this side of Swanage somewhere that hadn't been lived in for donkey's years, the water ran down the walls, he lived for four days, and the other one they put in a cottage in Kimmeridge, he lived quite a long time. He was in his own environment there, wasn't he?

Quite a few lived at Tyneham. You had the Lord of the Manor and that. The only fishermen were Tom, Jack and Charlie. They were old people, they did very little, and there was another old chap called Tarry, I didn't know him. I got pictures of them all. And all their stones are at the churchyard.

They had to get out within 24 hours. Tis true, 24 hours. They could have give them a bit longer than 24 hours. You can't clear a house out in 24 hours. You'd have a job getting the rubbish out of this house in a week, wouldn't you?

During the whole war I used to come home on leave. I don't think our family went short of much during the war. Lived on rabbits, I come home on leave once during the war and me father had about 30 rabbits up the allotment in hutches, he just killed one when he wanted one. When we was kids, before the war, seven rabbits was used a week in our house. We lived on rabbits. We never did drink, did we? I never used to drink. No. I had no vices at all. You'll believe that one…

We used to go out in the boat with my father when we was kids. Lobsters and crabs. We'd put a net out now and again to get a bit of bait. You get a few dead bodies now and again. Paddle steamers still come in here don't they? It was either the *Empress* or the *Victoria* or the *Premiere*. Sometimes they'd drag all your gear in and have it would wrap it up round their paddles till the rope broke. I've got two nephews, Norman and Ali and a son, Joey, they're all down there fishing now. Still doing crabs and lobsters. We'd toe the line at Kimmeridge, just by Worbarrow.

These are coastguard cottages. All these houses are two knocked in one. This is one room, and out there is the other room, this used to be the living room, and out there was the kitchen. And the shithouse was out there in the garden. Mother came from Hamworthy. Her father was a clay worker. They had big families, the coastguards. They used to come out of here like a load of rabbits. They only got two bedrooms, see. The old man that was born here, he said he was never allowed in this room, this was the front room, they all lived in the little kitchen.

I got married in 1948. I lived up the top of the village at one time, and then I lived at Sunnyside. About 1960 I suppose I came here. I retired when I was 60 and I've been hard up ever since. It's not easy living on just a pension, is it? I get £15 a week pocket money. That don't go far, do it? I don't buy much whisky. Have it all give me. Past favours. I'm the oldest local in the village. My old mate, he died, and I used to go to school with him. Tyrell up the top of the village. He only had one leg. He had diabetes. My two brothers are dead. When I stopped fishing I sat on me arse and make gear for the boys. Make his pots for him. I sleep in this chair some nights. I went to bed last night for the first time in a week. Upstairs. It's a good old chair this is. It's a Parker Knoll, one of the best chairs you'll get.

I was here when Dunkirk happened. I wasn't in the Navy then, 'cause a lot of them come back to Lulworth camp. Thousands of them. I think they dropped a couple of bombs on the old army camp. They used to get thousands of them out on the old football pitch on pay days, and of course you'd get the aircraft come along, rata tat tat.

The army camp still fires over the top here. You're safe enough, they can't hit F' all. I was fishing with my father, we had two boats, and I had one and me father had the other one, and

then I bought one and then I had another one built under some scheme. Wooden one. I always remember he cost just under £2,000. Early part of 1960. It was a scheme, you put so much down, not a lot, and I think they paid damn near a half. They give you a post office book and you put in what you could afford. Fishing isn't an easy way of life. People say 'Why d'you do it?' It's all you've done all your life. 'Tis like the Pitmans, their father was on the farm and the sons took over. It's the same with our mob. They've got a shop down there.

I collect things. Down the beach outside the boathouse there's a long bit of string. I pick up all the dummies I find. I counted them this morning, there was a hell of a lot. They drop them in the street. I hang them up on a bit of string. Until somebody pinches the lot. Have to start again, don't you. You ain't seen nothing, mate, you ain't seen nothing at all. It's under cover. I've got over 400 pipes. Clay pipes, ornamental ones. I've got all sorts. I don't know what I have got. All sorts of things used to come in the cove, so they said. There was one book next door called 'Contraband,' it says in there that a hundred horses used to go up and down the road here overnight, that's to carry stuff away, isn't it? Nobody bothered to look out the window. That's why they had shutters on, they used to pull the shutters. And nobody dared say anything did em? Or else something would happen to him. We heard about the coastguard that was slung over the cliff at Durdle. Another one say he was hung over. He didn't survive. I think his stone is in Weymouth or something like that. Must have been 1830s.

When me and me brother came home one time during the war, up home was a black whippet. Old Jack. Me and Dave walked through Durdle Door one day and we took Old Jack with us, and we went down the steps just underneath them caves, and Old Jack looked up there above them caves and his tail went up between his legs and he whined and whined and he shot off home. Now dogs can see things which you can't, so the next day we took Jack over, we tied him on a bit of rope, took him down over, and when he got on that beach he stuck his feet in, and we literally dragged him round there, and he looked up at that cliff, and he started howling again, and he flew round and straight on home. They can see things what we can't. I believe in ghosts, too bloody true I do, mate.

Children? I've got Joey down here, Pauline who lives with us, she's got a lovely daughter who's gone as far as she can go with schooling, sea biology or something, and another one somewhere abroad, two up the churchyard. So what's that, four or five, something like that.

I've got starfish here, buckets on the tree, chains… I've got anchors out the front, I've got every bloody thing. Everything bar money. I've got the best bunch of photographs I've ever seen. I've met people who don't even got a picture of their father. Grandfather died when I was at school, grandfather had a stroke down the beach, and he always slept in a bed downstairs at home, in the kitchen, and we used to go up and that. Old grandfather. I was seven or eight I suppose. He was 72.

I tell tourists all sorts of things. I tell 'em I've never seen a train. That's true as I'm here, and they believe it. 'I've never seen a train. Where you come from?' 'London' 'Where's London? Oh, t'other side of that hill!' They believe it. I wind them up. I had a watch like that, a wrist watch with no strap on, and I used to keep it in my hat just behind the peak, so when I used to put my hand up I could grab hold and see the time, and he wouldn't fall out. This woman was down the beach, I was doing a couple of pots, 'Can you tell me the time sir?' And I said 'Yes,' put me hand up here, got me hat, and I was facing that way and the sun was up there, 'Twenty past four,' I could see me watch, twenty past

four. 'Thank you sir,' she said. She come back half an hour later with more people. 'This is the gentleman who tells the time by the sun. Can you tell them the time?' I says 'Certainly.' Put me hand up here, grabbed hold of the peak, the old watch was there, and I held him up here, the sun was up here, held him up to keep the sun out me eyes. 'There,' she says, 'I told you he could tell the time by the sun.' Daft bugger. They think we're daft.

I was down on the beach one evening doing a pot, and a Yank come along, he had four cameras slung round his bloody neck, he said 'What's those things?' I said 'Crab pots.' 'What do you catch in them?' I said 'Crabs.' 'Where you catch the crabs?' I said 'See that hill there? Just on top of there.' He said 'Do you mean to say they climb up them steps?' I said 'Course they do.' 'It's amazing,' he said. Daft twats. You always agree with them, tell them what they want to know.

We've had torpedoes washed up in the cove. One was a test one. He went astray one evening and the Navy was looking for him. I spotted him running along and took my boat alongside him so they couldn't see and towed him into the cove. We'd get a fiver for a torpedo and ten bob for a mine. Several mines turned up here. There's lots of things washed up here. I found three dead bodies. I tell children they had shrimps for eyes and a conger eel coming out of their backsides. Teachers didn't like that… Then I done some grave digging as well.

There look, those photographs, 1911. That's my grandfather and one of his brothers, Levi. Ned, Charlie. Joseph Miller, born 1824. That's my great-grandfather. That painting above the mantelpiece is my father and old Lady Fripp. That used to hang in a gallery up London. And they want to borrow it back but I won't let them have it. Done in 1922. That's old Lady Fripp and the one that painted it was her brother- in-law, Heinz Fripp. Sir Albert Fripp was doctor to the King, wasn't he?

We've seen some strange things here. I've seen three big black panthers. The first one me and Joey saw just this side of White Nothe. That was a real big one. He was the size of a bloody donkey but not so high. And he had a tail longer than him. We was in a boat right under White Nothe. We was watching him for a good five minutes, and then he come all through the valley there, and then he got to the edge of the cliff, and he jumped over a patch of cliff where he couldn't land, and he landed on where a patch of grass and bushes was, and then he went to the edge of that, jumped over another space he couldn't get, and then he went on rougher ground and up into the cliff, just right by White Nothe. Then I saw one go across the car park here at half past seven in the morning, I was feeding the ducks and my two nephews were in a boat just going in the sea, and they swore he went across the car park, down to the beach, down one flight of steps and up another flight of steps and up the top of the hill. But the first one we saw was a whopper. There's small ones around as well. The missus' friend saw one up the top of the village. All the cats disappeared over there, and the pheasants. There's a wild cat about.

We've been fishing all our lives here, and we treat the ground proper. We chuck all the small stuff away, we even chuck the big ones away. The big ones is no good, no one will buy them, all they want is the ordinary size. So you chuck them away and let them breed. They always say 'There's plenty of lobsters up at Lulworth.' Course there is, because we treat the ground right. That's what you've got to do if you want to make a living and for your youngsters to come in the trade.

There was a dolphin here all last summer. Joe's kids would get in the water and play with him. They'd stand up in the water here and the dolphin lay alongside of them. They'd pat him and stroke him and all that. I wish he would come back, because I like all they things. But this electronic gear they get on these frigates, that makes them lose their way. When we used to go fishing, at about eight every morning, out of Portland Harbour would come four or five frigates or destroyers. Little flags on them and then they'd go in formation and that. Sometimes I'd be in Weymouth with Bert Randall spratting. Soon as them be about, not a thing. I think this disorientates them. And then they have these pingers on the net that they say keeps dolphins away. To me, they keep one thing away, they keep another thing away. They've got so many people today, they want to stop this, stop that and stop the other. They're trying to stop people catching bass. They got us right down to a limit, the size and the length, and the French are taking no bloody notice at all. We used to do long lining in the winter. We would catch skate. Skate, eels and tope.

And here's a picture in the paper of my grandaughter, Becci. She's only 13 but she wants to go fishing full-time. She's been out often 12 hours. Five in the morning till five in the afternoon. The boat's called *Silver Foam* PE 723.

There's my boat, *Four Girls* WH 67. It's my birthday next week, 11th November. Armistice Day. I'll be 85. Cheers you old bugger!

NOTES:
The coastguard who went over the cliff did not survive. This inscription from Weymouth sheds more light on the story.

Sacred to the memory of Lieut Thos Edward Knight, RN, of Folkestone, Kent, Aged 42, who in the execution of his duty as Chief Officer of the Coastguard was wantonly attacked by a body of smugglers near Lulworth on the night of 28th June 1832, by whom after being unmercifully beaten he was thrown over the cliff near Durdle Door from the effects of which he died the following day.

31. Major Mick Burgess – Range Officer, Lulworth Ranges. Born Whittlesey 1940.

It's been a passion of mine to improve the access and to ensure that when people walk on the ranges they enjoy what they see… You don't need to go to France or Spain. They go on about the Seven Wonders of the World… Well, Purbeck and the Dorset coastline…That'll do me.

I was born in the Fenland town of Whittlesey, in the Isle of Ely where it is as flat as the desert. Mother and father were teachers. The rest of the family were all farmers growing peas, beans and potatoes. Mother's father, he was Wisbech born and bred. Well I liked it because my father's friends were all into going up the Wash and we used to do wildfowling with the old blunderbuss on the end. The plovers, there was hundreds and thousands of them. That and of course we went back when Peter Scott took over Sutton Bridge, we used to go there and walk over where the Nene comes from the Wash, it's wonderful.

Education? I was lucky enough to pass the eleven plus. King's School in Peterborough. I hated it, I am not an academic. I am a practical person, I used to cycle to school and back every day. It kept me fit, it probably took half an hour. This was in the 1950s.

The 1947 floods were terrible. Mother used to send us with a pram down the gasworks to get a sack of coke for a shilling. The floods came right up the Wash and it froze. They used to hold the All England Ice Skating Championships down by the Dog and Doublet. It was very, very cold and it was tough. We wore big clothes and we didn't have central heating.

Anyway I joined the Whittlesey Army Cadets. I was a bugler and a drummer. There's pictures of me as a little kid when I was about seven dressed up with a wooden rifle. Two of my uncles went in the Second War, and one sadly was killed. He was in the Cambridgeshires and they were in Singapore. They got off the boat and all got killed. The second brother died last year, they were both in Naval Commando, 8th Battalion Suffolk Regiment.

Then I left school and signed up. Sergeant Vincent was the name of the recruiting sergeant. He was in Peterborough. I was 15 by then and I got off the train at Wool station here in Dorset. 4th September 1956. I was then in the boy's squadron at Bovington Camp. It was tough, you suddenly had a cultural shock of discipline. You could only change one sheet and one pillowcase every two weeks and you had to turn them over. No personal effects or food parcels.

A year and a half later I was posted. I joined the 14th/20th King's Hussars in Berlin, before the wall went up. Berlin was amazing. I was a regular, I think there was only three of us who were regulars in my troop, the rest were all National Service boys and they didn't have a lot of money. What we used to do, was for every round of drinks, we used to buy three and they used to buy one. Entertainment? Nightlife, not just the red lights, I mean there was concerts and gigs and musical festivals and cinemas and the buildings in West Berlin, some of them were absolutely magnificent. The NAAFI Club, it was like going back to the 1940s, there'd be a little quartet band playing in the officers part of the NAAFI Club. All you needed was Marlene Dietrich to come out with a bloody cigarette holder. And of course our barracks was right next to Spandau jail. Smuts barracks.

Guard duty? Yes absolutely. I never actually saw them but yes. There was Speer, Hess and I don't know who the other two were. And of course the night that he died, Hess, they bulldozed

Major Mick Burgess with Shiner and Winston, outside the head gardener's cottage, Tyneham

it down you know. They completely bulldozed it and built a supermarket and a NAAFI there, because they didn't want it made into a shrine.

Sadly I only spent 18 months in Berlin... Basically we had a bet to see who could get through the Brandenburg gates on the underground. Who could get the furthest and get back, they would win the kitty. We all put in a few Marks because we got paid in BAFS, British Armed Forces Sterling. We'd buy some Deutchmarks off the old barber. We'd had a few beers I must admit, and I went on the underground, got on this train, and stayed there. There was only about four people in the carriage, I can remember it quite well, we got stopped, and I thought hang on a minute what's it stopping for, and this German person then said to me, 'Out, out,' saying to me there is no more trains now until the morning run at four o'clock, to bring the East Germans back into work. He said 'Come, come,' so I went, and we sat in the waiting room. There was this Russian sentry in this big old coat, walking up and down. I tried to explain that. I fell asleep. He said 'All right as long as he stays here.' I gave him a fag, it was the usual thing, soldiers in different uniforms trying to make banter and he was probably as young as I was and doing his bit. Anyway he left us alone the new train came and I got back on. I was feeling a bit knackered. I fell a kip and went straight through the West Zone and the next thing I knew I heard 'Raus. Raus,' from one of the old Germans with black uniform, the East German police and I was taken prisoner.

An international incident? Yes, I was taken away and then grilled, taken to Potsdam jail. Well of course, my name being Burgess, and what with Burgess and Maclean, and this was 1959. So anyway they kept bringing me into this room and I can see him sitting there, blonde, blue eyed, fair skinned and speaking perfect Oxford English, asking me questions repeatedly. I had been in solitary in a cell. I had a bucket, there was a bulb, no windows, and this duvet, it had 2,500 squares on it. There was no books. I wasn't beaten up or anything like that. Of course they had my wallet. All your possessions were taken off you and you had to sign. I said I wouldn't sign, because you were always told you mustn't sign anything in German because you could be signing to say that you have defected. I wouldn't sign for ages and in the end he said 'Look I've put it in English, look we are not trying to keep you.' Then all of a sudden he would ask me a question. 'What regiment are you,' and I said' I'm not allowed to tell you.' 'Oh you're 14th/20th aren't you?' Then the next day he'd drop one in, 'Oh you are in Spandau, Smuts barracks, tanks?' And of course you go 'Yes.' Eventually I took the chance and signed it and called for the driver and he shook my hand and said 'Right come on,' he said 'I hope you don't get into too much trouble and here's the money for your fare back.'

When I got back to Smuts barracks. Corporal Scott who was the Guard Commander at the time said, 'Bloody hell mate, you are in the shit, get in that cell,' I said 'What?' He said 'The military police will be here in two minutes quick.' I was taken to Berlin headquarters and interrogated by the intelligence people. They were on the ball, they knew where I was. They wanted to know what they had asked me, who I'd seen, describe the uniforms and they had pictures of people. So I gave them the information. Luckily it never got in the press. I thought great I'm back in Berlin now, but no, I was banned from Berlin. I was put on the train and ended up in Celle, where C Squadron was.

Tanks? We were in Centurion Mark 3's. A twenty pounder. I was a driver in them days, it was an art. Double declutch first gear, crash box and we used to drive down the main Herr Strasser to the Olympic stadium. We didn't have rubber tracks it was steel tracks. They were a good tank but it was hard work, the maintenance and greasing.

I did my training at Lulworth on Centurion and Saladin armoured cars in Tyneham. I sadly remember shooting 'figure elevens' in the windows of post office row. As you went over near where the toilets are now in the old Tyneham farmyard which was a converted dairy place, there was little figures there, then we ended up down at Worbarrow and come back and we would start at East Holme, the final exercise, to make you a crewman.

You got to know the ranges very well. We would start somewhere on the Heath Range, at the back of the northern part and you just exercised your way down with targets. You'd exercise your way up the top of the ridge and then you'd scheme down through the valley using the tracts and the contours and end up at Worbarrow and go back.

The history of Lulworth Range is that it was taken over during the First World War. The Tank Corps at Bisley in Surrey moved to Bovington in 1916, with firing taking place at the Royal Naval Gunnery School at Whale Island or Chatham. Tanks were under the Navy then for some obscure reason. Then in 1917 the land was acquired for live firing and moved to Lulworth. 'Little Willy' was the first tank, they were called the Machine Gun Corps to start with, and well they only had machine guns, on the pods on the side. They were the secret weapon of the First World War. Yes, very, very secret. They called them tanks, to confuse people, to think they were water tanks.

In 1938 when the threat of the Second World War was looming the land around Monastery and Flowers Barrow was taken in. In 1943 the War Office had to look at expanding the tank ranges and because of the bigger weapons they needed a larger sea danger area, now six miles out to sea. When the Artillery come down now they fire a practice round and we have to use what we call an extended sea danger area. Another part of the agreement was that the ranges can only be used a certain number of days of the year because the MOD realised after the war that fishermen in Lulworth have got their work to do.

It's been a passion of mine to improve the access and to ensure that when people do walk on the ranges they enjoy what they see. I have always been a great advocate that it's a military training area first, that's what it's there for, and with what's going on in the world we still desperately need it. But at the same time when we don't need to use it, then why can't we allow our neighbours, our local people, to walk it and enjoy it.

I have been really privileged to manage it. When you are setting up the range early in the morning and the sun is coming up in the east and its lighting up all the limestone, the chalk, the Kimmeridge clay and everything else and the sea is a different colour and with the outflow from Winfrith into Arish Mell, the steam's rising up. You don't need to go to France or Spain. They go on about the Seven Wonders of the World, well Purbeck and the Dorset coastline…. That'll do me.

And of course the night times, it's different, because you look across and it's shining up Portland and Weymouth Bay, it's fantastic and you stand there and there's not an urban sound, but the birds. Once you get the other side of that ridge when the road is closed and we are preparing the range for the day's firing, there's not a car, a telephone, people shouting or talking, there's nothing but perfect peace.

All my staff, the wardens and the target boys, they used to say 'Oh boss this is fantastic,' and it is, you don't really appreciate it, until you are there or until you miss it, and then we break the silence by banging off. But also I really believe that because the military has been there in that space, the flora and fauna are not disturbed too much. It's a pre-1950s landscape. It's not buggered around by chemicals or intensive farming.

Once it was requisitioned then it was agreed, sadly for some people, but rightly by others, that it was never going to be handed back. The Cold War came and then we've had all the recent Middle East issues. I think I had about eight tenant farmers, who used to have a licence to graze, that was all. Now they have a tenancy agreement. They can claim subsidies but because they can only graze, they can't deep plough. And this part of Tyneham Valley just below Flowers Barrow Ridge you can still see the strip fields and the lynchets, and when you think about Tyneham it was medieval in a way, because everybody who lived there worked for the landlord. Tyneham was the Bond family, they weren't the original owners, they were the owners for the last 300 years. I've spoken numerous times to General Mark Bond who lives up here. His father owned it at the time and he was away in the war. The landowners were compensated but the people weren't because they were in rented accommodation. The evacuation? They were given very little warning, I think everybody was thinking that it wouldn't happen, I think it was the 19th of December, just before Christmas, 1943.

One of the nicest memories was that we've redone the church as an interpretation centre. I discussed it with a lady called Linda Price, and she did all the art work for me and we researched it all and what we have done is a human history. We have got pictures from families and anecdotes of how the village was, and who farmed it, and how they farmed it, and there's pictures of them, the fishermen down at the Worbarrow side, because they were all different communities as it were, and how the school operated and we have put that up and hopefully that will tell the future generations and local people how the village was.

I really feel that Tyneham should be kept as it is now. I've never tried to commercialise it, we didn't want burger bars. Take Worbarrow Beach. It was just like when I was a boy going to the beach, it's an epic journey, the car gets to the car park in Tyneham village, for which we ask for a donation of £1. Where can you park in Dorset all day for a pound and walk around the village for free? It's good value for money. You see them, there's dad with the deck chairs and he's wandering down, off they go and they have a lovely time and they haven't had to buy a football or ice cream. So hopefully we have got the balance about right, with public access, the range and the wildlife.

A lot of people think soon as last rounds down, check the guns are clear, that we can just go and undo the gates. You can't do that because we have got nearly 22 miles of footpaths and permissive ways and beaches to ensure that is okay. I have had hundreds of letters from people saying how wonderful it is. If we get some decent weather, the butterflies on the top of Gadd Cliff and Bindon Hill will just be there because there is not a lot of disturbance. The Lulworth Skipper is just prolific, you have got the Adonis Blue, the Marble White, and then on the Heathland we've got two of the biggest sites in Dorset for the Southern Damsel Fly. They started because we are still picking up 1st and 2nd World War ammunition and we used to collect them all together into a safe place and blow them up. It made a crater and if it was on wet heathland it would fill up with water and the next thing you know is that the aquatic plants are there. Pond life in the nicest sense of the word. Yes they are some horseshoe bats in the old Second World War bunkers. In those days, like in Germany, the range staff were down range. Here in Bindon, well everything is remotely done now, hard wired or radio controlled, so there is no humans down range at all.

Where else have I served? The Middle East. Libya. We lived in Benghazi for two and a half years. That Christmas we had only just got back from three weeks in the desert, doing the usual run from Tobruk to Benghazi. In fact my corporal had the front wheel of his Saladin blown off by a mine. That Christmas I was Guard Commander, then straight from Benghazi to Cyprus, we got there Boxing Day. We did the UN peace keeping. This was 1963, so Makarios was knocking around. We were stationed in the Ledra Palace Hotel, my bunk was in the squash court. The Turkish people, they had been kicked out. The worst thing was for the first three days we had to escort the RAF regiment from Akrotiri, the armed escort for them to pick up, sadly, all the corpses in the walled city. It wasn't very nice, but once that settled down our job was in the Panhandle, up the other end. We also did the first UN peacekeeping and were there for nine months, because Tripoli had shut down, when we moved out.

In between I'd been posted back to Lulworth as a gunnery instructor. I did two tours, once as a sergeant instructor and then went back as a Staff Sergeant. Then we went to Gosford Castle and Belfast. I was SQMS and SSM. We were the first ones to take Saladins in. The riots then, we were talking big riots. We're not talking 20, 30, 40 people, we're talking a hundred plus. Urban fighting with armoured vehicles, it's difficult. The milk bottles had petrol in…

I got the Ranger Officer's job in the end of 1991. Bindon Range. Now that was originally a 21-year lease, then they converted it to a 100-year lease. And in the last 10 years I was part of the team who renegotiated another 100-year lease for that part of the range. That is what we call a school range. The camp has all the trainers, the simulating buildings, the precision gunnery trainer for the Challenger, all the armoured infantry crews come through here as well, with the Warrior.

Basically they do the business for the first time using live ammunition, in whatever vehicle they are in, whether they are a recce, armoured infantry, main battle tank or artillery doing anti tank fire. But with the coastline we have the fishermen coming in.

We have a good relationship, we've got the telephone numbers. It's swings and roundabouts. Certainly earlier on when I was RSMI of the range, before I was commissioned, I used to work for the Range Officer and in the late 1970s there would be big fire power and sales demos and of course you would have everybody there, Chairman Mao and whatever. I'd be down at range control, I'd be operating the radar and the Safety Officer would ring me up and say 'Are we clear Mick? The General's arrived and all the people are ready to go.' And he starts the commentary 'No you can't go!,' 'What do you mean, Bloody hell.' I said 'No you can't go, Joey is still doing his pots.'

Well if they couldn't get to the pots for three or four days and they are tangled up there has to be a bit of give and take. Our major problem recently has been divers. Once they put a man down you can't get them out see and some of them are scallopers, they dive with just a flag on them and nobody in the boat. And they might not even have a licence.

Normally about May time we have a nice annual lunch with farmers, fishermen and local landowners. We pick a time when they are not lambing and we get them to come into the Mess and give them a free lunch and have a chat and let them have a whinge. We learn a lot and they learn a lot you see.

There's Arish Mell, there's still the effluent pipeline it comes from Winfrith. Its about to finish shortly, but they draw water up from the sea into it, it was to cool a reactor which I think is dead now, but they still do a bit of atomic research, and their waste product goes back down, and they come in regularly to the range control to say 'Can we go down and check the pump house?' That's Arish Mell because that's also where there used to be a big sheep wash there, when they were driving the sheep they'd wash them there, then shear them and take them on to Dorchester market for the May fair. And of course Mupe Rocks is a stunning place, had a few landslides, but of course Mupe Bay, yachts come in, moor up in the evening or at the weekend. We said it ought to be put on charts but it now comes up on their radar. And of course you have got Fossil Forest, which is amazing.

From Arish Mell you are coming back around towards Worbarrow Bay with half of that Iron Age fort there. This was part of Purbeck. Lulworth was a big market port. The Piddle valley was all flooded. Then you've got Little Bindon, where they built the first Cistercian chapel in England and then they moved on and built a farm. Bindon Abbey, that's where the telephone exchange name comes from. And Monastery Farm is there. This part of the range here, was all part of the monastic holding.

So they drive out in their tanks and they then go down these battle runs just like the ones in Germany. It's the same as the Glasgow Underground, powered, it's big, it's a railway, all singing and dancing and here we send out four controlled electric trolleys, with different silhouettes on them and we can expose them going left or right or right to left at different speeds to test the crew in their agility, dexterity and the equipment as well to see if they can pick 'em up, track 'em and hit 'em. This is the BIG BOY'S range. They start here, they are tested day and night.

We don't pull trees and hedges up, we need them for our skills, we need to conceal ourselves and things like that. We pick up the litter and don't allow any digging. We do have livestock out. In Tyneham basically, south of the route there and down by Kimmeridge. Oh yes we have got thousands of sheep. The main commercial side is sheep and cattle. And then we've got, for conservation reasons, we've got some agisters who run some horses for us. Well they used to have Welsh Cobs, but we have got some Exmoor and some Shetlands. And they are doing a grand job actually nibbling off the old gorse... I did about a year and a half as the RSMI Ranges which gave me an insight into running the ranges. I fell in love with Tyneham village.

The public are our ambassadors, if you look after them and you treat them well. It's their land anyway isn't it? How can you deprive people of walking across there? One of the things that came out from the inquiry and all the consultations in the 1970s, was that now, all the critics actually agree that if it went back to the landowners you'd have bungalows and it would be totally developed in a way which would be counterproductive. We are open 137 days of the year, that ain't bad. But I am adamant that it shouldn't be closed off but that is should be restricted, they are not public footpaths they are permissive ways.

When I first arrived the coastal section had two fence lines and it took me a number of years to convince my masters that we should get rid of the cliff top fence. That was 1996, but we had to do it in stages. I was also able to make better access for less abled people, from Tyneham car park down to Worbarrow. I got some money. We put a ramp so people could go into Tyneham church.

On the 60th anniversary of the evacuation it was my aim to get the new church interpretation done, and invite as many people as I could. We had a carol service. About 15 ex-residents of the valley came. People just say Tyneham, but they forget Worbarrow, Povington Heath and all of those further to the east. In the schoolroom we laid on coffee and biscuits and tea and everybody could mix and they hadn't seen each other for years and years. At the end of it the most satisfying thing to me, was one of the elderly ladies, who sadly passed away this year she came up she said 'Major Burgess I just want to say thank you very much indeed, it's been wonderful I never ever dreamt that I would be able to sing carols in my church again and it has been lovely.' That made it, it didn't matter about anything else, it was just lovely. It made all the work worthwhile, and little comments like that will live with me forever.

32. Alan Lander – Fisherman and Quarryman, Worth Matravers, Isle of Purbeck. Born 1934.

Crabs, they didn't really bother with crabs. Even when I started we just went for the lobsters, there were plenty of them.

I was born in Worth Matravers, just up the garden path in a railway carriage in 1934. They had a few problems getting the railway carriage up here, it came up on a timber carriage, I'm told, in 1920. I think housing was just as difficult after the First World War as it still is. Especially to get on the ladder today in a place like this, the property in this village is out of this world, it's telephone numbers they want for houses. Real local people left? Joan and Ron, myself, three. There is one of the Gillespie girls…Charlie Newman, no more than a dozen, I would think.

My father was a fisherman. We used to fish in the summer and quarry in the winter. I started fishing in 1950 and we were still using withy pots then, he used to spend most of the winter making them. Small inkwell pots. Crabs and lobsters. Some he would make a little bit bigger for crabs in the spring. Yeah, you used to get the odd starfish and octopus, quite a few octopus.

Father had bad eyesight. He never actually went in the war, he worked in the Telecommunications Research Establishment. They did some radar research. That was 'hush hush'. They had an RAF camp over by Renscombe farm, he worked there and then they moved up to Malvern more or less overnight, they were afraid they were going to get invaded, and he went to Malvern with them for a bit, then they sent him back to go fishing.

Grandfather was a fisherman. I am the fourth generation. I've got two sons that are fishing and one grandson, so we're up to the sixth generation. I think my second grandson's gone today, but he's still at school. Fish in the summer, quarry in the winter. Grandfather was quite a good mason and he used to work in Preston, near Weymouth. They used to walk down on a Monday morning to start at seven or eight o'clock in the morning and they used to walk back on a Saturday afternoon. They'd go along the cliff. It's a long way, especially to do a day's work after you'd done it. Grandfather died when I was 14 or 15.

Mother was born in Tolpuddle. She belonged to a family of carters, they ran the carts on the farm. She was a Gale, her family were carters at Broadmayne, then they moved to Tolpuddle, and from Tolpuddle they moved to Compact Farm up here, I think that's where they met. Mother said they moved their furniture here by horse and cart from Tolpuddle.

Grandfather bought this cottage. Worth was sold in 1920, before that it was the Rempstone Estate. Grandfather bought this with quite a bit of land, the garden and where the railway carriage is up the top. There is the railway carriage, up on the picture there. First or second class? It was a non-smoker! She was very proud that there was no smoking on the window. She did have running water in the end. No seats. It was completely stripped out. She had a kitchen range, father put a bit on the side, which was the front room, and then she had a bit of a scullery. Then father put a piece on to make the pots which she was allowed to use in the summer but it was his pot making shed in the winter. We should have taken more pictures of it. It was probably 50 years old before it got here. The floor was teak. Mother lived in the railway carriage until she died in 1982.

Chapman's Pool. Father fished from there. He walked down there, his mode of transport towards the end was a carrier bike, but they did have a donkey and cart and a pony and trap at times to take the catch in. But Chapman's Pool, it's a good mile and a half from here. There was also a boat fishing from Winspit, you

Alan Lander at Chapman's Pool

could push it off the ledge there. Father said at one stage there were six boats at Chapman's Pool, each with two crew so there were 12 of them working from there.

Crabs, they didn't really bother with crabs. Even when I started we just went for the lobsters, there were plenty of them. They used to take them on the donkey and cart. During the war a lot of barrage balloons broke away and they used to float in and they used to make bags out of the barrage balloon material which was waterproof, they used to pack the lobsters in these bags and take them to Swanage on the bus. You can imagine doing that today, can't you?

The lobsters were still alive? Oh yes, and at one stage they dealt with the liners at Southampton, and to get them there they used to get a taxi to Corfe station and put them on the train for Southampton, and we used to send prawns to London in the autumn. We could put them on the train at five o'clock at night in Swanage and they would be sold in Billingsgate the next morning. The last lot we put on took three days to get there, they weren't really worth selling then.

Quarrying was just to get through the winter, the fishing was the main thing. We used to start as soon as the weather settled a bit in March, and we would go through into October really. Father reckoned he used to row up off Swanage. Grandfather would never go to sea on a Sunday, he was a bit religious which was fair enough, he would never go to sea on a Sunday. I've got a couple of boys like that, they won't go to sea on a Sunday, but not because they're religious! Father said they left here at half past twelve of a Monday morning to row up to Swanage for daylight. There was no engine so they'd row up to Swanage for daylight. They were made of different material then. Every day they'd check their pots. They'd row all day long. And they had to walk home when they got back to Chapman's Pool.

We used to work about 60 pots, but when the tides were quiet, neap tides, we'd go off with 18 pots and we would haul 18 pots twice or three times a day, however many slack waters we could get. We'd go off, probably not more than a couple of miles, but we'd work off St Alban's Head and down off Kimmeridge, but there was nobody else fishing, and it probably only got touched once a year, perhaps twice a year depending how the weather was. So when you went out there you caught tons of lobsters. Two, three, four in every pot. It was full of them. It was good.

One of my oldest memories of Worth, Mother and I, looking out the kitchen door, two German planes go over when they bombed the camp over there. Now I can remember that as though it was yesterday. I can remember seeing the swastikas on the planes, they were quite low down, they bombed the camp and killed one or two there. I would have been six or seven. I can remember us kids used to go round the fields, they used to drop that shiny tape, that tin foil stuff, decoy for radar. There used to be loads of that in the fields.

Rationing a problem here? Not really, no. We never went short of anything. The coast was fairly well guarded, they had barbed wire entanglements at Chapman's Pool and they used to move the path through it. We went down the path one day and we had to find the opening because they'd moved it. There were some coastguard cottages down there and the army took those over, they had a pillbox down by the beach and all sorts of things. I can remember a ship coming aground on St Alban's head one afternoon in the fog and all you could see was the barrage balloon level with the cliff. You couldn't see the ship down below.

We haven't really seen any bad wrecks. The wrecks we've had, everybody's got off. I was involved with re-floating the

Sand Dart and *Lumey* was another one, there was the *TA Johnson* in 1945 which was a Liberty ship, that went off. Grandfather was involved with the worst one, that was the *SS Treveal*. He had the Royal Humane Society for helping with that one. She was a steamer on her maiden voyage, seven saved out of 42. What's it say on the citation? 'Frank Lander, Bronze Medal, Royal Humane Society, 10th Day of February 1920. Saving life from drowning.' I think that was when it was awarded.

I didn't do National Service as such because, as a fisherman, I could do ten years in the Naval Reserve, which I did. I was in Chatham when the King died. When I left school Father had a local village chap fishing with him, and he couldn't sack him, and I did a year in an ironmongers called Edgar's in Swanage. That was an education. It didn't hurt me. It gave me quite a good knowledge of tools and all sorts of things. There's a bank there now. After that I went fishing with father. He showed me where he put his pots. Yeah, same as I have with Charlie, the youngest boy. I wouldn't let them go fishing. In the 1970s the fishing got bad. '76, that hot summer, you couldn't catch a thing.

They both got a job on local farms, so the farming side of it got started again. The eldest boy came to me one day and said 'Will you come to Swanage and look at a boat with me? I want to buy a boat.' Well, it was a wreck, I knew the boat and it was a wreck, and I had quite a good boat, 18 foot, and I said 'I'll tell you what, I'll give you a boat, it wants a bit of sorting out, it wants another engine and that.' The boat was sound but the engine was rotten. So he did that and he used to go fishing in the morning, around four o'clock, and he'd be home for half past seven to go to work on the farm, until half past ten at night, and then he'd nip to bed and be down there fishing at four o'clock the next morning. He put a winch on. I was brought up hand hauling. We used to go out through the race when the tides were

right. It was good fun coming back in sometimes.

Quarrying? Yes, going back to father, father used to make pots for Bob Harris who had a quarry down at Winspit. When he'd finished his own pots he'd go and make Bob's pots, and my quarrying first started down there. One of the first winters when I was fishing, I went down there. Now back in 1932 the family had their own Purbeck stone quarry, the Winspit one was in the Portland beds and they had their own Purbeck stone quarry on the road between here and Acton. I said to father 'This is daft, coming down here and working for somebody else, we've got a quarry up there, let's go and open it up.' So we did and we worked out there. We've still got that quarry, it's still there, there's no name to it, it was just a part time winter job that got you through. So we went and opened it up. In those days you had a pick axe and a wheelbarrow and a shovel to get the dirt off the top, to get down on to the stone, there was about eight feet of dirt before you got to the stone, so you were there for three weeks with a pick axe and shovel and you didn't earn any money but you come home tired every night. And then some enterprising quarryman got a bulldozer in, and we used to have the bulldozer and push the dirt off the top, but when we got to the stone we still had to dig it out by hand.

Purbeck is much harder than Portland. Portland tends to come out in quite a thick solid block, whereas some Purbeck beds are only two or three inches thick, some of them are thicker. The Freestone is about 15 inches, it does vary from quarry to quarry. So after the bulldozer period we then got a machine in with a bucket…That was the fifties? That's right, and then we got a track machine with a bucket which dug the stone and all. Life had got so easy. We used to dress the stone, it was mostly building stone, but of course crazy paving, anything that was suitable went for crazy paving. We used to get jobs like making a fireplace for somebody, but the majority of it, because we weren't there all the year round, because you got orders you ended up working there when you wanted to be fishing, so we used to deal through one of the merchants.

Did people use explosives ? No, that would spoil it. We used to use explosives at Windspit. You used it to knock the rubbish out the top three or four feet, that's what you took out and then the block came out underneath. We had a crane there, crowbars to get it out, sometimes we had to chop bits off to get the first one started, but once you got it started it would come fairly easy. And to cut it up, you had wedges to cut it. All done by hand again. I knelt down there for two weeks on a heap of stone doing nothing but cutting holes in it and putting wedges in and cracking it down. I had two weeks doing nothing but that, and father probably dressed it.

You used to get chips flying around. People would come round and talk to you, and if you wanted to get rid of them you'd just bang a few chips out, they'd soon go! There were lots of quarries in the parish of Worth. There's very few today, and the way things are going I don't think there are going to be any quarries. They've got this landfill tax now. It's going to hit the quarrymen very hard. Two or three years ago there were a couple of quarries that were short of stone, and they wanted to open another field and the planners were dragging their feet, and one of them came to me, in fact it was the youngest boy's girlfriend, came to me and said 'We've got three day's stone left and we're out.' And I said to them 'There's a lot of stone there,' Charlie didn't really want it, and I said 'I don't want it, not at my age.' So we let them go in, two quarries, and they took a lot of stone out of there. When they filled it back in there wasn't enough dirt to fill it up, and you're not really supposed to tip anything else in there. Not even from the other side of the road, which is

absolutely ridiculous.

That quarry of ours, the Freestone was the easiest working bed of the lot. The Thornback and the whitestone bed were a little bit softer and needed a lot of banging, but the Freestone was the best of the lot, and the Roach along the top used to split out for wall stones and crazy paving. It's not always level, it runs in and one end of the quarry the stone will be nearly on top of the ground, and the other end it'll be 20 foot down. We had a wooden crane that was out there all during the war and the gibbet looked a bit dodgy. It hit me in the face once. I had about 15 cwt on the other end and I let go of the handle and it caught me across the nose, the dent is still there. Blacked both eyes, didn't it? That was before we were married, so a good 50 years ago.

Trouble with the Lobster Liberation Front? Yeah. Our son did. They didn't catch them? No. Charlie, the youngest boy, had quite a few pots ashore down there, about 50 in Chapman's Pool, it's out on a limb, there's nobody down there. They did it early Monday morning, and they got rocks and flattened the pots with rocks, about 50 pots. This was about two or three years ago, they came back about three weeks later, again early on a Monday morning and smashed the boat up. They smashed the engine up. We reckon all the way round it cost between eight and ten thousand pounds. They did a lot of damage, and he lost two weeks fishing.

Just our boat and his house. They chucked a lot of red paint around his house. They were fairly local. I'm sure the police know who they are. They went to Scotland and did someone there, again, it was a chap all on his own. I have got two sons fishing and a grandson. And the second grandson's gone today. It's his initiation.

Electronic gear on board? Yeah. Got the gear today. I think

he's got 12 strings of 20 pots. It isn't necessary to do them all every day. He works on his own, and he won't work from Chapman's Pool. He goes out from Swanage now. It costs him another tenner a day for fuel. The lobsters are a success. They're getting about £10 a kilo now. It was good when we first started dealing with Spain. And crabs. With father we never used to bother with crabs. Shortly after I started, we dealt with the fishmonger in Wareham and he used to come with the van and pick it up. He used to like a few crabs, not an awful lot, but he would have a few, and at times the brown crab got quite good. I could catch about £100 a day easily at one time, but it's gone off a bit now.

The quarries at Winspit finished in the 1950s. Dancing Ledge? They'd gone. Windspit was the last remaining one. Stone tiles came out of the Downsvein bed. There's still a bit of stone tiling around today but it's surprising how much of the stone tile was dug by the old men years ago. They seemed to know exactly where it was. They could find all the good tile beds. There was a quarry on the opposite side of the road to us out there, and I can't remember, I think father said there were 13 beds of tile come out of one stone. They'd be worth a fortune today.

Father was nearly shot during the war, it was only rifle stuff, machine guns I think, but it landed by the side of the boat and it was all a bit dodgy. I think they had the targets on the top of the cliff, but it was the overshoots that was the problem, and we were by one of the buoys off St Alban's Head, and the shell landed, they shouldn't have opened up. I don't think they knew we were there, it was a misty day, and they opened up and a shell landed a couple of hundred yards from us.

I've never been away, no. The trouble is, living here all the time, you don't appreciate the change. Worth has changed, when we were kids there was a whole mass of us kids. There was two

shops, firework night and that, we'd all get up on the village green and have a bonfire. Christ, now if you had a bonfire you'd have fire engines, police, God knows what out here. All the so-called locals would be after you. We used to have great times when we were kids, VE Day, VJ Day, firework night, we all used to congregate up by the pond. We used to pinch Eddie Reid's gooseberries from over the wall.

Commoners' rights? I think they did have some sort of rights, but not any more. They don't have any rights at all. I think the landowners own the mineral rights, but since the National Trust has taken it over, when Bankes had it he wasn't too fussy what you did with it, as long as you paid your shilling a ton, now you can't do anything with the National Trust. This house isn't very well built at all. It was added on to the one next door. The one next door is well built. This is rubbish. Absolute rubbish! We've got the view.

Which did I look forward to most, the beginning of the quarrying season or the beginning of the fishing season? Ooh. First of March! Let's get out of this mud. Terrible, dirty job, quarrying, and in the winter time you were out there in ice and snow. In 1963 the stone was frozen in the ground, you couldn't move it for three months. You couldn't do anything with it, and we went fishing when it settled down a bit in March, we put the pots out in March as usual, and we went down the next day, nothing. Nothing at all. And we went back again in the middle of April and we did start and catch, but it did put the fishing back a lot. Terrible. Of course by that time the ground had thawed out and at least we could get the stone up. The field we're in out there, we've lost several sheds to hurricanes. The railway carriage survived, very well built.

My wife, Barbara, we met at Poole Speedway. Originally she's a Brummie. She came from the wrong side of the bridge, as we say. The other side of Wareham bridge. She was one of the first outsiders to marry into the village. It was after we got married the first house was sold up here to an outsider for £4,000, Eddie Reid's. The first house was sold for £4,000. Oh dear. It would make half a million today, without a doubt.

Fishing out of Chapman's Pool? No. I think Charlie would have carried on, you know, because he still does more there. He still fishes that bit. He goes towards Kimmeridge, not quite that far. We still use the crab boiler. We can get about three-quarters of a hundredweight in. If you want all the legs to fall off, drop them in hot water, or bring them up quick from cold, but if you just get the water tepid, put them in there for a quarter of an hour they'll go to sleep, then you can boil them up. And they don't make a sound. Once you've got them to the boil, a quarter of an hour.

Global warming? I'm convinced it's not happening. They say the sea levels are rising. If they are, it's happening very, very slowly, and so little. The tide still goes out as far as it ever went out, and it still comes in as far as it ever came in, but triggerfish, the first one I ever handled, it bit until its teeth met. That was the first triggerfish I ever handled. We get congers but we've always got congers. Going back to the octopus, they had that year when they got all the octopus but that was the best part of 60 years ago.

Trouble with the Navy? No, not really. They used to come up the measured mile sometimes and they'd chew the pots, but not really. I did an exercise with the Marines at one time with Richard Clifford who was a major over at Poole SBS, he wanted me to do something down at Chapman's Pool one night. He said this chap will come onto the slip, to pick him up so he could pick up something out to sea, and bring him back and drop him on the beach, which we did. He came on the slip, I know not where from but he appeared on the slip, it was dark, dusk, we took him out. This buoy had appeared in the bay in the afternoon and they said 'Go out and pick up the buoy.' The buoy had been on a time switch, this was a Tuesday and they'd put it out on the Saturday on this timer switch and the buoy had popped up, the weighted canister contained ammunition and a bottle of whisky for me. When they'd chucked it out the whisky bottle had broken, so they were sorting out the ammunition from the whisky and the broken glass, he said 'When this chap comes, don't speak to him, if you speak to him he won't answer you.' This was only a small boat, but I didn't speak to him, I dropped him off on the beach, he walked up the beach and disappeared. Now I know Chapman's Pool, I know all the paths and bits and pieces, I haven't got a clue where he came from, I haven't got a clue where he went. And the next day that Major Richard Clifford was parachuted on to the QE2 in the mid-Atlantic, the one they had the bomb scare on. We were down Chapman's Pool at ten o'clock at night, the next afternoon he was on the QE2.

I found seven canoes down there one day. They were all hidden away down there. I found a bit of a rudder of a canoe one day, I thought 'That's odd.' And I thought 'That bit of corrugated iron, that don't look right.' So I lifted it up and I found seven canoes. I know there was one on St Alban's Head once, they'd piled stones over it, you could see the shape of the canoe under the stones! That was there for a couple of days, then it disappeared. But you know every stone in the cliff and all the rest of it with all the years and years.

NOTES

SS Treveal was wrecked on the Kimmeridge Ledges 9/10 January 1920. She was laden with jute and ore from Calcutta and bound for Dundee. She tried to pick up a pilot at Portland and as none was available she was ordered to proceed without one. Apparently the jute was washed ashore and salvaged and then draped over the hedgerows in an attempt to dry it out.

33. Brian Bugler – Master Mason, St Aldhelm's Quarry, Worth Matravers, Isle of Purbeck. Born Poole 1948.

I used to carve some nice foliated capitals. Thoroughly enjoyed doing them, they are now about 70 foot up in Chichester Cathedral. I did a barn owl for Eric Hoskins… I've even carved Purbeck Marble dolphins.

My grandfather's book that he wrote in 1939 was called *The Dead Bury the Dead*. He did 4 novels, *Bachelor's Knap* which is based around Worth. Then he did *Saul's Sons* which is based on a good quarrying family, then he did *The Dead Bury the Dead* which is about a chap who murdered people and buried them, he was a grave digger, and buried them underneath the coffins, so nobody knew where they were. I think it's fiction but the sexual side of it might have been something from his experience because he was married to my grandmother and they lived in the village and it was at the time when the Square and Compass was frequented by actors, sculptors and authors…

He met this author Mrs Wade and in the end in 1933, he ran off with her, leaving my grandmother and three young children. My mother was ten at the time. It was not the done thing in those days. Anyway, it was published by Obelisk Press in Paris in 1939. Jack Kahane wasn't it? I've been trying for 40 year to get this book, and it cost me $213 to get it from Massachusetts in America, and it hadn't even been read. We had to cut the pages. He is best known for his book *Purbeck Shop* which was based on the quarrying industry. His name was Eric Benfield.

When I came to leave school my father said, 'Well you ought go and get a trade, you don't want to go into quarrying.' At that time I went to Swanage and I was offered to become a plumber, painter or carpenter. I went to carpentry, but I worked in the quarries at the weekend for Dave Lovell up at Acton. I have been in the quarries since 1966. I was born in 1948, my father was a farm worker, my mother was Hazel Benfield. So I have carried on down the women's line, which of course, years gone by, the Marblers didn't really recognize this. That's why when I come to join the Purbeck Marblers I had to pay £5/6s/8d, penny loaf and a quart of beer instead of the normal 6s/8d, which the sons did. Anyway I had to pay that to get the line back again. Although my grandfather and my great-grandfather and his father before that, they had all been in it.

They were down at Townsend, Cowlease, I've been down it, we dug it out back in 1974, underground. Worked with Dennis Smale, Charlie Turner and Freddy Smale we actually dug it out. There were two cars that had been just dumped in the hole and they blocked the hole. We managed to cut our way around it and got in there and surveyed it. There was a planning enquiry, they wanted to put houses on Cowlease, but in the end because of all the unstable land, all they were allowed to do was put mobile homes on it, which is the Holborne Park now. So we surveyed all that area and that really got my interest going. I met Trev (Haysom) and I was looking for a job. It was at that time when inflation was so high that when you went into a timber company they would only quote you the prices of timber on that day, so when you went in the next day it had gone up again. So I decided to come up here and that was 1976 May, it was hot. Trev said, 'Well come on for a month.' I have been here ever since. He hasn't told me if he's gonna take me on or not yet… I've been here 31 years.

I did my apprenticeship as a carpenter, but I was doing dress walling and wall stones in the quarry part time, because

Brian Bugler in St Aldhelm's Quarry – a chip off the old block

everybody at my age was in the quarry and we all played football and cricket together so that's what I used to do at weekends.

I was born in Poole and I was conceived in a little house in Worth, opposite the Corn House in there. Quarrying is very much in my blood, I think Eric Benfield traced his ancestry back to the 1651 Articles in the Company of Purbeck Marblers. Sometime there is a De Bonville, he was the knight who came over with William the Conqueror and that became Bonfield and that became Benfield. There are both in the trade.

The estate owns the mineral rights, the families don't get to own them. This is the only one other than Swanworth which owns their own mineral rights, but that's Tarmac Roadstone. They are digging the same seams of stone as we are here, but we are the only ones digging what's known as the cliff stone, Purbeck Portland. That belongs to the Encombe Estate and Trev's got a licence to dig it, which runs for about 14 years I think. He has to renew that and you're covered by planning, 'cos the planners are now spying on us with satellite and they tell us that we have actually gone outside of our boundary…

When I left school in the 1960s you could get a job anywhere. My father worked as a farm worker here in Weston, his father was a carter and worked for the farm here. The three brothers came here as carters and they worked for James's on Renscombe around this quarry. I have traced the Bugler line back to Beaminster. There was Gertrude Bugler she was in one of Hardy's plays. There is a Bugler Lane I think in Beaminster as well. It seems as though a Bugler came over to work in this area in the1800s, he lodged with a Martha Bower who had an 18-year-old daughter and it wasn't long before he married the daughter and the Buglers have been around here since then. The Benfields have been in Swanage since 1651.

Where we quarry is called the cliff stone, which runs from Durlston Head to St Alban's Head. My theory is that most of those caverns that were dug out between 1750 and 1780 where when they did the Ramsgate pier. I'd been to Ramsgate and they said that all the documents were in Kew. So I went to Kew, I went in at nine o'clock and they kicked me out at half past four. I hadn't had anything to eat or drink and I had only got through two years of the thing. They had gone in for nine shillings a ton and they were going against Maidstone Stone and Portland Stone and they ended up doing it for six shillings and four pence a ton. It was all taken up by boat. You can go up there now and you can still see blocks of spangle. You can see it in the wall at low tide. It was a massive contract and they were having trouble supplying it. All the way along the cliff they were digging holes. This hole was probably started then. Obviously it didn't work well 'cos that's when they built Pier Bottom. There is a pier down there but you'll never find Pier Bottom actually marked on an Ordnance Survey map.

I actually found some staddle stones down there and lugged one up, and got it into the garden. It got rather heavy the time I got up here. I think the first Ordnance Survey was late 1790s so when they came to survey around here the pier had all been swept away, the contract ended in 1780. That's probably where most of the cliff stone went.

For cranes they used the old whim. I built one, two thirds life size scale, there is a photo of one in *Purbeck Shop*. It's basically simple, just a wheel with a drum where you take a turn around it with a rope, just take the weight and the actual gibbet goes through 90 degrees. You pick up the stone, sling it out and let them lower away. That's how everything went down off the cliff on to the boats. A one way process. You get these tales that perhaps brandy was coming up the other way sometimes. Trev's father reckoned that after the Ramsgate pier, much never went on up on the cliffs, but just a front for smuggling. They were up there 'working' but probably bringing in as much as went out.

They were all family quarries in the 1960s. There's Lovells, Locks, Bonfields, Keats, Hardens, Landers, Bowers, Lewis's, Cobbs. All family quarries two or three men working in each quarry. Landers, they used to fish in the summer and quarry in the winter, that was the sort of done thing in them days. I never went fishing though. I like looking at the water. I don't want to be on it necessarily, only when it's flat.

Here we work various beds, Bluebit, Spangle, Pond Freestone. The under Freestone here is so thin, they did go down for it, but it wasn't worth moving the amount of stone to get to it, whereas if you go to Seacombe or Winspit, that is worked in the under Freestone. Then they let it collapse and worked up on the Freestone and Spangle on top as it came down into the falls/faults, which you can see down at Winspit, where Bob Harris finished in the 1950s. He blew the legs out and let it tumble down and just go through it. Throw the waste down over the cliff. You wouldn't be able to do now. When they worked out the Head there in the 1930s again, all the waste went over the cliff and the block went into Wareham, it was processed and worked there.

The Spangle we use is for floors and fireplaces because it is a mass of shells and polishes up well, but the Pond Freestone is used mainly for memorial because it's slightly harder than Portland Stone. Letter cutters and carvers love it. We use it for building as well as fireplaces, for mullion windows etc. Most of our stone now is brought in from our other quarries which is the Purbeck Beds and that's between here and Swanage. Last ten years all we've been doing now is paving. We did Merrill Lynch European headquarters in London, Bovis they built office blocks at No 1 Paternoster Square, then we did the OBE Chapel in St Paul's. We are now doing the south churchyard in St Paul's. When the Great Fire of London in 1666 destroyed St Pauls, Wren put his on a slightly different alignment and they had an archaeological dig and found the cloisters. So now what they are doing is this paving which is a plan of the cloisters where it stood on the medieval building. Most of the paving in St Martin's in the Field is 40 mm thick, St Paul's is 75 mm thick and we're letting in 20 mm grub to give the outline of the columns. It's a bit more interesting. It's cut into slabs and interlocking shapes. When you walk up there you see the darker stone against the lighter one. When I came here in '76 we did carved capitals for Chichester, foliated Purbeck marble capitals. Proper architectural. We were doing a lot more of that work then than now. All the cathedrals have got their own masons and we just supply them Purbeck marble stones cut to size. We would dig it, saw it, then work it and then polish it in the marble case. It's quite labour intensive. It's sold by the cubic metre or cubic feet in some cases. I think Trev's licence is a guaranteed royalty, he pays the guaranteed royalties for how much stone he gets. The National Trust when you quarry on there, they work out how much stone is in the ground and charge for so much a ton in royalty and you have to pay that before you dig it…

The main Purbeck custom is Shrove Tuesdays. We meet at Corfe Castle and are summoned to the meeting by the ringing of the noon day bell at the church, which they still allow us to do, even though they have put new bells in there. They are a bit wary of us, they say we cracked a bell in years gone by. Then we have our meeting in the little town hall and apprentices are accepted into the trade. Well there aren't that many sons of freemen actually joining, so those who work in the quarry now all pay £5 6s 8d, instead of the just 6s 8d for being the son of a freeman. After that, we kick the football up through West Street just to maintain the right of way. We still take a pound of pepper down to our farm, which is supposed to be given as a rent for the right of way. In 1690s a pound of peppercorns was worth having.

At our meetings we usually get around 20-odd. I think at one count there was something in the region of 70 living members. There are no real rights to it. It's been going possibly since the 13th century so it's something that ought to be kept going. That appears to be when the football was first started. Football was often used to settle disputes between villages where they would have a ball and the first one to kick and hit the next village church door won the argument. They were really fighting amongst themselves. Several Kings tried to ban it, apparently. I heard the other day that Oliver Cromwell did ban it but it was allowed to be played again in 1660. Football hooligans have been going for the last 700 years.

You do everything you can by machines now. You got to, to compete. These shapes that we are doing, they were going to have it watercut, but they couldn't watercut three inches thick. So then they decided they had to inlay it. We do as much as we can with a saw with a wide blade but you still got to cut it and fit it all in. Getting a 2 mm joint is a pretty skilful job. The first frame saw they had here was a swing frame saw which had a rippled blade. One man used to spend all day just throwing the sand on to this blade so the water ran down and it was actually cut by the abrasion of the sand between the steel. Very old technique. The blades used to wear hollow in the middle and they would turn them over and then finally they would get so thin they would break. The sand used to come from West Bay, you just take it off the beach down there. These days we have diamond tip.

My hobby is photography and you think of the modern camera now, you lust after a Canon 1 DS Mark III, which is £6,000. You can start work at the £6,000 camera or a couple of lenses up to say £10,000, well £10,000 wouldn't buy you half a little crosscut saw. Your saws start at £30,000-odd just for a crosscut. For frame saws you are talking about a quarter of a million. The new ones we got up at the Landers are all controlled by a computer. We got them in here. The skill is fast becoming all about being a programmer. Even this has become computerised to some extent. No young people are coming into the trade because if you can programme a computer you are going to want to be sat in a warm office you don't want to be here in January and February in minus one degree C, programming a computer.

When you look out here, the youngest is 40, but most of us are pushing 60 by now. There are four of us working here. No apprentices coming on. Weymouth College they do courses. They go to the course they teach them to carve and work in stone, but that isn't what the trade wants now. We want somebody to just stand and think about nothing, squaring up Purbeck or polishing it. That's basically all it's been for the last few years. You want more pure architectural.

St Aldhelm's quarry has been worked since 1771. Trev's father came back here in 1935 and opened this site. When I came up here first in 1976 we dug it manually, drilling, putting plugs and feathers under the block and pulling it out with cranes. The Blue Bit and Spangle are reasonably easy, but the Pond Freestone is tighter. I always used to use the black powder. We used to have to go and get 24 hour licence. The black powder came in one truck, the detonators came in another, then the policemen came. Then you had to make sure it was all used up that day.. The black powder gives a slow heat, all you wanted was a *Whoom*. But if you got a Bang! you know you got it wrong. Then we run in with the forks on the front wheel of a loader and ease it out. We don't do that now, we have a big slew machine with a pneumatic hammer on it, it drives down the joints and prizes it all out and it all comes off in layers.

The last lot of burden we stripped off we put in through the road up here, made it a bit flatter and higher. That's now becoming a planning issue because they are now calling it waste. Now we can't get rid of it because it's waste. You can't backfill old quarries. The reason a lot of the flora and fauna along this coast is because it's all been quarried. All these orchids, they love lime soil, and are all growing on old quarries. They wouldn't be here if it wasn't for the quarry. There are cases where they, the nature wardens want to leave the rock formations stuck out so the future geologist students can come along and look at it, but they don't need to do that here because it's already here on St Alban's Head.

They say the chapel is 12th century, but it is built on sacred geometry it's not actually built on true east/west lines. I designed and made an altar for it and we had to put it in one corner, in the east corner, we did that a couple of years ago. Archbishop of Canterbury came down and opened it, blessed it, anointed it with oil. It's an amazing building, it's based on sacred geometry, the actual window that's left now overlooking the altar is actually on the line of the winter sunrise. Much earlier position. My son did archaeology at Bournemouth University and he had all the ground surveying stuff and I asked if I could do a survey around it, but they said the first thing we want is a health and safety policy and then a plan of how you are going about it and all this sort of thing. So I gave up in the end. All I wanted the survey for was to see if there were any holes for a timber henge, it is the ideal spot for the winter setting sun on the horizon, you can see it from there.

It would have set south of Portland and the actual chapel is facing that way. If you stand there at midwinter and if you had a timber henge there and on the 25th December you would have noticed that the sun is actually coming north again. They would have possibly been using Portland as a mark. We thought we would go and sit on the tumulus on Emmet Hill one midsummer's evening and watch the sunset, and the sun actually rolled down in Swyre Head, the sun went down in the dip. There is more to it than we know about. It would have been nice to have done the survey. On the south side during the war they had the radar there and they did dig it up and there is a manhole there.

Radar? Mum's biggest memory is of course that they were here one day all of them and then the next morning she woke up and they had all gone. They had all moved out overnight. Her other memory is that the Americans come in here and all the tins of fruit. They used to just knock a hole in the tins of fruit, drink the syrup and throw the fruit away and they in the village were nearly starving, they had hardly anything to eat, and this was all being thrown away. Dad he was actually in the camp because he used to take water from Swanage up on to Nine Barrow Down, because they were building huts up there as well. There are some up there now. He was actually here in the camp when the bombs dropped on the living quarters. I think a cook and an officer were killed. They had trenches just inside the gate to get into. His memory is seeing all the geese, the blast of the bomb had blown the geese all down the road. They were all right, they were far enough away it was just the blast had tumbled them along the road. But two were killed. The quarters that were hit were on the road between Weston Farm and Bonvils, they have knocked them down and put stone around them. That was the only real bombs that were actually pitched on Worth. I think that was after they had moved anyway. I think they were probably aiming for Hamworthy, which was the spot were all the arms were being made. The story was locally that they found out that the Germans were aware of the radar and that's why they moved to

Malvern, overnight. Another of Dad's jobs was, that when they put the pylon up, he had to go around and plough little areas so they could break up the shadow of the pylon for aerial photography. They were given potatoes to put in, they just ploughed and popped the potatoes under the furrow and he reckoned he had the best crop of potatoes that he'd ever had. They weren't really planted. They do a mixture here really, grow some corn around here, most of it is silage. They grow corn up in the east fields and it makes you wonder how it grows, the amount of stones there is. It's the nitrates that is actually making it grow.

There is plenty of stone left on the cliffs, it doesn't come up to the quality of the Portland. It doesn't come up to the block size, what we make out of, they throw away. There is always just enough to keep you going. This quarry wouldn't survive on just digging the cliff stone beds, it has to process the Purbeck beds as well, that's what most people like for their paving and flooring cover. The Pond Freestone, it does take a polish, but it's the Spangle that does, a bit harder, similar to the stone to Roach in Portland, their Roach got more holes, but they used to fill it and polish it. Our Portland stone is that much harder and it's more fragmented due to its hardness.

If you carry the beds across here they would go straight across to Portland about 17 miles away, it's changed in nature. Purbeck can change in a 100 foot, you can have a nice hard Thornback in one quarry and a soft one a hundred foot away. It varies so much. No one goes underground now quarrying. The last one was Harold Bonfield, he was underground about '76/77 up at Verney just above Swanage, but again he was using compressed air tools. A crane he had. He dug it out more like a well and he had a crane there to pull it out, it didn't make sense I don't think. I think the quarry inspectors came and looked at it

and told him that he had to put up supports here and there. Inspectors come periodically to tell us to do this and do that. Last one we had was a couple of years ago, she was actually a lady who worked at Swanworth Quarries. She worked for Tarmac Roadstone and obviously she left them and took on the quarry inspector job which actually covered Gloucester down through Devon, Cornwall and Dorset. I said to her, 'Are you gonna come back.' She said,' I'll be back in six weeks.' She can't do this in six weeks. We haven't seen her. Her area is so big. If somebody was killed in Cornwall, the time that goes to court and all that, she just spends all her time doing that.

They say we have the freedom to dig the stone anywhere in Purbeck, but I don't know about that. They say there is a charter. Planners will stop you nowadays digging stone out of a field, but it does appear that if you go back a couple of hundred years ago, because you were going underground, if the landowner was in favour, you paid him a royalty, which was just one thirtieth of the stone hewn. If you had a headstone, which was worth more than if you were doing wall stones, they got their royalties paid like that, and of course the farmer, he actually had the cart and he was hauling your stone, so there was a little bit in it for everybody.

Then you got merchants starting up in Swanage and they were having their own wagons and coming to collect the stone and then the farmers were getting cut out, they didn't get that then. So you got friction between farmers and quarrymen. Then in 1904 the landowners Bankes, would have been Kingston Lacey Bankes, they took on Lander. Our ruling was that if a quarry wasn't worked within a year and a day then the permission lapsed. Well he'd gone back to a quarry and promptly opened it up and the estate told him to stop, but he didn't stop and in the end he actually went to prison for contempt of court, because they took out an injunction and told him to stop. He still didn't stop. It would have been nice for him to actually have tested whether the quarryman really did have the right to do it. We were breaking one of the rules of our own company that we were going back to a quarry after it had been closed for a year and a day, which was breaking one of our own rules. For a quarryman who was fishing, he might have been away all summer, he could go as long as a year. There was a Brown who owned Swanworth quarry, which Tarmac have got now, and he used to go back and work some little dots as they call them, which were set six-inch squares, he would go back every year and knock out a few of them just to keep it going.

I can't see any real future much because of the planners for a start. Nowadays you can move so much more stone than you could before. If you granted a family a quarryman's quarter acre it was going to take them a good few years to dig that, but now they dig that within a year with all this machinery and process it with machines. The National Trust, all the planners just don't want to see the land quarried that quick. Almost need quotas like fishing. The planners and The National Trust have decided on an area for preferred quarrying, it turns out nobody asked the quarrymen about it and we know that the stone is deep. So now they have huge mountains of over burden up at Langton, which everybody is complaining about. Because it's so deep you've got to open a bigger hole because you need that ramp to come up out of the hole. So really they are digging the wrong place, the stone is not as good there as it has been in years past, but you can say probably that 200 years ago they had all the best stone. They dug in all the good places. They knew, probably by trial and error, that if they dug a hole down there and they found the stone near the surface and it was good, then that was it, they dug in that area. Everybody got in there.

The block wasn't as big as Portland, most that came out from underground was probably a ton by the time it was split usually in its beds to start with, and then just one man would be cutting it up. Most of the beds vary. From eight inches is good, inland Freestone is much more it's probably two-foot high, but it is very fragmented and of course they would have cut it underground to make it easier to get out. You probably had two men underground and then you might have one or two at the top working it. The carts were towed under ground by the men, they used to have one man in the front with a chain around him and one with the bar, then they would have the pony with the capstan at the top, and he would wind to bring the stone up and they would have four little quarry huts at the top, and whichever way the wind was blowing they would find one that would be out of the wind and that was it. Mainly in them days, 100 years ago, they would have been working window dressings for brick houses with bay windows and coigns. There was a big street in Cardiff all done in Purbeck stone. It went from the depot in Swanage but they are similar in Richmond Road and Osborne Road in Swanage.

You can have a soft Thornback and a hard Thornback, whereas we were buying Keat's Thornback back in the 1970s they were lovely hard stones. Well anybody who had a block we would buy it. Good quality Purbeck stone now, price wise it varies on the specification but you are talking for sawn paving, around about £70 for a square metre. If you are going up to the Purbeck Marble you can go up to £200 a square metre. Which is a lot more dearer than a carpet.

I used to carve some nice foliated capitals. Thoroughly enjoyed doing them, they are about 70 foot up in Chichester Cathedral now. I only really saw them in place when they were putting them in place. I have actually carved, I did a barn owl for

Eric Hoskins, he was a famous bird photographer, he actually came down here photographing barn owls and he said he would like a carving of a barn owl. I did it over three evenings while he was here staying. I often wonder what happened to it.

Photography is now my hobby, carving I don't do enough of it, because if you're working in it all day, you don't feel like going home and doing it. I've carved Purbeck Marble dolphins. I did one for the head of BP over at Wytch when he left. I did a tawny owl the other day for my wife's choir leader, retirement present.

My grandfather, he used to do stone carving during the General Strike in 1926 and the recession was on and he used to sell his carvings to the people who used to come to The Square and Compass like Leslie Banks and his crew. When he went off, he was writing his books and teaching sculpture in Park Prewett Mental Hospital in Basingstoke. He was at the forefront of actually teaching the craft to these people as a therapy. The *Nursing Mirror* did an article on him and his carvings.

Grandfather's other books. *Southern English* was his autobiography up till he left. Then he did one on Maiden Castle based on Mortimer Wheeler's dig. *Poison in the Shade* was a novel based on Park Prewett. Then he did Robert Hale's *Dorset*. Robert Hale did all the counties. He did the Dorset one. Eric had a stroke in 1955 I think it was and he ended up being a patient at Park Prewett, then he took his own life in December 7th 1955. I always remember it, because it was the same day as Pearl Harbour. Mrs Wade who he had lived with as man and wife came down. He was buried in Worth churchyard and there was only six people there because the local people still hadn't forgiven him for leaving my grandmother.

She coped with difficulty. During the war they were living off charity really. My mum can remember the Americans wasting food when they didn't have enough, that stuck in her mind. He used to send £3 a week home every week, he did send some money but it was never enough and they inherited the Hazelcot, the little tin hut that they lived in. Of course they sold that when my grandmother died. My uncle and aunt they wanted their money so they sold it for £300, it would be £300,000 now the plot, just the plot. They parted with it that a little bit too early, but there we are.

I am trying to get a little photographic exhibition of my own together based on Geoff Hooper's poems. He was a quarry man, he worked here up to 1963, he was a self-taught man. He taught himself to speak Russian and German, he could translate manuals. He did all these poems then somebody persuaded him it's about time he wrote them down. So he wrote them down and published them and in two years he had a heart attack and died. So hopefully I would like to do a little exhibition of my photographs with his poems by the side.

Eric Benfield also carved an interesting anti-war sculpture in 1935 warning about the terrors of bombs and war from the air. This was two years before the bombing of Guernica and of course five years before the London Blitz. The sculpture of the bomb was carved at the instigation of Sylvia Pankhurst who lived in Woodford Green, Essex. The sculpture can still be seen under the trees outside 587 High Road. It's the only known war memorial to future years!

34. Ron Hardy – Coxswain, RNLI Lifeboat, Swanage. Born Swanage 1918.

I did twenty-six years in the boat and then I did ten years as launching authority. Altogether I did 400 launches. It's about 384 lives saved.

I have lived all my life in Swanage. We were builders for 120 years in Swanage. My great-grandfather started the business and it was passed right down to my brother and myself. During the First World War my father was in the Naval Air Service and he was a fitter, because he was a carpenter and worked mainly on repairing early planes in the London area. String bags, all canvas and timber. There were Zeppelin raids at the time. He was at Chingford and then at Crystal Palace.

My grandfather George Hardy he was quite a local character, he restored Kingston Lacy for the Bankes family. That was in 1904. He had 50 men working there. He also built a hospital at Templecombe in Somerset and rebuilt the Hardy Monument above Portesham.

He was quite a go-ahead chap. When they were at Kingston Lacy he actually used to cycle along the southern beach to the ferry and hail the boatman and they would row him over. Then he would cycle to Wimborne, to see the job and then cycle back. After a while he had a 1904 motorbike, the first one around here. It was early days. He used to ride that around and terrorise the local countryside. Four-and-a-quarter horsepower BSA and it was the first motorbike I ever rode. Then he had a motorbike and sidecar, a twin Raleigh. And then he went into Trojans which were amazing cars, they had solid wheels and chain driven.

Well the earliest thing I can remember was one Sunday morning father got us up early. He said 'There's a ship wreck at Peveril Point,' and he took us out to see it, 1921 I think it was. The wreck of the *Diana* on the Peveril Ledges there. A sailing coastal vessel with a cargo of granite chippings from the Channel Islands. You can still go on the beach and find the chippings now. I couldn't have been more than about three years old then.

My family was involved with the RNLI from setting up all the way through. My great-grandfather William Hardy built the first lifeboat house in 1875. My grandfather George, when they had the first motor boat lifeboat, he rebuilt the house to raise it, made it bigger for the lifeboat, then put the slipway in. Before that they just launched off the beach. When they had the last lifeboat my brother and I raised the roof and did the alterations to take the boat. So we have always been involved in it.

The first lifeboat coxswain was my great-great-uncle, who was a Masters actually. And when Thomas Hardy the writer stayed in Swanage he stayed at their cottage in Belvedere Road. In fact that warming pan there on the wall, that came from the old cottage, the old lady used to warm his bed with it. Her husband was a skipper on the local trading boats then he was a fisherman. Actually he suffered from very ill health, so he was only coxswain for about a year, but he was the first coxswain.

Open boats with oars? That's right. Oh yes rowing. And we had another uncle and a great uncle who was in the rowing boat and another uncle who was signalman for years for the lifeboat.

In those days they had no radio, they carried a signalman to do morse and semaphore. These boats, they were about 36 foot and had a crew of about 15. They would have launched straight off the beach with oiled boards underneath. When I joined the lifeboat, the only thing they provided you with was a lifebelt and oilskins and we had to buy our own sea boots. We had thigh boots in those days and I think they were highly dangerous, I fell

Ron Hardy, lifeboat coxswain

over the side once. I went it head first and I floated upside down with just the two feet out of the water and no one missed me on the boat at the time. We were re-housing her. The coxswain noticed that something had happened and chucked a handful of rope over the side, because he saw a pair of boots, he thought the boots were just floating, but I was in the other end. We were going full to stern to keep her on the slip and I could look up the tunnel and see the propellers so I thought I was going to go that way. But I saw the rope come down, I grabbed it and it righted me. About 1955 that was.

In 1938 I joined the RNVSR, supplementary reserve. When the war started I was called up straight away and went to Hove. I had a fortnight's training in the Navy and I appeared as a Sub Lieutenant. I did six almost seven years in the Royal Navy.

I started off on armed trawlers. We carried a four-inch gun and two depth charges. My job was on one of the depth charges. Anyway we were a boarding vessel, we were out in the North Atlantic. Any neutral vessels we stopped and boarded. We used to go up to Iceland and the Artic Circle.

I did it for 18 months. Boarding, we did it in the open sea. You were always covered by your own ship with its four-inch gun manned. When the Norwegians and the Danes were overrun there was no neutrals north of Scotland, we were sent to Gibraltar. We then did like Nelson and we blockaded Cadiz and we used to lay off Cadiz or Lisbon with these trawlers. We stopped all ships coming in and out. I boarded a Japanese liner and the American ones as well. 'Heave to or I open fire,' we hoisted the signal, and they would be boarded if they stopped. Sometimes if they were faster than us they would get cracking. We only had a small trawler's boat, sixteen-foot boat. If we had an armed party we got aboard. About half a dozen of us, and we would go through the ship's papers and see what the cargo was

and where it was bound for. One of our ships got a lot of mail off a boat going to South America I think. It was when the Germans had a good hold in Argentina and they sorted through this mail and they were using accounts as a form of code I think. They got quite a bit of information out of that.

Then I went to a bigger vessel, a sloop. *HMS Rosemary* on convoy work, escort work down the Irish Sea mainly. Convoys from the North Atlantic. That's where we'd pick them up. Gradually I taught myself navigation, and I took over as navigator of the ship. Afterwards she was used for target practice for the Fleet Air Arm up in the North Sea. Towing the target? No we were the target…

Once in the Clyde they used to fire dummy torpedoes at us and then we went around into the North Sea and there we had to get through the minefields, which were all the way down through the Channel. It was the one gap we had and it was highly secret. We had to go through and out into the North Sea. We used to do various courses and alterations and the Fleet Air Arm would come out to check us and find where we went. It improved my navigation because we had to find this one buoy marking the gap. It was about 12 miles off and the target ship before us was sunk on one of our own mines, so it kept us on our toes.

D Day? I was at home on leave. I could hear the guns across the channel. Yes, they formed up in the bay here. Then it came through that I was on draft to the Far East. I joined a troop ship. Fortunately the Med had calmed down a lot by then. I went to Egypt. We flew from Egypt to Mombassa, it took us four days by the Empire flying boat. We took off on the Nile at Cairo, we landed at Wadi Halfa and then Khartoum. We only flew in the early morning because the plane didn't fly more than 2,000 feet high, and it was too bumpy with the hot weather and we used to land in the afternoons. At Khartoum we saw where Gordon did his last stand. Then Lake Victoria. We had to fly around Kilimanjaro. All the elephants and wildlife running about there and then we landed in Mombassa.

HMS *Falmouth* another Town class sloop. We were the East Africa Escort Force from Cape Town up to Aden. Then as the war progressed we went to the Maldives, to Bombay, Ceylon and then Burma and then we went up the Irrawaddy to Rangoon. That's one of the navigations I did and because there was no buoys we picked up a local pilot, and the skipper said 'I want you to observe what he does.' It's 45 miles inland. The mud banks kept moving, there were no buoys, there were wrecks in the harbour. Quite large vessels can get up there, about 5,000 tons. When we sailed back down I had to do the piloting backwards to what I saw. Real navigation? That's right.

We just had two or three days there. I remember there was a lot of Japanese money blowing about the streets where they had thrown it away. We went and saw the big pagoda there. We saw the Japanese planes escorted by Spitfires when they did the surrender. We were farther down the river when they actually used the atomic bombs. I can remember we celebrated and we fired distress flares and things on the vessel and there was a big merchant ship that was screaming and kept sending signals because she was loaded with ammunition, all the while fireworks were going over the top, they were a bit concerned…

Then we did get out on the China Sea on one trip and went back to Bombay and did a refit. We then went to the Persian Gulf and we'd pick up agents, drop them on the coast and pick them up a long way farther down. A lot of them were negotiating just after the war, between the British and the Americans. Yes Muscat.

Leave in India to Delhi then the Taj Mahal. On my demob I came back through Basra, train to Baghdad, lorry across to Jordan. It took us a week to get from there to Palestine, then train to Alexandria back on a troopship. *Empire Battle Axe*. Lt Hardy in charge of 250 sailors. All going back home with canaries in cages. Then we picked up another 200 in Malta so I had 450 sailors to look after. Then from Toulon to Dieppe by train and then Newhaven. Yes. I saw a bit of the world. It's a long story isn't it.

I got back to the business in the office, my brother was also in the Navy, he was demobbed before me. He was the second coxswain on the lifeboat, for about four years, but he had a back injury, an old one, from the submarines so he had to drop out. The coxswain stopped me one day in the street and he said 'Do you want to come on the lifeboat?'

Yes I didn't mention that, but I had been involved with a bit of a disaster and it was a disaster, when I was on the *Rosemary* in the Bristol Channel. Just when they started the invasions of Italy they had landing craft with two four-inch guns. They built three of them in a hurry in Belfast. We had been out on a convoy, it was a gale of wind. I remember we were glad to get into Milford Haven and as we were approaching we had a signal 'Would we standby. Two landing craft in difficulty off St Ann's Head.' So we spoke to the one we saw. She was hove to and said 'She was all right,' but 'would we look out for the other one which was then right in under the cliffs?' We steamed down there and as we approached her, she fired some flares. She capsized and went down by the head. Her propeller was out of the water and you could see the 40 chaps all swimming. We were close under the cliff ourselves. You get a very heavy sea there. It comes right off the Atlantic and the ship wouldn't respond to her helm.

Anyway we got alongside of her and the captain called out the whaler's sea boat's crew. You could see the people in the water and I was on the bridge with the Captain as navigator and the First Lieutenant. I was checking how close we were to the cliff, 4 cables. It was looking nasty. The First Lieutenant came up and said 'Shall I send Hardy in charge of the whaler?' and the Captain replied 'No, I want him here.' We sent away the whaler, we lost all our crew and I could have been one of them. They were all drowned. Forty marines were also drowned. We were recalled into Milford Haven, and that night the wind was recorded at St Ann's Head at 102 mph. We had two anchor cables secured to the mooring point and we snapped both of them and it was two o'clock and we turned out dressed in our pyjamas. We were adrift in the harbour. We had to get under way and we steamed down and re-anchored there in the convoy anchorage. At the same time the other landing craft capsized as well. Two were washed ashore a lieutenant and a sergeant and they managed to climb a cliff. The lifeboat in Milford Haven was having her engines repaired. She was out of commission, so they sent for St David's lifeboat, which was 15 miles up the coast. Then if you can imagine it...wartime...no lights...it's a rocky coast. They came down through there, and they picked up one. One sailor in the water I think. It must have been a hell of a trip. At the cemetery, they had dug a big trench and as the bodies were coming up, we were the only vessel there and we had funeral parties passing up and down there to the cemetery. Seventy-six lost their lives that day.

Years afterwards we went on a camping holiday at St David's and I met two of the lifeboat crew, they were the last two survivors who were in the lifeboat. Anyway I was always very impressed with what they had done, and it rather influenced me to join the lifeboat.

The one thing I was chuffed about it was that I had to give the position of the wreck, it was a 180 degrees, and four cables off Sheep Island. Afterwards in the inquiry they went and found the wreck. It was a 181 degrees, and four cables, so I was only one degree out. Considering the conditions....

Yes well I was second coxswain for 14 years. The *RLP* (*Reginald Lionel Pugh*) had an open cockpit – we used to get wet through every time. The crew? Seven or eight. A perfect boat, but you only had a compass and a lead line. I can remember an old inspector came down and I said to him 'Was it possible to have a chart table?' I was used to charts, and he said 'Huh you should know you own courses you don't need any charts, you should know you own area.' And so there you are.

We did a lot of cliff rescues, it came in just after the war this rock climbing craze. And we had no boat to do it. We only had the lifeboat. In one case I swam in. There was a woman lost in a cave, she was a bit strange I think, she had wandered off. She had managed to climb down the cliff and get in a cave and the police were searching all the area and asked us to keep a look out because we were on exercise. She had gone down to Tilly Whim and we came back along the cliff and she got in a cave there and we saw her. We couldn't get in and so I had to swim in. As kids, we used to go up there, there's a rock we called Smugglers rock we used to swim off it. She was in close to there and I knew there was a way to get up the cliff to Tilly Whim so I swam in and she said 'There's a little bird I am watching.' Anyway I persuaded her to come out and have a cup of tea and I got her back and up over the cliff into Tilly Whim. I didn't have any shoes on and I had to walk all the way from there to Durlston Castle with her and I asked the manager to ring the police. He refused. He said 'I won't ring them but if you want ring them yourself from my office.' I said' I'm wet through.' Anyway I had to go to the manager's office, and where I stood there was a big, big puddle. I got hold of the police. Then the manager gave me a mop and bucket to clean it up. They never even offered us a cup of tea. The ambulance took the lady off and the policeman said 'They're are a miserable lot here,' he said. He took me in the van and he stopped somewhere up near Argyle Road there and he must have known someone, he came back with half a bottle of whisky. He said 'Take that home.'

The coastguards phoned in and we used to fire the maroons then. That's all we had. The coxswain fired them. He got a phone call, then you'd rush down. Then later on we fired them from the pier. Well yes the guns were pretty loud. The coastguard is stationed at Peveril Point. To assemble, about seven minutes, it's amazing. They got bleepers now, we were almost as quick. Everybody lives quite close by. One time the second coxswain came banging on the door at four o'clock in the morning, our phone wasn't working or something, I hadn't had the call.

As coxswain you had to get the crew. We had a system then, most of them had got telephones in and I would tear on down and the wife, Joan, would phone Vic's wife, so we had it worked out so we would all phone different ones. You would keep your wet weather gear down there. Oilskins and sea boots and that.

The coastguard would give you the name of a vessel in distress and some indication of where she was. That's right yes. Then of course we were just fitting a radio and we worked with the Knighton Radio on the Isle of Wight. The coastguards didn't have any radios then. So to get a message to us they would phone from Peveril point to the Isle of Wight and they would radio to us. We would radio back and they would phone the coastguards. With these cliff rescues the old coastguards used to take off their caps and do semaphore. We had a signalman for that and I have seen coastguards do that, it worked quite well. We had a loud hailer fitted so we could direct them down the cliff.

One time the cox put the nose of the boat right up on the face of the cliff and I jumped from the bow on to the cliff and I had sea boots on. But this was for a boy who had fallen 300 feet down, by those little caves at Ballard Head. He was only about 14 or 15, bird nesting or something and the lifeboat drifted away. I was left in this cave place by myself. They fired a rocket line into me and I pulled the stretcher in, and by then the lifeboat, the tide had taken her, had drifted and I was left there on my own and I had to straighten his body out. I suppose it was just some natural reaction when I moved him, his hand came up and went like that. He was dead? Oh yes. His head was cracked. And I always said afterwards that I would never send one man in alone. It's a bit alarming. We have picked up other people but with two of you it isn't quite so bad. And then to get me back out they had to fire the line in again and they pulled me out on the end of the line. I had to swim again on that occasion.

Bronze medals? The first one there had been a heavy south westerly gale and a heavy swell, then the wind went around to the north west but there was still the swell coming in there, and at Blackers Hole down there on the cliff there, there's a ledge. You can get down the cliff to it and then there is a big sea cave on one side there, and this young lad with his father and uncle had gone there fishing off this ledge. And sometimes you get a rogue wave. The swell came in and washed the box off the ledge into the sea cave. We were called out. By then we were issued with a small inflatable rubber dinghy. There was a swell and there were a lot of rocks out there, but anyway I crept in, close enough in and we launched the rubber dinghy. We got it in and the boy was on the beach at the back of the cave. We managed to get him out. That was 1970.

The other one was 1976. That was hard, we earned that one. It was blowing a south westerly, it really blew hard, Force 10 to 11. They came out and said there was a French yacht, the

Campscharles with two people on board and one of those big Russian trawlers, the *Topaz*, had found her out in the Channel and had actually picked them up and was bringing them in. She wanted somebody to take them off. Well there was a difficulty of language, my brother was launching authority then and he found a Polish woman who could speak a bit of Russian and they tried to persuade them to bring them in close enough, but he wouldn't come in within the three mile. He was very suspicious. He laid off there. Anyway we were launched and it was very heavy sea and we got out to him. It was a big sea I remember, we had to get alongside and get these Frenchmen off her. The Russian was a big vessel, she was about twenty-foot high. At one time we were down here and the next time we were level with the people on the rail, there was a big swell. Where we were, the lifeboat was hitting her, our engine bulkhead and all the instruments, the lifeboat was buckling and the paint was chipping off, the actual bulkhead was buckling. This was in the cabin and you couldn't see out, we were going up and she was coming down smashing the cabin roof, we broke the rails off the top.

Anyway we got them off and she had a big thick hawser secured to the yacht and that had got around the trawler propeller. They let go of their end and we were tied to the trawler propeller in the sea. Anyway she started her engines up, this trawler and although it was a big hawser, it cut it through. We were left with this rope hanging down below us and when we started up, we picked it up in our engines. So we were stuck out there then with the yacht tied on. We had to let the yacht go. To clear it I got two of the crew to go around, we had a grappling iron, to go right around, throw it out and it pulled empty. I think one of them, Tony, or his mate said afterwards 'Oh we are wasting our bloody time here.' But luckily on the last throw we did it. So we brought the hawser up so we could clear the port

propeller. You got open hatches and you can look down into the propellors. The poor mechanic had to be hanging head first down there till it was clear. Anyway we cleared the port propellor but the other engine, the starboard engine, they were just like one mass of fibre, nylon. There wasn't a hope in hell of clearing that, so we had one engine and on our way in we started looking for the yacht. We picked her up, put one chap onboard and we towed her, we only had one engine then and we towed her up into Poole.

Luckily there are not many ships wrecked. I have been down to the *Sand Dart*, they were on the shore, and got the people off there. They were on the rocks and there was also a German, a little coaster, down on the rocks at St Alban's Head. Usually bad navigation. The accident with the German one, it was a beautifully quiet day and a coaster was following her down and obviously the bloke on the wheel had gone to sleep. The coaster said they saw her go in and she went aground. They steamed on right behind her and she went straight in on to the cliff. And another one did that off Ballard, I had two, afterwards.

I did twenty-six years in the boat, and then I did ten years as launching authority, where you get the phone call. They generally request a lifeboat but you could make up your mind and say 'yea or nay.' We kept ourselves separate from the coastguards.

As the coxswain it was always in my mind, because you have to go into situations which every instinct as a seaman was to keep out of. But if you had to go in there you had to make up your mind. Well you had six other blokes with you and you had to consider those as well. One time and I think even more so now, it was one big family, you knew everybody right from the top. The centre was in London, Grosvenor Street was our main offices at one time, and their stores were in Borehamwood. It only came to Poole about 20 years ago.

I know when we was struggling at one time we was very careful with money, we did all our own repairs and we used to get in touch with Borehamwood. We did one rescue there with a chap off a barge and he had gone ashore at the entrance to Poole harbour and the shallow water, we were hitting the bottom, we smashed our rudder and that was when I was the second coxswain, Bobby Brown was coxswain then and we only had one bloke on the barge and we got him off, but we had to send to Boreham and they sent us a new rudder down by rail and we fixed it.

We cover more or less from Lulworth up this way yes. There is a bit of argument, well of course Weymouth has got a fast lifeboat, we usually go down to Kimmeridge. We rescued a chap off a cliff in Kimmeridge, I was sent in, in a rubber dinghy then and that was rather a strange affair. It was a thick fog, one of the fishing boats was fishing off there and they come back and they said they thought they heard somebody whistling. That was one day and they went down the next day and they heard it again and they reported it and asked us to go down and look. I think we took one of the crew with us and he pointed out where it was. It was so foggy. You could hear someone shouting on the cliff and he had got himself into this cave and up into the roof of it. We anchored off there and I went in, in the rubber dinghy. I couldn't get in but I could see him, he got up in the roof of the cave somehow. It's 1965.

So then there had been a murder done and the chap, he was thought to have come this way, they were looking for him. So they were all interested, they turned out in force, the police turned out, and it was a complicated business. The coastguard up at the top, they decided to get the Lulworth coastguard and lower them down the cliffs to get in the cave and they couldn't

see where to go. We had to try and direct them in the lifeboat. They couldn't receive signals up there, we had to wireless Portland, who phoned Dorchester who radioed the police car and then told the coastguard at the top what our message was, well then it went a long way around. He turned out to be a vagrant sort of chap.

The early boats were all wooden but they are now fibreglass. I liked the old 'RLP.' She was a real sea boat, she was non-self-righting, so she sat in the water and you felt you was a part of the sea. The *J Reginald Corah*, she was a self-righting one, she was lighter on the water. I saw the capsize trials for her, they put her on a crane and turned her over.

With the waves, the main thing is, I think, running before the wave. You can broach on a big wave and I must admit we was going to Poole once and we had been out all night searching and I was coxswain then and I was sitting down dozing. We had been up all night and I think the second coxswain was on the wheel, and on the entrance to Poole harbour, just on the bar there was two or three big waves and I heard a bit of shouting and she had actually put her nose down and she was running away. She started to broach but she didn't go over. But I remember I stuck my head out quick and we were in broken water then, you know how it is there. But the *Reginald Corah* she will run before big seas happily as you like, a nice little boat and she never broached or anything like that. Almost surfing some of the waves? Yes. If you were handling it she would. Her turning circle was tremendous. I like a twin screw boat. You go ahead on the outer one and astern on the inner one and twist her around on it.

What were the engines like? Well that's quite interesting, when I was on *RLP* she had two 35 HP petrol engines, Webbers I think they were called. They were changed to diesel. She did eight knots before that. And then I think they had two, 50 HP fitted. It went up from 75 HP to 100 HP and increased our speed by about point one of a knot. Eight knots was their maximum speed but she did get a bit more power for towing. In the boat now I think, just under 300 horse, something like that. We used about two gallons an hour, but this one uses about twelve gallons of diesel an hour.

The other crew members? Well originally they were more fishermen in those days. There was Bobby Brown, he was the coxswain, you know who the lifeboat now is named after. He had been in there almost 50 years. He joined in 1916 in the First World War when there was nobody about, he was in the crew then, he was about 16 years old. And there was two mechanics, they were two brothers, they were Arthur Dyke and Sid Dyke, and Sid was the boat mechanic and the other was the second mechanic, myself and my uncle Ken was the signalman and we had Gusser Norman, and he was crew and then we had the Inman's and Johnny Brown he was Bobby's brother, and there was one of the Marsh's I think, not Sid, Sid Marsh was a launcher, Jack Marsh, that was in the early days.

These crews are in that picture there. That one was on the *RLP*, by then Gusser Norman, Vic Marsh, myself, Donald Dyke, he was the second coxswain, Vic was the bowman, with me and Donald was the second coxswain, John Bishop, and Johnny Johnson. We still had the old fashioned radio, you had the twin aerial so we weren't on VHF. So we reckon it's about 1960 or 1962.

Modern oilskins are much better. Lifebelts are much less cumbersome because we had the big kapok ones you know, but the thing with those was you could be chucked around in the lifeboat and you could bounce off things, but these modern ones you get a dig in the ribs it gets so bad.

Bad weather? The real south west gale I always dread. Down on the freshwater ledges you know the other side of St Alban's Head, they run out a long way about three-quarters of a mile long, the ledges there and the only good thing is they run near enough south east, if you got in them you would run out south east, not the other way.

Our boat did one there after I left the boat, it was the second coxswain. A fishing boat had got right in there and he had to get hold of her and tow her out, it was a pretty tricky one that was, close up under the cliffs. The thing was about the cliffs, 'cause we had that awful one down at Penlee when they lost so many, our cliffs they are very much the same as theirs, deep enough for a small coaster to go right in against the cliffs.

The only lifeboats were the small pilot gigs. But that was how we got a lifeboat here. In 1875 the brigantine *Wild Wave* from Essex, sailing from Exeter was wrecked on Peveril Ledge with her cargo of coal. The coastguards went out in those gigs and they tried a couple of attempts and they couldn't get to it. They managed to fire a line aboard, but then she rolled over the line, it was trapped underneath. They couldn't use it to get to shore. By then they couldn't see any people and they thought they were all lost. The next morning they realised there was still some people huddled onboard and they went out again in these gigs and rescued the crew and at the same time the Poole lifeboat came down but they had rescued them by then. The Poole lifeboat took them back to Poole. Lieutenant Lose of the coastguard, I think was the name of the coastguard in charge, and he got a silver medal I think. After that Mr Robinson who lived in Newton Manor wrote and suggested that there should be a lifeboat in Swanage.

Interestingly my grandmother was a Masters and they owned stone vessels. These other pictures are of Swanage harbour. They owned that one the *Brisk* and there is the

Purveyor. She was built in 1810, for the Government to carry stores for the fleet and this picture, Spencer Masters, was my great-great-great-grandfather. He bought her in 1819 off the Government and she had a copper bottom, so he got it stripped off, sold the copper and had her re-rigged and she was in the stone trade and he gradually built up until he had a little fleet or about three or four vessels, he had the *Brisk, The Rising Sun* and the *Purveyor*.

He was collecting stone from the quarries on the cliff. This is where they loaded the stone. A horse would go out up to his neck with a load of stone there you see. A horse and cart going almost out of its depth. And then there was a heavy rowing boat which would take the stone. She has got a little ginny wheel rigged on her mast and used the ship's winch. That stone would go up to London because half of Swanage has bits of London, the tower by the lifeboat house, called the Wellington Tower came from the London Bridges.

The Purveyor – I traced this one's history, she had all kinds of adventures – built in 1810 And then in 1860 when the son took over from the father, he had her sawn in half and lengthened and changed her into a ketch. They put a 14 feet in the middle of her in Southampton. And she went on until the train came here in and then sold her down to the westcountry and that's where I got this photograph from. She was wrecked once at Padstow on the sandbars and anyway they must have got her off and she carried on and in 1912 she was a 102 years old, a Norwegian bought her to go sealing in the South Arctic.

And these two chaps, they sailed her and she got to Durban, the same year in May, and then I haven't got a real good check on her, she must have fished for only a year or so, and then she was bought by the Cape Town Fishery Company. She was re-registered on the British registration and I think the last we heard of her it was 1920 she was still owned by this fishing company, and she was the a 110 years old.

But I have forgotten one of the most important things…. The Ladies Lifeboat Guild. They raise money by various means. They ran a shop and unfortunately the shop's been pulled down. They make about £50,000 a year. Joan my wife, she joined the Ladies Lifeboat Guild and she became the secretary. We used to do a lot of fairs and things, money raising and that sort of thing. She was awarded a silver medal and then she was awarded a gold badge, and finally she was awarded a gold badge and bar for fund raising activities. And she still is the president of the Ladies Lifeboat Guild now.

Rescues? Sometimes 20 or 30 a year. Altogether I did 400 launches. It's about 384 lives saved. I have been at sea enough times to know what was safe and what wasn't.

1 cable = 100 fathoms or 200 yards

POOLE HARBOUR AND MUDEFORD QUAY

35. Clive Tyler – Water bailiff and Fisheries Inspector, Environment Agency, Wareham. Born Weymouth 1957.

So I was on my own. I suddenly had to become a water bailiff… Most of the poaching activity occurs in Poole Harbour.

My mother was a housewife from Weymouth. We lived in a prefab left over from the Second World War. Things were basic to start with. She was always having to do little cleaning jobs to make ends meet. When we got older she ended up working at Universal Engineering in Weymouth. I have got one sister. The prefab didn't leak but I vaguely remember it was a bit damp. They lasted a lot longer than they were meant to.

I hated school. Absolutely hated it. When I was about 12 years old, I got a job on the Montevideo Caravan Park selling Calor gas bottles just outside Chickerell. At 12 years old I used to lug about these huge great gas canisters. I didn't used to get paid a lot I know that. But it kept me out of mischief, especially in the summer, out of mother's hair. I think I did it for about two summers. Then paper rounds. I did one in the morning, the daily papers, one in the evening, doing the Echo and I used to do two on a Sunday. Through the letterbox. Never had a problem with dogs. I still had to ride three miles on my bike to get to school. Westham Secondary Modern. I left at 16.

I had a job in a restaurant, down in Weymouth, just the washer up and then I progressed to cook, that's simply because the chief chef spent most of his time drunk in the corner. My mother said, 'I don't mind you cooking as a living, becoming a chef, but I don't want you painting bloody restaurants all winter, because there's no future in that at all.'

I didn't know what I was going to do, so I went down to the council yard. And I said 'I'm looking for a job,' and he said 'What do you want to do?' 'Plumber, I would like to be a plumber.' And I went there and I must have gone in and out about a dozen times. Eventually he made a phone call and said 'Yeah start on Monday.' So I did an apprenticeship for five years. I went from Weymouth day release to Poole Technical College. I got my qualifications but I got a bit bored with it. When you are an apprentice you are on cheap labour basically. There wasn't enough work to keep us occupied.

So I ended up moving down to Burton Bradstock, Bay View Hotel, up on top of the cliffs. I did the cooking and a bit of cleaning and I eventually got a job in a factory, North Mills Textiles in Bridport. They used to make blue rope for the GPO, pulling rope but the main activity I was involved in was making yarn for carpets, huge great machines, terrifying things, I mean they'd kill you if you fell in them. This would have been 1975-76. Yes we lived in a caravan at the back of the hotel. It was quite nice there. The only fishing I did was a bit of mackereling off the beach, though I started fishing when I was ten or eleven, off the Stone Pier in Weymouth.

But after a while in the factory I was on nights, and that was good because you could do your eight hours at night and have the whole day off the next day. But then they put me on shift work and it didn't agree with me at all, it was two till ten, ten till two, and six till two. I thought that's it and I thought time for a move, so I went into the Wessex Water depot down in Bridport. I was passing by one day and I went and saw the manager down there and I said' I'm looking for a job.' And he said 'What do you want to do?' And I said 'I'm a plumber by trade.' He said 'There is definitely a future for you here if you want it,' He said 'Let's see how we get on.' So about a week later he offered me a job as

Clive Tyler with the patrol boat on the River Frome, Wareham

'service layer,' which is repairing burst water mains and service pipes, stop taps set in the road and that sort of thing. I did that for about nine months, and towards the end of 1977 we decided to move to Dorchester and it coincided with me being offered a job as a store keeper in Dorchester, so I spent three years in the stores. Wessex Water depot stores.

Then a job came up in Poole, as a supply inspector, dealing with complaints about the taste of water, burst water mains etc, but instead of actually repairing them, you just turned the mains off. I did that for about ten years, then this job that I'm doing now turned up, this was 1989.

The job varies. If you read the Salmon and Freshwater Fisheries Act, which is the legislation we use, you are a water bailiff. All rivers and sea, so that's the legal definition, a water bailiff. Then it became Fisheries Inspector, which is the normal title we use, but now we are actually called Environment Officers. It's a bit confusing. First I worked for Wessex Water, which went PLC, then Wessex Rivers South, then National Rivers Authority and now it's the Environment Agency. So you take your pick.

I work beside the River Frome in Wareham, the Environment Agency boathouse behind the pubs on the quay. *The Granary* is directly next door and then *The Quay*. There's always been a site here as far back as records go. The Victorians used it for hiring dinghies. The River Authorities took it over in 1957. The boathouse that was here originally bears no resemblance to this. They took it over and they rebuilt it over the years slowly into what it is now, which is now falling down. So I was on my own. I suddenly had to become a water bailiff.

Based here at Wareham, my jobs are many and varied. The agency owns the bed and soil of the river, the Frome and the Piddle, up to the tidal limit. We control 129 moorings on the river which we actually own on the Frome. We also let salmon and sea trout fishing on the Piddle. That is for rod. There is a net but it's for salmon and sea trout. It is actually for use in the harbour more than in the rivers, but it's something else I used to control. I used to maintain all the moorings, earning the Agency a great deal of money. We have a boat that does the moorings, looking after the chains and looking after the boats. I used to do the speeding. There is a four knots speed limit but that is purely to protect the flood banks. I also make sure there is no illegal fishing going on in the river with nets, checking rod licences. When I started the only place you could get them were the tackle shops, but now you can get them online by direct debit, on the Internet, there is no excuse.

Problems with poaching here? Not a great deal no, a few rumours on the river over the years but nothing. I never ever caught anybody on the River Frome or the Piddle. I have caught people in the past but the only thing I have caught people for are minor infringements, like eel fishing or no rod licences, most of the poaching activity occurs in Poole harbour.

It's a bit complicated but Poole harbour comes under the jurisdiction of Southern Sea Fisheries, but one of their byelaws prohibits the use of setting a net in the harbour from the 1st April to the end of September. That is purely for the protection of the salmon and sea trout, but they don't police that, we do. You can net in the harbour, there is no problem, but you must not fix it. These are gill nets, the sort that you could get at Gundry's. So that was one of my major jobs, going in the boat around Poole harbour. You would vary it, it depends on what the weather is.

The fish are migrating, they are going up river to spawn. We are coming to the time of the year now a lot of the fish have probably moved up the rivers anyway, they would still be in the deep water of the river.

April to September they are just hanging around. In winter

time our focus shifts from the harbours to up the rivers, because the salmon are spawning in six inches of water. Some people seem to think it's a good idea to try and take them while they are cutting their eggs. It's a real shame. So our priorities then move up the rivers.

What they are looking for is the gravel, but that could be on the Frome, it could be on the Piddle, it could be at Salisbury, it could be anywhere, on the Avon, the Stour. You have actually got a very wide area. We go up to Salisbury, the Nadder and the Wylye. The problem with Salisbury is that the main Avon runs right through the town, and you get a lot of locals use what is a treble hook, trying to snatch them out. I haven't ever caught anybody doing it, but close a couple of times. One of the other jobs we do is fish rescues if we get any trouble with pollution in a river, anything where the fish start dying. If a silage clamp leaks, anything like that, we will go out and investigate it and take samples.

All I have ever seen has just been with nets. You get seine nets, the mullet fishermen use a huge net, it can be anything two to three hundred metres long, but the way the net is designed it is not designed to catch salmon and sea trout. Believe it or not very rarely do they actually catch one, they are good for catching mullet and that's all.

Anytime you go into night time it's two men, if you know you are going into a situation it is two men or more. With Poole Harbour if I see anybody doing anything wrong, I have to call for back up, whether that be the police or colleagues. If you have seen an offence being committed you may not be able to stop them straight away but you get them in the end. We have good lights on the boats if we need them, and the night vision equipment is quite good.

No set to's out in Poole Harbour, but I have been threatened with death three or four times. One was actually in court when I was assaulted. Yes I have had a couple of court cases this year where people have threatened to kill me. But I have been very lucky. I have never actually been touched by anybody. I prefer to go in nice and calm and try and explain it's not right. And if they don't comply then look out, because then I start to use the powers that I am entitled to use, but I prefer to go in softly, softly and it has always worked.

The only law that is covered by the Sea Fisheries people is the fixed engine or the fixed nets in Poole harbour. The fixed engine refers to any fixed method of fishing. Traps? Yes it could be anything. There are powers that are derived from the 1975 and 1986 Salmon and Freshwater Fisheries Act. So we are helping to protect those fish to live a reasonable life and to spawn without too much intimidation. That's the idea. And of course there are byelaws made under those acts as well.

We are there to protect the salmon and sea trout, because the fish doesn't belong to anybody until it's caught. You could argue that we are protecting the estate's fish, but they are not their fish until you catch them. A lot of private bailiffs who work on rivers in estates call themselves water bailiffs, but technically they are not, they are keepers like ghillies, but they are not bailiffs, it's just a term they like to use.

If we found a net that was fixed in Poole Harbour from the 1st April down to September, if there is nobody there and it doesn't look like anybody is going to come back to it, in Salmon and Fresh Water Fisheries Act, it states that we don't have to make a case of it, we can seize that net and destroy it, without prosecution, which is pretty unique. But the trouble is unless it's a very dark night they see you and they say 'It's not mine mate.' You know. 'Someones nicked it.' That's a favourite one.

We actually go six miles from the coastline, directly out. Our actual area is from Lyme Regis to Christchurch, almost the same as the Southern Sea Fisheries. The recent case in West Bay it would have been ours. Yes £600. And a man a few years ago, one of our torches was found in the nets. I wasn't actually involved in that job, I nicked him the year before. One of my colleagues was telling me, it was quite funny, because he knew he had lost his torch and didn't know where it was. And this guy pulled the net out, got the fish, the sea trout and as he was sorting the nets out my mate said 'Argh there's my torch.' And the penny dropped, by which time it was too late.

Yes we are very lucky down here. The rivers take a lot of fish, but they don't hold the fish, they spread out over the whole system, we haven't got very many deep pools. The main areas are down the estuary, at the entrance, if we get a very dry year. There are one or two down at Lyme Regis. Sea trout come in shore and go in the little rivers like the Brit, Char and places like that, the salmon normally tend to stay a bit off-shore until they go back to the Avon, the Stour and the Frome.

The Centre for Ecology and Hydrology, CEH they do all the tagging. We used to do a little bit, that's going back a little bit now. One of the big jobs we used to do was electric fishing during the summer. We used to do it week after week. All on the gravel beds, we had a tiny little par. Electric, fishing, mind numbingly boring. Two stop nets, a hundred-metre site, it just depends on the survey. Yes, hand-held with a generator on the bank. You do it two or three times. Eels. Longham, Yes there is a rack along there, you see it as you drive past, you need a licence. We still monitor those guys that have got those racks. They can operate through out the year. The only stipulation is that you have got to man it all the time, because if any salmon or sea trout or par get stuck on it they are going to croak. Brown trout and pike. We look after them, or try to. Again it's the rod licence and bye laws.

The coastal side of it there's not much that goes on that concerns us. All the problems we get are at West Bay. Nets that are within one or two hundred metres of the shore, close into the shore, but it's stopped now. A colleague of mine has worked very hard and has got a new byelaw in, so they don't do it anymore. Well at least this is the first year it's been in.

One of the biggest objectors to that, when we were nicking him for poaching sea trout, he was telling us about how he managed to conserve more sea trout and salmon than we have ever done. We saw him put the nets out on a Friday night and we decided that we'd go back on Saturday morning. I found out who the boat belonged to, and having spoken to my colleague we set up an operation because we had a lot of new staff who hadn't done that sort of thing before. So we thought we might as well set up an operation, show them what its all about, the vantage points and the rest of it. He went out next morning and the first thing he did when he started pulling the nets in, I was looking at him through my telescope and binoculars, was, as he was pulling the gill net in, another bloke on board went towards the net with a landing net. I have never ever seen anybody do that before and I said to my colleague on the radio, 'there is something occurring here and I couldn't identify the fish,' but I said 'he's just pulled this first bit of the net in.'

Yes. And I said 'He's gone towards the fish that I saw and scooped it up with the landing net while it was still in the net.' I said 'It is either a very good bass or something else entirely.' He said 'This is going to be interesting isn't it.' So we carried on and all I could see from the distance was a small fish, it could have been mackerel. It could have been anything, so we waited and he then went off to sea.

Now the important thing is, once he's got the nets onboard

and you suspect he's caught a fish, and you can't identify them, you know it's worth giving them the pull on the beach, or in the harbour or whatever. The important thing to remember is what he does next, because if he goes beyond our six-mile limit, right, disappears off to sea, you have got to prove that he had caught those fish within the six-mile limit. If he goes six to twelve miles he's ok. So he didn't. He just sorted the nets out with this other chap and he came into West Bay Harbour, tied up, and I basically went down this ropey old ladder. I told him who I was, and as I was going down the ladder I was a bit defensive because I thought, 'I don't know how he is going to react.' I got half way down, said 'Environment Agency mate, just going to come and check your catch.' He said' Yeah, yeah no problem.' I stopped and he picked up two fish boxes and he handed them to me as I was coming down the ladder. And I said, 'Well put them on the deck and I will get onboard first,' because I said 'I ain't letting go of the ladder.' 'Oh yeah, no problem mate here you are look, you can see what I have caught, a few horse mackerel.' And I thought 'There is something wrong here.'

So my colleague then joined me, checked the fish, a few mackerel, a few horse mackerel, a few small pollock, and my colleague says something like 'Right, what else have you got onboard?' 'No I ain't got nothing else onboard.' And my colleagues says 'Are you sure now?' He said,' Yes.' 'Right,' he said, 'I am going to carry out a thorough search of this boat.' So he went into the cabin, 'Well, uh, actually I have got to tell you there might be something in there that shouldn't be in there.'

Fair enough he brought out a bin liner, it was a bloody sea trout about two foot long. And I thought 'Result'. My colleague then came out with a bucket, I think there was about 16 in there. Sixteen sea trout, all small ones, and I think 75 per cent of them were under the minimum size. Not only had he poached them

but they were undersized. This was in West Bay Harbour. Nice little job that was.

We have had minor ramming incidents but nothing too serious. When I first started you had nothing, in terms of protection, only as fast as you can run basically. And about four years ago we were issued with handcuffs, but we were never trained to use them in combat with a baton, which is what you want, because unless someone is very compliant, you would have to handcuff them to arrest them. You have the power of arrest. You are a constable. You are classed as a constable and it says so in the Salmon and Freshwater and Fisheries Act.

Everybody else calls the police it, but two years ago the agency had a complete rethink about the whole way that its staff were being looked after. We have got two choices, we can either stop catching poachers or we protect the staff as much as we possibly can. So they decided to protect us. So they issued us with ballistic stab vests, batons and handcuffs. And we are fully trained on the use of them.

I mean when you are dealing with 19-year-old lads all they want to do is fight you. Somebody with a little bit of commonsense has written into the working practice that if you are on a boat and you are carrying out fisheries work you have got a choice, you can either wear the stab vest with a life jacket on top, or if you feel it will impede your operation you can take your life jacket off. Six months ago they were doing tests on the stab vests, because the stab vest is buoyant. We have night vision goggles, Yes we have all got digital, I have got a Canon 65.

A lot of the poachers that I have caught have been totally anonymous. We chase them until we catch them. Check the vehicle or follow the boat, or call the police in. We have had a bloody helicopter out and all sorts, filming them at it. The police take us seriously. They know if we catch someone we are going to nick 'em, we don't muck about. Yes we have got a lawyer who works for the Agency, but we also employ barristers, based in Exeter. So we have got our own legal teams as well. Basically you have still got to catch the person red-handed. I mean even with a boat, if somebody's off netting and catches a salmon or a sea trout, until they actually land it, but that's the difficult bit catching them, because it's the definition of the word 'taking'. We have had many discussions over many hours.

Mesh sizes? That's Southern Sea Fisheries, nothing to do with us. It doesn't matter what net it is, the only legislation we have got on net sizes is, a guy who is licensed to catch salmon and sea trout, and his net must be a certain size. Up until 16th June all salmon go back. Even in the net. Yes there is one in Wareham and he's got the agency's license. I think there is five or six in Christchurch.

What they do with the salmon up to the 16th June is release them. After that it is the Wessex Salmon Trust Association. They buy the salmon off the fishermen to release them and they put them in cages and take them up river. I did it a couple of times, but basically you have this tube, they catch the salmon, you weight it, so they get their money for it. You put it in the tube, in the back of the vehicle or in the trailer with a water tank on it, and you take it up the river. Saves the salmon a journey. We take it up the river for the simple reason if you put it back in where the net is they catch it again, because salmon are stupid. Then it will turn around and come back again.

Seals? There was a report about four years ago, me and my mate had a crisis on the Avon, there was a report that the seal was eating all the salmon, so we went on a big seal hunt but we never found it. We went up and down, we were chasing this bloody thing, we had the woman from the Sealife Centre on board, to identify the seal, how we were going to catch it. It was

a major operation, and we didn't see the damned thing. And three days later my mate and I were stood on Mudeford Quay and the bastard swam by, and I swear he was smiling at us.

The patrol boat. We call it a Poole canoe, it's an aluminium flat bottomed boat, for going across mud. The hull only used to draw about six inches, but now she draws about a foot, simply because of all the safety kit we have to carry. The actual hull is 20-foot, plus you have got the net tray on the back which is about another three-foot overhang. The bare boat weights about a ton without the engine and all the safety kit. It's a lot of weight. It's a 75 Honda on there now. When we first got it, it had a 15 Mercury. Before they had a 60 Mariner.

My bosses are in Blandford. Rivers House. Poole harbour is enormous, 460 acres, 100 square miles and Christchurch to Lyme Regis, yes it has got to be 60 miles I suppose. And then there's the rivers. It's a massive area. Plus the other things as well, pollution, is probably one of the biggest things. Farm pollution, fly tipping, waste sites, scrapyards in the end of use, decontaminating cars before they are put through the crusher and recycled, waste packaging is another thing. Polystyrene packaging from fast food, fishing lines and lead weights. Yes that's all part of our job.

We are covering most of Dorset and half of Wiltshire. A lot of maintenance. Everything is falling apart, then the paperwork, then the moorings, that was three or four week's work during the winter, to tidy them up and maintaining those. Police? Mostly the marine section down at Poole Quay. We deal with them a lot. Coastal poaching and then on the small rivers like the Sherford and the Corfe River which run into the harbour, people tend to forget those two. One of the jobs we had last year, which we got a very good result out of, £800, we had three or four fisheries officers, us, I don't know how many police were there, because I lost count, but we had two dog units, we had three officers in the vehicle I was in, plus there were two or three other cars, plus the firearms unit. Salmon and sea trout, and we got 'em. We got a good result out of that. We went from Cobbs Quay to Turlin Moor beach and I don't think she did under 80 all the way there, I was shitting myself, I didn't know a Land Rover could go that quick, I don't know what she had under the bonnet but it didn't half hit on, cor, Jesus, the wrong side of the road all the way through Hamworthy. I was bricking it, I thought we was going to die. And we went down Turlin Moor road and there is speed ramps, I swear to God she hit the first one she didn't touch the ground until she hit the second one. We screeched to a halt on the beach, with all these oiks hanging around, and they sort of looked up and said 'Oh yes, it's only the police.' And then suddenly they saw me, and as soon as they saw me the penny dropped that they were nicked. Because they thought they had had so many problems with the shellfish that that was what they were there for, course they saw me and thought 'oh shit.'

Kit? We have a one-piece flotation suit, a special order for us in the dark blue. Plus we have camouflage clothes and black clothing, depending on what the mood is at the time. Binoculars and telescopes. All the gear. Plenty of insect repellent. The SBS? Well funnily enough I had a good contact down there and we were planning to do some operations together, training operations, I said 'we'll look if we are out at night and you are out at night. We know where their vehicles are, and the vessels they use and what they are up to. I said 'what if we are the enemy and you are trying to find us, with our kit. Escape and evasion.' But it never came off. I went sick and that was the end of it. It was a bit of a shame,

My real interest is in aviation archaeology, where planes crashed. A lot of the information I picked up out of books. Knowing a few locals here in Wareham helped, people who were actually alive during the war, two or three of them used to help. We used to go around the graveyards. Wareham is one of the few graveyards in the country that has still got German airmen from the Battle of Britain. Quite a few went straight into the sea. There is probably about another 50 or so that aren't on the map. I remember my step-grandparents telling me about it, because they used to live down in Chickerell. They had seen the dog fights over Portland. In the early part of the Battle of Britain that was. It was very intensive. The chap on the *Foylebank*, he got the VC. Later on the Germans used to fly over here. Apparently they used to fly along the Piddle Valley, going to Bristol, trying to bomb Filton. They used to come across here quite low, through the Piddle Valley and as soon as they went by, somebody must have worked out how long it used to take them to get to Bristol, drop the bombs and come back, and from RAF Warmwell, they used to be waiting for them and they used to knock them out of the sky, the ME 110s.

36. Brian Mullins – Fisherman, Poole Harbour Commissioner. Born Parkstone, Poole 1936.

I've been a wooden boats man all through my life. Too old to change now. I have worked most of my life fishing single-handed. Still you've got to respect the weather. Always got to remember to respect the sea.

My father was a carpenter and joiner. My grandfather was a gardener in the big houses that were here, went from house to house, a regular gardener. I always remember him with a green/beige apron on. My mother came from Salisbury. Her father delivered mail years ago then he actually did work in a fish shop, I can just remember, in Salisbury. Not sure how they met, obviously they are both gone now.

My first memories of growing up here are being taken up to the primary school near St Peter's church at the beginning of the war. I remember barrage balloons and some troop movements. The Americans were in a garage just on the road to Ashley Cross and obviously in the port at Poole. I left school when I was 16 and did an apprenticeship as a ship's joiner, solely in wood. RA Newmans which was by the Lifting Bridge at Poole, actually where Sunseekers is now. Did a five-year apprenticeship. While I was an apprentice I did go out with one or two of the men that worked there that had fishing boats. I think that's how it started. Got the taste of the sea from them. They were building yachts, they did some admiralty work because they had a big slipway there which was built for the war. Royal National Lifeboats they used to do, but mainly yachts. They actually built two lifeboats for the Royal Yacht Britannia. I did finish the apprenticeship just when the first signs of fibreglass were appearing.

I had then to go and do two years in the army. I didn't really enjoy it. I was in the Hampshire Regiment based in Germany in the forests. I wasn't so lucky as some of them, 'cos all the apprentices in the different boatyards went to a college and they all got posted to the Isle of Wight to work on boats. I came back out of the Army and my father was employing about four people in his carpentery work, repairing houses and that. I went back to the boatyard for a year and then worked with him for a year but didn't really settle.

I then worked with a well known Poole fisherman for four and a half years. His name was Ron Stevens. His boat was called *Cathron*, and he had it built actually, so it was a nice boat, about 30 foot. It was a bit of lobster fishing, a little bit of trawling and then in winter in them days we used to go sprat fishing, not done now. The sprats came from Chesil, they sort of worked up into Poole Bay, you either got none or loads. We used to have to go as far as the Freshwater Bay in the Isle of Wight looking for them. We wouldn't go any further, a good four hours there and four hours back. So you hope to catch them nearer home. With the potting we always worked in the bay. Poole Bay has got small outcrops of rocks and rough ground. Never anywhere further than Swanage. Always afraid of bad ground with the nets. I worked for him for four and a half years then one day he said, 'I'm finishing.' His boat was up for sale for £3,000 not much these days. My father wasn't keen on me going fishing in the first place and he always said to me, 'Never buy anything until you can afford it.'

I never bought that boat, but I bought a small clinker-built boat, about 19 foot, and worked on my own, called the *Smiling Through* PE 36 in the early 1960s. I kept that and worked in the harbour mainly. I used to go hand picking for cockles with it, and I used to do a bit of trawling with it at night. In those days it

Brian Mullins with PW159, Elizabeth Shaun, Poole Harbour

was plaice and sole, in the harbour. It was a very old boat it had a petrol/paraffin engine. The engine was made in Bridport. In those days you could make a living, you wouldn't now. The harbour held a lot of feed, a lot of mud and channels, they breed in there. The fish were always full of rag worm and that, gradually the seabed changed. I don't know why, the rushes started to disappear, long before any real dredging took place and it was other estuaries that suffered. Of course then we used to get what was called eel grass laying on the seabed.

I didn't have that boat terribly long and then I did go trawling at night with another fisherman. He kept his promise and offered his boat to me so I sold the *Smiling Through* and bought a boat called *Jewel* PE 40 which was a Poole yawl, lead keel, deep draughted, very stable. So I kept that for about 18 years, trawling and pots. She had a two-cylinder heavy engine in there and I kept that. She was built pitch pine on oak and she was built solely to the length of the log of wood, there were no butts in the planks at all. I did sell it to someone local and they let it go in a state. Then one of the old retired dockers in Poole said to me one day 'I saw the old *Jewel* going up the road on a trailer,' and I've never known what happened to her.

Then I bought the present boat I've got, she is called *Elizabeth Shaun* PW 159. I bought her from Padstow, typical Cornish-built boat. Quite strong. She's built iroco on oak grown frames, built in 1971 in Polruan in Cornwall. Toms still builds wooden boats now. I've been a wooden boats man all through my life. Too old to change now. Lot of maintenance on a wooden boat. If you use it for your living you've really got to overhaul it and paint it once a year. If you leave some part of it inside or out for a couple of years it all goes to pieces, you've got to try and maintain it. Most of the winter was spent maintaining it.

When I had to earn a living I didn't have her much out of the water, because I also did some oil survey work, with both of the boats in the harbour. I worked for BP and British Gas on some surveys in the 70s. British Gas first and I used the *Jewel* for some survey work and then I bought this boat and did some more work. They would come out with their equipment and I would take them around. They usually had a fisheries officer with them, and in the early days they set posts across the harbour with explosives all connected with cables. I looked after, best I could, for the interest of the fishermen and the harbour. The seismic survey, that's how they did it in the early days. Just prior to extracting oil from Wytch Farm. They were extracting there at Kimmeridge, but they did some bore wells there then, I don't think it was in production then. There haven't been major pollution incidents with the oil, no major spillage. They got booms and equipment all ready for emergencies.

Did explosives affect fish? Only if the fish was directly over the explosion, it was all in shallow water. Obviously now they don't need to survey, they are taking oil from out under the harbour now and out in the Poole Bay. They are able to extend it to get more, it goes down and out to Poole Bay and I did work out there for them in seismic survey.

The history of Poole. It's a very ancient harbour, there is an old causeway over by Green Island which linked the mainland to the island. The trade was with Newfoundland, strong links with Newfoundland, wood and fish. A fine example of Newfoundland trade is in the parish church, St James's. The pillars are made from wood which came from Newfoundland, some people say they are masts of ships and some say it was specially for it. A lot of visitors from Newfoundland have come to the church and there is an association in Poole. Some of the big houses like the Mansion House and Jolliffe House they belonged to the ship owners. There was a lot of other trade apart from the cod. Also there were small coasters and of course all around the UK the small coasters are disappearing.

I was accepted on the board of The Harbour Commissioners to represent the fishing industry and I did 25 years on the board. I retired from it about five years ago, started about 1976. It was a great honour. The number of fishermen in Poole stayed pretty level because the harbour is important. You've got fishermen full time, mainly only working in the harbour and just outside the entrance. And then the boats go up in size and you've got Poole fishermen working 25-30 miles out in the Channel working pots. All over the UK there is a decline in the fishing industry, but the numbers have stayed here because of the shellfish beds in the harbour, but less to catch. About 70-80 fishermen are now earning a living from it.

Shellfish in the harbour, it started with oysters, there was always oysters in Poole since the Romans. A lot of oysters. The two rivers coming down, there's good silt or feed in the Piddle and the Frome. Then they built the power station and they sucked the water in by Poole lifting bridge and it discharged in the harbour warm, that helps a lot of clams. There was a lot of oysters in the harbour then. Years ago the Ross group had some beds, they lease the beds from the Southern Sea Fisheries. Then there was a disease in some French oyster beds and they restocked with Poole oysters. Along with all the other fishermen there was no hard regulations then, they fished heavy in the harbour for two to three years for restocking the French, which unfortunately reduced the oysters. So the public fisheries, there are some leased beds where you are not allowed to go and there are some public fisheries where, with a licence, you could dredge, but the government body the Southern Sea Fisheries closed the public fisheries and they are still closed to this day. But the oysters are coming back. No one harvests them now, only the people who own the beds. So when the oysters decreased they started laying the beds with seed mussels. Some of the mussels came from Ireland but I think a lot came from near West Bay. Fishermen there had them so they brought them up, so they restocked the beds.

And then there was a fisherman started on his own with clams and breeding them, and it was him, Gary Wordsworth, that really put the clams in the harbour, because they spat two or three times a year and spread all over the harbour. It's a winter fishery for the fishermen. It's got better if anything. It needs tight regulations on any fishery really. Being shallow you get quite good temperatures in the water. But then it's fishermen that fish in the winter and then they go out with nets out in the bay in the spring and the summer, so the harbour is very important. Poole harbour I think is 100 miles around, there is a debate, but I always say it's the second largest harbour in the world.

It's very big and very important because the fishermen know it's important. At Harbour Commissioners' meetings we discuss everything. Obviously if a fishing industry question came up you would expect to help, but once you were a commissioner you got to help to run the port. It's a Trust Port, no shareholders, just the commissioners, so any profit that was made in the harbour is ploughed back into the harbour with the benefit for yachtsmen, fishermen and all the people that use the harbour. They are getting a turnover, but they've just had to move with the times. sixty-odd acres had to be used. Started with one ship coming over from Brittany farmers, Truckline, it's moved from there, and in my time on the board the link with the Channel Islands started with Channel Island Ferries then Condor. They have recently since I left dredged the harbour to a deeper draft boat and just recently they have taken a bigger ship to pick up empty containers, and they've moved into the scrap iron, timber and bricks. Yes, I was honoured to serve on the board. Up till the last six years I didn't get paid nor any commissioner, it was voluntary, but you didn't think about it. I was honoured to be vice chairman and I was acting chairman for a while.

When Condor Ferries come in they go to Cherbourg, St Malo and down to the Channel Islands. You do get many French coming this way and it's very popular because in the summer months the fast ferry leaves at 7.30 am for Cherbourg and I think it gets in at a quarter to ten and you can have all day there and then come back on the conventional ferry for 10 o'clock at Poole. That's quite popular. It's the commissioners that I miss more than anything. There were some big things we did you know, the boat haven which you see on the Town Quay was another big project. A lot of work that I took on with another fisherman to get a ministry grant for the fishing part of the boat haven, just don't happen overnight.

All the water that the Port Authority controls goes right out to Old Harry and a bit beyond and it comes in like a triangle to Shore Road and all the harbour right up to a line at the entrance where the Piddle comes out where the River Frome comes out. The islands are Brownsea, Green Island, Furzey, Round Island and Long Island, they are the main ones. Very ancient sites these.

When I joined the board the chairman then was Major Ryder, they farmed all the ground where Wytch Farm is now and down to the harbour. It was very good, but I was very nervous when I first joined I only knew the harbour master. Major Ryder was a formidable man sat in an upright chair and had rim glasses. Had to collect harbour dues, day-to-day things. Obviously you do get a bit of conflict now and then. People have realised you had to develop the port to carry on and then the fishing industry, yachtsmen and harbour authorities and all the ones connected with the harbour. You sort of had to work

together, which meant a lot of committees and different meetings. Everybody likes to try and carry on as they did, like yacht racing and that. We have trawler racing here, it has diminished a bit since, because the harbour has got so much busier.

The whelks are out in Poole Bay, for years I have been taking samples of whelks. They go to the ministry's laboratories at Lowestoft. They always wanted them cooked and frozen. Perhaps they eat them! They still do cook and freeze them, I'm obviously semi-retired now and I said I'll give up the whelks, but they keep coming to me each year because nobody will do it. They used to do it twice a year, I think it was four times a year to start with, but then when Winfrith scaled down in recent years it's only once a year.

The Customs House? It's a restaurant now on the quay, it was the Customs and Fisheries office, and Ministry of Fisheries as it was then was underneath there. And it so happened not so many years ago, I was asked if I could scatter some ashes in the harbour for one of the old fisheries officers at Poole. The family came down and we scattered the ashes then we went back in there for breakfast and actually had breakfast in what was the Fisheries Office. Rather nice, if only he'd known. Obviously the harbour office in them days was just opposite on the quay, it's lost a bit of the character now.

The Navy and the Marines? They keep to themselves. If they fly the white ensign they are on practice so they can go over the speed limit. That's how it was arranged in the beginning. The speed limit is ten knots in the harbour, six knots in the little channel leading to the quay. Outside you can do what you want. Basically it is a lot better than it was. Some of these RIBs like to rev it a bit. When some of the Sunseeker type of boats go at slower speed they still pick up a bit of wash. Lifeboat headquarters and big training area here now. They train a lot and take the crews out. The SBS is part of the Marines, don't really see them. The harbour is important for shell fish but also for mullet and bass. Fishermen for netting and that, there is a nursery area where you are not allowed to fish with fixed nets. That's important too.

I think it's something to do with global warming why there is so many bass around now. There has always been bass here, but in the pots now we are catching trigger fish which when they were first caught you got your name in the paper: Trigger fish - rare! But I have landed four or five a day out of 100 pots and then they go again. I only work 100 pots now, semi-retired, I used to work 180 to 200 pots to earn a living. A lot of work even with a winch. If I had to earn a good living now you would want 700 or 800 and then somebody working with you. I have worked most of my life fishing single-handed.

When you started whatever you used you made, whether it was a trawl or pots, because there was nowhere to go and buy the actual gear. Bridport to buy the actual twine and the ropes and that, but you had to make the rest, but now you can go to a firm and buy it all ready-made to fish. And the electronic age GPS, echo sounders and all that has all improved. You just had to learn it from somebody else to start with.

Weather? Still you've got to respect the weather. Always got to remember to respect the sea. Some of the old signs are still working, ring around the moon is as true as anything. I've never changed the names of any of the boats, never even changed the numbers. I'm registered under Padstow PW, it's PE for Poole.

I have seen extraordinary changes in Poole harbour, in the fishing methods and the commercial shipping as well, because the main two things that have been reliable at the port is the import of steel which is I believe nearly gone now and the roll-on roll-off. There is a new ferry coming. That's been important.

There are still pilots, they come under the port authorities now. There's always been pilots in Poole. Ships now have bow thrusters, but in an emergency the ship owners like to know there is a tug on stand by, it's expensive to have them not doing a lot.

Shellfish export is quite big here. That took off with the ferries, Vivier trucks. Poole was a centre part for most of the UK and Ireland and it was traditionally Tuesday night, still is. Used to be 20-25 lorries go out. They come right down from Scotland and there is a wholesaler in the port that handles shellfish as well and some of the fishermen sell direct to the Vivier lorries. Most direct to Spain, France. In season spider crabs and velvet crabs. There is no demand in this country unfortunately. Spider crab, velvet crabs, whelks, cuttlefish all rubbish that used to throw away. The bay is shallow and they never have stayed in the bay. From Weymouth on down you can guarantee it. There has been a run of salmon up the Frome river. How it is now I don't really know. And eels, there used to be quite a big fisheries in the harbour because there was mud and a lot of deep channels but it has levelled out a bit now. There is one family that I do know of that still have a go at it, but I would imagine there might be one or two in the river. You used to have to keep them alive and they were shipped to Holland in the days of ships coming in with steel mainly Dutch skippers. Two of them had smoke kilns on board to smoke the eels. They always wanted eels when they come here.

I mentioned St James's Church because I'm a churchwarden there and that is the parish church of Poole. The future? Difficult to give the fishing up. Have made up my mind the boat I've got now, that's it. I'm not going to downsize.

37. Stella Stride – Vice-Chairman, Southern Sea Fisheries Committee. Born Tuckton 1950.

I think fishing should favour the smaller inshore fisherman. Here most of the fishing is sustainable because it is with pots, whether it's whelk pots, crab pots or lobster pots. Whelks have become quite big here and cuttlefish. Fishermen know their fishing grounds almost inside out. There's a wealth of fish in our waters and people don't eat as much as they should.

I was born in Tuckton, which is in Bournemouth. My father, Ron Edgell, was a fishmonger in Purewell, Christchurch. In those days, Purewell was in Hampshire but I would say I am a Dorset girl. My grandmother had the shop before him and my mother also worked in the fish shop. I am not sure if it went further back. I have pictures of the shop from 1936 when my father took it over and a picture of the shop with his mother, Daisy Edgell, in front of it from 1927. Even before that you can trace the Edgell family, which I was before I was a Stride, right back to 1694.

The Stride family as well, go back to the early 1800s in Mudeford and they were also a fishing family. I grew up with the fish shop always in the background, I would help with serving in the shop, and we also did fish and chips. It was a game shop as well, particularly during the war and my parents used to buy the salmon from Mudeford. Now all the salmon caught is 'catch and release.' Still netsmen here, they catch and release and the fish are taken up the river to spawn. The Stour and Hampshire Avon rivers are extremely good fishing rivers.

My husband's name was Brian, his family were all fishermen, his grandfather as well. My father used to buy fish from his father. We actually met at a dance though rather than through fishing. Brian was also born in Tuckton. There are no farmed fish or shellfish here at all. It's all 'organic' as natural things are now called.

I'm Vice-Chairman of the Southern Sea Fisheries Committee. It's not actually a full-time job, my main job is working for the Southern Fish Industry Training Association which trains fishermen in safety at sea. I work from home where I do all the accounts and administration. It is run by a volunteer committee and we employ a training co-ordinator who lives in Fareham. The training association covers a large stretch of the coast from Lyme Regis right through to the Medway. Young people wanting to take up fishing, have to, by law, to go on safety courses. There are four courses they must take; Sea Survival, Fire Fighting, First Aid and Safety Awareness. It is all basic health and safety at sea. It's practical as well, we hire a swimming pool and the trainees have to right a life raft in the pool and undertake practical exercises in fire fighting. The first aid training is similar to all first aid courses in that we use the dummy to practice resuscitation. The safety course is more theoretical. All these courses are important as fishing is the most dangerous industry in the UK.

There were many more fishermen here when I was growing up, I would say at least 30. Old Christchurch families made up the bulk, families like the Strides, the Derhams and the Edgells. The Derhams operated the ferry during my childhood, which was then a rowing ferry, now that ferry is owned by Paul Derham, it goes across to Hengistbury Head. The fisherman were fishing mostly for lobsters, crabs and prawns. They did do netting. Shellfish was the main catch during the summer. Brian's grandfather was born in the Black House, which is just across

Stella Stride with cuttle traps, Mudeford Quay

the Run over there, and lots of his family were fishing. They probably would have been involved in the Battle of Mudeford which occurred between local smugglers and the Customs men, I haven't read up history of the battle recently... Certainly I think the Burseys were involved, my husband employed Doug Bursey for a while. He died some time ago and he had also worked with my father-in-law and Brian's grandfather. It was a very close knit community, two or three families, but this has all changed. Thirty fishermen, 30 different boats, they were all very small boats. In fact we encourage smaller boats in the Southern Sea Fisheries, we have got a byelaw that limits the size of boat that fishes within our area. Our jurisdiction goes to six miles out.

I think the under-12-metre byelaw is by far the best one. We are the only Fisheries Committee along the south coast that has got that byelaw. Other people, for example from Brixham, can fish in our area only if they have 'grandfather's rights'. The French are not supposed to come within the 6 miles. There is a box off Christchurch where you don't net because it's Environment Agency territory and you mustn't put nets in that box at certain times of the year because of the salmon run. All fish for the Rivers Avon and Stour have to come through the Run. The salmon season is much shorter now than it used to be, it used to start on the 1st February but in recent years that has changed and is now far less than it used to be. The number of netsmen has reduced as well, my eldest son use to watch his father and up to five other teams fishing the Run. But now there has been a net limitation order and the numbers have reduced in accordance with that. Each net limitation order has set the numbers. These rights are not hereditary rights, although they have in fact in practice perhaps passed down from generation to generation, it's whoever applies for the licence. Fishing is quite prohibitive. You've got to buy a boat, licence, fishing gear. This is expensive and a heavy investment. To pay, fisherman have to be out in all weathers and at all times.

The fish and chip shop? I would describe it as smelly! We had regular customers. Cod didn't come from these waters, there has never been vast quantities of cod off here. We bought it in from the merchant and that comes from wherever it was available, so it could come from Iceland or anywhere. It's difficult to get people off cod, they are moving to pollack and things a bit more now – but this is either for environmental issues or due to the TV chefs. Pollack is an underrated fish. From 12 years onwards I worked in the fishmongers. But it wasn't my full-time job when I left school, I only assisted. I was a secretary and PA to a managing director of a building firm when I left school.

My husband? We got married in 1970 and he was then an apprentice marine engineer and he didn't get his first boat until 1973. He only ever used one fishing boat at a time, but he had several boats to use for different jobs, eg netting, oyster dredging or to renovate. Once he bought a boat he didn't like selling it so he kept them. The boatyard was his father's, his parents live at the boatyard. His father had a stroke and then Brian helped out at the boatyard. It's only a very small yard, mainly just with moorings. When my husband arrived they did repairs, never building boats. There was a hire business there as well, his father used to fish and give sailing lessons. He did not take trips around the bay, that was more the Derham family which have been doing that till recently. Others take mackerel fishing trips. My husband mainly used a dory in the last two decades, he had a catamaran built when he was ill, he never got to use that. He died earlier this year. His first boat was called *Stella Barbara*, then he had one called *Band of Brothers*, one called *Kit* which was my son's boat, *Anton* which he bought from his second cousin, *FI*, and finally *Star*. I have two sons, they like fishing and have got salt water in their veins, they both love being on the water.

I have been involved in fishing associations for most of my working life. The first one was the local fishermen's association which is the Mudeford and District Fishermen's Association, I'm still secretary of that. We used to organize the trawler race, but that doesn't happen any more. It used to run from here on the quay out to sea around a course and back. We raised a lot of money for a number of different charities such as the lifeboats, the Guide Dogs and Cystic Fibrosis. There are less fishing boats and trawlers around now and it got more and more difficult to organise and with less people to help.

The training is vital. Each area has got its own group association. Ours is quite a big area: it stretches from Lyme Regis to the Medway. Southern Sea Fisheries Committee goes up to Langston near Hayling Island. The SSF committee holds statutory joint quarterly meetings and then we have sub-committee meetings. We have an eastern and a western sub-committee, we discuss byelaws and we also have a staff sub-committee. In fact we are interviewing prospective fisheries officers this Thursday. A fisheries officer's main job is to enforce the byelaws of the committee, the new one will probably have more of an environmental role, and we also sponsor work from the universities. They get as much data as they can from fishermen. I think the fish stocks out here are better than is widely reported. Some of the scientific evidence is a day crab sampling, whereas a fisherman has got a daily trip to sea, scientists might go once every few weeks or once every few months. Fishermen know their fishing grounds almost inside out, but that is not scientific enough. That's what we are told anyway.

Minimum sizes? Yes, and some of them have been suggested by fishermen in the past. They have suggested upping the size limit in the past, there are quite a few regulations. For example, edible crabs have a minimal size of 5·5 inches across the shell, Scallop is 4·3 inches in area VIId. There is a measure you have for the crabs and the lobster, it's across the widest part of the shell. It's 100 mm in area VIIe. The area boundary is at St. Albans Head. Mudeford is in area VIId. The lobster is 87 mm which is 3·43 inches from the top of the shell to the point. The spider crab, female is 4·7 inches and the male is 5·1 inches that's lengthwise. We do get many spider crabs here, sometimes it is difficult to get a good market for them. But the Spanish like them. My husband caught mainly lobster and crab, he did a bit of prawn fishing, he used to net as well but not in recent years and he did have an oyster licence in the Solent. There were very specific dates, ancient oyster beds, in fact Christchurch Priory was built on oyster shells. There used to be quite a lot of oyster between the piers at Bournemouth, but the sand replenishment has probably wiped them out. There are no oysters here in Christchurch that I know of.

Mullet, flounders and a few small bass are caught here in the harbour. You can see Royalty marks strung half way across the harbour and you can mullet fish up to those, you would have to have a mullet net. Another of my husband's boats was called *Chance It*, it was a Poole canoe, which can be used for mullet fishing, which he had done in the past. He would fish off Barton-on-Sea that's about as far as you can see to the east, he would net off there, but again not so much recently, probably the last time was about perhaps ten years ago. He would also fish off Southbourne. He had an ancestor who would only go as far as he could put the oar down and touch the bottom.

There are a lot of pots out here. Each fisherman has a few hundred. Poole is the main exporting port for crabs and lobsters in the whole country. Certainly my husband's grandfather used to take the catch to the railway station, it used to go up to Billingsgate on the train in those days. Now they go in a truck to Poole and go across to France and Spain on the vivier lorry.

We get a double high tide here. In later years, my husband had more dories and shallow draft boats so he wasn't restricted by the tide. I never went to sea fishing, he said it was bad luck for me to go fishing with him. He hated green on the boat, he would not allow green on the boat. He had even had a blue Lister engine on the *Stella Barbara* – where most were green. We did eat fish, but not all the time obviously. I'm quite busy with the different committees. The South Coast Fishermen's Council covers the same area as the Southern Sea Fisheries District and any fishermen's association can belong and we then put the fishermen's views to the Marine Fisheries Agency and DEFRA, MPs, local authorities or whoever needs to be advised. I look after my grandchildren when needed as well.

Oil? The channel is divided into plots and there was a lot of exploration in the 1980s and the fishermen had to either move their gear or move it into different sections for the seismic surveys. Fishermen needed somebody to go to meetings and I set that group up. It has now disbanded. There is oil off here, BP have got Wytch Farm and they do direct drilling which goes underneath the sea. I don't know if they have reached the distance they can drill.

The fishing industry? Yes, slightly sad that it seems to be in decline and also that some of the species are said to be in danger when the fishermen can see no signs of that. I do think the discards problem is dreadful when fish are caught they should be eaten and they should not be discarded. If you kill any animal it should be used to its optimum, whether it's shooting a pheasant or catching a fish, I think that once it's been killed it should be used. It's a bit like growing vegetables, they should be eaten. I don't like these mountains of food going to waste because they should be used somewhere. I don't think there should be any such thing as 'black fish' because fishermen can't always target the right species there is no sign on the net saying: 'We don't want any cod in here.'

Lobster seems quite healthy at the moment. Yes, a lot of small ones I understand. Most areas have a byelaw to put the small ones back. For details you would need a copy of the byelaws book, it's more complicated than you think where you can fish and for what species and when. And the other thing that is sometimes not quite right, the national limits don't always marry with the local ones and sometimes there is a loop hole where people say: 'Oh yes it was caught further out,' so that needs to be tidied up, it might be in the Marine Bill. Virtually everyone has been consulted on the Marine Bill, it's quite complicated and there is not much detail so you can't always make constructive comments until they get the detail into it.

I think fishing should favour the smaller inshore fisherman. Here certainly most of the fishing is sustainable because it is with pots, whether it's whelks pots, crab pots, lobster pots. Whelks have become quite big here and cuttlefish.

There's a wealth of fish in our waters and people don't eat as much as they should. Friday was always such a busy day. People ate fish on a Friday, a lot of younger people aren't even aware of that I don't think. Good Friday was certainly extremely busy, I don't know whether it's as busy now as it used to be. But then different things happen now, you get a good fish recipe on these celebrity chefs programmes and then there is a huge demand for it. People are definitely more keen to experiment today.

Finances? Young man with a family? Yes, that is difficult because you do get outside pressures whether it be from all sorts of legislation, people wanting to do all sorts of things with areas of the sea and they think the fishermen are not important and they always think the fishermen can go somewhere else, when they can't always because it's somebody else patch or you've got a small boat. You are restricted around your particular port and you are also restricted with the type of investment you have made. The type of fishing gear you have, you have got to get a return on that choice of fishing gear.

My husband didn't tell me if he nearly didn't come back and he didn't tell me about accidents to other fishermen, I found out through other means always. I would hear and being on the training association I would hear, but he wouldn't come home and tell me. There is about 440-460 boats in the Southern Sea Fisheries, there used to be double that. There used to be about 900, but then perhaps some of those have gone out of the industry. Only large boats get bought out and decommissioned.

Seine netting? Not a lot. Salmon netting is seine netting. I would have thought the Avon is better, Stour is more for coarse fishing. There are some eels caught on the rivers, but further up, not so much locally. Grayling? It might be too salty for them down in the harbour.

We can see the Isle of Wight and the Bar from Mudeford. The Bar is quite tricky, very dangerous. I think some people underestimate the dangers there. You see people taken unawares, lots of rescues in the Run. There has always been a lifeboat station here that I can remember and the Trawler Race used to raise a lot of money for them. Now there are about 20 members fishing from the quay here. Mostly older fishermen, we have only a few young fishermen there, which is a shame. They have to work very hard and they have to have the capital in the first place, it's not that easy to get into and they have also got to take the courses that I've mentioned. I don't issue licences, they are issued from Defra. I am appointed by the Minister. We have trouble getting new byelaws usually, it's not easy. We make the byelaws but only with the Minister's approval. He has to confirm them. It can take months or even years to get a byelaw passed, so often we think national legislation is a good route.

We've got our own patrol boats, they move around within the area. I shall carry on with my administrative roles. Meetings with fishermen all the time, I have a monthly one with the Mudeford fishermen so I can find out what's going on. I represent their views whenever I can.

POSTSCRIPT

It is very obvious having read these life histories that there is a vast depth of knowledge and expertise along the Dorset coast, a knowledge which in some cases we are in danger of losing forever. This is a clear case of oral history being a vital link to the past. The Dorset coast is visually one of the richest I know but it has also been industrially important, from the cement works at Lyme Regis to the quarries of Portland and Purbeck, as well as the clay and shale deposits to the east. Interestingly BP brings oil and LPG ashore from underneath Poole harbour at Wytch Farm and at Kimmeridge Bay. Despite numerous phone calls, BP did not want to be interviewed, which is a shame as their onshore oil fields in Dorset are some of the most successful in Europe. The nodding donkey at Kimmeridge has been nodding its head wisely since 1959. Production was once over 300 barrels per day and although it has slowed up a little, it has never ceased in nearly 50 years. The oil is taken out of Middle Jurassic limestone from about 1,000 feet depth. With the oil price now at over $100 a barrel that is quite a good little earner, almost as good as the car park at Lulworth Cove…

Interesting industrial experimentation is nothing new to the Dorset coast. In the early 1620s there were several attempts at glassmaking on the beach near Smedmore by the Clavells which resulted in court cases being taken out against them by Admiral Mansell for infringement of his monopoly. With the lack of firewood, which had been used for iron smelting and charcoal burning, they experimented with oil shale to provide the basic fuel. There were great clouds of sulphurous smoke which upset the neighbours and led to other court cases. Around this time the invention of bottle glass took place with the trace elements of iron and manganese, in all probability by accident. And without bottle glass there is no bottle-fermented sparkling cider and certainly no champagne. Every dark cloud has its silver lining.

My own grandfather, whose father had been born at Lulworth Cove, not only extracted oil from shale in 1912 but also used the quarries near Swanage for experiments to test the physiological effect on soldiers of strenuous work in bulky anti-gas clothing. This was just before the Second World War. Luckily the gas clothing never had to be used. Interestingly he used those quarries because on a still summer's day it was the hottest place he could find in the south of England. Early experiments which mirrored conditions in the Middle East.

The final word should go to the fishermen. Hopefully by reading these stories the public will come to understand the dangers of fishing, as well as the constant barrage of regulations that the fishermen have to deal with. International politics often lurk just beneath the surface. Sadly the number of full time fishermen has dropped but the quantity of fish being sold locally is increasing steadily. Support your local fishermen. Support your local economy. The fishermen are the last in a long line of hunter-gatherers. We ignore their plight at our peril. The sea is your oyster. Don't forget the coastguards and the RNLI, they are nearly all volunteers and if you are in trouble at sea or wrecked, your life is in their hands.

Researching *Dorset Coast* has been a marvellous experience and if this book helps you to learn more about the working lives of those who live here, then that is better still.

James Crowden *November 2007*

USEFUL WEBSITE ADDRESSES
for people, places and organisations mentioned in Dorset Coast

LYME REGIS

www.amherstlodge.com/lymeregis/aquarium

www.cefas.co.uk

www.lymeregis.com/marief

www.boatbuildingacademy.com

www.lymeregismuseum.co.uk

CHARMOUTH, WEST BAY AND ABBOTSBURY

www.charmouthfossils.co.uk

www.jurassiccoast.com

www.axisweb.org/artist/lalhitchcock

www.samwaysfish.com

www.bridportmuseum.co.uk

www.abbotsbury-tourism.co.uk/swannery

www.featherart.co.uk

www.chesilbeach.org

WEYMOUTH AND PORTLAND

www.judithfrost.co.uk

www.deepsea.co.uk/boats/wildfrontier   Clem Carter

www.portland-port.co.uk

www.hotelaqua.co.uk

www.divedorset.com

www.weymouth.gov.uk/main.asp?svid=271   Weymouth Museum

www.weymouth.gov.uk/main.asp?svid=252   Portland Museum

www.underwaterexplorers.co.uk

www.wpnsa.org.uk   The Sailing Academy

www.crabhousecafe.co.uk

www.seafares.net

www.weymouthrowingclub.org

www.poultonpuppets.co.uk

www.sculpturesinsand.com

www.dovecotebooks.com

LULWORTH TO SWANAGE VIA WORTH MATRAVERS

www.lulworthonline.co.uk

www.lulworth.com/ranges

For recorded message on the Lulworth ranges: 01929 404819

www.purbeckstone.co.uk

www.swanagelifeboat.org.uk

www.swanagemuseum.org.uk

Langton Matravers Museum

POOLE HARBOUR AND MUDEFORD QUAY

www.warehammuseum.fsnet.co.uk

www.defra.gov.uk/marine

www.defra.gov.uk/environment/water/marine/uk/policy/marine-bill

www.environment-agency.gov.uk/subjects/fish

www.phc.co.uk   Poole Harbour Commissioners

www.southernsfc.org.uk   Southern Sea fisheries Committee

www.mudefordferry.co.uk/battle   Battle of Mudeford Quay

www.dorsetcoast.com

Poole Museum

www.russell-cotes.bournemouth.gov.uk   Bournemouth

www3.hants.gov.uk/redhouse-museum   Christchurch + Mudeford

NOTES ON AUTHORS

Photo by Tessa Gilks

JAMES CROWDEN was born in Plymouth in 1954 and grew up on the western edge of Dartmoor. He joined the Army, read civil engineering at Bristol University, then travelled widely in the Middle East, Eastern Turkey, Iran and Afghanistan. In 1976 he spent a year in Ladakh on the northern side of the Himalaya and lived in a high altitude Tibetan Buddhist valley called Zangskar. After studying anthropology at Oxford he worked in the Outer Hebrides, Bristol Docks and North Dorset. It was around Shaftesbury that he kept sheep and worked as a woodman, shepherd and sheep shearer. His first book, *Blood Earth & Medicine* charts the annual cycle of farm work as seen through the eyes of a casual agricultural labourer. He then moved to Somerset and took up cider making in the autumn. Other books followed, *In Time of Flood* and *The Wheal of Hope - South Crofty and Cornish Tin Mining* with George Wright, *Bridgwater - the Parrett's Mouth*, *Working Women of Somerset*, with Pauline Rook, as well as *Cider the Forgotten Miracle*. More recent books include *Waterways* for the National Trust and *Silence at Ramscliffe - Foot and Mouth in North Devon* with Chris Chapman, *Dorset Man*, *Dorset Women* and *Dorset Footsteps*. James now writes full time.

www.james-crowden.co.uk

Photo by Edmund Wright

GEORGE WRIGHT was born in London in 1950. From 1970-1973 he studied graphic design at Wimbledon School of Art and in 1975 he became a freelance photographer. He has worked internationally for many newspapers, magazines and book publishers. His pictures have appeared in *The Independent Magazine, The Observer, The Independent on Sunday Review, Departures* (USA) and *Instituto Geografico De Agostini* (Milan). He has also worked as a stills photographer for Channel 4. His work has been exhibited at the Metropolitan Museum in New York and the Chicago Botanic Gardens. He also has a number of photographs in the National Portrait Gallery collection. His books include *English Topiary Gardens* (1988), *Ceramic Style* (1994), *Print Style* (1995), *In Time of Flood* (1996), a collection of photographs of the Somerset Levels and *The Wheal of Hope* (2000) about the demise of South Crofty and Cornish Tin Mining. He has lived in Dorset since 1983 and has undertaken many local commissions and arts projects. A large collection of his work is on the permanent display at the Dorset County Hospital. George Wright has also just completed a major series of portraits of council employees – *Council Works* for Dorset County Council. George lives in Bridport.